Imperial Networks

Imperial Networks investigates the discourses and practices of British colonialism. Focusing on the colonisation of the Xhosa to the east of the nineteenth-century Cape Colony in South Africa, the book places this episode in the context of a much broader imperial network. The book reveals how British colonialism in the region was informed by, and itself informed, imperial ideas and activities elsewhere, both in Britain and in other colonies.

Drawing on materialist South African historiography, postcolonial theory and geographical conceptions, *Imperial Networks* examines:

- the origins and early nineteenth-century development of three interacting discourses of colonialism – official, humanitarian and settler
- the contests, compromises and interplay between these discourses and their proponents in South Africa and Britain
- the analysis of these discourses in the light of a global humanitarian movement in the aftermath of the antislavery campaign
- the eventual colonisation of the Xhosa and the construction of colonial settler identities.

Imperial Networks introduces students to key debates in the historiography of nineteenth-century South Africa, as well as in materialist and postcolonial constructions of the past.

Alan Lester is Lecturer in Human Geography at the University of Sussex. His previous publications include *From Colonization to Democracy: a New Historical Geography of South Africa* (1996) and *South Africa Past, Present and Future: Gold at the End of the Rainbow?* with E. Nel and T. Binns (2000).

Imperial Networks

Creating identities in
nineteenth-century South Africa
and Britain

Alan Lester

London and New York

First published 2001
by Routledge
11 New Fetter Lane, London EC4P 4EE

Simultaneously published in the USA and Canada
by Routledge
29 West 35th Street, New York, NY 10001

Routledge is an imprint of the Taylor & Francis Group

© 2001 Alan Lester

Typeset in Garamond by BC Typesetting, Bristol
Printed and bound in Great Britain by MPG Books Ltd, Bodmin

British Library Cataloguing in Publication Data
A catalogue record for this book is available from the British Library

Library of Congress Cataloging in Publication Data
Lester, Alan.
  Imperial networks: creating identities in nineteenth-century South Africa
  and Britain/Alan Lester.
    p. m.
  Includes bibliographical references and index.
  1. Xhosa (African people)–History–19th century. 2. Xhosa (African
  people)–Colonisation–South Africa–Cape of Good Hope. 3. British–South
  Africa–History–19th century. 4. Kaffraria–History–19th century.
  5. Cape of Good Hope (South Africa)–History–1795–1872.
  6. Great Britain–Colonies–Administration–History–19th century.
  7. Imperialism–History–19th century. I. Title.

  DT1768.X57 L47 2001
  968.7'00496e985–dc21   2001018726

ISBN 0–415–25914–2 (pbk)
ISBN 0–415–19850–X (hbk)

Contents

Figures

Preface

This book is ultimately about the processes through which Xhosa-speaking peoples were colonised in the eastern Cape frontier zone of modern South Africa, particularly during the first half of the nineteenth century. But the book's main subjects are not the Xhosa. In the belief that colonialism was 'shaped as much by political, social and ideological contests among [British] colonisers as by the encounter with the colonised', the main subjects of the book are those who considered themselves British.[1] While it situates these Britons within a network of extraneous influences, this remains primarily a study of their colonial cultures and practices.[2]

Just as British metropolitan identities were being forged in relation to others during the late eighteenth and early nineteenth centuries, different kinds of British identities were being carved out in diverse colonial settings. These colonial identities were constructed in relation to the cultures of Indians, Maoris, Aborigines and West Indian slaves, to name but a few examples. In the eastern Cape, a British settler identity was constructed in tension with those of Khoesan- and Dutch-speakers, but especially, I will argue, in relation to the material and symbolic practices, and not least the resistance, of the Xhosa.[3] In each settler colony, colonial identities were also created through communication with, and often out of antagonism towards, certain metropolitan social and political groups that concerned themselves, even if only periodically and half-heartedly, with events at the margins of empire. It is thus not only British colonial, but also British metropolitan identities, and the discourses of colonialism connecting them that provide the substance of this study.

The Britons on whom the book centres include governors and administrators, missionaries and their metropolitan directors, Members of Parliament and colonial politicians, settlers, journalists, travellers and merchants. If they did not themselves shuttle back and forth between the eastern Cape frontier and Britain, the people studied here sent dispatches, compiled reports, wrote letters, participated in official inquiries and moved capital along circuits connecting these two places, together with other nodes, within an imperial network. I aim to consider the ways in which they imagined and contested colonialism on the eastern Cape frontier and else-where, the ways in which they were changed by it and some of the ways in which, through it, they participated in the construction of the modern world both in South Africa and in Britain.

I hope to achieve all this by building upon the foundations established by a generation of materially oriented South African social historians over the last twenty years. However, I seek to contribute to the literature that they have produced in two main ways. First, by critically and highly selectively incor-porating certain 'postcolonial' notions that have been regarded with some suspicion by many South African historians,[4] I hope to illuminate the colonising culture that gave rise to those material interactions lying at the heart of the existing historiography. Secondly, I intend to highlight those discursive/political transactions conducted across a broad imperial terrain, between Britons in the metropole, in the Cape Colony, and in other colonial sites. In the introductory chapter, I will elaborate upon these two 'innovations'.

Acknowledgements

This book would not have been possible without the forbearance and encouragement of Jo Nash, and the unfailing support of my family: Patricia, Brian, Gary and Tracy Lester. The book's completion has been much delayed, but for the most wonderful reason: the birth and rapid growth of my daughter Daisy. This book is dedicated to her and to her cousin Jessica.

A number of friends have always been supportive of my academic endeavours and broadly if resignedly tolerant of my South African reminiscences. This seems a suitable place to thank, in alphabetical order, Fe Burbage, Ian Chitty, Matthew Davis, Ewan and Sarah Edwards and Chloë Jolowicz.

Robert Ross consented to read the manuscript before its publication, while Saul Dubow assisted by providing me with drafts of his work in progress. I am grateful to both of them for their help. They, of course, cannot be blamed for the weaknesses that remain. Finally, material included at various points in this book has been published elsewhere, as *Colonial Discourse and the Colonization of Queen Adelaide Province, South Africa*, Royal Geographical Society–Institute of British Geographers, Historical Geography Research Series, no. 34, London, 1998; 'Reformulating Identities: British Settlers in Early Nineteenth Century South Africa', *Transactions of the Institute of British Geographers*, 23, 4, 1998, 515–31; '"Otherness" and the Frontiers of Empire: The Eastern Cape Colony, 1806–c1850', *Journal of Historical Geography*, 24, 1, 1998, 2–19; 'Settlers, the State and Colonial Power: The Colonization of Queen Adelaide Province,1834–37', *Journal of African History*, 39, 1998, 221–46, and 'The Margins of Order: Strategies of Segregation on the Eastern Cape Frontier, 1806–c1880', *Journal of Southern African Studies*, 23, 4, 1997, 635–53. I want to express my gratitude to the editors and publishers of these journals and research series for permission to reproduce this material.

1 Introduction

Histories of the eastern Cape and postcolonial theory

Most current histories of the nineteenth-century eastern Cape frontier zone, like those of nineteenth-century South Africa more generally, are broadly materialist in orientation. Materialist endeavours to explain British colonisation in the eastern Cape can be dated to the early 1980s. At this time, Martin Legassick, Basil Le Cordeur and Jeff Peires sought to challenge two kinds of established interpretation.[1] On the one hand, they attacked a cluster of 'settler narratives', dating from the mid to late nineteenth century, which had proclaimed the beneficial progress of colonial 'civilisation', brought by British officials and settlers on the frontier, and its triumph over African 'barbarism' or, even worse, 'savagery'. On the other hand, these revisionists challenged a set of liberal accounts dating from the 1920s, which had argued that the genesis of the white 'attitudes' underpinning modern systems of segregation and apartheid lay in early frontier 'racial relations'.[2] Critiquing the latter tradition, Legassick emphasised that there did not seem to be a systematic racial ideology among British and Afrikaner farmers on the pre-industrial Cape frontier. He located the construction of such an ideology instead in South Africa's late nineteenth- and early twentieth-century 'mineral revolution', and traced it to British industrial capitalists based on the Witwatersrand, and the British imperial state, rather than to their early nineteenth-century predecessors.[3]

Le Cordeur and Peires took a different kind of approach, but one that still focused on material aspects of the eastern Cape's history. Rather than considering the early nineteenth-century colonial frontier only to dismiss its 'claim' to be the arena for the development of a modern racial ideology, they held that the British colonisation of the region was significant in its own right. This was because it represented the first penetration of a pre-industrial, agrarian form of capitalism into African territory. For Peires, the 4,000 British settlers located on the frontier in 1820 in particular acted as 'apostles of free enterprise and free trade'.[4] It was these settlers who rapidly became agents for the Xhosa's dispossession and subjugation under a

regime of settler capitalism. That regime was based above all on the production of wool for the metropolitan market, on white-owned farms, using a subordinated black labour force.[5]

Le Cordeur's and Peires' emphasis on the British as harbingers of capitalist
social relations and Xhosa labour-domination has received new impetus of
late. In a review marking his reconsideration of the eastern Cape frontier
zone in 1993, Legassick saw the agrarian capitalism of the British as the
main reason why 'the emphasis in the shaping of twentieth-century South
Africa is decisively shifted from Afrikaners to British settlers'.[6] For the
same reason, the arrival of the 1820 settlers marks a turning point in Noël
Mostert's acclaimed epic narrative of frontier relations, and in Clifton Crais's
more theoretical treatment of colonial power and Xhosa resistance.[7] Finally,
British settler capitalism looms large in the more recent, impressive synthesis
of the Cape's colonial history written by Timothy Keegan. Keegan argues that
it was the British settlers, backed by the colonial state, who 'undermined
Xhosa self-sufficiency, eroded chiefly prerogatives, and re-oriented economic
activity to new patterns of [capitalist] production and consumption'.[8]

Peires' and Le Cordeur's early interest in British activities on the frontier,
then, seems to have been vindicated in Keegan's synthesis. If, as Legassick
argued, South Africa's modern system of industrial segregation did not
have its origins on the frontier, at least one can be confident that some of
the first full-blown capitalist relations systematically predicated on racial
stratification were constructed there.[9] The penetration of the eastern Cape
by settler capitalism thus played a central role in prefiguring 'the transformations that were set in motion by the mineral discoveries in South
Africa in the last third of the century'.[10]

Over the last decade, however, the currents of postcolonial thought, which
have affected so many arenas of academic enterprise, have brought challenges
to materialist renditions of South African history as a whole. They have
initiated, at times, fairly heated debates among South Africanists.[11] According to Crais, most historians engaging in these debates 'have sought dry and
safe land far from the dangerous breakers of post-modernism'.[12] Nevertheless,
'the appearance of studies more closely attuned to questions of culture and the
mind . . . are beginning to fracture an earlier coherence'.[13] Postcolonialism
challenges the materialist notion of an extraneous capitalist 'logic', which,
having been imported by European colonisers, underlies racial 'ideology'
and generates a particular pattern of historical change. Against such a conception, postcolonial scholars have emphasised the more contingent power
relations embedded in that 'congeries of values [and] beliefs . . . that have
come to carry the force of nature', and which are generally referred to as
culture.[14]

In postcolonial readings, capitalism cannot be thought of as having a logic
or structure which exists somehow prior to, or outside of, culture. Culture
mediates relations of power across social boundaries that are constructed in
relation to one another, rather than 'given' by any extraneous framework.

Thus, 'culture is not some sort of residual category, the surface variation left unaccounted for by more powerful economic analyses, but it is the very medium through which social relations are expressed, experienced and contested'.[15] And these social relations consist of far more intricate inter-meshings of race, gender, ethnicity, religion, language and locality than those that a class-based analysis alone can supply.[16]

However, I do not believe that the established historiography of capitalist penetration in the eastern Cape on the one hand, and the relational insights of postcolonial theory on the other, are irreconcilable. First, we can recognise that developments within the materialist South African historiographical tradition as a whole, including that portion focusing on the eastern Cape, have led it away from any orthodox and structuralist Marxism and closer to postcolonial conceptions of identity and change. They demonstrate that the social boundaries of class, race, ethnicity and gender are dynamic and flexible creations, generated through contingent power struggles. Some seek to deal with these social boundaries in an integrated way, and, in common with recent analyses of colonial India in particular, they draw attention to the failures as well as the successes of capitalist endeavours.[17]

Furthermore, although most South African historians writing of 'race' prefer to use the more traditional terms 'racial ideology' or 'racial attitudes', in the ways in which they deploy these terms, they have included many of the meanings that postcolonial scholars invest in the word 'discourse'.[18] Indeed, they have been engaged in an historically embedded form of discourse analysis for some time, without necessarily theorising it as such.[19] Thus, they write implicitly of 'race' as an enframing set of representations, rather than merely as a screen of 'bias' or 'prejudice' that obscures some objective 'truth' about difference or sameness. It is in this unstated rejection of the notion of ideology as 'false consciousness or an imagined representation of the real conditions for existence' that we find the clearest connections between current social historical and postcolonial approaches.[20]

Like the prevailing historiography, this book insists on the significance of the transformations engendered by settler capitalism as a set of practices on the eastern Cape frontier, but it also gives more explicit recognition to three things that are more generally associated, at least overtly, with post-colonial analyses: first, that such practices were culturally conditioned, legitimated and regulated through discourse.[21] Secondly, this discursive regulation of capitalist practice took place across an extensive imperial terrain connecting Britain's colonies, and its settler colonies in particular, to the metropole. The geographies of flow and connection within a broad imperial network are central to this account. And thirdly, that, for settler capitalist practices to 'work' in the eastern Cape they had to be formulated in response to the conditions which settlers found there. Not the least of these conditions was Khoesan resistance to material exploitation and the Xhosa's 'primary' resistance to the settlers' very presence in the region.

Without wishing to construct them as being mutually exclusive, three main early nineteenth-century British colonial discourses are identified and analysed in the following chapters – governmentality, humanitarianism and settler capitalism. This book is about their differential and overlapping effects, both in the eastern Cape and in Britain. Although any attempt to delineate these discourses runs the risk of creating artificial boundaries and an unhelpful impression of internal homogeneity, I nevertheless believe that each of them, at least in the early nineteenth century, constituted a particular 'ensemble of regulated practices'.[22] Despite their multiple points of origin, each was internally consistent enough to be considered a broad imperial programme in its own right These discourses were created initially as a result of competing 'projects', devised by differentially situated British interests to be carried out in a variety of colonial spaces.[23] It was the incompatibility between the Colonial Office and its governors' agendas for producing order at minimal cost, philanthropic and evangelical humanitarians' schemes of proselytisation among 'aborigines' and their eventual assimilation, and settlers' more targeted visions of capital accumulation and security that brought these discourses into being and into collision with one another. Thereafter, they were continually being refashioned in relation to each other.

Critical to each of these discourses in the Cape (and elsewhere), and to the contests that were waged between them, were representations of 'the disputed figure of the African'.[24] Within each discourse, Africans were reduced to stereotypes and each such stereotype necessitated a specific set of colonial responses. Governmental discourse, I will argue, produced the Xhosa and Khoesan of the eastern Cape (and to a certain extent the Dutch-speaking colonists too) as unpredictable objects, predisposed to irrational acts of violence – objects to be located, ordered and disciplined in line with the efficient administration of the Cape at minimal expense. Humanitarian discourse tended to produce them as pliant and childlike brothers and sisters, fellow human beings and creations of God awaiting the blessings of Christianity. Within this discourse, the Khoesan and Xhosa were merely one component in a global enterprise aimed at nothing less than the redemption of souls, the extension of legitimate trade and the diffusion from its British heartland of a spiritually and materially progressive Utopia. In settler discourse, these indigenous Others came to feature primarily as a potent, threatening presence, ominously lurking beyond or, even more dangerously, within the colonial frontier, and requiring to be either removed or rendered tame and productive. Only then could mutual prosperity spread, specifically through sheep farming, infrastructural development, labour control, further emigration from Britain and the supply of the British manufacturing market.

We must be careful to remember that the colonial projects identified in this book could converge around particular imperatives which were necessary for any of them to be realised, thus giving the impression of a more unified and totalising colonial discourse. Philanthropic evangelicals, government officials and settlers were all concerned with the effective British 'management' of indigenous peoples in the eastern Cape. They agreed on the imperative for orderly, well-regulated behaviour on the part of colonised subjects, and there was consensus that a British example was needed to show 'natives' (as well as recalcitrant Afrikaners) how to improve their situation. But while the colonial forces at play in the eastern Cape never 'worked from irreconcilably different positions', there was certainly vehement dispute over precisely which British example should be employed.[25]

On questions of crucial material importance, such as whether 'natives' were to retain access to their land, missionaries and settlers might squabble, while officials generally took less principled and more contingently pragmatic approaches. But to state that the combinations and permutations of colonial interests and their discourses were diverse is only to go part way towards defining the complexity of British colonial culture. Not only was it possible for individuals to shift their allegiances, to reproduce other kinds of discourse and pursue other colonial visions; it was also possible for the same individuals to engage with different discourses, reproducing elements of more than one of them at any given time. Thus, during a period of humanitarian political ascendancy in Britain, colonial officials felt the need to legitimate their decisions in the light of humanitarian concerns, and to deploy rhetoric most often associated with humanitarian discourse – even when humanitarians in the Cape disputed those decisions.

In other words, the analytical boundaries between the colonial discourses delineated here were not so clearly defined that individuals were unable to transgress them. Rhetoric from one discourse could be 'borrowed' to serve the purposes of antithetical projects and political, military and material expediency allowed the fractures between colonial interests to be crossed in the long-term pursuit of shared colonial ambitions.

Imperial networks

Before proceeding in the next chapter to examine the genealogies of the colonial discourses that interweave throughout this account, it is important to identify one other of their characteristics – one that is deserving of much more attention than any parochial account of the eastern Cape would recognise. Crucially, each of the colonial projects and the discourses associated with them that are identified here was forged not just within the Cape, or even within multiple colonies or the metropole, but across a network linking these sites together. Histories of the Cape such as Keegan's, Bank's, Crais's and most recently Ross's, certainly recognise the material and ideological connections between the colony's frontier and Britain, but in the following account I want to give more emphasis to the ways in which the two sites were knitted together within a global cultural and political fabric. I want to suggest that British colonial discourses were made and remade, rather than simply transferred or imposed, through the 'geographies of connection' between Britain and settler colonies like the Cape in particular.[26]

Colonial and metropolitan sites were connected most obviously through material flows of capital, commodities and labour. By the late eighteenth century, British material culture was already located within intensively developed circuits connecting Western Europe, Africa, Asia and South America.[27] As Susan Thorne has pointed out,

> The extraordinary scale of British imperial expansion at the end of the nineteenth century has obscured the magnitude of Britain's colonial involvement at the eighteenth century's turn . . . By 1820, the British Empire had already absorbed almost a quarter of the world's population, most of whom were incorporated between the Seven Years War, which began in 1756, and the Napoleonic Wars, which ended in 1815.[28]

The nodal points holding this expanded imperial web and its extra-imperial trading partners together were ports and, the means of transmission between them, ships. Within these ships, Indian calicoes moved to Africa to purchase slaves, Tahitian breadfruit was taken to the Caribbean to feed those slaves, Caribbean molasses was transported to New England where it was made into rum for trade with Native Americans, and tea, coffee, chocolate, tobacco, sugar, rice and potatoes converged, from sites dispersed across the globe, on the British metropole. Although they were incomplete and subject to disjunctures and delay, the construction of such material networks by the early nineteenth century had created 'a new set of relationships which changed what was grown, made and consumed in each part of the world'.[29]

However, colonial and metropolitan sites were articulated discursively as well as materially, and through the same kinds of network infrastructure that serviced a global commerce. While each different site within the imperial network had 'its own possibilities and conditions of knowledge' these differentiated knowledges were connected by the communicative circuits of empire, and could thus be mutually affecting.[30] British ships carried information between colonial sites, in the form of newspapers, dispatches and letters, as well as produce and personnel, enabling far-flung colonies and the metropole to participate 'in a coordinated metasystem of meaning and action'.[31] Reinforced later in the nineteenth century by the telegraph, such technologies allowed representations of indigenous peoples in one part of the world to act as precedents, guiding imageries of subsequently colonised peoples elsewhere.[32] Indeed, as Bayly argues, precisely because of the development of an imperial network, 'the period 1760–1860 was a critical one in the epistemological and economic creation of "indigenous peoples" as a series of comparable categories across the globe'.[33]

While their relative significance oscillated within metropolitan imaginations according to multiple local contingencies, the major components of the early nineteenth-century empire of settlement – India, British North America, the West Indies, the Australian colonies, New Zealand and the Cape – became the most significant locales for the production of such imageries. Images of the empire's racial Others travelled from these colonies during the early nineteenth century in the form of settler newspapers and letters, we well as in official dispatches and travellers' reports. Parliamentary commissions, with their interrogations of colonial and metropolitan witnesses, their minutes of evidence collated from various colonies and their comprehensive reports on matters ranging from slavery to trading trans-actions and evangelicalism, were a particularly significant mechanism by which news of social relations in these settler colonies arrived at the centre of the empire. From there, the news was frequently disseminated outwards again, via the colonial press, to other colonial sites. The Colonial Office's per-manent under-secretary, Herman Merrivale, noted in 1841 that in building an empire of settlement, the British had constructed 'channels of inter-communication' throughout the world.[34]

A number of analysts, both postcolonial and materialist in orientation, have now begun to recover the complex ways in which 'knowledge' traversed these imperial circuits of information, impacting upon both Britain and each of its colonies.[35] Among historians of South Africa in particular, Shula Marks has pointed out that by the nineteenth century 'daily life in [the British Isles] – from diet to industrial discipline, from sexual mores to notions of governance – had been permeated by experiences of empire', generated in the colonies as well as the metropole.[36] As far as governance is concerned, Ann Stoler has shown that a consideration of colonial and metropolitan affairs within the same terms of reference, meant that the very 'inclusions and exclusions built into [metropolitan] . . . notions of citizenship, sovereignty and participation' were influenced by colonial social boundaries.[37] Catherine Hall has also emphasised that continual communication allowed nineteenth-century elites in the British imperial 'centres' and in its 'peripheries', to engage in debate about the proper status and treatment of their respective subordinates. She has thus advocated the recognition of power relations embedded in cultural exchanges that 'criss-crossed the globe'.[38]

In this book, I share the 'founding premise' of Stoler and Cooper, that 'social transformations are a product of both global patterns and local struggles'.[39] In particular I highlight the significance that settlers, mission-aries and officials on the eastern Cape frontier consciously attached to their participation within British imperial discursive networks. I also indicate some of the ways in which their activities, reinforced by similar activities in other settler colonies, impacted upon metropolitan representations and practices.

Acutely aware that marginalisation from imperial discursive networks could lead to the loss of access to political support and material resources, and that most Britons could only imagine what their colonial environments were like, each of the colonial groups studied in this book strove continually to fashion circuits of communication with vital metropolitan interests, and thus to shape British understandings of the Cape's places and peoples. Further-more, each colonial interest had a vital stake in maintaining correspondence with other, similar interests elsewhere in the colonial 'peripheries'. This, then, is very much a situated history of the Cape – one that conceives of it as a place partly constituted through its relations with other places.

As this book progresses, the focus expands and contracts, alighting on different components of the imperial network at different stages of the argument, but most frequently on the eastern Cape itself and on Britain. Chapter 2 begins with a brief narrative of Cape frontier history and historiography, covering the period from the late eighteenth century to the 1820s. This is intended to establish a context for the reader who is not already familiar with the Cape frontier's historiography. Thereafter the genealogies of British official and humanitarian discourses are traced over the same period. The framework of analysis here has its hub in Britain, but extends to incorporate diverse colonial locales, including India and the West Indies as well as the Cape in particular. In the tracing of an eastern Cape British settler discourse, chapter 3 engages more thoroughly with the colonial side of the Cape frontier, but highlights the material and discursive connections that the settlers there maintained with the metropole. In chapter 4, British colonising officials are followed across the frontier and their first endeavours to subordinate the Xhosa within 'Queen Adelaide Province' (1834–6) are examined in some detail. The close reading of colonialism 'on the ground' in this chapter is followed, in chapter 5, by a dramatic expansion of focus. This chapter consists of an analysis of the terms in which the British empire as a whole, as well as the Cape especially, was conceived within an ascendant humanitarian discourse. In chapter 6, a broad, mid nineteenth-century discursive shift towards biological determinism and away from the assumptions underlying humanitarian discourse – a shift incorporating both metropole and colonies – is identified. Finally, in chapter 7, the focus rests once again on the eastern Cape and British Kaffraria (the former Queen Adelaide Province), with an examination of the local implications of this discursive shift. This concluding chapter also contains a synopsis of the findings, about imperial networks and colonial discourses, that the writing of this book has engendered.

2 Colonial projects and the eastern Cape

I cannot but feel myself the Representative of a Body who cannot speak for themselves and for whom I must act without other guide than my own Conscience.

(Thomas Fowell Buxton, 1832)[1]

The Cape colonial frontier

The British government first decided to seize control of the Cape of Good Hope in 1795, during the war with Revolutionary France. The decision was taken in order to prevent the strategically vital harbour at Cape Town, currently held by the Dutch East India Company, falling into the hands of the enemy. Although the Treaty of Amiens allowed the colony to be handed back to the Dutch republic in 1803, the resumption of the Napoleonic War meant that it was captured again by British forces in 1806. By 1814, it was clear that the British government would be holding on to the Cape for the foreseeable future.

The western part of the colony inherited by British officials was already marked by clearly defined status groups and a broadly mercantilist economic structure. Most of the Cape's population, consisting of 20,000 Europeans, 25,000 slaves and 15,000 indigenous Khoesan and people of mixed descent, would have understood where they were positioned relative to others in the social hierarchy.[2] At the top of this hierarchy were those colonists of Dutch, French and German descent who had accumulated land and wealth through commercial wine and wheat production in the hinterland of Cape Town, a region which Dutch East India Company forces had begun to seize from Khoesan pastoralists from the late seventeenth century. This dominant class is known to historians as the Cape gentry.[3] By 1731, colonists of this stature, comprising some 7 per cent of the European population, owned over half of the colony's landed wealth.[4] However, private accumulation of the most valuable land around Cape Town had guaranteed relative poverty among those colonists who were deprived of access to it. The poorer sons of western Cape farmers or discharged company employees who acted as farm

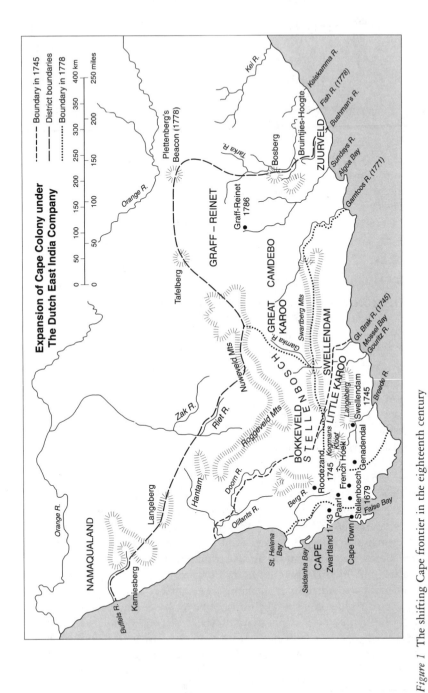

Figure 1 The shifting Cape frontier in the eighteenth century

Source: A. Lester, E. Nel and T. Binns, *South Africa Past, Present and Future: Gold at the End of the Rainbow?* Prentice Hall, London and New York, 2000, p. 57

servants, or *knechts*, had been propelled into the interior, where only livestock could be transported profitably to the Cape Town market.[5]

In the interior 'frontier' districts, colonial settlement had been achieved during the eighteenth century by small groups of men co-operating in mounted and armed units known as commandos. They had concentrated first on monopolising access to the most valuable land in a semi-arid environment – that surrounding a spring or a watercourse – subsequently getting their claim to it recognised by the company. Control over water supplies and the game which they attracted had often enabled dominance over far more numerous local Khoesan populations without the need for direct conquest. By such means, dramatic colonial expansion had been effected by just a few thousand colonists and their families.[6] Towards the end of the eighteenth century, however, the further extension of the frontier was proving much more difficult. The boundaries of the colony, ranging from some 100 miles inland of Cape Town to the north, to 400 miles to the east, became spaces of bitter and enduring warfare.[7]

In the east, colonial expansion ground to a halt after colonists entered lands between the Gamtoos and Fish Rivers, lands that were being increasingly densely settled by Xhosa-speaking chiefdoms. In 1776, the colonist Hendrick Swellengrebel noted that unless colonisers 'succeed through industry in reducing the amount of ground necessary for grazing on each farm', competition with the Xhosa meant that it would not be possible for many more colonists to settle in the region.[8] By the time the British first took the Cape in 1795, many of the colonists in the eastern frontier district of Graaff Reinet were already *bywoners*, or landless tenants. In the face of Xhosa resistance to encroachment, even those who had managed to obtain farms had been forced to evacuate them on more than one occasion. They had discovered that although colonial commandos could destroy Xhosa homesteads and drive their inhabitants away from grazing land, once the commandos were disbanded and their members dispersed to remote farms, they were often incapable of defending those farms from Xhosa raiding parties.

For Xhosa chiefdoms, of course, the marginal area around the Fish River comprised the western, rather than the eastern, frontier. These chiefdoms shared one of the family of Bantu languages, worked iron and practised crop cultivation as well as keeping cattle – attributes defining them in distinction to those Khoesan groups that colonists had first encountered in the west. Some Xhosa chiefdoms had exercised a 'loose sovereignty over Khoekhoe chiefdoms' in the area between the Fish and Sundays Rivers from the first half of the eighteenth century, and others had used the same territory for occasional grazing. But it was not until the 1760s that the first Xhosa chiefdoms erected permanent settlements there.[9] At that time, the succession of the Xhosa paramount, Phalo, was disputed by his sons Rharhabe and Gcaleka. Fighting between their followers resulted in Gcaleka's dominance to the east of the Kei River and Rharhabe's crossing of the river, along with his followers, to the west.[10] Rharhabe's crossing of the Kei prompted the smaller Gqunukhwebe chiefdom to move further west in turn, entering what was then the limit of colonial settlement. After the Gqunukhwebe came the Mbalu and the imiDange chiefdoms, also settling during the 1770s in areas abutting vanguard colonial farms.[11]

Largely disregarding these minor chiefdoms settled between colonial farms on the western fringes of his new territory, Rharhabe set about founding a new and autonomous branch of the Xhosa polity through the conquest and absorption of Khoesan groups that had, until now, retained their independence just beyond the colonial frontier. His project of constructing tributary relations, or of achieving the direct assimilation of subordinate groups, would be continued into the nineteenth century by his son, Ndlambe.

From the 1770s, the 'eastern Cape frontier' was thus a space of interaction between colonial, Khoesan and Xhosa polities and structures of authority. In a sense, it would seem to have been a region approximating Mary Louise Pratt's conception of a 'contact zone'. Here, 'copresence, interaction, interlocking understandings and practices', rather than simple binary oppositions and conflicts, characterise the meeting between previously separated populations.[12] Aside from the frequent sexual contact between colonial men and Khoesan women (only rarely formalised in marriage), relatively isolated and impoverished colonists' housing, dietary, clothing and hunting practices, their techniques of labour control and even their language, were certainly inflected by Khoesan material and symbolic cultures.[13] However, the clearest evidence of understanding between colonists and Xhosa in the late eighteenth century does not derive from projects of cultural hybridisation. Rather, it points to expedient political and, above all, military alliances forged between colonists acting independently of the colonial authorities on the one hand, and stronger Xhosa chiefdoms on the other. These alliances were orientated largely towards the conquest, expulsion or domination of militarily weaker Khoesan and Xhosa groups.

During the first two, full-scale, but inconclusive 'frontier wars' of 1779–81 and 1793, colonists acted in a loose alliance with Ndlambe against the other Xhosa chiefdoms claiming rights to the Zuurveld – the seasonal grazing land between the Sundays and Fish Rivers. Their co-operation was designed to guarantee colonists exclusive access to land and Ndlambe political paramountcy over rival chiefdoms.[14] Such colonial–Xhosa transactions were by no means conducive to the dilution of either an exclusive colonial sense of identity, which was being forged primarily in the slave-owning society of the western Cape, or of a Xhosa sense of identity, which was being established through the absorption of tributary groups within a dominant lineage to the east. Indeed, colonists' continuing preoccupation with the founding of new, privately owned farms militated against anything more than an ephemeral alliance with any independent Xhosa authority and embroiled the first British governors of the Cape in two further conflicts along the frontier during the 1790s.[15]

Even the Cape's relatively impoverished frontier colonists were determined to create and maintain social boundaries founded on ethnicity and 'race', rather than perpetuate a balance of power that was conducive to the transgression of such boundaries. In other words, cross-frontier borrowings, exchanges and alliances with the Khoesan and Xhosa were, from the start, conceived of as being temporary measures, engaged in until such a time as colonists felt able to construct more robust systems of white dominance. The colonial community on the eastern frontier may not have conceived of their intended subordinates in the biologically determinist ways that would later characterise white racism, but they nevertheless shared both an established discourse and a political project of ethnic superiority.[16] However much Afrikaner farmers and Khoesan came to resemble one another in clothing, language and material culture, and however enduring were the political alliances forged between colonial commandos and Xhosa chiefdoms, relations between these self-defined groups in the late eighteenth century were 'founded on violence' and 'shot through with fear'.[17] This was the over-determining characteristic of the frontier zone that the British would inherit for a second, and more permanent time, in 1806.

British governmentality and the problem of the Cape frontier

After 1806, the turbulent margins of the Cape became the responsibility of a new set of officials embedded within a novel framework of global power. In this section I will consider on the one hand the implications of the frontier for a British discourse of colonial governmentality, and on the other hand, the effects of that discourse on the frontier zone.

Colonial governmentality

During the late eighteenth and early nineteenth centuries, Britain's 'second empire', along with British identity as a whole, was being forged out of the wars with Revolutionary and Napoleonic France.[18] Having seized the empire, it was the military who also governed it. As in other new colonies, government in the Cape after 1806 rested in the hands of officers with aristocratic connections, most of them having served under Wellington in the Peninsular campaign or at Waterloo. These men were participants in the 'network of relationships and an *esprit de corps* which carried the military, diplomatic and colonial services into the Victorian Age'.[19] They had received their administrative appointments in much the same way as they had obtained their military commissions, through their ability to exploit aristocratic connections 'at home' and in the colonies. One of their major functions was to oversee strategically placed garrisons (the Cape had 6,500 troops in 1810 – more than at Gibraltar or Malta). This meant that their ties with

the British army's headquarters at Horse Guards in London, were as significant as those with the War and Colonial Office.[20]

Early nineteenth-century governors thus comprised a globally distributed
network centred upon two metropolitan hubs – military and civilian. The
policies that they implemented in any one place can be conceived of only
in the light of those adopted elsewhere, since they reflected both what
Bayly calls a 'style' that was established for the governance of new colonies
in general, and the British ruling class's own, shifting domestic concerns.[21]
Together, military governors and War and Colonial Office officials formulated their own rules and procedures, their own knowledges of contrasting
colonial situations and of their relation to metropolitan ones. Their construction of a coherent system of representation was facilitated by the close-knit
nature of colonial officialdom, itself partly the result of the few men considered able enough to govern colonies who made themselves available for
the purpose, given the other opportunities available in Britain itself.[22] One
administrator would often serve in a variety of colonial locations during his
career, carrying his package of favourite techniques with him, and building
a 'knowledge' of colonial situations in general.[23] He could also transport
his own small-scale network of patronage, with acolytes transferred between
postings.[24] Despite their global distribution, as Cell points out, 'there was
enough real or imagined similarity among local administrators to enable
reasonably coherent books to be written on the subject of the forms and processes of colonial government'.[25] Colonial governmentality, then, was being
constructed by these military and often aristocratic men as a discourse of
its own.

This discourse may have been constructed within a colonial frame of reference and with regard to colonial conditions, but it was always conceived of
very much in relation to metropolitan preoccupations. The period from
1806 to 1815 was one in which the land-owning aristocracy and gentry
who comprised the British governing class, were besieged. They were fighting
not only Napoleon's armies on the Continent, but also political radicalism
and unrest 'at home'. In Britain, 'apocalyptic fears concerning . . . invasion,
blockade, food shortage, national debt, a mad king, and a general appre-
hension [to which we will return below] that England was about to be singled
out for divine punishment', were interwoven with destabilising economic
currents.[26] Fearing that an established ethos of paternalistic, aristocratic hegemony was collapsing under the strain, Tory governments were reacting with
repression, cracking down on public meetings and political agitation with a
series of legislative and judicial measures.[27] From the local autocracy of the
landowner and squire to the representation of landed wealth in the parliamentary parties, the British establishment was trying to construct a 'revivified
conservative regime'.[28]

The metropolitan elite's emphasis on stabilising fraught relations between
apparently 'naturally' defined social classes immediately became the concern
of colonial governors too, if only so that the newly expanded empire could

be governed at minimal expense, and so that troops could be spared for other commitments. British governors' first, limited attempts to intervene in Cape colonial society after 1806, like those in other colonies, were accordingly conservative.[29] Policies which bolstered colonial masters' control over their labour force were necessary to secure adequate finance and manpower to maintain the garrison and supply transiting British ships at Cape Town.[30] Just as corveé was being newly implemented by British authorities in Java, forced labour in Ceylon and debt bondage in India, so in the Cape, Afrikaner masters' control over their Khoesan servants was effectively reinforced.[31] In 1809, Earl Caledon, the new British governor, issued the 'Caledon Code', which required Khoesan servants to obtain a colonial farmer's pass before leaving their 'place of abode'. Otherwise they could be arrested and jailed. Similarly, in 1812, a Proclamation of Caledon's successor, General Sir John Cradock, forced Khoesan children to be apprenticed to colonial masters until the age of eighteen.

Afrikaners and Khoesan

Such measures, however, were accompanied by a skein of protective legislation, as had been promised to the victims of colonial 'brutality' by governors during the first British occupation of 1795–1803. Then, coherent representations of the Dutch-speaking colonist, or Afrikaner, had first been generated within British official circles, and they were generally unfavourable. Aside from the Cape gentry, whom British officials found conducive to projects of commercial and cultural 'improvement', Afrikaners were quickly constructed negatively within a wider configuration of British patriotic and class discourses.[32] Many of the 'problems' posed by the Afrikaners were ascribed to the effects of Dutch East India Company rule. The company had apparently always stood as a barrier between the Cape's colonists and the Dutch metropole, allowing only an intermittent assimilation of new European ideas, and even then the worst kind of republican ones, to filter through to the Cape.[33] At the same time, the company's enforcement of restrictive and mercantilist 'monopoly' measures had apparently stifled individual 'industry'.

Despite the common antipathy to Catholicism, which would help bind Dutch gentry and British officials into an elite colonial class,[34] many officials felt that Dutch 'peasants' in the Cape, like those of Britain's Catholic enemies on the Continent, had become lazy under a corrupt and rigid regime. The colony's agricultural potential had not been realised because of the master class's dependence on poorly motivated slaves and oppressed Khoesan servants. The traveller Robert Percival remarked that 'even when gain was evidently the ultimate reward, the indolence of these degenerate colonists prevailed . . . over their avarice'.[35] As Robert Ross points out, in John Barrow's 'classic' account of Graaff Reinet burghers, the 'main motif is fat, whether on the boers' table, belly or floor. In this land of grease, in which all forms of cultured entertainment were lacking, indolence . . . prevailed, sustained by systematic brutality towards the [Khoesan] labourers'.[36]

The further one travelled away from Cape Town and towards the frontier, the more poverty-stricken, indolent and brutal, the more generally degraded, Dutch colonial burghers seemed to become within British official discourse.[37] Two frontier burgher revolts within the space of four years during the 1790s had only reinforced such notions. Not only were frontier colonists in particular condemned in British aristocratic, governing eyes for their tendency towards rebellion and republicanism, they were also despised for eroding the vital distinction between colonist and 'native' through their 'squalid and wretched' lifestyle.[38] What made Afrikaner degradation even more contemptible than that of the indigenous Khoesan, however, was that the former was the result of a slide out of a civilised condition, whereas the latter was at least 'original' or 'inherent'.[39]

Even under a conservative British regime, the physical punishment of labourers had to be taken out of the hands of these 'degenerate' masters. It became the responsibility of government instead, and the institution of circuit courts in 1813 gave Khoesan servants an avenue for direct appeal against abuse.[40] If British administrators hoped that slave and Khoesan 'industry may be excited . . . by equitable treatment barbarously withheld from them by the Dutch',[41] they also hoped that the customs and manners of the Afrikaners would be reformed in the process. As in Ceylon and Java, soon after their assumption of government in the Cape, British officials publicly destroyed instruments of Dutch torture. This was partly in order to demonstrate a new benevolence to the Cape's servile classes, one which would reproduce the Tory ideal of paternalism 'at home'. But it also unambiguously pressed home the message that British rulers did not need to rely, like their predecessors, on archaic and brutal forms of punishment.[42] When the first British settlers to arrive on the eastern Cape frontier were told that Britain, 'had now sent her Sons and Daughters to cultivate the arts of civilised life amidst the long neglected natives of the third Quarter' the word 'natives' was taken to mean Afrikaners as much as it did Africans.[43]

The frontier and the Xhosa

While effective, paternalist government was being instituted within the colony 'proper', the official approach to the eastern Cape frontier was informed by the geostrategic imperatives of European governmental discourse. Focusing on the need for government power and its objects to be contained within policed territorial limits, the British military governors' concept of order in the Cape was based upon neat and discrete 'national' boundaries.[44] The emphasis in military and political strategy was to secure those boundaries on terms favourable to the state, and seal them off from external economic and demographic forces. Only then could the projects of improvement being contemplated for the western districts be extended to the east. As Governor

Cradock admitted in 1811, 'I can only reason and act upon such general [European] principles as will apply to every case of the present nature'. This meant that 'British territory' must be maintained 'inviolate . . . resisting under any pretence the inroads . . . of any neighbouring state'.[45]

In 1778, the Dutch governor van Plettenberg had launched the first official attempt to make political subjectivity congruent with territoriality along the colony's eastern borders. He had endeavoured to negotiate a mutually recognised boundary between the colony and 'Xhosaland' running along the line of the Fish River. However, van Plettenberg had managed to secure the consent only of the minor Gwali Xhosa chiefdom. Despite the fact that the Ndlambe and other chiefdoms inhabited and grazed lands to the west of the Fish River (that is, within the colony as it was now thought to be defined), they were not consulted. Even had the river marked a discrete boundary between colonial subjects on the one hand and independent Xhosa on the other, it was an extremely awkward one, since it ran from west to east for much of its length, before providing a barrier of sorts between the mass of the Xhosa and the colonists by turning south towards to ocean.[46] Nevertheless, the first British governors recognised this treaty as the only one in existence that defined a recognisable boundary and, accordingly, assumed that they were entitled to exclusive control of the Zuurveld, and that the Xhosa presence in the area was anomalous.

One of the earliest British intelligence reports on the Xhosa was written by Colonel Collins after a tour of the eastern districts in 1809. Collins clearly considered himself a rational product of the Enlightenment. His initial response to the unfamiliar Xhosa was to enumerate and classify them.[47] Having done this, he set about tracing the genealogies of each of the major chiefly lineages, so that the new British administration would know exactly with whom it was dealing.[48] Collins concluded that he would have been 'exalted' if he had been able to recommend that the Xhosa, like the conquered Khoesan should be integrated within colonial economic networks and uplifted by British civilising projects. He expressed his wish that the colony could contribute to 'the laudable endeavours of those humane persons whose labours have been so worthily employed in rescuing a portion of the original inhabitants of Africa from the miseries of barbarism'.[49] However, he continued, 'when that pleasure can be indulged only by sacrificing the interests and compromising the safety of one of the best appendages of his Majesty's crown, it becomes a duty to resist such agreeable illusions'.[50] Since the Xhosa could not easily be made 'loyal Protestant servants of His Majesty',[51] the parameters of governmental power in the Cape were best defined by excluding them entirely from the colonial order.

Despite the requests previously made by the chiefs Ndlambe and Chungwa to the Batavian Governor Janssens, that Xhosa commoners be allowed officially to work among the colonists, British officials identified with Collins' 'maxim of the first importance . . . that all intercourse between the settlers and the Caffres should be scrupulously prevented, until the former should have increased considerably in numbers and are also much more advanced in arts and industry'.[52] Collins' official predisposition to construct the Xhosa presence on the margins of the colony as a 'foreign' intrusion was reinforced by a series of memorials from colonial farmers in the Zuurveld to their new rulers, describing 'the Kaffers' as 'naturally insatiable beggars and thieves'.[53] Invariably, these memorials complained about stock loss at the hands of Xhosa raiding parties seeking to maintain their own access to contested grazing land.

Governor Caledon soon became determined to stamp out the 'trifling depredations committed by wandering caffres'.[54] In 1809, he ordered that the hundreds of Xhosas unofficially earning livestock by working on frontier farms, and those independent chiefdoms engaging in transhumance furthest within the colony, were to be expelled east across the Sundays River. In 1811, however, Caledon's successor, Cradock, received further memorials from burghers, again representing the Xhosa consistently as rapacious cattle thieves. The new governor was convinced that the Xhosa were imbued with a fundamental 'spirit of depredation [and] thirst for plunder and other savage passions'.[55] Stating that 'it should be our invariable object to establish the separation from them, as intercourse can never subsist to the advantage of one party, or the other', he expressed his determination to carry into effect the expulsion of all Xhosa across the Fish River 'boundary' itself.[56]

As far as Cradock was concerned, not only had the Fish River been 'agreed' as the border between van Plettenberg and the Xhosa chiefs, it was also a defensible and therefore 'natural' frontier line. Throughout the first half of the century, British military officials would continue to conceive of the ideal colonial border as being 'a large unfordable river running through the country with unlimited visibility and no prospects for concealment'.[57] If the Xhosa could be expelled across the Fish River, Cradock believed that colonial territory could be more easily maintained as 'inviolate . . . resisting under any pretence the inroads, even for permanent or even temporary purposes of any neighbouring state'.[58] The attempted securing of the colonial margins was carried out by Colonel Graham in 1812, employing troops who had just become available following the expulsion of the French from Madagascar. Graham's colonial, Khoesan and regular British commando finally forced the Ndlambe and other Xhosa across the Fish River by 'destroying kraals [and] laying waste . . . gardens and fields'.[59] Those Xhosa who resisted the 'clearance', known conventionally as the Fourth Frontier War, were shot, so as to instil a 'proper degree of terror and respect'.[60] Graham himself expressed regret that such action, 'tho' strongly repugnant to my own feelings' was unavoidable given 'the character of the Kafir nation'. He was convinced 'that by no other means whatever can a hope be entertained of putting to an end the encroachments and accompanying cruelties of this savage nation'.[61]

While the military action against Ndlambe may have brought incipient prosperity to a colonial frontier on which a permanent garrison had now to be supplied,[62] it failed to ensure security for local colonists. Ndlambe's followers were forced onto the territory of Ngqika, Ndlambe's nephew and great rival for paramountcy among the frontier Xhosa. The contest between these men on the eastern side of the Fish River, resulted not only in intensified raiding between their chiefdoms, but also in further incursions by warriors from both chiefdoms into the colony.[63] When Lord Charles Somerset, an illustrious and conservative descendent of the Plantagenets, arrived to take over the administration of the Cape in 1814, he inherited the same problem as his predecessors: an eastern frontier that simply refused to be rendered 'orderly' in the terms defined by the British governmental imagination.

The 'messy' interpenetration of colonial subjects and independent Xhosa within the colonial margins seems to have been particularly and personally galling to Somerset. With his grand, requisitioned buildings and his own 'court' situated just outside Cape Town and comprised of favourites who benefited from substantial official salaries, Somerset was resolved to represent his authority as a seamless power that was easily and naturally exercised. He made determined efforts to insulate his political and personal activities in the Cape (which included a penchant for horse racing, 'fox' (jackal) hunting and the appropriation of government resources for private use) from 'interfering ministers in London'.[64] Like many other governors of his time, Somerset made full use of the latitude allowed him by an understaffed Colonial Office that was prepared to tolerate a degree of 'ancient corruption' in the colonies as long as it saved on expenditure. Even in the event of Colonial Office disapproval, Somerset could follow the example of governors in India and cite the exigencies of war, in his case on the eastern frontier, 'as an excuse for a personal and often despotic style of rule'.[65] This new governor soon came to be 'looked upon as the embodiment of [corrupt] High Toryism by Whigs and radicals in England, and as an oppressive autocrat by many at the Cape'.[66] If his authority was to continue to hold undisputed sway within the colony, it was particularly important for him to impose order on the colonial borders.

In the face of continued cattle raiding, Somerset thus made his own distinctive modifications to frontier government from 1816.[67] His strategy was dualistic. On the one hand he intended protecting the colonial border as had his predecessors, consolidating it as the barrier against foreign Xhosa 'intrusion'. But on the other hand, with the frontier Xhosa having recently been subjected to a display of superior British might at the hands of Colonel Graham, Somerset articulated a hope that the Xhosa might now be made more amenable to long term cultural transformation. This was a significant, if politically expedient departure. For the first time in Cape official discourse, there was the expressed intention to protect and consolidate the colonial order not only by sealing off its margins from Xhosa 'depredation', but simultaneously by neutralising the Xhosa's 'otherness' which was so threatening to that order. Somerset's adoption of a 'civilising mission', was, however, guarded and suspicious. Military techniques still provided the essential backstop to colonial security. The governor held that

> So long as the habits of savages remain unbroken the colony will . . . be exposed to the changes incident to the fickleness of that character . . . That the most beneficial result may be expected in due time from [an] attempt [at Xhosa civilisation], I do not permit myself to doubt, but . . . this system is not solely to be trusted to . . . it is essential that it should be supported by that prudential strength which shall tend to overawe the restlessness of our hostile and wily neighbours.[68]

The more effective sealing of the frontier would be achieved, as Collins had recommended, through the denser settlement of the Zuurveld with Britons, providing a new colonial population and one more easily governed than the existing colonists, as well as one more capable of dealing with the Xhosa. The margins of the colony would be filled 'with men superior beyond comparison to those savages who have plundered [colonists] so grievously and rendered their abode there irksome and unprofitable'.[69]

The gradual and guarded cultivation of the Xhosa as more docile neighbours was to be achieved by two means. First, missionaries were permitted to introduce 'agriculture and civilization' to frontier chiefs.[70] Somerset selected two men whom he felt had the necessary piety, and the kind of conscience that would lead them to refrain from engaging in colonial 'politics'. At the same time, however, he instructed them to send him intelligence from the Xhosa side of the frontier. In 1820 John Brownlee was sent to establish the Tyhumie valley mission, located at a strategically vital point at the foot of the Ngqika's Amatola Mountains stronghold. He was later joined by William Ritchie Thomson, who proved himself a particularly avid collector and transmitter of information on Ngqika's activities.[71] Secondly, Ngqika himself was to be accorded a special status in the expectation that he would control further Xhosa 'outrages' against colonial farms. Contradicting the general prohibition on intercourse across the frontier line, Ngqika and his councillors were given access to the colonial garrison town of Graham's Town for trade. Through such interactions, Somerset hoped that 'civilization and its consequences may be introduced into countries hitherto barbarous and unexplored'.[72]

Somerset, however, soon found that if the Xhosa could not be prevented from raiding frontier farms through expulsion from adjacent lands, neither could their political order be controlled from without. A form of 'indirect rule' over the frontier Xhosa through Ngqika proved impossible. In 1818, much to the Governor's consternation, Ngqika was overthrown by his rival Ndlambe. Ngqika was given British support and a devastating punitive cattle raid was led by Colonel Brereton against the victorious Ndlambe.

In turn, Brereton's raid precipitated a full-scale Ndlambe attack on the British garrison in Graham's Town, led by the wardoctor Nxele.[73] The British soldiers were saved only by the timely return of mounted Khoesan troops, who had been out hunting. British reinforcements then launched a counter-attack, securing Ndlambe's surrender and concluding this 'Fifth Frontier War'.[74]

The war convinced Somerset to press ahead with plans to further protect the colonial margins during the interval before the Xhosa could be transformed into more tractable neighbours. The land lying between the Fish and Keiskamma Rivers, which had been occupied largely by the colony's Ngqika 'allies', was seized as a strategic buffer between the colonists' farms and the Xhosa's kraals. Although Somerset officially reported that this strip of land was a neutral territory, and stated his intention 'not to permit [it] to be inhabited until our endeavours to civilize the Kafirs had been successful', it was very swiftly described as being 'ceded' to the colony.[75] With the Ngqika being expelled from the territory as the price of British support against the Ndlambe, colonial farmers saw the land simply as an extension of the colony.[76]

Some smaller Xhosa chiefdoms, notably the Gqunukhwebe, were allowed to retain their land within this 'ceded' strip in recognition of their having refrained from raiding colonial farms, and even some of the Ngqika were subsequently 'permitted' to graze there in times of drought, but a number of colonial homesteads nevertheless became permanently established there. Furthermore, colonists and regular soldiers, organised in commandos, could traverse the territory, supposedly in pursuit of stolen cattle, under a notorious set of regulations known as the 'spoor law'. Any farmer alleging the theft of stock could call out a commando accompanied by British cavalry and confiscate an equal or greater number of stock from the first Xhosa kraal to which the 'spoor', or track, was traced. Frequently, scant regard was paid to the precise spoor being followed or to the culpability of the particular kraal being punished. This incensed even those frontier Xhosa who had thus far been left in possession of their land, and thus provoked further Xhosa raiding.[77] So the 'essential gesture' of Xhosa 'savagery' in British official discourse – depredation – continued.

I will return to officials' schemes for the frontier in chapter 4, where the departures in governmental imagination of the 1830s are considered. But at this point, I want to assess the points of origin and the early evolution of such schemes before outlining the genesis of a competing humanitarian discourse of the frontier. By the mid 1820s, British officials had achieved much in gaining the general support of the white population of the Cape, largely by reinforcing master-servant relationships in new ways. As Freund points out, 'administrative dispatches had become self-satisfied and conventional compared to the crisis-ridden hand-wringings of the first occupation'.[78] However, while governors had consolidated projects of governmentality in the west, they had also become inextricably involved in, indeed had unintentionally exacerbated, the conflicts of the eastern frontier. On this point their dispatches were far from complacent. British officials had become reluctant participants in the violent struggles of the colonial frontier, I would argue, largely because of the way that they framed and understood certain experiences and events as 'problems' with which they had to deal.[79]

It was the notion of a necessary kind of 'order', generated at first within a recently elaborated European discourse of governmentality, which created the frontier as a 'disorderly' space in need of administrative intervention. As previous mercantilist Dutch authorities had demonstrated, it was not *necessarily* the case that the frontier should generate a rationale for forceful governmental action. Colonists who chose to live there could be, and for much of the eighteenth century, had been, left largely to their own devices and their own means of negotiation with, and defence against, the Xhosa and their own Khoesan subordinates. The frontier became a 'problem' for British governors because the governmental project of demarcating and defending territory and population in conjunction had travelled with them from the metropole to this colonial periphery. Within the British governmental imagination, all attempts possible had to be made to render political and national subjectivity congruent with territoriality. Out of all the colonial interests, officials who acted within this discourse of governmentality had the greatest need 'to fix and order all social sectors, especially those least susceptible to the rulers' self-disciplining practices'.[80]

In a vicious cycle, the military techniques which had provoked the Xhosa to raid 'colonial territory' prompted yet further military responses. When planning for the reception of new British settlers along the frontier in 1820, Somerset's temporary replacement, Acting Governor Sir Rufane Donkin could think only in strategic terms. He wanted the settlers, who were to be located in the Zuurveld, protected by 'two strong posts at their flanks' within the 'ceded territory'. One of these posts, in the Kat River area, would be occupied by Highland Scots 'with the military view of having them, a strong and warlike body of mountaineers, to form the left flank of the military line of defence'. The Scots party's leader, Captain Grant, having been an officer, 'will be able to keep these people [the settlers] in such a sort of military discipline, as to be able to act against the Caffres in defence of the frontier'.[81] Although the anticipated Scottish settlement did not materialise, the party having been shipwrecked before it reached the Cape, the subsequent filling of the ceded territory with other military units simply provoked further Xhosa raids.

Despite their consistent failure to realise their governmental imperatives on the frontier, governors' actions there were just as consistently legitimated, and their failures perpetually explained, by a coherent representation of the Xhosa as rapacious and incorrigible depredators. This was a construction which officials made sure would travel to the metropole, contained as it was in a succession of dispatches to the Colonial Office. As Governor

Sir Lowry Cole put it in 1829, and as metropolitan officials came to 'understand' and 'know', 'The very general disposition to plunder which appears inherent in the Caffre character, and the open and exposed state of the frontier districts of the colony, render the Caffres most troublesome neighbours'.[82]

The construction of humanitarian discourse

If military governors tended to see the eastern Cape as the front line of a fragile colonial order, for many largely middle class British humanitarians, in the Cape and in Britain, it was conceived in a very different light. Their approach to the frontier was active and professedly benign rather than defensive and strategic. The essence of their critique of colonial government in the Cape is contained in a question put by Charles Lushington to the former colonial official Andries Stockenström in 1835:

> We have tried the system of military coercion for many years and to a great extent; we have had great public commandos in 1818, in 1819, in 1823, in 1829, in 1830 and in 1831; we have had besides those, military patrols and inroads for the purpose of seizing cattle stolen, or said to be stolen by the natives; notwithstanding the extent to which we have carried this, does it appear that it has wrought the effect which was anticipated from it, and that peace upon the borders has been obtained?

Stockenström's reply was 'Decidedly not, on the contrary'.[83]

Rather than constructing the colonial margin as a zone of military operations, British humanitarians saw it as an advancing arena in which a utopian order of Christian, British civilisation could be continually extended over those previously denied its benefits. In order to comprehend these representational differences, we need to conceive of a humanitarian politics of the Cape frontier as but one aspect of the construction of a new bourgeois subjectivity in Britain and its empire as a whole.[84] An entire, uneven global network, and a discourse of humanitarianism was constructed during the late eighteenth and early nineteenth centuries, at least in part through middle-class opposition to aristocratic reaction at both colonial and metropolitan sites.

Evangelicalism, patriotism and anti-slavery

As Davidoff and Hall note, the 'middle strata' of late eighteenth- and early nineteenth-century British society, that was propertied and yet not landed, 'was criss-crossed by differences of interest and riven with internal dissension. The large sector of professionals and merchants in London differed from the manufacturing families in the north and Midlands whose experience differed again from the market town tradesmen and solicitors of the farmers whom they serviced'. Religious and political distinctions among the 'middling sort' also reflected profound differences in social standing. And yet, during the first decades of the nineteenth century, 'these disparate elements welded together into a powerful unified culture'.[85]

In contrast to an aristocratic identity founded on natural hierarchy, heredity and stasis, middle-class British identity was being constructed around a universalist conception of human nature; of the capacity of each individual, given freedom from confining regulations, to progress spiritually and materially, thus contributing to the greater good of society. Middle-class culture was characterised by the interlocking of religious and secular imperatives to generate a new 'moral code', both for the individual and for society at large, in order to achieve this greater good.[86] A number of interweaving programmes, including evangelicalism, patriotism and abolitionism, informed this middle-class code and underpinned its diverse political agendas. Each of these programmes was linking metropolitan and colonial spaces in powerful, politically enabling ways, at the very time that British governors were attempting to govern the Cape through more reactionary discourses.

Evangelicalism became particularly important in the contests that were waged over colonialism in the Cape and elsewhere. It was one means by which metropolitan middle-class groups, marginalised from 'the world of rank and land', could establish their own 'associations and networks', challenging 'the existing apparatus of power'.[87] For this reason, it was eyed warily at first by an Anglican, aristocratic elite (including the influential Somerset family). However, by the early nineteenth century, Britain's ruling class was beginning to identify evangelicalism with more comforting prospects than subversion or revolution. Through its uplifting message to labourers and artisans, it promised a more acquiescent, or at least a more resigned, working class.[88] This more conservative promise was pursued in particular by the Anglican Church Missionary Society. As its founders explained, 'The husband and wife, the father and son, the master and servant, at once learn from [Christianity] their respective duties, and are disposed and enabled to fulfil them . . . Rulers become the fathers of their people, and subjects cheerfully yield obedience'.[89] Evangelicalism could thus be made 'part of an established consensus' by ruling groups, its liberal, progressive aspects' underplayed and its 'power to mute popular protest and prevent rebellion' brought to the fore.[90]

During the war with France, Protestant evangelicalism contributed to a patriotic discourse which bound the British classes together rather than tearing them apart. The persecution of Protestants on the Continent and the threat of a Jacobite invasion supported by a French or Spanish Catholic army of occupation, were events that had occurred within many Britons' living memories. In the 1810s, the Napoleonic War was popularly coded as a struggle against continental Catholicism, with Britain's very religious identity felt to be in peril. Evangelicals' spiritual efforts could thus be represented as part of the collective project of national survival. By the end of the war, it was not just the bourgeoisie, but Britain's aristocratic rulers themselves, who had been persuaded 'of the necessity of grounding their authority in religion'.[91]

The incorporation of evangelicalism into a set of hegemonic representations was by no means, however, an isolated, metropolitan affair. It was inextricably connected with Britain's imperial expansion, and in particular with the debate over the slave trade.[92] As Thomas Lacquer has argued, within a nascent evangelical morality, the eighteenth-century concept of individual 'virtue' was being superseded by a notion of collective responsibility for the plight of distant others. This shift was manifested in a 'new cluster of narratives' including fiction, coroners' reports and post-mortems, all of which 'came to speak in extraordinary detailed fashion about the pains and deaths of ordinary people in such a way as to make apparent the causal chains that might connect the actions of its readers with the suffering of its subjects'.[93] What lay behind this sense was an awareness of the relations between distant peoples forged by modern capitalist practices that were stretched across space. Such relations, of course, reached their extremes of brutality and exploitation in the trans-Atlantic slave trade and an increasingly powerful evangelical sensibility required urgent political action to obtain redress for its victims.[94] Slavery was, accordingly, constructed by the British middle classes as 'one of the major questions over which . . . the notion of a "civilised" nation was defined'.[95] The abolition of the trade in 1807 served both to secure national atonement for the wrongs which Britons had inflicted on the world through their participation in the trade, and to reinforce patriotic discourse by distinguishing freedom-loving Britons from tyrannical Continental Catholics.[96] By the early nineteenth century, then, anti-slavery had become 'a defining quality of being British; a proof of the distinctive and divinely-inspired qualities of the British people'.[97]

However, as well as consolidating a particular kind of evangelical Protestant nationalism, abolition of the trans-Atlantic trade in itself gave rise to new techniques of political mobilisation. The anti-slavery campaign had co-ordinated Baptist missionaries in the West Indies, Quakers in Britain and America, evangelical businessmen and middle-class women in the British provinces, Members of Parliament in London and, for a brief period before the great bourgeois fear of revolution in the 1790s, large numbers of working-class radicals in Britain's industrial and agricultural towns. The London-based Committee for the Abolition of the Slave Trade had mobilised this uneven trans-Atlantic network through books, pamphlets, prints and artefacts, using all the resources which late eighteenth-century modern print capitalism, the 'birth of consumer society' and the growth of the 'public sphere' put at its disposal.[98]

After 1807, similar techniques, built around networks linking evangelical reformers in the colonies to allies in Britain, would be deployed not only to secure the freedom of existing slaves, but to reform colonial governmentality more broadly, in an attempt to alter the subjectivity and behaviour of both colonisers and colonised. The nineteenth-century debates about intrinsic human worth, conducted between official, settler and humanitarian groups, not only drew many of their reference points from the preceding debate over slavery; they were also conducted through similar imperial networks extended into Asia, Africa and the Antipodes, and through similar techniques of public mobilisation.

Reforming Britain and the Cape

After the abolition of the trade in slaves, the continuing campaign for emancipation and colonial reform was led by the Clapham Sect (often referred to as 'the Saints'), a group of largely Anglican evangelicals centred in south London. The sect included among its 'members' great abolitionist heroes like the Thorntons and Wilberforces as well as luminaries like Zachary Macauly (Governor of Sierra Leone), James Stephen the elder (whose son would become Permanent Under-Secretary at the Colonial Office), and Charles Grant (an evangelist on the board of the East India Company, whose own son, Lord Glenelg, would later be Colonial Secretary).[99] As well as being engaged in campaigns to improve conditions for distant, colonised others, the Clapham Sect was at the centre of those domestic reforms which helped the propertied classes as a whole to weather the storms of unrest in early nineteenth-century Britain. Indeed, the implementation of reform across colonial and metropolitan sites was an indivisible project as far as most 'Saints' were concerned.

Their opportunities to influence ruling groups were enhanced during the years of domestic instability which followed the ending of the slave trade. Resentment at the erosion of paternalistic protections during the Napoleonic war, together with a sharp economic downturn after its conclusion in 1815, prompted unprecedented unrest among Britain's labouring class, manifested most spectacularly in the Luddite disturbances of 1812, the 'Corn Law riots' of 1815, the 'Pentridge Revolution' of 1817, the 'Peterloo massacre' of 1819, and the 'Cato Street conspiracy' of 1820. 'The suspension of Habeas Corpus in 1817 and the passing of the Six acts two years later were the response of a government that reflected the general alarm among the propertied classes.'[100] As well as outright repression, including restrictions on the freedom of the press, the searching of houses without a warrant and the prohibition of meetings, these post-war years saw the panicky consolidation of property rights created by the landed classes through measures such as enclosure and the Black Acts. The right of the state to defend property was also 'extended into other areas of capital accumulation', so as to protect the commercial and industrial classes.[101] It was in this context of fear about the sanctity of property as a whole, that Britain's aristocratic elite, having already come to terms with bourgeois religious morality, was additionally obliged to come to terms with middle-class political aspiration. Some kind of alliance with the middling classes represented in so many ways by reformers such as those of the Clapham Sect, seemed the only way left to defend against more serious threats 'from below'.[102]

A growing liberalism within Tory politics was the first indication of Britain's political elite being increasingly swayed by the agendas espoused by bourgeois reformist constellations. While eighteenth-century Tory tradition had held that the current order of things was God-given, early nineteenth-century liberal Tories like Peel and Canning maintained that the present hierarchy had to be reformed in certain respects before it approximated God's intentions. For these reformist Tories, only if 'one could rid the natural machine of friction – by stripping away anomalous powers, monopolies, preferences, special favours, and backstairs influences', could society run itself according to Divine intention.[103]

In Peel's policies as Home Secretary, this meant that surveillance through secret contacts, spies and *agents provocateurs* would have to be replaced by a police force visible to the public through its uniform, 'encouraging individual citizens to weigh up, with some degree of certainty, the probable consequences of different courses of action'.[104] In Canning's foreign policy, it meant that 'cabal and intrigue' would have to be replaced by permanent principles of diplomacy. In colonial policy, the shift meant that the venal and corrupt regimes of autocratic governors (of which Somerset's Cape government was exemplary), would have to be replaced by a form of government that was regulated, principled and consistent. R. Wilmot Horton, Permanent Under-Secretary at the Colonial Office, wanted to convert those colonies that Britain had recently conquered into productive, and partially self-governing possessions, while William Huskisson at the Board of Trade was agitating for the removal of restrictions on trade with the settlers who had emigrated to them.[105]

What made this logic of renewed Toryism all the more compelling in the case of the Cape Colony was its reinforcement by local reformist interests, each of which was forging its own direct and indirect contacts with the British government and with pressure groups like the Clapham Sect. On the one hand, Cape humanitarians, as we will see below, were mobilising allies in Britain against Somerset, because of his frontier policy. From their position within the Cape's slave-holding society, they were also joining in abolitionist demands from the West Indies for the speedier amelioration, and eventual abolition, of slavery itself.[106] On the other hand, expediently joining them as part of a local reform complex were British merchants operating out of Cape Town. They were concerned to remove the restrictions on trade which accompanied Somerset's *ancien régime*. At the same time, liberal British colonists with journalistic interests, most notably John Fairbairn and Thomas Pringle (formerly co-editor of the Edinburgh *Blackwood's Magazine*), whom we shall also encounter again below, were making very public protests about Somerset's refusal to grant a free press in the colony. With these diverse appeals arising from well-connected colonial interests, in 1822 the Tory British government appointed a commission of enquiry to examine the Cape administration, along with those of Mauritius and Ceylon. The commissioners, J. T. Bigge (Chief Justice of Trinidad) and W. M. G. Colebrooke (Indian army officer and later governor of a series of West Indian islands) were busy accumulating evidence against Somerset's government when the governor departed from the Cape on a leave which turned out to be permanent, in 1826.[107]

If Tory reform during the 1820s embraced both metropolitan and colonial sites, so too did the projects carried out as a result of more thoroughgoing bourgeois influence in the early 1830s. 'At home' the Tories' Whig successors were determined to

> break the radical alliance by driving a wedge between the middle and working classes, buying off the one with votes and representation, leaving the other, isolated and weak, outside the pale. The tactic, in [Earl] Grey's words, was 'to associate the middle with the higher orders of society in the love and support of the institutions of government of the country'.[108]

Rather than sweeping away aristocratic political domination, the cornerstone of a new bourgeois political power – the Reform Act of 1832 – helped to underpin it. Women and workers were excluded from citizenship under the Act's £10 male property franchise, but at the same time a 'remarkable consensus in national aims' was forged between the men of 'a revived and prosperous landed class' and those of 'an emboldened professional and business class'.[109]

In admitting the 'respectable' bourgeoisie to shared political representation however, the aristocratic order was also accepting its claims to the representation of social truth and thus paving the way to middle-class cultural hegemony. With middle-class notions of a proper, moral social order 'becoming the common sense of the Victorian age', projects of prison, asylum, sanitary and housing reform were all taken up with more vigour, often by exactly the same networks of individuals that had fostered the anti-slave trade campaign, including the members of the Clapham Sect.[110] It was through the proliferation of such reformist endeavours on behalf of suffering individuals that the anti-slavery of the late eighteenth century became the humanitarianism of the early nineteenth.

Humanitarian prescriptions: 'at home' and overseas

Perhaps one of the most profound instances of bourgeois-led reform 'at home' was the Poor Law Reform Act of 1834.[111] It can usefully be seen, however, in conjunction with colonial developments, and in particular, with the abolition of slavery itself. It was passed during the same year as the emancipation of Britain's colonial slaves, and was partly a result of the same reformist discourse of proper relations between employers and employees.[112] Both measures, colonial and domestic, were immensely revealing of the prescriptions that middle-class reformers held out for government and its subjects during the first half of the nineteenth century.

Since the abolition of the slave trade in 1807, the 'machinery of print propaganda' had continued to be wielded in the debate over slavery, by the West India interest on the one hand and by the abolitionist network on the other. By the 1830s, though, it was above all the missionary societies that had capitalised on the growing commercial market for books and pamphlets.[113] Colonial missionaries, and especially Baptists in the West Indies, were able to persuade the literate metropolitan classes that the plantation owners had 'rejected the teachings of Christ [and] stained the good name of Britain with the national sin of slavery'.[114] Such propaganda was crucial in bringing the humanitarian campaign against slavery in Britain to a crescendo in the early 1830s, with a mass petition to parliament signed by one and a half million men and women, manifesting widespread moral repugnance.[115] Within this atmosphere, the British government once again overrode the material interests of the West Indies planters and other colonial slave-owners. However, once the slaves were freed, a question remained over their proper social role, just as it did over that of the British labouring classes. It was around this question that the domestic Poor Law Reform Act and the colonial emancipation of slaves most clearly manifested their commonalities.

First, we should note that while both poor law reform and the abolition of slavery may have been products of an emerging set of bourgeois representations, they were also specific measures adopted in response to outbreaks of resistance at different sites of empire. Reform of the domestic relief system was spurred because of the Swing revolt of agricultural labourers in the south-east of England, while the emancipation of Britain's colonial slaves was prompted by rebellions on the plantations of Demerara in 1823 and Jamaica in 1831.[116] Each was thus a measure designed to head off further revolt by encouraging workers' 'self-exertion'. Critically, in both cases, this would be achieved 'by forcing "free" labour onto a competitive market', constructing on the one hand, 'a world of autonomous individuals contracting freely', and on the other, 'a landscape of moral discipline and government'.[117] In Britain that landscape would be filled with workhouses constructed as much like prisons as possible; in the colonies it would be occupied by 'freed' slaves who continued to labour on their masters' farms and plantations for a further four years' 'apprenticeship' in order that they might learn the responsibilities of freedom.[118] As far as British reformers were concerned, then, the enslaved abroad and the poor at home 'occupied similar moral space', and had to be treated in similar, if never identical ways.[119]

The prospects that British reformers held out for the emancipated slaves were further conditioned, however, by a revised set of representations of Africans. These challenged the lurid images of savagery, sloth and cannibalism that had been generated on the one hand by travellers who had visited West Africa and on the other hand, by West Indies slave-owners, during the debate over the trans-Atlantic trade.[120] While both travellers' and planters' representations 'stressed precisely those aspects of African life that were most repellent to the West and tended to submerge the indications of a common humanity',[121] it was this very common humanity that missionaries sought to convey to metropolitan audiences. In missionary representations, African slaves were the vulnerable, innocent, child-like victims of European brutality.[122] As Catherine Hall puts it, 'While the icon of the planters was the imagined figure of "Quashie" – evasive, lazy, childlike and lacking judgement – the missionaries and their allies constructed new figures, the Black Christian man and woman . . . ready to learn, ready to labour and to live in families. These men and women were human beings, with feelings and thoughts and with the capacity for redemption'.[123]

Although evangelical humanitarians by no means always portrayed non-Europeans in a positive light, advocating the necessity for missionary work against East India Company opposition in India by constructing the Indians as 'immersed in the most appalling depths of bestial superstition and social corruption', for instance, they nevertheless proved persuasive in arguing the point that 'mankind had sprung from one stock imbued with some knowledge of divinity'.[124] However, it was precisely middle-class Britons' knowledge of their own superior access to this divinity which meant that Africans freed from slavery, again like the domestic labouring classes, were in need of further instruction before they could take their rightful places in a morally sanctioned social order.[125]

At both metropolitan and colonial sites, middle-class humanitarians thus claimed sovereignty over those whom they sought to protect. As Lacquer suggests, humanitarians spoke 'more authoritatively for the sufferings of the wronged than those who suffer[ed] [could] speak for themselves'.[126] And in speaking for the British working class and the freed slaves of empire, it was by no means a bourgeois humanitarian intention to elevate them to an equal status in society. Even if systems of slavery were increasingly being identified as incompatible with Christian practice, as Todorov has pointed out, the Bible (Galatians 3:28) makes it clear that social distinctions do not dissolve simply because 'all are one in Jesus Christ'. 'Christianity does not combat inequalities . . . but it declares them irrelevant with regard to the unity of all in Christ'.[127] The humanitarian desire to assist distant strangers, then, was always accompanied by a caveat. As Nicholas Thomas puts it in the case of missionaries, their 'benevolence and their will to control were indissoluble'.[128] Thomas Holt's description of the humanitarian prospectus for Jamaican slaves applied just as well to British workers: 'They would be free to pursue their own self-interest but not free to reject the cultural conditioning that defined what that self-interest should be. They would have opportunities for social mobility, but only after they learned their proper place'.[129]

Humanitarians in the Cape Colony

Not all of the missionaries in the Cape Colony, as we will see in chapter 4, subscribed to the metropolitan-centred humanitarian network, but many of them did. Through their correspondence with other missionaries and their directors in Britain, they partook of the 'global intoxication' that infused the early nineteenth-century bourgeois reformist movement as a whole.[130] Their representations of the independent Xhosa were cut from the same abolitionist and monogenesist cloth which fashioned the metropolitan abolitionists' images of Africans. Despite their portrayal as rapacious depredators in official circles, within a hegemonic evangelical and abolitionist framework, the Xhosa could be described, even by the conservative *Times*, as merely 'an uncivilised people, whose character is for the most part as inoffensive as their powers of annoyance are unworthy of serious notice'.[131]

For metropolitan humanitarians like Beverly Mackenzie, who publicised information received from missionaries in the Cape under the pseudonym of 'Justus', it was important for Britons to appreciate the Xhosa's 'traits of generosity and kind feeling . . . their good-natured attentions to strangers and visitors, their quick and grateful perception of friendly feeling; and especially their placable dispositions'.[132] Indeed, noting the Xhosa's laudable respect for a hierarchy of social rank, 'Justus' drew a favourable comparison between the Xhosa and the British labouring class:

> It appears to me, that setting aside the externals of clothing, and conveniences of civilised life, and viewing the savage mind in a moral and philosophical light, the lower order of the English nation are in many places far more *savage* than the Caffres – more savage in coarseness of mind and manners, more desperate, unrestrained, and uncivilized, and in one word, very far below the Amakosæ [Xhosa] in the scale of recovered humanity.[133]

By the mid-1820s, humanitarian discourse was articulated most consistently and eloquently in the colony by Dr John Philip, the superintendent of the London Missionary Society (LMS) in the Cape and a director on the board of the society in Britain. The Congregationalist LMS had been established in 1795, but given that it was founded in the conviction that 'the knowledge of Christ shall cover the earth as the waters cover the channel of the sea', it would not remain a merely national institution for long.[134] It had been the first society to send missionaries – Johannes van der Kemp and James Read – to the Cape in 1803.[135] Indirectly, it was van der Kemp and Read who had brought Philip out to the colony. They were both loathed by labour-hungry colonists. Not only did they fight against colonial oppression in general on behalf of the 2,000 or so Khoesan attached to missionary stations, they also resisted specific colonists' enforcement of contractual obligations made under duress or false pretences.[136] Of greater concern to the metropolitan directors of the LMS, Read, who had married a Khoesan woman, had been found guilty of adultery, and van der Kemp, who had married the daughter of a slave, seemed to have abandoned bourgeois respectability altogether for a Khoesan lifestyle. Philip was sent out in 1819 to restore the propriety of the mission and put its affairs in order after the scandal. However, he soon became embroiled in the same struggle for the liberation of the Khoesan that van der Kemp and Read had begun.

Philip had been raised within a lower middle-class Scottish Enlightenment tradition. He was convinced that, 'education, evangelical Christianity and freedom from feudal restraints had created the prosperity [and the enlightened morality] of the Scotland of his youth'. Furthermore, 'The same combination of factors could do the same for all humankind'.[137] He 'corresponded widely with the organisers of other missionary societies and their employees in the field'. Indeed, he felt that too few people appreciated 'how much of our active benevolence we owe to our sympathy with the great affairs of the world, and these great things cannot affect us if they are not known to us'.[138] John Fairbairn, Philip's son-in-law and the editor of the Cape Town-based *South African Commercial Advertiser*, was similarly brought up within the context of the Scottish Enlightenment and the broader humanitarian network, and he was Philip's most influential ally in the colony.[139]

Both these leading Cape humanitarians were vehemently opposed to the military, aristocratic culture through which the Cape was governed, especially under Somerset. Fairbairn wrote that 'If England is determined to use us only as a depot for the dregs of her Aristocracy − if her surplus Idlers are to be quartered upon us at this rate − we would . . . advise our countrymen to avoid these shores'.[140] With Fairbairn fighting an additional battle against Somerset over the institution of a colonial press, he joined forces with Philip in campaigning for the amelioration of the Khoesan's as well as the Cape slaves' conditions. Indeed, they portrayed the Khoesan's plight as one akin to slavery and mobilised the humanitarian network through propaganda that rivalled that of the anti-slavery campaign in its depiction of brutality and horror.

The foundations of Cape humanitarianism were set out publicly for the first time in Fairbairn's newspaper, once his struggle for a free press had been won. In 1829, Fairbairn derided those colonists who attempted to 'search for new principles of action in the minds of men who differ from us only in the colour of their skin'.[141] But it was Philip, similarly convinced that 'the actual capacity of the African is nothing inferior to that of the European', who led the first effective humanitarian crusade on the Khoesan's behalf.[142] The publication of his book, *Researches in South Africa* in 1828, caused a furore both in the Cape and in Britain.[143] An indication of its influence can be derived from the proceedings of the Aborigines Committee of 1835–6. One of the witnesses before the committee, the frontier official Major Dundas noted scornfully that 'Every body [in England] has got the book; I dare say it is on this table'.[144] In this notorious work, Philip wrote that 'to give a faithful sketch of [the Khoesan's] past sufferings, and of their present condition, is my chief object', but he was well aware that his work would have to compete with colonists' and officials' representations for a claim to veracity.[145] He, in particular, faced an imperative to 'lay my authority before the reader'.[146] As well as personal recollections, he used the writings of travellers such as Le Vaillant, Sparrman, Barrow, Thompson and Pringle, all of which were well known to metropolitan readers interested in Africa, as substantiation for his allegations. In addition, he drew on government records, newspaper reports and LMS missionary letters. Nevertheless, Philip's narrative of '"violent dispossession", "hopeless bondage", "wrongs and outrages" inflicted on the innocent and defenceless' was challenged in court.[147] When he was successfully sued for libel by a number of colonists, his costs were paid by subscription among metropolitan humanitarian sympathisers, including churchmen, philanthropists and Whig politicians.[148]

While Philip's *Researches* took in the whole span of the Cape's colonial history, what was particularly significant about it as far as bourgeois reformers and allies in Britain were concerned, was its attack on British colonial officials. As Bank points out, 'The bulk of Philip's history was dedicated to the period between the late 1790s and the 1820s in order to demonstrate "how little their condition had been improved by the change of masters [from Dutch to British]". British occupation of the Cape had only seen Khoesan being "sacrificed at the shrine of a Boer–English union".'[149] Philip's message was reinforced when Saxe Bannister, a humanitarian former Attorney-General of New South Wales and visitor to the Cape and Canada, now based in Britain, drew attention to the divergence between expressed humane intention and official practice, on the part of both Dutch and British governments in the Cape.[150] His own swingeing critique of the Cape regime, published in 1830 as *Humane Policy; or Justice to the Aborigines of New Settlements*, drew on Philip, but it was also based on Bannister's own distinctive claim to veracity – one resting on a scientific approach and the inclusion of a compendium of official documents.[151]

Humane Policy had on its frontispiece an inscription from Dutch law, the application of which to the Cape could only be ironic: 'The Aborigines shall be undisturbed in their liberty, and never enslaved; they shall be governed politically, and civilly, as ourselves, and enjoy the same measure of justice.'[152] Bannister concluded that, like the Dutch before them, the British authorities in the Cape had submitted 'to evil local influence; although furnished with far better opportunities for checking it than ever before existed'.[153] The British-innovated Caledon Code came in for particular criticism from Bannister, Philip and others, for its restrictions on Khoesan mobility, its refusal to recognise their right to own land and its general effect of 'consign[ing] the Hottentots and their posterity to universal and hopeless slavery'.[154]

With all the radicalism of Philip's critique, his prescriptions for reform were very much in line with those of humanitarian discourse as a whole. Philip made it clear to the Khoesan that he could alleviate their plight only if they conformed to the expectations of their missionary benefactors. He urged on the converts of the LMS's Bethelsdorp mission station, for instance, 'the advantage which an improvement in their houses, and in their industry and mode of living, would afford to their friends, in pleading their cause'. He continued: 'I pointed out to them, that it was in vain to attempt to plead their cause, while their enemies could point to Bethelsdorp in its present state; that the world, and the church of Christ, looked for civilization and industry as proof of their capacity and of the utility of our labours; that the men of the world had no other criterion by which they could judge the beneficial effects of the missions'. The criteria for assessment which he had laid out were summarised in Biblical fashion: 'By their fruits ye shall know them'.[155] Similarly Bannister reassured metropolitan middle-class readers that the humanitarians did not envisage reforms in the Cape which could lead to revolution. Rather, they hoped that improvement among the Khoesan would bring about 'a gradual restoration of the fair equilibrium of the different classes'.[156]

In the late 1820s, Philip and his metropolitan allies were aware that 'the times . . . seem favourable in many respects' for 'a fresh impulse' to be given 'to the enlightened principles which alone can save [Africa's] unfortunate tribes'.[157] In 1828, the same year that the *Researches* was published, it was primarily Philip who was responsible for the ratification by the British parliament of Ordinance 50, passed in the Cape by Somerset's more liberal successor, Acting Governor Sir Richard Bourke. This was a measure which effectively undermined the Caledon Code. Although the Ordinance still classified 'hottentots and other free persons of colour' differentially from the white colonists, it did so, according to Philip, in order to provide them with 'additional protection . . . in the same manner as orphans, apprentices and soldiers have additional protection afforded them in England'.[158] Having made this association between the colonial Khoesan and marginal groups within metropolitan society, the ordinance abolished the pass laws and released the Khoesan from the legal requirements which bound them and other free blacks to serve those colonists. Furthermore, it explicitly recognised their right to own land.[159] Philip's agitation for Ordinance 50 was justified both by free market economics and by the incontrovertible evidence of Britain's progressive history. Drawing a parallel between the conditions of the Khoesan and those of the medieval English serf, Philip wrote: 'To what does England owe the subversion of the feudal system, and its high rank among the nations of the world, but to the emancipation and elevation of its peasantry?'[160]

Philip was able to circulate this message within the corridors of government in Britain, as well as to a popular readership, through the services of the most prominent metropolitan humanitarian of the time, Thomas Fowell

Buxton. Buxton was Wilberforce's successor as the leader of the anti-slavery movement in Britain, vice-president of the Church Missionary Society (CMS) and chairman of the annual meeting of the Wesleyan Methodist Missionary Society (WMMS). He had close ties with the London Missionary Society as well, but what was more important, he was a respected proponent of the broader complex of bourgeois reformist projects, including prison reform, sanitary improvement and poor relief.[161] With Buxton's support, Ordinance 50 was hailed within metropolitan humanitarian circles as a first, painful step towards the reform of pre-emancipation labour systems in the empire as a whole. In spite of the 'wrath and spleen' of the 'slave-driving colonists', the Ordinance had changed the Khoesan 'from brute beasts into men'. 'As free labourers', they could now 'demand lawful hire for their services'.[162] As far as metropolitan humanitarians were concerned, the Ordinance was 'a sort of Magna Charta to the Hottentots'.[163]

The Kat River and the frontier

While the new opportunities available to most Khoesan 'freed' by Ordinance 50 remained limited, humanitarians in the Cape were able to establish a grand experiment for a small proportion of them on the eastern frontier.[164] In 1829, Ngqika's son Maqoma and his followers were expelled by colonial troops from a stretch of relatively fertile land along the Kat River. Ironically, it was this callous expulsion that provided humanitarians with their first opportunity to construct a model settlement from scratch – one designed to demonstrate the progress that the freed Khoesan were capable of making.

Maqoma's expulsion had been ordered by a significant, but ambivalent figure in frontier affairs, the Afrikaner Commissioner General Andries Stockenström. Stockenström had been a friend of Philip's since he had accompanied him as a youth on one of his tours among the Xhosa, and he was later to be a vital witness for humanitarians in their campaigns against other colonial officials and settlers. There are some indications that he may have drafted Ordinance 50. But he was also a clear-sighted military strategist, an effective colonial commander in times of war against Xhosa chiefdoms, and a generally loyal frontier official. Perhaps more than any other individual, due to the extent of his personal connections and allegiances, Stockenström uneasily straddled humanitarian and official discourses, contributing to the projects of each in various and often contradictory ways.[165] By the late 1830s, he was loathed by British settlers in particular for the paradoxes that he embodied.[166] But I will return to this in a later chapter.

In 1829, Stockenström ordered Maqoma's expulsion from the Kat River area for strategic reasons. The decision was ostensibly taken in response to a destabilising raid that the chief had launched against the neighbouring and 'friendly' Thembu. But as early as 1822, Stockenström had considered it a 'most injurious measure' to allow Maqoma's continued occupation of the Kat River valley, which connected the highland strongholds of the

Xhosa with the fringes of the British settlement established two years before.[167] Stockenström's resolve to uproot Maqoma's followers and move them deeper into Xhosaland was condemned by both local and metropolitan humanitarians. Bannister quoted approvingly a sympathetic colonist who felt that 'The sudden and violent proceeding against Macomo was equally impolitic and unjust. The country he believed, and rightly believed, to be his own. It is not even part of the neutral ground'.[168] However, in a demonstration of its flexibility, Stockenström was able to counter within the same humanitarian discourse, focusing on its respect for property and 'order':

> Whilst the voice of humanity is justly raised in favour of the long and cruelly oppressed blacks, that of justice and prudence remind us that the whites also have a claim to protection; that they also have lives and property and rights to lose, and that the wanton abandonment of these to the ferocity of a few desperate gangs among the native tribes will not benefit and civilize their brethren in the aggregate, but must generate that irritation and despair which ultimately no Government can prevent from terminating in the most unrestrained indulgence of revenge.[169]

Since, by the end of 1829, the Xhosa's expulsion from the Kat River was a *fait accompli*, humanitarians were delighted when Stockenström proposed that Khoesan recently 'emancipated' under Ordinance 50, be allocated land there. With Stockenström appealing to the imperatives of military officials by arguing that 'no other set of men can be rendered more efficient auxiliaries towards the object [of frontier defence] in view', the scheme was approved by the new governor, Sir Lowry Cole.[170] As far as the government was concerned, the Kat River settlement was established in order to provide an effective militarised buffer between the expelled Maqoma and vulnerable colonial farmers. As far as colonial and metropolitan humanitarians were concerned, it was an experiment in what could be achieved with formerly bonded, but newly freed and Christianised subjects.

In order to give this humanitarian experiment its greatest chance of success, the Khoesan and 'mixed-race' 'Bastaards' initially chosen to reside along the Kat River were 'respectable' individuals and families, selected mostly from the mission stations. However, they were soon joined by relatives and other Khoesan escaping the colonial farms as well as by some Xhosa from across the frontier, seeking land and commercial opportunities within the colony. By 1834 there were some 5,000 inhabitants. Plots of land were allocated to family units and Lowry Cole appointed the Dutch Reformed Church missionary, W. R. Thomson to the settlement. Thomson proved most popular with those 'Bastaards' who claimed social superiority by virtue of their lighter skins. He was not best pleased when many of the Khoesan in the settlement demanded the LMS missionary, James Read (the same Read whose unorthodox behaviour had played a role in bringing Philip out to the Cape ten years before). Read helped set up missionary schools in the settlement and assisted in securing the material necessities for a flourishing agriculture. By 1833, the Kat River 'settlers', as they were called, already owned 250 horses, 2,444 head of cattle and 4,996 sheep. Moreover, it was reported that they had built twelve substantial stone houses, planted thirteen orchards and completed fifty-five canals for irrigating their allotments.[171]

As Keegan notes, humanitarians now had 'a community of the imagination which could be evoked against those who were inclined to a pessimistic view of life after slavery'.[172] James Read exulted in 1835:

> The improvement of the Hottentots was such that their friends supposed them now to be taking their final exit from that state to which slavery naturally reduces a people. Their enemies stood aghast. It was quite pleasing to a contemplative observer to see how gradually the people threw off the shackles which their circumstances had put on them, to see ignorance fall from the eye of the mind as it had been scales and they receiving sight; the sunken eye of despondency brightened at the hope of a better day.[173]

In Britain, after receiving the latest news of the Kat River settlement in one of Philip's letters, Buxton's daughter reported that 'My Father walked up and down the room, almost shedding tears of joy to hear of the prosperity and well-being of these dear people'.[174] The positive lesson of the Kat River settlement was soon utilised by Buxton in parliamentary debates to agitate for the early ending of freed slaves' apprenticeship in the West Indies.[175]

By 1833, with Ordinance 50 in a protected position on the statute books and the Kat River settlement flourishing, Philip felt confident that the Cape's 'Hottentot question was settled'. But, he wrote to an American colleague:

> there is another evil of great magnitude which I have to contend against. In the second sentence of my *Researches* you will perceive in what manner the colonial boundary has been extending for the last thirty years. The system is as much opposed to sound policy as it is to the interest of justice and humanity; but the colonists will think of nothing but an extension of territory and more land, so long as they can hope that they will be indulged in their wishes . . . The indulgence of those feelings by the extension of the colonial frontier is attended with . . . the destruction of the natives who have been killed in defending their territories, or have perished by the evils which have followed their expulsion.[176]

Philip, Fairbairn and their metropolitan allies now extended their critical gaze to the affairs of the eastern Cape frontier, where, 'Independently of those who are reduced to almost helpless beggary by the Dutch and English Governments in South Africa, there are many others not yet crushed, towards whom there has also prevailed, and still prevails, a signal disregard of justice'.[177]

It had long been a humanitarian aim to make sustained contact, and even to develop a 'legitimate trade', with 'pristine' African cultures that had not yet been exposed to the corruptions of the trans-Atlantic slave trade. During the late eighteenth century, abolitionists had financed expeditions to find West African chiefdoms far enough removed from the coast to have avoided being 'degraded' by contact with European traders.[178] The experiment of establishing freed slaves and other blacks in the colony of Sierra Leone had been designed to show that even Africans already 'tainted' by slavery were 'capable of useful cultivation, social organisation and legitimate trade', provided that they were shown a better example.[179] However, in a foretaste of later, and much more widespread, humanitarian disillusionment, the inhabitants of Sierra Leone had failed to fulfil their benefactors' expectations of them. After displays of 'drunkenness, sexual promiscuity and obscene language', which humanitarian sponsors found mortifying, there was open rebellion in 1800 and an assumption of authority by the British Crown in 1807. While humanitarians did not give up the Sierra Leonean experiment just yet, and the African Institution was founded partly in order that it may be extended, there still seemed greater possibilities for the 'improvement' of Africans who were within reach of British influence, and yet unaffected by slavery. For Philip and Fairbairn, the Cape eastern frontier was an absolutely critical arena of interaction precisely because it presented the only existing opportunity to 'cultivate' such an African people. Although time was short, and the ravages of the existing colonial system had first to be halted, the Xhosa were 'upon the very eve of becoming the first national fruits of the civilisation which may be given to Africa by means of English exertion and integrity'.[180]

Both Philip and Fairbairn visited the frontier in 1830, and spoke with Xhosa chiefs including Maqoma, Tyhali, Bhotomane and Dyani Tshatsu (who had adopted Christianity). They also made fruitful contacts with LMS and Glasgow Missionary Society (GMS) missionaries in Xhosaland, as well as consolidating their connection with the now rehabilitated James Read in the Kat River settlement. Most of these missionaries would become vital channels of the Xhosa representations which Philip would relay to Buxton and other metropolitan humanitarians. Philip's initial response to the Xhosa he met on his tour was the standard humanitarian one of identifying a need for collective and individual reformation, but also of emphasising the presence of those 'universal' characteristics of humanity which rendered such a reformulation possible. Although, 'contemplated through the medium of their own superstitions, or that of their general condition, we might hastily pronounce them [the Xhosa] to be inferior to the white race', Philip felt that 'on these points they lose nothing by a comparison with our own European ancestors'. They were therefore capable of regeneration through Christianity and civilisation in the same way that those ancestors had been. Philip stated that 'In point of abilities and good feelings, I consider the Caffres on the borders of the colony as most decidedly superior to that portion of the refuse of English society that find their way to this country'.[181]

After his tour, the humanitarian agenda for the frontier was clear to Philip, and he set about making it clear to his friends in Britain, as well. This agenda, as Mackenzie put it, was to bring 'into a cheerful and friendly obedience those barbarian neighbours, who have expected to find in us examples of moral pre-eminence'.[182] Even if the humanitarians were mistaken about the Xhosa 'character', and the Xhosa really *were* the rapacious raiders that officials and frontier colonists portrayed, then it was up to those officials to 'improve' them by introducing them to the benefits of Christian civilisation. As far as humanitarians in the Cape and their contacts Britain were concerned:

> If it could be proved, that after a thirty years' dominion we had done nothing at all . . . to bring the barbarian tribes under the mild and trans-forming power of the Gospel – that the government had in no way advanced the civilization, or improved the condition of the Aborigines of its colonies – then we are weighed in the balance and found wanting; but when we advance beyond this, and prove that our Christian sway has been applied to purposes of spoliation, wrong and cruelty, how shall we find words to express our guilt and degradation?[183]

It was just such colonial 'guilt' and 'degradation' that Philip and Fairbairn communicated to their metropolitan contemporaries from 1830 onwards. They condemned both official and settler approaches to the colonisation of the Xhosa. First, they attacked directly the strategies employed by a succession of governors, describing their 'cruelty and injustice'.[184] In a series of letters to Buxton, Philip foresaw the Xhosa sharing the historical fate of the colony's Khoesan: land deprivation and servitude.[185] The Xhosa frequently appeared in exactly the same light in Philip's communications as those West Africans whom Wilberforce had so successfully represented to British public opinion some fifty years before. It was not only along the Atlantic 'slave belt' that 'We have stopped the natural progress of civilization . . . cut off Africa from improvement [and] . . . kept down that continent in a state of darkness, ignorance, bondage and blood'.[186] In the Cape too, as Bannister declared, 'much blood has been shed without the slightest justifi-cation [while] the valuable exertions of missionaries . . . are . . . greatly dis-turbed . . . by the violation of the most obvious duties'.[187] Bannister's own book, along with those of Pringle, 'Justus' and others was an endeavour to render 'the whole British public . . . more deeply impressed with . . . improved principles' for frontier relations, and thereby, 'to carry them into effect'.[188]

Using Philip and Fairbairn's testimony, itself gathered from the LMS and GMS missionaries in touch with the Xhosa chiefs, 'Justus' wrote sarcastically about the strategic Xhosa expulsions carried out in 1809, 1812 and 1819:

'The proper boundary in a military point of view was secured, "military men" were set at ease, and the colony was safe!!!' However, he continued, the authorities should have known 'that justice is a stronger wall for a frontier than . . . valleys gained by rapine, and that national integrity is worth a thousand cannons, and a hundred thousand soldiers'.[189] Predictably, Somerset's unreconstructed regime came in for particular condemnation. Philip castigated the former governor's conception of 'civilisation' for its neglect of those internal reformations of manners, morals and sentiment that were so central to the missionary project: 'the question between us and the government was one of civilization. The criterion of a people's civilization with Lord Charles Somerset was whether people used knives and forks'.[190]

Focusing on Somerset's more specific acts of frontier policy, Bannister described 'the mischief we have caused for years' in first selecting Ngqika as a privileged colonial ally and then giving him up by seizing his land in the 'neutral' territory, 'in a way the most insulting to him'. The subsequent absorption of his territory into the colony seemed almost to have been designed as a provocation to the Xhosa. 'A series . . . of plunderings and expensive commandos may reasonably be looked for, if we persist in this unfortunate enterprise of occupying the neutral ground without due arrangements for the benefit of all the parties interested in it'. The latest colonial boundary on the far side of the 'neutral' territory, the Keiskamma River, 'we may be assured . . . is only acquired as a step towards another river, to be inevitably reached with more havoc and expense, unless new principles be steadily established'. Bannister concluded that there was 'something altogether unworthy of our own character' about Somerset's actions.[191]

Somerset was of utility to humanitarian campaigners precisely because he, more than any other governor, symbolised an official and military culture that was conditioned by the discourses of the *ancien régime*. As such he epitomised the way that official discourse was 'misled by views, which will be discountenanced in but a very few years . . . as they now are by all who have derived the most immediate instruction from the spirit of the times'.[192] Attacks on Somerset could capture the modernising thrust of the entire bourgeois reformist project. However, Somerset was not the only target for humanitarians. Indeed, by the late 1820s, when the most influential humanitarian treatises on the Cape were written, his regime had already come to an end.

Somerset's replacement as acting Cape governor, Sir Richard Bourke, was generally approved of by humanitarians and thought to be a well-meaning man. Although government in the Cape as in other 'reformed' colonies 'remained militaristic and monopolistic in practice in spite of the softer protestations of constitutional political theory',[193] Bourke nevertheless encouraged unprecedented expectations concerning the Xhosa's 'civilization'. In 1828, partly in response to the British settlement's continuing labour shortages, but also as an official indication of his faith that work for colonists would expose Xhosa men to the influence of colonial civilisation, Bourke passed Ordinance 49. This allowed large numbers of pass-bearing Xhosa and other Africans from the interior to enter the colonial margins in order to find employment.[194] Although many stayed on in the colony as labour tenants, Bourke's intention was that those who returned to Xhosaland at the end of their contracts would 'gradually and naturally introduce' the 'blessings of civilization . . . among these ignorant tribes'.[195] Bourke, who, as we have seen, was also responsible for the passage of Ordinance 50 in the Cape, provided a further cause for humanitarian congratulation when he expressed the intent behind his frontier policy: 'to maintain those situated immediately on our front in possession of their country as long as by their friendly and peaceable conduct they prove themselves deserving of our protection. This will be the easiest and cheapest way of preserving the colony itself from plunder and disquietude'.[196]

However, Bourke's optimism was undermined in the last two years of the decade by a period of increasing frontier instability.[197] In an episode conventionally known as the 'Mfecane', competition over trade and environmental resources between polities in the interior and on the eastern coastal strip of southern Africa had been fuelled initially by drought and subsequently by slave raiding from across the Cape's northern frontier, and from the Portuguese-held Delagoa Bay. The enlargement of some states through conquest, including the Zulu and the Ndebele, had been accompanied by the fragmentation and flight of numerous smaller polities, resulting in widespread turmoil and violence to the north and east of the frontier Xhosa chiefdoms.[198] During the mid-1820s, Sotho and Tswana-speaking immigrants to the frontier region, many of whom were refugees from these conflicts, were already being settled as clients within Xhosa chiefdoms or absorbed as labour tenants on colonial farms. By 1828, though, the Xhosa side of the frontier was being further pressurised by the arrival of additional groups of refugees from the east and north. Simultaneously, drought set in on either side of the frontier itself.[199] More Xhosa commoners, and especially those recently expelled from the colonial side of the frontier, were obliged to raid into the colony for sustenance, threatening the 'good order' which Bourke felt he had been helping to construct. Henry Somerset, the former governor Lord Charles' son and the officer commanding the frontier garrison, began publicly to express his loss of faith in the governor's 'civilising' process: 'with a race of determined plunderers it becomes very difficult to suggest any measures securing ultimate tranquillity and success'.[200]

It was in this context that Bourke committed, or rather permitted Henry Somerset to commit, what humanitarians saw as one of the gravest and most brutal of official acts in the Cape. Henry Somerset already had a certain unenviable reputation among evangelical humanitarians in the colony. In 1826, Fairbairn had written that 'when he made love in Cape Town and war on the Frontier, the inhabitants of the immediate country had frequent occasion to regret that he did not dedicate himself entirely either to the soft passion or to the glory (they were indifferent to which)'.[201] Nevertheless, fearing that both sides of the frontier were about to be overrun from the east, either by refugees fleeing King Shaka's advancing Zulu armies, or by those armies themselves, in 1828 the governor allowed Henry Somerset to lead a British force through Xhosaland, acting in alliance with the Gcaleka Xhosa and the Thembu to expel the 'Zulu invaders'.[202] Rather than attacking Shaka's forces, however, the colonial troops launched a devastating attack on a group of unthreatening refugees known as the Ngwane at the 'Battle of Mbolompo'. Somerset's 'mistake' (which incidentally gave colonists acting alongside British regular soldiers the opportunity to enhance their labour force by taking captives) was to provide humanitarians with a compelling reason to criticise even Bourke's colonial government.[203]

Bannister felt that the 'Battle of Mbolompo' 'abounds in circumstances which illustrate the [reformist] purpose' of the humanitarians: 'we cannot justify the slaughter that took place . . . The errors . . . are without parallel in the history of any wars, and they indicate an origin in the imprudent manner in which we are acting in South Africa'. While Bourke was heavily implicated in the humanitarian outcry, however, the most damaging criticism was reserved for Henry Somerset himself. It was clear to whom Bannister was referring when he wrote that 'the most experienced officers are utterly ignorant of the obvious means of executing their duty, and make no scruple of sacrificing human beings without offence and on mere conjecture'.[204]

If the 'Battle of Mbolompo' provided humanitarians with their most spectacular single example of military incompetence, provocation and callousness, the most evident manifestation of a systematically 'tyrannical' official discourse in the Cape was the 'spoor law', instituted by Somerset and continued under Bourke. As we have seen, 'spoor law' regulations enabled frontier farmers to form commandos in order to retrieve supposedly stolen cattle from the nearest Xhosa kraal to which tracks were traced. The practice had been condemned by the same official enquiries, conducted by commissioners Bigge and Colebrooke, that had resulted in the reform of Somerset's administration. In 1826, they had noted that 'cattle have in some instances intentionally been driven by the depredators near to peaceable kraals, with the object of eluding pursuit, and of making them the object of suspicion and attack, and that some chiefs have complained of the repeated seizure of their cattle for the thefts committed by others'.[205] The practice's continuance after this damning report was blamed by humanitarians partly on Somerset's successors, but also on 'those insatiate robbers the Boors [*sic*]' and their British neighbours, who used it [the spoor law] to enlarge their own herds at the expense of innocent Xhosa.[206] The decision taken in 1833 by the new governor, Sir Lowry Cole, to endorse the practice of even minor frontier officials, mostly Afrikaner farmers, calling out commandos against the Xhosa, provided the grounds for Philip's first specific and targeted reformist campaign for the frontier.

Supported by the published writings of Thomas Pringle, Philip produced a weighty memorandum on the injustice of the spoor law and of Cole's decision.

It was sent in the first instance to Buxton who, in turn, publicised it in the House of Commons. In the meantime, drawing on further correspondence from the Cape humanitarians, 'Justus' persuaded a more popular metropolitan readership that 'nothing was so easy [for colonists] as to augment their own herds without the trouble of purchase; they had but to complain to the military stations, and immediately, without examination, the patrols were set in motion, and brought back to the complaining farmers anything they wanted'. The spoor law was thus a peculiar 'wickedness to be found nowhere but in the British colony of the Cape of Good Hope'.[207] With mounting popular support from within the metropolitan mission society and evangelical nexus, Buxton was able to persuade the Colonial Secretary to disallow Cole's ordinance.

This was a minor victory, however. By the 1830s, humanitarians and their British supporters were objecting to a set of practices and representations that went far deeper than the actions of ill-informed and aggressive individual officials, or the policies of specific Cape governors. Humanitarians had as their target the whole complex of colonial official-military thought and action.[208] As 'Justus' put it, 'military habits of acting and thinking' in general were 'inconsistent with the development of justice'. Such habits could 'so confuse the understanding as to make the noblest dispositions assent to the propositions of tyranny, as if they were wise and virtuous maxims'.[209] The problem, then, was that the Cape frontier was being governed by men who, well-intentioned as they might have been, were participants in a militaristic discourse which was totally unsuited to the maintenance of civilised behaviour on the colonial side of the frontier, and therefore, to the promotion of such behaviour on the Xhosa side.

Just as abolitionists held that 'it was slavery that made men cruel and inhumane, not inhumane men who made slavery bad',[210] humanitarians in the Cape and their allies in Britain held that it was the prevailing discourse of colonial officialdom that made colonial governors consent to acts of British barbarism, and not just in the Cape itself. As Bannister acknowledged when drawing in comparative material drawn from New South Wales and Canada, 'the evils combated [in the Cape] are not confined to one spot, and therefore are unlikely to originate in mere local circumstances . . . on the contrary, they are so widely spread as to indicate a deeply rooted origin in our general government of distant dependencies'.[211]

Arising from their critique of official colonial discourse was the humanitarian suggestion of a revitalised colonial programme. Far from leaving the Xhosa to their own devices this programme would involve their upliftment through Christianity and civilization. Even to contemplate a total withdrawal from colonial intervention in Xhosa society would be morally unconscionable to humanitarians when British rule had such potential benefits to offer, and not just in the here-and-now, but in the hereafter. For evangelicals, after all, 'it is not sinful activity but lack of faith for which men are condemned to Hell', and 'an apparently innocent life', which many humanitarians believed that the Xhosa generally led, 'is often more dangerous spiritually than a career of heinous crime'.[212]

Leaving aside evangelical discourse, in purely secular terms it was widely understood that Britain itself would not be in the civilised state that it was if the Romans had refrained from its colonisation. Colonisation *per se* then, was far from harmful. As Saxe Bannister argued:

> If we, the civilised, could not, physically, exist in the same land with the barbarian and the savage without destroying them, it would be a paramount duty to discourage the extension of colonies; but history, early and recent, where the civilised have been just, shows all men to be capable of improvement; and the same experience also shows, that doing justice is the grand means to ensure the amelioration and the mutual safety of the most dissimilar races. The opinion of our inevitable hostility with our neighbours and weaker subjects abroad, must consequently be rejected: and so long as it is open to us to cease from being wilfully unjust in our daily relations with them, we must not despair of raising the most simple to the true point of political well-being, – a state of self-protection.[213]

If the Xhosa were to attain this 'state of self-protection', and if their cultivation as new, model Christians were to be achieved, they would, of course, ultimately have to be shielded from less savoury colonial elements through a more benign system of government. Philip wrote:

> On the subject of it being desirable that the caffres should be retained as British subjects, I have long made up my mind . . . The caffres cannot otherwise be saved from annihilation. Were the Colony surrounded by belts of Native Tribes under the British government, nations would get time to form beyond us, but no Tribe will be allowed time to rise into civilisation and independence on our borders, if they are in immediate contact with our colonists.[214]

The programmes of those colonists themselves are the subject of the next chapter.

3 British settlers and the colonisation of the Xhosa

Oh what a gay, what a rambling life a Settler's leading!
Spooring cattle, doing battle, quite jocose;
Winning, losing; Whigs abusing; shopping now, then mutton breeding;
Never fearing, persevering, on he goes!

                (A. G. Bain, *The British Settler*, 1844)[1]

This chapter focuses on the creation of a new cultural identity among the British colonists who settled on the Cape Colony's eastern frontier in 1820. As we saw in the introduction, these settlers have increasingly been regarded by historians of southern Africa as a salient influence in the region, and it is the economic aspects of their social identity which have been emphasised. The historiographical tendency has been to highlight their impact as proponents of capitalist enterprise, forcing the colonial penetration of the subcontinent.[2] As Clifton Crais, Timothy Keegan and Martin Legassick, as well as Jeff Peires, have argued, material aspirations and capitalist ideology united a substantial portion of the settlers around common interests.[3] Accordingly, it has been argued, they shaped the social identity to which the settlers generally subscribed.[4] In this chapter too, I argue that rapid adoption of the colony's racial division of labour and a public discourse of capitalist 'progress' first encouraged certain of the British settlers to redefine social divisions carried with them from the British Isles, and helped to generate a new, colonial identity. However, I also suggest that the settlers' positioning as a dominant capitalist class takes us only part way towards explaining an emotive sense of identity which was capable of vociferously challenging humanitarian representations.

Because of the new possibilities that were involved, the process of colonisation is particularly revealing of the ways in which social identities can be reshaped. Studies of unifying colonial identities during the late eighteenth and early nineteenth centuries, such as those by Ann Stoler on Sumatra and Jack Greene on Barbados, emphasise the experience of collective insecurity as much as that of material endeavour.[5] The 1820 settlers were no exception. In 1819, they departed a Britain in which, as we have seen, the ruling classes considered themselves acutely vulnerable to 'sedition' and revolution. Even before 'contact' with indigenous peoples, colonisation of the Cape was seen as harbouring the potential to upset a fragile social hierarchy among those who emigrated. By opening up new opportunities for the creation of privilege within a racially stratified society, colonisation raised fears among a threatened elite of the rapid social advance of their 'inferiors'. Immediately following the settlers' transplantation, those discourses which helped maintain the upper classes' social supremacy were accordingly intensified. But with skilled labour shortages, the mutual domination of a Khoesan workforce and the prospects for lucrative trade, the material and social advance of lower class settlers was soon a *fait accompli* in the Cape, and the settlers as a whole were coming to appreciate a shared vulnerability.

By the early 1840s, the British settlers' collective exploitation of Khoesan labour had *necessarily* raised fears of rebellion and their expropriation of Xhosa land had *necessarily* generated anxieties about Xhosa reprisals. Furthermore, a programme of future capitalist expansion was accompanied by insecurity over the level of support which could be expected from an unsympathetic metropole. These connections between the settlers' new-found material status and a collective anxiety were inextricable and it is unrealistic to imagine them separately. Within the British settlement, initially divisive discourses of class, gender and nation were remoulded in the interests of solidarity, and solidarity was an imperative because capitalist penetration of the British kind had its unwelcome counterpart in communal insecurity.

Towards the end of this chapter, the cultural strategies which were deployed by the British settlers to reformulate their imported social boundaries are examined. First, there was the invention of a shared past, relying on imageries of a landscape being civilised through mutual endeavour. Here, Robert Godlonton was a central figure. Not only did his newspaper, the *Graham's Town Journal* provide settlers with a public political voice and an arena for the shared representation of settler 'enemies', but his writing of history constituted a collective biography of the settlement. A second strategy stemmed from notions of a unifying settler 'character', which could serve to obscure real differences of personality and politics. A third was a shift of emphasis in daily gendered routines, with women, initially constructed as 'boundary markers' for class identity, being positioned more as harmonisers of an inclusive sense of 'British-ness'. I will argue that each of these strategies, whether they were consciously formulated or not, reinforced the boundaries by which a British settler identity was defined in the eastern Cape, and helped perpetuate a sense of affinity embracing not only political agitators and aggressive capitalists, but settlers from a variety of class, religious and ethnic backgrounds.

While the emphasis in this chapter is on the construction of an embracing sense of identity, it should not be assumed, however, that this implies homogeneity or the erasure of difference. As the example of Thomas Stubbs will demonstrate, settlers could conflict, sometimes violently, in their political

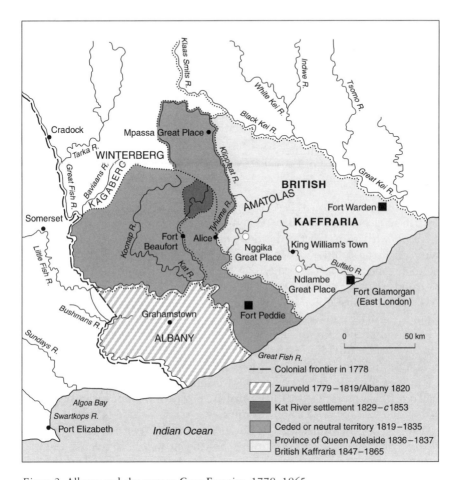

Figure 2 Albany and the eastern Cape Frontier, 1778–1865

Source: A. Lester, E. Nel and T. Binns, *South Africa Past, Present and Future: Gold at the End of the Rainbow?* Prentice Hall, London and New York, 2000, p. 73

opinions, their ethics, their material status and their lifestyles. Conflicts among them simmered, and on occasion, exploded, and, even if it was muted, a common sense of class differentiation remained among them. And yet the point is that the 1820 settlers became remarkably consistent in defining themselves against the same shared threats, and in replicating those central tenets of an identity constructed around notions of racialised class, gender and nationhood. The flexibility of this identity, its capacity to reconcile difference, itself enhanced its utility and its sustainability. In creating it, the Cape's British settlers were also forging a distinctive discourse which had much in common with that of other British settlers facing similar imperatives elsewhere. This was a discourse opposed in fundamental respects to that of the humanitarians, and in occasional tension with that espoused by the colony's officials.

Creating a settler identity

The emigration scheme

As we have seen, in 1817, Governor Somerset advocated the location of British settlers along the Cape Colony's eastern frontier in an endeavour to settle it 'with men superior beyond comparison to those savages who have plundered' the colony.[6] British settlers, the governor believed, would also be more amenable to the projects of improvement that British officials had in mind, than were 'degenerate' Dutch-speaking colonists on the frontier. As well as securing the colony from the Xhosa then, British emigrants would Anglicise and 'civilise' it.

The Colonial Office in London eventually backed Somerset's proposal largely because British resettlement in the Cape was seen as preferable to continuing emigration to the USA. More importantly though, in 1819, the Tory Cabinet as a whole developed further reasons for supporting a resettlement scheme. It was prompted by the immediate prospect of domestic insurrection. While radicals opposed colonial emigration on the grounds that it undermined the urgent imperative for social reform, the increasingly influential theories of Thomas Malthus and Adam Smith lent weight to colonial resettlement as both a demographic safety valve and a source of new markets. Ruling class anxiety that Britain lacked the manpower to fight the French had mutated by the late 1810s into fears that a surplus population was fuelling Britain's agrarian revolt and industrial unrest. Ministers were giving official encouragement to private schemes removing people from the western Highlands of Scotland, Ireland and the English counties and relocating them in colonial sites such as the St Lawrence River Valley.[7] Parliament ultimately voted £50,000 for subsidised emigration to the Cape.

However, while the Tory government wished to be seen to be doing something about the plight of 'paupers', it was the Colonial Office that would actually select the emigrants. Neither Somerset himself nor Colonial Office officials in London had any desire to see the already unstable Cape frontier zone populated with the 'indigent'. As a result, the scheme was directed in practice not at the poor, but largely at those who could form a sturdy, self-reliant community.[8] In the midst of unprecedented 'emigration fever', fuelled by the kind of inflated expectations that Cruikshank satirised when he portrayed the new settlers living among pigs already stuck with knives and forks, and with bread and milk growing on trees, 4,000 settlers were chosen from 90,000 applicants.[9] Of the emigrants, 36 per cent were men, 20 per cent women and 44 per cent children.[10]

Just such a rough balance of gender in any British settlement was a measure explicitly endorsed by the Cape merchant George Thompson, who had travelled among the Afrikaner frontier farmers. In a comment on the kind of frontier relations to which British settlers would help put a stop, he warned that thus far, 'the illicit connexions of Europeans with females of the coloured population has but too obviously tended to the degradation of both classes'.[11] Endogamous marriage, beginning even as the transports arrived at the Cape, was one of the practices which would help to sustain a collective 1820 British settler identity and maintain the settlers' social distance from both the indigenous peoples and, to a lesser extent, Afrikaners, on the frontier.[12] As Thomas Philipps testified before the metropolitan Select Committee in 1835, 'in the Dutch part [of the frontier] there has been a greater amalgamation [with the Khoesan]. Mr Read the missionary is the only European who has married a Hottentot woman'. When asked, 'Has there ever existed any amalgamation as to the tribes called the Caffres?', Philips replied 'No, none whatever'.[13]

The emigrants were organised into three kinds of parties. First, there were proprietary parties, consisting of a wealthy leader and ten or more indentured labourers. Wherever possible, aspirant proprietary leaders pulled strings of patronage to be accepted as a party head, and the well-connected arrived in the Cape with letters of introduction to the Governor. These men, such as Major Pigot, Thomas Philipps and Miles Bowker, generally wished to recreate in the Cape the lifestyle of the gentry which they could no longer afford in Britain. Bowker explained that he was

> Presently upon a large farm . . . where I can make a living, but cannot provide for a family of eight sons and one daughter without reducing them to the lowest ranks in Society, which ill accords with the previous knowledge of being descended from *the first*, we are unanimous in the decision to emigrate.[14]

Joint stock parties formed the bulk of the settlement. These were comprised mainly of artisans or professionals and their families, and many were attracted by the Colonial Office's promise that 'To small capitalists, say of £100, an opportunity is presented of employing it most advantageously, and thereby acquiring a handsome independence for themselves and families'.[15]

The members of these parties elected nominal heads to pay their deposits and secure land on the party's behalf. But the largely middle-class joint stock parties were themselves stratified. A quarter of Bailie's party, one of the largest, were London tradesmen experiencing declining material status as a result of technological innovation and competition. As one of them, George Anderson wrote to the Colonial Office,

> our own active exertions . . . are now paralysed in this Country thro' the Extreme deadness of trade ours having so fallen off that we have not been able to get any work for more than two years past . . . having lived Respectable and in one house for near twenty years the near prospect of absolute Poverty is the more Dreaded.[16]

At the other end of the social scale within these parties were 'gentle' men and women who brought their own indentured servants and requested separate grants of land. Many of these settlers were as concerned as the gentry to maintain the 'finer distinctions' of class within the colonial environment. As Mr Bishop Burnett, a half-pay officer, asserted, 'gentlemen or females of delicate habits altho' reduced in life cannot expose themselves to an association with Labourers and Mechanics'. Daniel Hockly, a goldsmith, enquired with the 'solicitude of a husband and father . . . whether there will be an indiscriminate mixture of all persons applying' for emigration.[17]

Finally, four parish parties were formed from those dependent upon relief. Their costs could not be covered from the poor rates, but had to be raised through extra parish donations. They were not to be granted land in the Cape. Instead, 'responsible' men, appointed as party leaders, would oversee their hire as labourers for the more 'respectable' settlers.

Protecting class boundaries

At its inception, the British settlement in the Cape was riven by divisions. Reflecting the contemporary insecurity of British national cohesion, English, Welsh, Irish and Scots parties were located separately, the Scots still on the frontier but far inland, the Welsh near Cape Town and the Irish at Clanwilliam in the western Cape. Within the Irish parties sectarianism provided another, potentially violent source of division.[18] Even as Irish, Welsh and some Scottish settlers left their original locations to join the main body of English in the Albany district around Graham's Town on the eastern frontier (see Figure 2), ethnic distinctiveness remained marked through the early 1820s.[19] Religious identity served further to divide the settlers.[20] Unlike the Anglican gentry, many of the joint stock party members were nonconformists, Hezekiah Sephton's party being explicitly defined and recruited according to its Wesleyanism.[21] Nevertheless, the primary divisions in the early settlement were self-consciously constructed in terms of class.

As we have seen, in Britain, the early nineteenth century was a period in which established relations between classes were being threatened. The Napoleonic War years and their immediate aftermath witnessed an increasing social distance between landowners and their landless workers, as farm servants made the traumatic transition to casual labourers. This transition was especially acute after the Battle of Waterloo, when the labour market was flooded with demobilised men. Most no longer had the bargaining power to insist on board and lodging as payment in kind. Their exposure to the vagaries of the market price for food contributed considerably to rural social tensions.[22] Already feeling that the class hierarchy was vulnerable, those members of the gentry who emigrated to the Cape expressed their fear that transplantation to a colonial environment held the potential completely to overthrow that hierarchy. Thomas Pringle's prognosis was hardly reassuring. He felt that with colonisation,

> the piramid [*sic*] of civil society is . . . turned topsy-turvy, the classes who once occupied the upper grades . . . must necessarily sink . . . and will, ere long . . . be degraded into the servants and dependants of the more fortunate mechanics and mendicants who came out under them.[23]

Evidently, the highest official at the Cape upon the settlers' arrival, Acting Governor Donkin (Somerset's temporary replacement) concurred, noting that 'great and disagreeable changes must take place in regard to many of the particles now floating in the heaving mass of Colonists, while it is working and arranging itself into social strata'.[24] Even on the voyages out, lasting four months or more, party leaders sought to ensure that social distinctions were maintained as far as possible, through minimal contact between passengers of different rank. Thomas Philipps was compelled to admit that 'it is well perhaps for the Colony to have a stock of labourers', but he felt that the parish party sharing his naval transport were 'a most horrid dirty set and the pest of the ship'.[25] Like the ships' berths, the tents housing the settlers temporarily on their arrival in Algoa Bay, were segregated strictly according to class.[26]

The struggle to maintain class boundaries began in earnest once the settlers were located in the Zuurveld, now renamed Albany. Proprietary leaders attempted to secure privileged access to the Cape government, and thought that they had succeeded when they found an ally in Donkin. However, while the Acting Governor was willing to use official appointments and land grants to bolster the authority of 'a sort of aristocracy or gentry who might lead and encourage the labouring classes',[27] upon his return, Somerset proved far less obliging. Personally infuriated by what he saw as Donkin's high-handed treatment of his son during his absence, and holding a Tory ethos of aristocratic paternalism not shared by the Whiggish Donkin, Somerset immediately set about countermanding his predecessor's influence.

By the beginning of 1823, he had reversed many of Donkin's appointments, and elevated more commercially minded joint stock settlers instead. Somerset declared that it was 'unwise to make Dukes of Bedford of Heads of Parties', since they might use their power (unlike the paternalistic Duke, who wished only to 'bless and comfort' his 'vassals'), 'to increase their rapacity'.[28]

The politics of the new settlement became polarised. On the one hand were those whom Somerset, rather ridiculously, labelled the 'Albany Radicals' – members of the gentry such as Thomas Philipps, Major Pigot and Donald Moodie, who had fallen from official favour on his return. Their fall from grace was exacerbated by their attempts to organise charitable relief for those settlers who were faring worst in the new settlement – attempts which drew attention to the failure of the Cape government to protect its new immigrants.[29] As Shula Marks and Stanley Trapido argue, Somerset constructed their dissent in the Cape in the same way that he constructed 'the British Radical challenge to the authority of Tory rule' in Britain, from whence, of course, he had only recently returned from leave.[30] On the other hand were those whom these men called the 'serviles' – settlers like John Bailie, Alexander Bisset, Walter Currie and William Cock, who had recently gained from Somerset's patronage.[31]

The dispute between 'radicals' and 'serviles' became discursively structured overwhelmingly in terms of inherited class boundaries. The success of 'servile' joint-stock settlers in trade and commerce, at a time when the gentry were struggling to farm successfully in the face of drought, disease and then flood led Donald Moodie to complain that 'the lower classes' had become 'too upish'. Thomas Philipps agreed, holding that 'it would have been better for [the lower classes] themselves, for the larger landed proprietors, and for the country at large, to have allowed them to fall at once into that scale in which they were intended to remain by habit and by profession'.[32]

Nevertheless, in the Cape as in Britain, strategic alliances were soon forged between gentry and middle classes in order to maintain mutual domination of the lower orders. The 'respectable' settlers were united first on the issue of labour control. Following the abolition of the slave trade and the injunction on British emigrants employing slaves, the settlement suffered from severe labour shortages.[33] Given their scarcity, working-class settlers found that they could attain far better conditions and pay by escaping the indentures with which they had arrived. Most abandoned the middle- and upper-class 'employers' to whom they were contractually bound and many set up as independent tradesmen in the settlement's only urban centre and garrison, Graham's Town. Thomas Philipps expressed a common sense of grievance among their original employers when he complained that his servants had 'mutinied and struck', tempted by 'the enormous wages given in the Country'.[34]

By the end of 1823 virtually none of the labourers was left on the original rural locations. Both proprietary and joint stock employers agreed that 'a Crisis has now arrived' and campaigned, ultimately unsuccessfully, for the punishment of absconding labourers.[35] With former servants often 'in far better circumstances than the men of means to whom they had originally been indentured',[36] it seemed that the gentry's early fears of an inversion of the class order within colonial space were about to be realised.

Representing class and gender

This crisis of class relations was one for which an appropriate discourse had long been established in Britain. In their combined agitation for more stringent controls over the workforce, wealthier settlers drew on the familiar imagery of the 'idle poor'. Pringle for instance, noted the tendency of servants to become 'spoiled' in 'new colonies', and bemoaned their 'reprehensible idleness, improvidence, and presumption'.[37] But the 'respectable' settlers' class concerns were also expressed in terms of gender relationships, which were themselves being refashioned within Britain. There, the late eighteenth and early nineteenth centuries saw the more rigid and gendered differentiation between public and private space – a development to which I will return below. With their rapid loss of control over labour, and their material circumstances deteriorating both relatively and absolutely, the 'respectable' settlers attempted to make the women of their class, as Frosh puts it, 'the boundary of what can be tolerated'.[38] John Philip sought to advertise the upper- and middle-class settlers' plight using an image of female degradation which would be particularly shocking for his bourgeois metropolitan readers:

> You may see the fingers, which seldom moved but to paint for the eye, or to charm the ear, tying up cattle, or stopping the gaps of their enclosure: females, on whom, in England, the wind was scarcely allowed to blow, exposed to all the rage of the pitiless storm; mothers with large families, who used to have a servant to each child, without an individual to assist them in the drudgery of the house, the labour of the dairy, or the care of their children.[39]

Similarly Major Pigot's daughter Sophia complained that settler women were being 'Obliged to lay aside the accomplishments of the Drawing Room, for those of the Kitchen and farm yard' and Pringle was aghast at the daughters of 'gentlemen . . . washing clothes and digging potatoes!'[40] Although Henry Dugmore found the image of settler women having to capture and slaughter a runaway sheep rather comical, an alarmist report in Cape Town was taken far more seriously.[41] It went so far as to suggest that formerly respectable settler women were being forced to resort to prostitution on the frontier.[42]

It was the descent of the upper-class woman to the labouring function long associated with women of the working classes which was most frightening for wealthier settlers. This, after all, suggested a subversion of more than one naturalised order. Not only was the established class hierarchy being undermined; so too was the 'respectable' male's patriarchal ability to shield the women of his class. In the early years of the settlement then, anxieties of class and gender intersected and reinforced one another.

Yet, within twenty years of their arrival, settler politics were no longer centred on discourses of internal class division, nor of uncertain gender relations. Economic and personal divisions undoubtedly remained among the settlers and the jockeying for material and social status continued. But fractures which, in their marginal colonial environment, were potentially dangerous, were being stabilised within an enveloping settler identity. The remainder of the chapter examines the processes by which individual subjects, with varying backgrounds and agendas came eventually to produce and internalise this identity.

Constructing race

As one might expect, mutual constructions of race would form an important unifying influence for the settlers. As Simon Dagut notes, many settlers would have been informed of colonial constructions of race, and prepared to adopt them by advice literature on emigration, even before their voyage to South Africa.[43] The first direct experience that many settlers had of eastern Cape Africans, however, was that of being carried ashore at Algoa Bay on their backs – an ambivalent experience involving notions of African sub-servience, strength, potential threat and sensuality that had to be taken light-heartedly by emigrant women in particular if it was not to offend their sense of decency. As this initial juxtaposition of sensations suggests, the processes through which the 1820 settlers forged a shared discourse of the frontier's black population were far from straightforward.[44]

Official separatist policy meant that the new settlers were expressly discouraged from interacting with the Xhosa after their establishment on their farms. Upon Somerset's return from leave late in 1820, strictures on contact across the frontier were tightened in an attempt to use the settlement to delimit the colonial edge more firmly. Britons crossing the Fish River boundary were made liable to corporal punishment, and trading, which Donkin had tolerated at an official fair on the Keiskamma River, was restricted. However, an unwelcome form of 'contact' nevertheless took place as a result of Xhosa warriors' continuing efforts to drive colonists from parts of the Zuurveld/ Albany. In September 1821, settlers were shocked to hear of an isolated raid in which a herd boy was killed.[45] In 1822, with raiding continuing, British soldiers made matters worse by leading the attempt to capture the colonial 'ally' Ngqika and force his more emphatic compliance with colonial terms.[46] While the mass of the British settlers generally remained ignorant of those historic and contemporary Xhosa grievances, many certainly felt the brunt of Xhosa retaliation.

The experience of cattle raiding quickly stimulated antagonistic representations of the Xhosa among certain settlers. Within a few months, almost all of the most exposed, easterly settlers' livestock had been taken.[47]

Thomas Stubbs wrote that, for those Britons located right on the frontier line, 'books were now exchanged for guns', and in a statement of grievances sent to the Colonial Secretary in March 1823 and signed by 374 settlers, farmers warned that 'existing measures can only lead to a war of mutual extermination'.[48] Even the Romantic and humanitarian poet, Thomas Pringle, exasperated by stock theft, excused a commando which he had mounted against a group of raiding Khoesan, explaining that 'we back-settlers grow all savage and bloody by coming into continual collision with savages'.[49] In these conditions a stereotype of the Xhosa developed rapidly among many frontier farmers. It was one expressed clearly by S. H. Hudson, for whom the Xhosa were a 'cunning' and 'dangerous enemy'. He continued, 'When a settler has produced stock and fancies himself comfortable in his prospect of success these depredators make an inroad by night and sweep the whole of his hope away, perhaps fire his home and murder himself and his family for daring to resist'.[50]

Settler representations of the Xhosa, however, were far from homogeneous in the 1820s. While those who had sunk the capital that they had brought with them from Britain in exposed land and sought to prosper through pastoralism, had good reason to fear Xhosa 'depredation', a minority, like the well-informed Thomas Philipps, did sympathise with the frontier Xhosa's plight: 'We have driven those nearest us to encroach on the other tribes . . . can it be supposed then . . . that the settler can ever be free from such depredations?'[51] George Thompson agreed that after colonial land appropria-tion 'there is scarcely sufficient pasture for their cattle', and Pringle himself believed that Xhosa raiding was 'not so very "enormous" as some of the settlers have been prone to consider it'.[52] Especially those located at one remove from the frontier itself, and to some extent insulated from Xhosa raids, could claim to 'have not the least dread of them'.[53] Most of the upper-class settlers who made a point of 'educating themselves' by visiting Xhosa homesteads in fact initially paid the Xhosa the barbed compliment of drawing analogies between their physiques and lifestyle and those of admired Greek and Roman antiquity.[54] Such a classically informed, Romantic portrayal was itself of course, a stereotype, and it was one which cast the Xhosa backwards in time. But it was, superficially at least, a benign one, allowed by the fact that the Xhosa whom these particular writers had observed were safely 'in place' across the frontier line.[55]

Carrying more weight than the sympathy of a few gentlemanly visitors were the constructions of settlers who interacted with the Xhosa on a more regular basis. Soon after their arrival, over 120 settlers, including former labourers like Montgomery and Goldswain acquired generous credit from British merchants in Cape Town, in the form of beads, iron-ware and guns, to carry on a lucrative but largely illegal trade in ivory, hides and cattle among the Xhosa. William Southey boasted that 'we get from 20 to 100 per cent profit on goods' and Benjamin Norden, who had also started life in the settlement as a labourer, was able to earn between £40,000 and

£60,000 over twenty years in the 'kaffir trade'.[56] Aside from those who entered Xhosa territory themselves to trade, others profited from the enterprise through wagon manufacture and repair, and by transporting Xhosa goods to Algoa Bay and British and Indian manufactures to Graham's Town.[57]

In their memoranda applying for a more extensive exchange to be legalised, the traders' constructions of the Xhosa differed from that of the rapacious raider of whom many frontier farmers complained. Some traders made representations about Xhosa land loss to the British authorities and over 170 settlers petitioned the governor, stating that raiding was stimulated only by official sanctions on trade which denied the Xhosa the chance to acquire colonial goods legitimately. One trader even berated the colonial authorities for failing to understand the humiliation which their overbearing conduct had inflicted upon Xhosa chiefs like Ngqika, implying that raiding was simply a natural reaction.[58] Aside from their material interest, these settlers' more accommodating approach was perhaps influenced by the trust which they placed, and found fulfilled, in the Xhosa (a trust shared by many missionaries). In entering Xhosa territory, early traders were flaunting explicit colonial regulations, and could expect no support from the authorities. Laden with valuable commodities, they were conducting, as Dugmore put it, a 'life-in-hand venture into the power of the Kaffers'.[59] And, more often than not, it was a successful one.

Settler stereotypes of the Xhosa in the early years then, were personal, shaped according to individual experience rather than any public discourse of savagery. Whether these stereotypes consisted of the suffering farmers' cunning depredator or of many traders' put-upon clients, they were primarily mechanisms by which individual settlers could 'map their self' into a new world of differentiated interaction with an unfamiliar people.[60] As we shall see, it would take other, more emotionally disturbing and more collective experiences, for a general settler discourse of a 'savage' Xhosa other to be created. In 1826, and without fear of universal contradiction, Thomas Philipps could still write 'What a noble race of People all the neighbouring Blacks are . . . Of all that I have yet seen the Hottentot [Khoesan] is the lowest in the scale'.[61]

As Philipps' remark suggests, if the settlers' constructions of Xhosa 'otherness' did not initially bind them together, their defence of the more immediate colonial racial division of labour, based on 'Hottentot' service, did. With the eastern frontier districts suffering from an acute shortage of labour, even some of the settlers who had emigrated as indentured servants were soon employers in their own right, and were themselves experiencing the economic constraints brought about by a lack of workers. Towards the top of the settlers' social hierarchy too, Charlotte Philipps complained that 'the great want and difficulty of procuring servants . . . renders it impossible for us to get on with the improvements on our new place'.[62] Ideas of bringing out further labourers from Britain, 'perhaps from a poor house', were discountenanced once the rapid social mobility of even the 'pauper' settlers had become evident, and in 1823, an official Commission of Enquiry into the colony's affairs was instructed to investigate 'the means of introducing [Khoesan] labour . . . especially in the frontier districts'.[63]

The commission's recommendations merely legitimated the steps that the settlers had already taken. Many attempted first to hire individual Khoesan, but finding that they would not be separated from their families, employers adopted instead the Dutch colonial practice of incorporating Khoesan house-holds as labour tenants. Others, like Montgomery, simply bought Khoesan servants illegally from their former Dutch masters.[64] By 1827, Thompson felt able to advise other prospective emigrants that 'the Hottentot population affords an important resource . . . and, when judiciously treated, generally prove useful and obedient dependants'.[65]

Despite Thompson's assurances, though, the domination of Khoesan labour could not be taken for granted. During the late 1820s, as we have seen, John Philip was campaigning on the Khoesan's behalf, identifying their condition, under the Caledon Code in particular, as analogous to that of slavery. His agitation in the colony and in London culminated in the abolition of the Khoesan pass system under Ordinance 50 of 1828. Stubbs spoke for many settlers when he described the ordinance as 'that abominable false philan-thropy which made [the Khoesan] free and ruined them . . . They were a people that required to be under control, both for their own benefit and the public; the same as the slaves in this country'.[66] Well before their agitation on behalf of the Xhosa, the Cape humanitarians' role in securing 'freedom' for the colony's Khoesan labour force alienated them from the most vocal of the settlers. J. C. Chase, one of the most voluble of a select group of self-appointed settler spokesmen, felt that the colony's Khoesan had been favoured by 'the pious but gulled John Bull', duped by the repre-sentations of Philip and his allies. He wished that the 'overjealous friends of the Cape Hottentots' had been with him on a tour that he had recently made among independent Khoesan and Griqua to the north of the colony. Had they witnessed the 'defects' in the Khoesan's 'natural character', they could no longer have blamed the bad example of the whites, nor the oppres-sive laws of the colony for their 'acknowledged viciousness'.[67]

It was not only the publicly vocal settlers who shared a post-Ordinance 50 disillusionment with humanitarians and with their Khoesan workforce. The private writings of Mary Anne Webb, for instance, include a reference to the Khoesan being shown 'such favour . . . that they have the assurance to think themselves equal to other people and will not contract for work nor work without [a contract] . . . they say they are their own Masters'.[68] Threatened by the loss of control over their labour force, a consensus developed among the settlers as a whole that the Cape's 'coloured classes' were potentially rebel-lious and criminal.[69] As Major Dundas, an artillery officer stationed on the frontier put it, 'The Hottentot by disposition is little disposed to labour; he is idle, drunken and improvident, and required to be held under restraint'.[70] Colonel Wade, military secretary at the Cape in the late 1820s and early 1830s and subsequently acting governor, felt that a 'considerable increase of crime throughout the colony' was 'the inevitable consequence . . . of the unhappy gift of unrestricted liberty conferred on the free coloured population by the 50th ordinance, without any attendant measure for controlling their irregularities, and saving them from the worst enemy they ever had to contend with, namely themselves'.[71]

During the early 1830s, many of the settlers agitated for a colonial Vagrancy Ordinance, modelled on West Indies planters' suggestions, which would effectively re-impose the pre-Ordinance 50 legal constraints, obliging 'these people to be useful to the community'.[72] Chase maintained that 'we do not want a vagrant law for particular classes, but for the whole community; and if the Hottentots are really the industrious people they are represented to be, they have nothing to fear from any enactments directed against idleness'.[73] The Khoesan, then, were condemned by the new British settlers for not being diligent and sober workers, and humanitarians were condemned for failing to make them so before bringing about their freedom from necessary restraint. As Acting Governor, Wade, as we have seen, backed the settlers' proposal for a vagrancy law, but with the legislation disallowed in London, alternatives such as the use of the treadmill and the local implementation of former Dutch colonial vagrancy laws were advocated in order to control those Khoesan who refused to work on settler farms.[74]

Pringle voiced his disappointment that settlers had, 'with lamentable facility adopted similar sentiments towards the "native labourers" as the established colonists',[75] but such 'sentiments' were perhaps the first which settlers from a variety of class, ethnic and religious origins in Britain, now colonial employers in their own right, had shared.

British labour relations and public morality

Despite their adoption of 'similar sentiments' towards Khoesan subordinates, most British settlers nevertheless 'managed' them in ways that differed from those employed by the Dutch colonial master class. As John Philip's son wrote, 'the Dutch Boers . . . are by no means so bustling in their habits or so strict in their supervision of work as English settlers'.[76] Historians of South Africa have long implied that Britons were responsible for the introduction to the Cape of a new kind of 'social distance' between master and servant.[77] More recently, this distinction has been analysed in passing by Clifton Crais and in more detail by Simon Dagut.[78] Dagut suggests that the British settlers were influenced by the labour relations that they found on surrounding Afrikaner farms, but examines the ways in which they adapted those relations.

Among Afrikaners, even if it was not always practised, and particularly not on isolated frontier farms, there existed an 'ideal' form of paternalistic relation between master and slave or servant. This idealised paternalism had long provided a sense of self-legitimation among slave holders in the Cape, as it had on the American plantations.[79] But it had recently been articulated more forcefully as a result of the abolitionist challenges facing slave-owners. Encountering metropolitan condemnation for the first time, as Stanley Trapido argues, 'the Cape [Dutch] elite was at some considerable pains to stress its commitment to such paternalism and to express resentment of outsiders – whether missionaries or travellers – whose interpretations suggested otherwise'.[80]

However, Dagut suggests that, while British settler ideals were based on this Afrikaner model, they came to diverge from it in a number of respects. Not only were more subtle and commercialised forms of punishment than the 'paternalistic' beating, such as the docking of wages, often employed as responses to dependants' transgression, but other distancing mechanisms, such as payment in cash rather than kind, were adopted.[81] Dagut argues that British settlers generally retreated from the social and domestic proximity between master and servant inherent in local Afrikaner practices, and resorted instead to practices which he labels 'pseudo-paternalism'. This novel set of practices 'retained a comfortingly benign vocabulary', but implied 'none of the onerous duties and uncomfortable intimacies of the genuine article'.[82]

While Dagut has concentrated more than any previous historian on identifying the discrepancies between a British settler discourse of labour relations, and that which was applied to varying extents among Afrikaners,[83] Crais has sought in a less systematic manner and as part of a larger project, to trace the origins of the settlers' discourse to practices recently adopted in the British metropole. He ascribes the settlers' ideals of labour relations to their experience of the disciplinary regimes which Foucault has identified as being forged in Europe.[84] In contrast to most Afrikaner farmers, and in line with bourgeois metropolitan approaches towards the working class, Crais argues that 'British settlers resisted close contact with blacks. The elite neither wanted blacks sleeping in their bedrooms nor were willing to take a whip to disobedient workers: they preferred the treadmill to the sjambok'.[85]

Although the genealogy of British settler labour relations can indeed usefully be traced to contemporary Britain, I would add that it is possible to track these relations to more specific developments *within* the broad institution of Foucaultian disciplinary regimes. As we have already seen, the early nineteenth century, and particularly the post-Napoleonic War years, witnessed considerable instability in Britain, associated with economic depression, 'surplus' rural labour and the move to a more commercialised economy. An increasing distance between agricultural labourers and landowners was one manifestation of the shift in social relations which accompanied these changes. It was reflected in both the stripping away of old poor law protection and the expulsion of the labourer from the intimacy of the employing family's dining table.[86] As Davidoff and Hall point out, this metropolitan transition was itself mediated by the construction of new forms of paternalism which moderated potential class polarisation.

It was not just among Afrikaner colonists attempting to control a potentially rebellious slave and Khoesan workforce, that employers strove to be seen as paternalistic guardians of their dependants' well-being. In Britain too, middle-class businessmen saw themselves ideally as 'the "providers" not only for their wives, children and servants, but also for their employees. Wives, children, servants, labourers, all could be described in the language of paternalism as the dependants and children of their father, their master, their guardian'.[87] Among the British bourgeoisie, who were managing an innovatory phase of capitalist transition, then, a 'pseudo-paternalist' discourse, to use Dagut's term, had already been forged from the remnants of older practices. It was this discourse, combining social distance with paternalistic remnants, along with the racialised reaction to Ordinance 50, I would suggest, that provided a more directly relevant model for settler practices than the Dutch colonial ideas that the emigrants encountered in the Cape itself.

What most distinguished the imported metropolitan model of paternalism from the slave-holding colonial form, was its combination of a closely monitored bourgeois morality and a more commercial orientation. In Britain, the sanctity of Christian paternalism in regard to one's servants was a justification in its own right. But paternalism would also 'lighten the cares of business [and] brighten the scenes of prosperity'.[88] The British settlers' payment of Khoesan servants in cash rather than in kind reflected the wider, and contested shift away from payment in kind in Britain. It was an outcome of a growing middle-class imperative for responsible, closely recorded and regulated business transactions – transactions that enabled employers to lead their families upon a morally sanctified path to self-reliance and moderate accumulation.[89]

Despite the lowly class origins of many of the British emigrants to the Cape, as employers they had come to share the moral discourse of the employing classes in Britain itself, adding a new racial twist to the depiction of their subordinates. It was largely because of the requirement for 'morally legitimate' rather than blatantly rapacious capitalist behaviour, that settler protests about the effects of Ordinance 50 were couched in terms of the irrepressible criminality of the Cape's lower ('Coloured') classes. Measures such as pass controls were needed not simply so that settlers could acquire a labour force, but so that 'naturally' unruly and amoral elements in the population could be subject to proper restraint of the kind contemporaneously advocated in Britain for the uneducated labouring classes. For both colonial 'masters' and the domestic bourgeoisie, 'the overriding objective of pursuing a moral and genteel life made it almost impossible for employers to acknowledge the price paid by their employees . . . The processes, however distasteful, which had made such a life possible were but a means to a divinely sanctioned end'.[90]

Legitimate capitalist enterprise and the public sphere

After the establishment of a free port at Port Elizabeth, during the early 1830s the growth of woollen production promised the significant and legitimate commercial expansion that settlers had long anticipated. A realisation of the eastern Cape's potential for sheep breeding corresponded with a massive increase in the demand for raw wool in Britain, and the easing of tariffs on imports from the colonies.[91] Both Graham's Town merchants (mainly from the joint stock parties) and landed proprietors (many of them proprietary leaders) saw in wool the economic future of the Albany settlement, and both became involved in its production and sale.[92] They were encouraged by settlers such as Chase, who had established himself in an official position in Cape Town, from where he was able to act as an agent for sheep farmers, buying imported sheep and sending them east to the frontier.[93] Capital for investment in the industry was newly available in the colony, since British merchant houses were acting as agents for the Dutch slave-owners, who were in turn receiving compensation from Britain for the freeing of their slaves. Much of this compensation money was ultimately recycled to the sheep farms of the Cape frontier.[94] It was due to the money being made through woollen production and its ancillary services that Graham's Town grew in the 1830s to become the second largest town in the colony.[95]

A settlers' newspaper, the *Graham's Town Journal* (*GTJ*), was founded in 1831, partly in order to extol the virtues of sheep farming among the settlers, partly to frame moral arguments for its expansion onto Xhosa land and partly to defend the settlers against humanitarian allegations of greed and brutality towards their dependants. Although in the first instance the paper articulated only the concerns of an acquisitive elite centred around its editor, the former London printer, Robert Godlonton, it soon became the settlers' 'public voice'. The *GTJ*'s status as a medium of communication was enhanced during the 1830s, as the settler population expanded and dispersed north along the frontier, and the public meetings, which had at first secured consensus on political strategy, became less inclusive. From the mid-1830s, more settlers bought the *Journal* simply in order to stay in touch with developments that were of collective concern.[96] A relatively high circulation of 700, and a readership that would have been far greater, gave Godlonton a virtual monopoly on public expression in Albany. Such was his grip that Dr A. G. Campbell's rival humanitarian paper, established in 1840, was stifled and Campbell himself forced to leave Graham's Town.[97] By the 1840s, Godlonton's paper was being circulated not just among settlers in the eastern Cape itself, but quite widely in the western Cape (over a hundred copies of each issue were sent to Cape Town), Port Natal and the interior, and also in Britain, North America, India, St Helena and Mauritius.[98]

Godlonton and settler contributors used the *GTJ* to bemoan incessantly their insecurity in the face of Xhosa raiding.[99] For them, the Xhosa's raiding habits supplied all the moral authority that could be required for punitive action. They called for the imperial authorities to take this action by confiscating the frontier Xhosa chiefdoms' land. By 1834, a number of settlers who had suffered stock losses reached a consensus, aired publicly through the newspaper, that the expansion of settler farms into Xhosa territory was effectively synonymous with 'progress'. Not only would the confiscation of their land teach Xhosa culprits the sanctity of private property, it would also expose them decisively to the disciplined morality of the settlers' own commercial system.[100]

At the same time as it advocated the seizure of Xhosa land, in standardising and reproducing the stereotype of them as 'cunning depredators', the *GTJ* was also creating a new, public representation of the Xhosa themselves.[101] With the repetition of this stereotype, and its accessibility to settlers, earlier, differentiated constructions of Xhosa difference were being challenged. However, they were not yet generally being supplanted. It would not be until after the collective experience of a massed Xhosa attack that the *Journal*'s imagery became, almost universally, the settlers' own.

Within the first fifteen years of the British settlement in Albany, the acceptance of an established racial division of labour, its structuring according to a model of labour relations imported from Britain, and the diffusion of a public discourse of settler 'progress' based on wool production, had helped to forge shared values and material aspirations among many settlers who had previously been divided by class boundaries and by individual experiences of, and responses to, the colonial environment. Nevertheless, neither a 'pseudo-paternalistic' domination of the Khoesan, nor the desire for the advancement of sheep farming into Xhosa territory yet bound individual settlers together in any truly *emotive* sense. These imperatives had not yet generated a consistent discourse of racial difference among the settlers and nor had they yet established the morality of seizing the Xhosa's land. It was, above all, the experience of warfare that would bring about these more potent cultural effects.

Warfare and the 'irreclaimable savage'

During late 1834, Maqoma forged a coalition of frontier Xhosa chiefdoms willing to embark on a full-scale endeavour to reclaim the Zuurveld. For a decade, most Xhosa chiefs had counselled against war with the colony and attempted, with varying degrees of commitment, to restrict stock theft from colonial farms. But three successive expulsions of Maqoma's followers, combined with other incidents of colonial aggression had made the exercise of restraint increasingly difficult. The shooting of the chief Bhotomane's brother, Xhoxho, by a colonial patrol, and incidents in which Xhosa commoners had been fired upon by British soldiers acting under the 'spoor law', prompted commoners to apply increasing pressure on their chiefs to retaliate. At the same time, a severe drought, which had begun in 1833, was undermining the chiefs' ability to dispense patronage in the form of cattle loans. A reassertion of chiefly authority was overdue and, for the first time since 1819, a number of chiefs came together to sanction and plan a violent response to colonial aggression. The Ngqika under Tyhali and Maqoma himself, the Mdange under Bhotomane, the Langa under Nqeno and those Ndlambe who refused to follow their chief Mqhayi's policy of neutrality, launched a co-ordinated attack on the colony in December 1834. Albany in particular was singled out for retribution and twenty-four British settlers were killed within the first few hours of the attack.[102]

The war of 1834–5, or the 'Sixth Frontier War', as it came to be known, was the most vicious yet and it was beyond anything that the British settlers on the frontier had experienced. In total, forty-three colonists were killed and 765 farms burnt or pillaged. Most of the settlers outside Graham's Town lost a significant proportion of their property, even while those within it engaged in war profiteering.[103] It was the collective experience of the war, and the metropolitan and colonial debates to which it gave rise, which prompted most of the settlers to close ranks and to forge an unprecedentedly clear and embattled political identity. This was an identity extending far deeper than the public discourse of settler 'progress' that had thus far been established. It was defined in opposition to two challenges. The first was the personal threat represented by the Xhosa themselves and the second, the Cape and metropolitan humanitarians who sympathised with them. Neither, opined one of Miles Bowker's numerous sons, John Mitford, 'ought for a moment to be allowed to thwart in any way the general progress of improvement'.[104]

The Wesleyan missionary Rev. Shaw, who had been in England during the war, found upon his return to Graham's Town soon after its conclusion, 'a great revolution in the sentiments of the British Settlers in reference to the Caffre race', and the military commander, Harry Smith, noted 'a spirit pervading all classes of society . . . to teach everyone to view and treat the Kafir as a beast'.[105] Prominent settlers declared themselves convinced that 'many of the missionaries have been labouring under the greatest delusion and although living for years amongst the Kafirs, they have not been able to form anything like a correct estimate of the character of the people around them'.[106] A party of traders, returning from deep within Xhosaland, articulated the prevailing view when they claimed that 'we have lost all confidence in the Caffres'.[107] The Xhosa were also widely credited with the heinous war crime of having destroyed the mission stations that had been established for their own improvement.[108]

In the wake of the war, the *Graham's Town Journal* took the lead in reconstructing settler representations of the Xhosa, in an attempt to rationalise the recent display of 'savagery'.[109] The paper printed a range of assessments of 'the Kafir character', from relatively mild and anecdotal descriptions such as 'incorrigibly dishonest', through analogies between the Xhosa and incurably spoilt children, to contributions that were genocidal in nature.[110] One anonymous letter, for instance, advised the use of a spring gun for 'Kafirs and wild beasts in general', mentioning that the Bowker brothers had recently 'destroyed' two 'Kafirs' in this way.[111] A 'scientific' attempt to grapple with the problem of the Xhosa took an environmentally determinist line, describing the Xhosa as having 'all the ferocity, cruelty and craft of some of the lower animals' adjusted to the same 'bleak, rough and uncomfortable' climate and vegetation.[112] But the wartime presence in Grahamstown of a Dr Macartney, allowed for a newer strand of 'scientific' thought to be applied. He offered a series of public lectures on the 'now popular science of phrenology' using model skulls of different nations, including those of Xhosa 'lately received', presumably as trophies of the war.[113] The lecture series' enthusiastic reception by the settler community was applauded by the *Graham's Town Journal*.[114] In the face of such settler hatred for the Xhosa, dissenting voices, like that of Captain Fawcett, a visiting East India Company army officer, were overwhelmed with invective whenever they dared make their views known to the journal's readership.[115]

John Mitford Bowker, in particular invested considerable emotive energy in his post-war representations of the Xhosa. A speech which he gave in 1844 is worth quoting at length for the unparalleled insights which it gives into the blend of intense anxiety and newly aggressive materialism which also characterised the range of more modest post-war settler men's responses:

> The day was when our plains were covered with tens of thousands of springboks; they are gone now, and who regrets it? Their place is occupied with tens of thousands of merino sheep, whose fleeces find employment to tens of thousands of industrious men: are they not better than the springbok? Yet I must own that when I see two or three of them on the wide plains, and know that they are the last of their race, my heart yearns towards them, and I regret that so much innocent beauty, elegance, and agility, must needs be swept from the earth. My feelings towards the Kafir are not of that stamp. I know that he has disregarded the zealous missionary for years. I know that he has once overrun and destroyed these districts, and I fear him, knowing him to be ready and willing to do it again. I know him to be the great bar to all improvement amongst us. I know that rapine and murder are in all his thoughts, and I see them in his looks, and hate him accordingly . . . and I begin to think that he too, as well as the springbok, must give place, and why not? Is it just that a few thousands of ruthless, worthless savages are to sit like a nightmare upon a land that would support millions of civilised men happily? Nay; Heaven forbids it.[116]

Settlers found moral authority for such views in the speeches and letters of frustrated Wesleyan missionaries, some of whom had themselves emigrated as settlers and turned to missionary work only after their arrival. Encountering widespread resistance to his evangelical efforts across the frontier, the

Rev. Shrewsbury had declared even before the war that 'were it not that I desire to promote the salvation of their souls, I would not dwell amongst such a wretched people another hour'. After it, he suggested the execution of any Xhosa who had taken colonial lives and the tagging of others so that they could be monitored while they were put to 'merciful' hard labour building colonial roads.[117] With the new governor, General Sir Benjamin D'Urban, passing on Shrewsbury's recommendations to the Colonial Office and himself describing them as 'irreclaimable savages', it was determined, as we will see in the following chapter, that after their surrender, the frontier Xhosa's land should be seized by the colony. Over 400 settler men put in applications for farms in the conquered province.

However, the settlers' post-war plans for the simultaneous punishment of the Xhosa and expansion of sheep farming were resisted by humanitarians in the Cape and in Britain. From within the colony, Philip and Fairbairn remained in favour of extending British authority over the frontier Xhosa in principle, but with Xhosa access to the land guaranteed and with govern-ment-sponsored 'civilisation' rather than settler acquisition in mind. Philip therefore set about publicising the grievances of the Xhosa in London more vigorously than ever before, once again invoking the assistance of Thomas Fowell Buxton, as a conduit for his representations. I will return to this humanitarian campaign in chapter 5. What is most significant here is that the opposition of local and metropolitan humanitarians to the Cape govern-ment's and British settlers' colonial projects after the war, was critical in prompting a clearer, reflexive definition of settler affinity.

Metropolitan condemnation seems to have been a spur to settler com-munality well beyond the Cape. In eighteenth-century Barbados for instance, 'the continuous bombardment of calumny to which settler communities were subjected [from Britain] gave them an early and powerful incentive to develop a more favourable image of themselves if only in self-defence'.[118] The British settlers in the Cape found themselves in a similar predicament to those in other colonies during the age of abolition and humanitarianism, or, as Bowker put it disparagingly, of 'Aborigines' protection societies, Anti-slavery societies [and] Mission institutions'.[119] Colonists were utterly dependent on the metropole for protection and they thrived materially through their links with metropolitan manufacturers and merchants. And yet they were simultaneously threatened by metropolitan humanitarian reformist currents. Just as abolitionism threatened the West Indian planters, so labour reform and sympathy for indigenous land rights worried the settlers of the eastern Cape. As Bowker complained, '[t]he very laudable exertions to suppress the slave trade, have induced a feeling of pity and commiseration for the swarthy nations of Africa, in which the Kafirs, unfortunately for them-selves and us, have largely participated'.[120] It was the ambivalence in their relationship with the metropolitan bourgeoisie, generated by these tensions, that lay at the heart of a settler identity that was becoming simultaneously assertive, defensive and loudly loyal.

In the months immediately following the end of the Sixth War, Albany settler men aroused themselves into a political frenzy, both to justify the punitive annexation of more Xhosa territory and to salvage their own reputation in Britain. The issue of the *South African Commercial Advertiser* which had been printed just before the Xhosa attack on the colony, and which arrived among frontier settlers during that attack, contained prescient warnings to colonial officials, and to settlers themselves, about the consequences of provoking the Xhosa further, but was interpreted by many settlers as a direct encouragement to the Xhosa to attack. It was widely considered among the settlers that Philip, Fairbairn and their metropolitan allies had 'usc[d] us most rascally', and that they were, in fact, 'unprincipled scoundrels'.[121] What really rankled with the settler men who expressed their opinions in public was that Philip and his allies, 'with the assiduity of purpose that Satan himself might envy, have gained their object in persuading our countrymen, to whom we looked for sympathy and succour, that we are monsters'. Humanitarian 'betrayal' had led to the possibility of imperial abandonment. As Bowker continued,

> England, instead of protecting us, accuses us, who were born and bred in her bosom, and have the like feelings as the rest of her sons, of cruelty and oppression . . . I begin to believe that the charge of cruelty fixed upon our West Indian planters has originated more in cant, helped out with a few solitary instances of cruelty, blazoned well forth as examples, than in anything else.[122]

The emotive effect of humanitarian and metropolitan condemnation can be gauged in the writings of Donald Moodie. Moodie had arrived in the eastern Cape in 1820, but not as part of the Albany settlement scheme. Before the war, he had been generally sympathetic towards the Xhosa, informing the Commission of Enquiry in 1823, for instance, that the 'spoor law' was 'cruel and unjust', and describing it as 'sufficing cause' in itself for the Xhosa's propensity to steal from colonists.[123] After the war, however, he expressed his anger that the settlers should have been blamed by colonial and metropolitan humanitarians for provoking the Xhosa attack through their hunger for land. Like other settler men, he articulated his grievance by corresponding with the *GTJ*, vigorously attacking the accusations of Philip, Fairbairn and Pringle. He also assisted Chase in the writing of a settler polemic, *Some Reasons for Our Opposing the Author of the 'South African Researches', The Rev. John Philip.*[124]

Thereafter, Moodie devoted his energies to compiling a record of colonial documents intended to refute the claims about the abuses of the Khoesan that Philip had made in his *Researches*, and to establish that official policy in the Cape, despite its good intentions, had only ever been taken advantage of by indigenes in order to plunder the colonists. Colonists certainly appreciated his efforts on their behalf. As one of them wrote to a western Cape, humanitarian-inclined paper:

If the Editor of the *Cape Mail* could collect together every copy of every book which has been written to the prejudice of the Colonists and burn them – and if he could restrain the would-be philanthropists here, as in England, from bringing false accusations against us, we might then dispense with Mr. Moodie's Records. But while the books above referred to exist, and we have 'friends at the Cape' to write that which is untrue to . . . England . . . I maintain that such Records are indispensable.[125]

In their vocal post-war representations to the authorities in London, settler men certainly displayed elements of a consciously moulded, unifying political strategy. But it was also a strategy which expressed personal feelings of an emerging colonial identity, shaped at great distance and in different conditions from the metropole. They stressed their value as capitalists, contributing to the wealth and prestige of the British empire as well as the comfort and security of their own families. They asserted the morality of their own actions in trying to build a civilised culture on a dangerous frontier. They emphasised the lengths to which they had been forced to go in order to defend that culture from Xhosa 'savagery'; their need, as men, to exercise continuing surveillance over this racial foe, and the 'madness and despair' caused by humanitarian allegations that they themselves were to blame for their misfortunes at the hands of the Xhosa.[126] They also pointed out their differentiation from the Dutch-speaking colonists who seemed at the time to be deserting the frontier zone on what would later be called the 'Great Trek', and they pressed their special claim to patronage as British subjects.[127] It was around such legitimations and external representations that a broad, emotive and defensive sense of settler affinity first coalesced.

Maintaining settler discourse

Landscape, history and identity

The British settlers' post-war affinity could have been an ephemeral phenomenon were it not for considerable, continuing investment in the construction of a collective, legitimating past. In post-war settler discourse, the class and other divisions which had characterised the early settlement were retrospectively obscured or trivialised through the acceptance of such notions as a civilised landscape, a shared settler 'character' and a transplanted 'Britishness'. These notions allowed not just settlers themselves, but also many of their subsequent historians to create and nourish the idea of a united and 'natural' settler community.

One of the first published works of South African history was Robert Godlonton's *A Narrative of the Irruption of the Kafir Hordes*.[128] Purporting to be an explanation of the causes and course of the 1834–5 war, it was a reconstruction of the settlers' past, an analysis of their present predicament and, above all, a conscious defence of their activities. In the *Narrative*, Godlonton

provided the first widely available outline of a collective settler history, focusing on their persistence in bringing 'civilisation' to the frontier landscape.[129]
A series of landscape imageries was developed in his text, with wilderness,
ruggedness and impenetrability associated consistently with the pre-colonial
Khoesan and Xhosa.[130] The wildness of the landscape prior to colonisation
is an exaggerated motif running through many of the settlers' individual
reminiscences too. Henry Dugmore, for instance, describes an Albany overrun with elephants, rhinos and lions, animals which most settlers never
encountered unless they went hunting for them.[131]

The settlers' sense of self-legitimation was attached firmly to what they saw
as the 'improvement' of this landscape, partly through the construction of
European-style 'towns and villages, fields of grain and vineyards'.[132] As
Michael Taussig has put it in another context, the Khoesan and Xhosa
'could all the better reflect back to the colonists the vast and baroque projec-
tions of human wildness that the colonists needed to establish their reality as
civilised (not to mention businesslike) people'.[133] Godlonton's *Narrative*
sketched the settler habitations within a landscape made tranquil and John
Mitford Bowker was convinced that they were raising 'for the interest of
the Empire, a garden in the wilderness'.[134]

Such a claim would have appealed to a metropolitan audience familiar with
the notion of the cultivated garden proclaiming 'the values of privacy, order,
taste and appreciation of nature in a controlled environment'.[135] As David
Bunn argues, Thomas Pringle's poetry too represented the settlers' landscape
'as a center of gentle . . . control far removed from the violence associated with
the actual colonial process'.[136] This domesticated vision allowed settler
women as well as men to survey the eastern Cape landscape from the perspective of an 'imperial', if gendered 'eye'.[137] Rather than imagining urban centres
and cultivated fields, for example, a Mrs Armstrong identified the utility of
the Ngqika Xhosa's Amatola Mountain range as lying in its 'fine rich black
soil suggesting rhododendrons etc. etc. for the gardens of future settlers'.[138]

These landscape representations were, of course, enhanced by the physical
ordering of the landscape which the settlers managed to effect. In settlements
like Salem, 'the majority of homesteads had sightlines to the church and
village green. In many of the houses one could stand at the doorway and
look toward the symbols of safety, community and religious leadership'.[139]
In 1826, the Rev. Shrewsbury, working among the Xhosa across the frontier,
articulated the considerable comfort that his visits to the landscape constructed around the 'delightful English town' of Graham's Town habitually
afforded him:

> The houses, the farm-yards, the cross-barred gates, the inhabitants in
> manners, dress and appearance are thoroughly English, and while looking
> at every object I met, and the fields of oats and barley, and the gardens
> with abundance of vegetables of the same kind as are met in my native
> country, it seemed almost a reverie to conclude that I was in Africa.

It certainly is pleasing to think that from my circuit in the heart of Caffraria I can at any time ride on horseback in the short space of 5 days to Graham's Town and behold England in miniature.[140]

The settlers' 'improved' landscape was not just more gentle though; it was also more profitable. Like the earlier settlers in Barbados, profitability 'legiti-mated their enterprise in their own eyes and also – or so they hoped – in those of their fellow countrymen'.[141] By the mid-1830s, it was not the leisured, pastoral imagery of Albany, first generated by genteel settlers like Major Pigot, which was being reproduced.[142] Rather, it was a busy, productive and utilitarian landscape. Bowker wrote that the development of docks and a railway in the eastern Cape were 'things which Englishmen will do where they prosper and are protected' and for Thomas Philipps, it was '*British industry*' which 'will soon overcome the . . . obstacles which appear'.[143] We will revisit this conception of 'British-ness' below, but the point driven home in Godlonton's reconstruction of the settler past was that a civilised *and* pro-ductive landscape would have been in prospect for the frontier as a whole, were it not for the Xhosa and humanitarian obstacles impeding settler 'progress'.[144] The Albany landscape was being fashioned by Godlonton as the context for a sense of self arranged around active 'improvement' – a sense which could unite the settlers against common enemies and express a collective spirit.

Godlonton's *Narrative* was the product of an immediate sense of anger and betrayal in the wake of the war, but settlers from a variety of backgrounds found in his writings a template for their collective history. The narrative which he disseminated, in both the *GTJ* and his book, allowed an array of settler experiences to be orchestrated around certain themes and it was the repetition of these themes which gave them their aura of 'naturalness'.[145] Not only did many of the individual settlers' own later reminiscences mirror the *GTJ*'s concerns and the *Narrative*'s sequence of nature overcome, prosperity won and hopes dashed, but even apparently personal recollections made in later life, were often drawn straight from their pages. Henry Halse, for instance, clearly reproduced the *Journal*'s self-serving interpretation of the subsequently named 'Great Trek' as personal memory.[146] According to the editor of his *Chronicle*, Jeremiah Goldswain was similarly influenced: 'One feels that, unconsciously, the paper moulded not only his style but his emotional responses'.[147] Even Thomas Stubbs – as we shall see, hardly the archetypal settler – had lodged 'in his memory . . . attitudes . . . derived partly from his own personal experiences and partly from Robert Godlonton and the pages of the *Graham's Town Journal*'.[148] It was not only John Ayliff, writing his largely autobiographical *Harry Hastings* then, who drew upon the 'common fund of settler tradition'.[149] This 'common fund' was in many respects one originally narrated by Godlonton and, subsequently, more generally reiterated.

Gendered celebrations

If the settlers' collective memory was initially stimulated by Godlonton after the war, its apotheosis came at the commemorative ceremonies held in Albany in 1844. Just as middle-class men in Britain were consolidating their networks of association and their public political voice through formal clubs, societies and commemorative committees,[150] so settlers in Albany found new bonds of solidarity in the establishment of a committee to celebrate the twenty-fifth anniversary of the emigration scheme that had brought them to the Cape. The 1844 celebrations have been aptly described by M. J. McGinn as the 'self-conscious beginning of the cult of the 1820 settlers'.[151] Published by Godlonton as *Memorials of the British Settlers of South Africa* and purchased by Queen Victoria herself, the proceedings present a hagiographic recreation of united settler endeavour. Both Godlonton in his introduction to the *Memorials* and the Rev. Shaw in his printed dinner speech stressed that the settlers had survived and prospered because of the attributes that they had always shared. These were attributes not of class, nor of regionalism, ethnicity, nor religion. Rather, they were attributes of *character*, the invocation of which, as Stoler has shown, could serve to unite otherwise disparate colonial populations.[152] Despite the fact that the settlers' 'pursuits and circumstances differ widely from each other',[153] their 'character' could be made mutual. The settlers, proclaimed Godlonton,

> were not money capitalists; but they came hither provided with what is of far more importance in the establishment of a colony – they possessed indomitable resolution, ceaseless industry, and a spirit of enterprise, the ardour of which no disappointment could subdue, no danger appal, no difficulties frustrate.[154]

There was no mention here of the frequent references made by settlers in the 1820s to Graham's Town as a 'dismal, depressing place', nor of a high rate of suicides within the early settlement, nor of the *GTJ*'s own 'countless stories of failed settlers returning to Britain'.[155] There was only triumph in the face of adversity. And it was made clear that this adversity had not been occasioned solely by the Xhosa. In his address to the celebrations held at Port Elizabeth, Chase lauded the settlers for their persistence in the face of insults received from their 'wretched and degraded calumniators', the humanitarians. 'While a favored colored race was bepraised', Chase fulminated, 'we were denounced as having been *often* engaged in Commandoes against the aborigines, – all which representations, industriously propagated and greedily received in England, had the effect of arresting sympathy for our sufferings, and seriously endamaging [*sic*] the Colonial character for a time'.[156]

By no means all the settlers wished to think of themselves as sharing the same character as the self-righteous Chase and Godlonton (later nicknamed 'Moral Bob'). Thomas Stubbs was certainly alienated by Godlonton and other 'leading' settlers' smugness. He explained the 1844 celebrations as being the result of 'a lot of men . . . [who] had somehow or other managed to fill their coffers . . . [taking] it into their heads to have a rejoicing'. Stubbs could not resist attending the public dinner held in Graham's Town, but during a speech by Henry Somerset, he became so angered by the seemingly deliberate official omission of some settlers' travails, that he declared the speaker to be a liar. An ensuing fist-fight brought the proceedings to what the organising committee described as a 'disorderly and reprehensible' conclusion.[157]

And yet, for all his resentment of the self-proclaimed settler leaders, and all his combativeness, Stubbs, as we have seen, reproduced the *GTJ*'s attitudes as his own. His *Reminiscences* suggest that he also considered himself, alongside the other settlers, as being besieged by the Xhosa on the one hand and the humanitarians on the other. Settlers did not have to reproduce Godlonton's priggish conceit in order to adopt the settler consciousness expressed by him. Stubbs and others, like the alcoholic Thomas Shone, who occupied a similarly marginal position within 'respectable' settler society, were compelled to the same communal rallying points, and were encompassed within the flexible boundaries of a settler identity.[158] Articulations such as those which Godlonton provided are important 'precisely because they are polyvalent, providing an all-embracing concept which can contain the multiplicity of individual objectives and expectations'.[159]

Public events such as the 1844 celebrations reaffirmed Godlonton's original discourse of the past as speaker after speaker reiterated the *Narrative*'s themes, transforming individual recollection into the 'ordered memories of a [collective] biography'.[160] However, one significant component of this public discourse – an inclusive sense of 'British-ness' – was also being shaped within the private surroundings of the settler home. Despite the fact that the biography of the settlement left to posterity by the *Memorials* and, indeed, by the *Graham's Town Journal*, is an almost entirely male one, it was settler women who played the crucial role here.

Until recently, the historiography of colonial settler women rested on a simple dichotomy. In some accounts, female colonisers were too oppressed by European patriarchal structures, too confined to the domestic sphere, to have made their own distinctive contribution to the racial structures erected by colonising men. By contrast, in other accounts, colonial sites were seen as positions from which women could challenge the patriarchal structures which hemmed in their metropolitan counterparts, but in creating space for their own agency these women themselves became active agents of racial oppression. However, we don't have to accept either of these dichotomous versions in its totality.[161] We can begin by recognising that, due to patriarchal constructions, women colonists generally played a less significant role in the construction of racial hierarchies than their male counterparts, but that they nevertheless had a substantial stake in the maintenance of colonial cultures. As Alison Blunt and Gillian Rose put it, 'Colonizing women . . . were

positioned both inside and outside colonial discourses'. They 'were marginalised within patriarchal contexts where they were perceived primarily in
terms of gender inferiority. However, within colonial contexts, constructions
of racial superiority could overcome those of gender inferiority, and thus
colonising women could share in colonial discourses of power and
authority'.[162] Settler women thus 'carved out a space amid the options available to them: options for the most part created by imperialism and limited by
male dominance'.[163]

The options available to many of those women who emigrated to the Cape
in 1820 were most constrained by a relatively new discourse of femininity
associated with domesticity. The late eighteenth and early nineteenth century
in Britain was a period in which 'the energy, organizational skill and sense of
commitment which middle class women had [previously] put into economic
activity were deflected into domestic affairs.' The home was 'strongly
associated with a form of femininity which was becoming the hallmark of
the middle class', while 'a masculine penumbra surrounded that which was
defined as public'.[164] But the extent to which metropolitan women's domestic
confinement was reproduced in colonial settings has been disputed. Sara
Mills, among others, has argued that 'once one begins to move the analysis
of the public/private sphere away from a concern with British middle-class
women, the distinction becomes untenable'. She has called for 'a reappraisal
of analysis of gender and colonialism where it is assumed that colonising
and colonised women are confined to the private domestic sphere'.[165] Nevertheless, it is noticeable that the examples of women breaching the confines of
domesticity in colonial India that Mills deploys to substantiate her argument,
relate almost exclusively to metropolitan travellers paying visits to colonial
communities, rather than to female members of those communities.
Permissible activities could be structured very differently for these differentially situated 'women of empire'.[166] As the work of Ann Stoler among
other historical anthropologists has indicated, 'to maintain colonial authority
along the lines of race, European women [who lived in the colonies generally]
had to submit to [even] stricter rules than was common in the metropole'.[167]

Albany settler women certainly seem to have been expected to make their
primary social contributions within the home, regardless of their metropolitan class backgrounds while, as we have seen, masculine roles were
fulfilled by venturing forth to improve the land, engaging in politics and,
if necessary, waging war. Just after being placed on their location, for
instance, it was up to Sophia Pigot and her mother to make their temporary
marquee tidy and sort out the family's clothing while her father cut paths
through the local scrub, taming the wilderness outside in order to facilitate
the women's construction of interior domesticity.[168] As Natasha Erlank
points out, given the material hardship encountered during the early years
of the settlement, many poorer emigrants found it difficult to reproduce
the domesticated feminine ideal on the Cape frontier: 'Women needed to

work, either apart from or alongside their husbands . . . [and] Unmarried women and widows were often required to support themselves without assistance from any other quarter'.[169] But when settler women did work outside the home, they felt the need to explain it to their contemporaries in the Cape and in Britain. One of Erlank's main subjects, Mary Anne Webb, for instance 'seems to have felt some uneasiness about her status as a working woman and felt the need to justify this to her husband's family by claiming it was necessary in order to keep her family financially solvent'.[170]

The work of the settler naturalist and illustrator, Mary Barber breached the confines of feminine domesticity and, despite its impact on both local and metropolitan science (she corresponded with Darwin and revised his thinking on some finer points of evolution), her research was never a part of the settlers' collective memory, nor she a member of its pantheon. Her permitted sphere of activity in the Cape closely paralleled that of both educated women and male artisanal collectors in Britain, who could collect, identify, draw and paint specimens on behalf of genteel male scientists, but generally could not collate or present their own research findings. Like other women naturalists who managed to obtain a scientific male audience, Barber's papers were read to learned societies in the Cape and Britain by male members of those societies[171]. Even Mary Barber, though, was privileged, in terms of her mobility over most of her female counterparts. The experience of many more settler women during the first half of the nineteenth century was one of domestic confinement, and an associated sense of isolation. Many settler women, as Helen Dampier has demonstrated, experienced acute fear and loneliness on the frontier.[172]

However, as Strobel argues, 'the apparent triviality of the lives of some European women in the colonies masks their important functions within the male centred colonial system of domination'.[173] Even in their domestic role as wives and mothers, settler women could vitally assist in the maintenance of social boundaries between coloniser and colonised. For a start, with settler men frequently away on hunting, trading or office-seeking trips, wives would manage the farm's workforce, deploying the same imported techniques of paternalism that allowed metropolitan women to manage their husbands' employees in the shop, the dairy, and the printer's establishment.[174] But settler women's contribution to the culture of British colonialism in the eastern Cape went well beyond acting as substitute patriarchs when occasion demanded.

Women's provision of familiar domestic appearances, of household routine, and of reconciliatory diversions, lay at the heart of the settler community's reproduction. As Sibley argues, the domestic environment 'reflects an expanded boundary of the self', and domestic objects 'are signs of . . . ties to a larger system of which [one] is a part'.[175] In the Albany settlement, that wider system was constituted by links to the metropole. While settler men endeavoured to stake their claims as British subjects through public political representation, the preoccupations of women like Sophia Pigot, with clothes-making, furnishing, letter-writing and the receipt of goods from England, were vital to the maintenance of 'British-ness' within domestic space. And that 'British-ness' in turn was vital to the settlers' claim to metropolitan protection and support.

Just as in Britain 'many families, having increased incomes, were preoccupied with new patterns of consumption' in the late eighteenth and early nineteenth centuries, so the Albany settlers, and women in particular, concentrated on recreating changing metropolitan taste, even if after some time lag.[176] In metropolitan middle-class homes, carpets, sofas, settees, stools, tables, cabinets and sideboards were for the first time becoming ubiquitous. While most settlers managed to obtain only those items which would allow for bare furnishing during the 1820s, by the late 1830s, many were more successful in emulating metropolitan interiors.[177] The maintenance of such connections was itself dependent on settler women's determination to stay in touch with metropolitan relatives and friends through letter writing. Before steamers brought fresh metropolitan magazines, it was only through a continual correspondence that they could find out about shifts in British fashion and be in a position to requisition dresses, tablecloths, curtain fabrics and other domestic sundries from relatives 'at home'.[178] Distanced from the material stratification and the ethnic divisions of British society itself, settlers by the 1840s were able to indulge in the uplifting sense of national origin and powerful connection which British-style commodities and interior surroundings could furnish.[179] Even if the men's attempts at exterior architecture could not always replicate 'British-ness' in the frontier environment (Philipps, for instance, mocked Major Pigot's attempt to build an English stately home, describing him as 'Pigot Park mad'), the women's attempts at interior domesticity often could.[180]

A domestic sense of shared origin extended beyond furnishing and commodity. It also included the recreation of British rhythms and rituals within household life. In one of the few explicit recognitions of the settler women's 'sphere', made during the 1844 celebrations, the Rev. Shaw pointed out to 'the Ladies' that a scheme for the improvement of a local harbour would enable them to procure tea and sugar at a reduced price – 'a subject connected peculiarly with their domestic economy'. Godlonton also commended settler women for making 'the tea table a shrine sacred to cheerful, social and domestic enjoyment'.[181] In early nineteenth-century Britain, 'tea, from being regarded as a harmful intoxicant, became a beverage identified with women and afternoon tea gradually a feminine light meal'.[182] Thus located at the centre of feminine household rhythms, tea was one issue over which women's public political activities could be indulged.[183] During the campaign for reform in late 1830s Birmingham, for example, women were exhorted to agitate alongside men against taxation on tea.[184] In the colonies, as well as in Britain, 'The taking of tea together by chosen individuals fostered a sense of group membership and involved a complex set of obligations and reciprocity in the repayment of hospitality that facilitated the long-term maintenance of social bonds'.[185] Women's concentration on the maintenance of tea-drinking habits in Albany, then, provided 'beacons of constancy and recognition through which a familiar social order . . . and stable collective rhythms [could be] maintained'.[186]

Women contributed, however, to more than just the domestic repro-duction of metropolitan connections. They were also participants in the generation of the settlers' racial discourse. As Natasha Erlank has shown, settler women as well as men read the *Graham's Town Journal* and reproduced its racial discourse within their private writings.[187] Mary Barber's writings also suggest that 'women could be involved – though as unequal partners – in . . . the hardening of racial attitudes in the later nineteenth century Cape'.[188] Furthermore, they innovated their own variants on that discourse within a domestic setting. The imperative of recreating the ideal, metro-politan middle class domestic environment, with its atmosphere of order and discipline, meant that settler women encountered particular frustrations in regard to African servants, exceeding even those which most bourgeois women in Britain were experiencing in 'training' servant 'girls'.[189] As Elizabeth van Heyningen notes, 'given the fact that [African servants] usually possessed a precapitalist work ethic, a high degree of stress could result' from settler wives' endeavours to 'educate' them.[190] Women's remarks about the persistent difficulty of tutoring Africans in the daily routines which consti-tuted 'civilised life' could only have contributed to the entire settler com-munity's early disillusionment with humanitarian notions of African 'reclaimability'.

Finally, it was the construction of settler women as being 'above politics' in most respects which enabled them to fulfil yet another unifying role within the settlement – that of assisting in the critical reconciliation of community conflict. When the social cohesion of polite Graham's Town society was threatened by a rift between the civil and military authorities, it was the town's genteel women who acted to restore a community of interest by organising a round of soirées in the warring parties' houses.[191] They could restore harmony because they were able to mediate between the public sphere of their husbands and the private, easing the contests of politics through the tranquillity of the domestic.[192]

If we consider in combination the projects of replicating metropolitan appearances, reproducing customary rituals, securing civilised standards of cleanliness and order and smoothing over potentially divisive contests, the 'domesticated family' could well be said to have 'provided the "cradle"' for a new, British colonial culture in South Africa just as it did for a new bourgeois class culture 'at home'.[193] Settler women's activities contributed (although with less recognition) both to a sense of greater communality in the colonial settlement, and to endeavours 'to improve morally and to render [that settlement] worthy of the British name and nation'.[194]

Settler identity and discourse

John Montgomery emigrated to the Cape as a single youth, by attaching himself to a proprietary party of 1820 settlers from Wicklow in Ireland. He was
expelled from a berth on the transport ship by other Irish settlers for proclaiming himself a Protestant and, soon after his arrival at the Cape, denied
an apprenticeship with an English settler in Graaff Reinet for being an
Irishman. Yet, when trading in the Transvaal in 1868 and encountering
prospectors with a Union Jack attached to their wagon, he wrote: 'The bare
sight of the flag that has braved for a thousand years the battle and breeze
made me for a moment forget my troubles. I paid the gold seekers a visit
and felt more than I can express at being once more under the glorious
standard of Old England'.[195] During the celebrations of the settlement's
anniversary in 1870, Montgomery accepted proudly his public laudation as
one of the few surviving 1820 British settlers.

Montgomery's own shifting array of identities is perhaps an extreme
example, but other settlers too, came to weave the various strands of their
identities around the concept of 'the British settler'. Differentiated senses
of social position, ethnic origin, religious adherence and, of course, differentiated gender positions, remained among the settlers. But as they invented
a shared past and a mutual character, perceived a landscape being civilised
through collective endeavour, represented their 'enemies' in common terms
and adapted public and domestic gendered roles, they were each helping to
construct this more embracing concept.

As materially inclined historians of the Cape have suggested, a shared and
publicly expressed programme of accumulation, entailing the dispossession of
a racial 'Other', did prompt certain of the settlers to transcend their social
divisions. But the settlers' refashioned identity was deeper, more personal
and more complex than any acquisitive strategy taken in isolation. Their
new-found status as capitalists, itself constructed on a metropolitan cultural
model, and their collective anxiety as colonists in an insecure frontier space,
were two sides of the same coin, and their distinctive settler identity was
experienced primarily as a response to the latter. During the 1870 celebrations, Montgomery, rather than proclaiming the triumph of the settlers'
capitalist endeavours, thought 'here I stand with those who have experienced
wars, troubles, disappointments, losses and difficulties too numerous to call to
mind'.[196]

Soon after their arrival, the settlers had discovered that they were positioned not only on a contested frontier, but on the remote fringe of a some-
what reluctant empire. Within the colony, the spectre of Khoesan labour
rebellion had hung over them as soon as they participated in an established
racial division of labour, and devastating Xhosa attack had ultimately
become a frightening and similarly shared experience. The settlers' culturally
framed capitalist endeavour, indeed their very location on the frontier had

necessarily generated these most immediate fears, but Cape and metropolitan humanitarians had raised the additional prospect of imperial abandonment. In their marginal space, the settlers' divided past was, as Revill puts it in a different context, a 'spectre of great menace threatening to break any communal security'.[197] This was why that past had to be reinvented and a corporate identity constructed differentially by settler men and women.

4 Queen Adelaide Province and the limits of colonial power

> Treacherous barbarians will be converted into Christians and peaceable neighbours.
> (Colonel Harry Smith, Commander of Queen Adelaide Province, 1836)[1]

As we saw in chapter 2, an overriding experience for officials posted to the Cape had been frustration in their attempts to secure the conditions for governmentality on the frontier. The war of 1834–5, however, gave them their first opportunity to construct a more realisable vision of effective domination. Military victory over the offending Xhosa would be followed by an exercise of state power that now seemed both morally justified and economically possible. In this chapter I want to examine the official fantasy of control that developed in the mid- and late 1830s, to tease out the ways in which it was translated into a very different set of realities, and to outline some of the ways in which the Xhosa themselves defined the limits of colonial power. However, I also want to examine some of the coincidences and contests between official visions for the colonisation of the Xhosa, and the projects pursued by the 'imagined community' of settlers, whose genealogy was traced in the preceding chapter.[2]

A colonising government

Official fantasies

A new Governor, General Sir Benjamin D'Urban, arrived at the Cape shortly before Maqoma's attack. D'Urban had previously served in British Guiana, where he had opposed immediate emancipation of the colony's slaves.[3] Nevertheless, for the first time, this governor came with instructions from the Colonial Office to settle the frontier 'problems' through treaties negotiated with individual chiefs, rather than through punitive military measures. The Colonial Office, still desperate for economies on this most troublesome of imperial margins had been swayed, as we will see in the following chapter, by humanitarian critiques of the prevailing frontier system. Metropolitan officials had decided that if military forcefulness could not bring order and economy to the region, then perhaps a formal recognition of Xhosa independence and an agreement over mutually beneficial trade and mission interaction could. D'Urban's arrival in Cape Town did not promise the humanitarians' preferred extension of a more protective British authority, but it was nevertheless welcomed by Philip and his allies as heralding a great improvement in frontier policy. Aware of frontier Xhosa chiefs' mounting anger, Philip and his missionary colleagues toured the frontier zone assuring them that D'Urban would soon remedy their grievances.[4]

However, the Cape humanitarians' attempts to counsel patience among the Xhosa failed. Maqoma and the allied chiefs launched their attack before D'Urban, who was busy making arrangements for the emancipation of the colony's slaves, found the time to visit the frontier. When the new governor did arrive there, it was not to sign treaties, but to examine a landscape of abandoned and burnt-out farms and to meet dispossessed and grieving settlers. All thought of treaties was dropped during the war and D'Urban, reverting to a familiar Cape official rhetoric, wrote to his superior in London of 'the devastation and horrors' which the Xhosa, 'these merciless barbarians, have committed'.[5] While the colonial troops were launching their counter-attack, D'Urban was planning a new, unambiguously military post-war strategy.

In January 1835, together with Colonel Harry Smith, the commander of the colonial troops engaged in the war, D'Urban first envisaged the expulsion of the offending Xhosa to beyond the Kei River. This, the two military men believed, provided a shorter and more secure line of defence for the colony. Smith later formulated his own justification for the expulsion, invoking the historical 'law' that 'Conquest establishes the right of possession'. He continued, 'are the Kaffirs, the possessors of this soil by right of conquest, not to be ejected by the same right? Are they alone, of all the rest of the Aborigines from whom England has wrested her possessions to be thus favoured?'[6] Smith intended first securing the new territory by building military posts, roads and fords. Then, despite his view that the Xhosa were 'irreclaimable savages . . . whose extermination would be a blessing', he would ensure that their ejection from it was as peaceable as possible.[7]

However, it was not the entire Xhosa population of the conquered territory that was to be expelled. Some Xhosa chiefs were not fighting against the colony, but collaborating with it. The Gqunukhwebe chiefs Phatho, Khama and Kobe let it be known that they had ordered any men who stayed with them during the war to desist from attacking the British and to return any stolen cattle that they came across. They stated further that, if communications with the colony had remained open during the fighting, they would have punished any offenders according to the governor's wishes.[8] The Ndlambe chief Mqhayi also claimed that he wanted no part in the war, and the Ntinde chief Dyani Tshatshu's people were forced by other Xhosa to leave the Buffalo River because of their support for the colony.[9] It was Phatho though, who went furthest in his collaboration, assuring the governor that he would pass on any relevant intelligence and informing him that he had placed his men along the Keiskamma, doing his 'best to prevent the hostile Caffers from crossing that river'. He put 1,000 of his own men at the disposal of the British forces and garrisoned a colonial force of 200 men. Furthermore, he claimed to have killed two of the hostile Langa chief Nqeno's men, including his chief councillor, on behalf of the British.[10]

These 'friendly' chiefs, who had proved their capacity to be docile, were to be allowed to remain, D'Urban having clarified his implicit intention to expel the Xhosa *en masse* in May 1835. D'Urban also made it clear that he wished Suthu, Great Wife of Ngqika and her son Sandile, Ngqika's successor as Rharhabe paramount, to remain under British influence within the conquered territory.[11] Finally, the Mfengu, discussed below, were to be located there. But for the remainder, Smith wrote 'it is absolutely necessary to provide for the future security of the colony . . . by removing these treacherous and irreclaimable savages to a safer distance'. These 'irreclaimable' Xhosa included the chiefs Tyhali and Maqoma (both sons of Ngqika), Bhotomane of the Mdange, Nqeno and the remnants of the Ndlambe Xhosa, all of whom, as we have seen in the previous chapter, had invaded the colonial margins.[12]

On 19 May 1835, after colonial troops had expelled the hostile Xhosa from the colony and invaded Xhosa territory up to and beyond the Kei River, King William's Town was declared the capital of the conquered Queen Adelaide Province.[13] The province, which came under Smith's direct military authority, extended across some 7,000 square miles between the Keiskamma and Kei rivers south as far as the coast (see Figure 2). Initially the northern boundary was indeterminate, but in November 1835, D'Urban annexed the territory up to the Orange River in order to extend jurisdiction over Afrikaners already grazing there. A strategic wedge of land was later annexed extending deep along the main trading route into Gcaleka territory on the other side of the Kei. This was extorted out of the Gcaleka paramount Sarhili in lieu of the cattle that his father Hintsa had been expected to pay as war reparation.[14]

Smith's declaration of King William's Town as the capital of the new province of Queen Adelaide, however, was premature. Even the military head-quarters there could not be secured in the face of 'hundreds of kafirs . . . watching every post night and day for the purposes of murder and plunder' and the colonial forces still had little prospect of controlling the remote fastnesses of the province's Amatola mountains.[15] There, the colonial troops continued to find it almost impossible to penetrate the steep thickets and flush out resisting Xhosa, let alone round them up and expel them across the Kei as Smith had intended.[16] Queen Adelaide Province in fact began as a compromise between British official intentions and what the frontier Xhosa could be forced to accept.

D'Urban's first realisation was that, if the war were to be brought to a satisfactory conclusion, the Xhosa would all have to be guaranteed continued occupation of their land within the new province. Even after the granting of this 'concession' though, the Xhosa retained sufficient residual power to amend the terms of the peace. In August 1835 D'Urban tried to insist that, among other things, the surrendering Xhosa hand over their guns and be confined to locations outside the Amatola mountains, terms which Charles Lennox Stretch, serving with Smith, considered to be 'unreasonable'.[17] But Maqoma's and Tyhali's refusal to accept these terms, combined with an escalating fiscal crisis brought on by the war, forced the governor to concede further.[18] The Xhosa were to keep their arms and their chiefdoms were to remain, by and large, *in situ*. Queen Adelaide Province thus became the first British attempt to extend direct rule over a large body of formerly independent and definitely hostile Africans. No such ambitious scheme had ever been attempted before in southern Africa and no such scheme would even be seriously contemplated elsewhere in Africa until the late nineteenth century.

An official census of the Xhosa population was completed and the locations of the various chiefdoms assigned, again with concessions being made to Xhosa chiefs who threatened continued resistance, in February 1836. Each location contained missionary and military stations for its supervision. The most significant component of the province's population were the Ngqika Xhosa, numbering 56,000. They were to remain within a location larger than that originally envisaged around Burn's Hill mission station on the upper Keiskamma. The smaller chiefdoms comprised the remnant Ndlambe under Nqeno, who had also fought against the British during the war (9,200); the largely 'friendly' Gqunukhwebe under Kobe (7,600) and the Ntinde under Dyani Tshatshu, the most Christianised chief (1,000). The Xhosa therefore numbered some 73,800 in total. Combined with the debatable figure of 16,800 Mfengu who were escorted into the colonial margins by Smith during the war, the colonial government now had 90,600 new subjects. John Fairbairn pointed out that in theory this would give a population density within the province of between ten and eleven per square mile – about ten times that of the colony proper.[19]

Once the colonial authorities had been forced to accept continued Xhosa occupation within the new province, their first priority was to exert effective military domination over it, so as to gain, in Smith's words, 'a firmer hold over these slippery vagabonds'.[20] King William's Town, some forty miles east of the previous advanced colonial post of Fort Willshire, was to be the province's military headquarters with two forts of its own. From there along the one hundred miles of wagon road to the Kei, and around the Amatolas, a string of forts was to be built, descending, as Mostert puts it, 'like an imprisoning grid upon all the Xhosa'.[21] Not content with this, Smith, delighting in the idea that 'it would appal the Kafirs to see me coming out of the water [with three or four hundred men]', proposed the construction of ports at the mouths of the Fish and Buffalo Rivers.[22]

Having put this infrastructure in place, Smith intended to supplant the power of Xhosa chiefs with direct military control. Gradually, the chiefs would be 'reduced to the more wholesome position of subordinate magistrates . . . acting under . . . the subjection and subordination of . . . salutary authority'.[23] The chiefs would be allowed to retain their own jurisdiction over minor matters, but anything significant was intended to come under the sway of the British Resident Agents to whom they were attached. With their chiefs emasculated and 'military posts of occupation . . . within, around and among their locations', D'Urban anticipated that 'the means will be ever at hand to subdue any serious resistance'.[24] The Xhosa were to be allowed to enter the established colonial territory only if issued with passes by the Resident Agents and these were to be granted 'very sparingly and with great discrimination'. Those holding them were to be unarmed and were subject to being shot if the conditions on which they were admitted were broken.[25]

Despite the continued occupation of the Xhosa, D'Urban and Smith hoped to leave some land within the new province 'for the occupation and speculation of Europeans', but in the early stages, this was less their concern than an effective post-war strategy of control.[26] Having established military supervision, the next and most ambitious aspect of their plans involved nothing less than the mass cultural transformation of the Xhosa, who were now, whether they liked it or not, British subjects. As if intended all along, a discourse of their experimental 'civilisation' was grafted into official documents. Although this scheme had much in common with Somerset's earlier exploration of the 'civilising mission', D'Urban wrote that 'it was indeed high time to devise and adopt some new measures at the conclusion of *this* Kafir war differing in character from those pursued after all former ones'.[27] Smith declared that those who had previously been 'irreclaimable savages' now possessed 'the same attributes as ourselves' but remained 'poor degraded sinners' who could be saved only by 'the necessary restraint of just laws and the diffusion of the doctrines of our blessed religion'. He vowed to 'reclaim these savages unless the Devil himself has so established himself that he cannot be cast out'.[28]

The Xhosa first learnt of this new colonial strategy when Smith, in his inaugural address as commander of the province, informed them that they wished to become 'real Englishmen'. He went on to explain that once the English had been as naked, as ignorant and as cruel as they were, but love of the true Christian God had been their first step towards redemption. Soon they had learnt to respect property and cease thieving and to use money, earned through daily industry, in honest transactions. It was this which had enabled them to wear clothes rather than skins. Having thus become civilised, the English were able to 'cast away our vicious habits and put to death and banish by the law everyone who by his crime and wickedness was a pest and an enemy to society at large'![29] If the Xhosa were to emulate such remarkable strides towards civilisation, Smith continued, they should no longer tolerate certain activities. These included the system which Smith, believing himself the master of Xhosa idiom, liked to call 'eating up' (fines in cattle levied by chiefs as an expression of their authority and for the distribution of crucial patronage), murder, the belief in witchcraft (which had apparently deluded the Xhosa into thinking that they could overcome the British in war), perjury, arson, rape and treason (as resistance to the British administration was now defined).[30]

Smith's programme for the conversion of the Xhosa would be realised through four main institutions. Magistrates, police, churches and schools would effect transformations in every aspect of the Xhosa's social life. Crime, religion, agriculture, the gender division of labour and clothing were especially targeted. The attack on crime (defined widely so as to include 'eating up') was to be marshalled through the magistrates and a new police force. But it was the more powerful chiefs themselves, those who had traditionally held this prerogative, who were to implement British laws as co-opted magistrates under the supervision of British Resident Agents. They were therefore guaranteed initially an annual 'rent' in cattle from each kraal, and then an annual salary, in order to secure their compliance.[31] In addition, they were favoured with European clothes and a magistrate's medal.[32] The magistrates were to deal with minor cases themselves and bring the accused in more serious cases before the appropriate Resident Agents. With the province under Martial Law, they in turn were initially to report directly to Smith as military commander, although Hudson in Graham's Town was later appointed Agent General for all the Resident Agents.[33] Smith promised to make whole kraals responsible for thefts if individual culprits could not be traced by his police force. This was comprised of Xhosa and Mfengu men attached to each magistrate. While the police were to carry their own brass-knobbed sticks as signs of office, Smith characteristically reserved the largest stick with the biggest gold knob for himself. He boasted that 'when I seized the stick, held it myself, and gave a decisive order, that was formal and irrevocable'.[34]

Transformation in Xhosa religion, clothing and agriculture was to be achieved largely through the missionary churches and schools and Smith let it be known that clergymen would be the Xhosa's instructors. He was, however, particular to request of D'Urban only a certain type of missionary for this task: 'those of active and industrious habits are to be preferred, who would enforce an observance of the Sabbath, and occupy the rest of the week in practical lessons of industry to the natives'. In a reference to Philip, Read and other humanitarians, 'Your fanatical preacher is to be avoided'.[35] He told the assembled Xhosa 'You must send your children to School, or you are wicked and base Parents'. Particular attention was paid to exhorting the mothers of the paramounts to this injunction, and the Gqunukhwebe chiefs who had mastered the use of the plough, were upheld as examples of what could be achieved with a willingness to learn.[36] Chiefs such as Phatho, asserted Smith, 'are rapidly progressing towards civilisation, they are clothed by their own industry, some have ploughs drawn by bullocks, all know the use of money and attend to the Clergymen'.[37]

For Smith, the use of ploughs in Xhosa agriculture was merely part of a wider transformation of gender roles, bringing Xhosa culture in line with English. As early as 1809, Colonel Collins had reported that the Xhosa's gendered division of labour produced thievishness as a national characteristic: 'The Kafirs are naturally insatiable robbers All domestic and agricultural labour being performed by the women, and the cattle being herded by the boys, the men have nothing to do but to hunt and to wander about among the colonists'.[38] One of the main reasons that missionaries brought their wives with them, or 'acquired' wives before they entered Xhosaland, was so that they might themselves provide the Xhosa with models of more proper gender relations. As Natasha Erlank points out, 'Without wives, the missionaries would have been unable to transmit the virtues of nuclear families, monogamous marriages and the sorts of gendered behaviour considered normal under the emerging middle class ideology of the nineteenth century'.[39] With ultimate authority within the new province in his own hands, Smith now wanted to convince the Xhosa that

> it is the duty of men to work in the fields – not of women – *they* ought to make and mend you clothes and *their own*, and to keep the children clean, wash your clothes, cook your food, take care of the milk – you will know from observation what the Englishmen and what their women do – this you must imitate, and not sleep half your time.[40]

Spiritual conversion, the practice of European-style agriculture and the adoption of European rather than African forms of gender discrimination were all desirable attributes of the Xhosa's transformation, but the most visible and therefore most politically potent manifestation of that transformation, was the adoption of European clothing. Smith held that 'It was one of my great endeavours to make them regard appearing naked as a grievous sin, now that they were British subjects'.[41] Accordingly, in his address to these new subjects, he declared in heroic Nelsonian fashion, that 'England expects of her subjects – leave off this trash of brass, beads, wire, clay . . . and replace them by soap, linen and clothes'.[42] A change of clothing, above all else, would signify the systematic neutralising of Xhosa otherness.

In all of this, Smith felt encouraged by his new powers as military commander of a province under martial law. As such, he 'held more direct power and authority than any other frontier official ever had been allowed to possess'.[43] He felt that he had quickly learned the traits of Xhosa society and therefore knew just where they could best be undermined. Even Smith though, occasionally demonstrated that he was not entirely lacking in realism. With all his faith in 'parsons, magistrates, secretaries, religious institutions and schools of industry', he felt forced to admit that 'the only institution for the suppression of vice for some time to come is the hand of power wielded by innumerable Patroles and thief catchers'.[44]

Queen Adelaide Province and settler politics

In materialist accounts of Cape history, of which the most recent is Keegan's synthesis, D'Urban and Smith are characterised as becoming 'captive' to settler capitalist interests in the aftermath of the 1834–5 war. Queen Adelaide Province is represented as the first manifestation of the allegiance of the colonial state (not yet the metropolitan state) to the cause of settler expansion onto Xhosa lands.[45] A broad coincidence between official and settler projects is thus established and, indeed, in some accounts, the colonial state and the Albany settler community become almost synonymous, with no distinctions being drawn between their respective representational practices or material goals. While settlers often occupied positions of local authority, and while there was certainly a convergence of the governor's and settlers' imperatives around certain aspects of the planning of the conquered provinces' administration, however, I suggest in the analysis which follows that, at least in the 1830s, tensions remained between official and settler aspirations, representations and practices concerning trade, land, labour and security.

Once the Xhosa were on the defensive during the war, the most immediate concern of many settlers was agitation for the severe punishment of those who had acquired colonial livestock during the initial attack on the colony, largely through complete expulsion from their lands.[46] However, some settlers had done fairly well out of the war and hoped to do even better out of spurious claims on livestock to be extorted from the Xhosa.[47] It was presumably commissariat commissions which enabled Thomas Stubbs, a saddler to 'make some money besides doing lots of duty' and move to larger premises in Graham's Town, for he felt able to condemn others for making extra money through false applications to the Board of Relief set up to help the destitute.[48] Other wartime ruses were noted by Charles Lennox Stretch, Resident Agent to the Ngqika within the new province. He wrote of one George Wood who reaped £7,000 from supplying the Provisional Colonial Infantry with inferior cloth. Stretch continued, 'This person soon after purchased Mr Cock's house for £2,000, who had also not been indolent in filling his pockets. It is therefore not surprising these Graham's Town worthies were desirous the *"war should proceed. The Caffres were not sufficiently punished"."* Stockenström concurred in this assessment, describing the Graham's Town 'faction' as 'those who pant for war and money'.[49]

It may be true that the war stimulated higher commodity prices which would have benefited most of the settlers,[50] but settler acquisitiveness was not the only colonial response to the war. It must be remembered that for those Afrikaners and British located on the exposed frontier away from Graham's Town, as well as for many within it, the war would be remembered as a genuinely catastrophic experience. The Xhosa attack had demonstrated how tenuous was the colonial occupation of the frontier and undermined the nascent sense of security which had been developing among British settlers during the 1820s. It was not just established Dutch-speaking farmers who threatened to emigrate from the colonial margins in the aftermath of the Xhosa attack. Several British settlers too, 'instead of resolving to maintain their ground on this frontier, have resolved to quit it, and either return to Britain or go to some other country. Many others seem determined to leave the frontier only and remove further back into the colony'.[51]

As we have seen, D'Urban was unable to meet the settlers' expectations of Xhosa punishment after the war. Although supportive, he also found it impossible to extract compensation money from the metropolitan government for the losses that they claimed to have suffered. Once immediate expectations of large gains in land had been shelved, the most direct economic opportunity opened to settlers by the new province was trade with its Xhosa occupants. By the end of 1835, it was estimated that the Xhosa within the province were consuming £30,000 per annum's worth of British manufactures.[52] The commander of the province, though, was not entirely happy. First, Smith's hope had been for the rapid replacement of barter with a trade in money, which would be more conducive to his programme of 'civilisation'. But this proved impracticable in the light of a shortage of silver. Secondly and more seriously for the traders, Smith disagreed with their methods. The commander stated that British settlers were 'carrying on a most unfair, unjust and fraudulent trade' with his new subjects, and he therefore fixed a scale of prices to which they had to conform. In response the *Graham's Town Journal*, remarkably given its general support for military supervision of the Xhosa, confessed 'that we do not like military law . . . We trust that the legislative council will see the necessity of immediately promulgating such . . . regulations for the new province as shall give free scope to industry'.[53] In this case, it was Smith who backed down. Not only did he apologise for any offence caused to the traders, but in ordering the survey of the Fish and Buffalo River mouths as possible ports he claimed to be facilitating easier trader, as well as military, access to the Xhosa.[54]

Far outweighing even trade profits in settler visions of commercial expansion, however, was the prospect of expanded wool production. If D'Urban's measures for Queen Adelaide Province were confirmed, there might be potential for long term expansion to the east.[55] Settler expectations were first raised by the initial promise of a mass Xhosa expulsion and then by the subsequent prospect of smaller grants among the Xhosa locations. When Xhosa expulsion had still seemed likely, another of Miles Bowker's sons, Thomas Holden, had anticipated the whole of the new province becoming 'excellent sheep farms'.[56] Some four hundred odd applications for land in the new province, largely from British settlers, arrived on the desks of colonial officials.[57] Godlonton attempted to persuade metropolitan readers of the *Graham's Town Journal* that if the province were retained, within eight years the colony could double its current consumption of £150,000 worth of

British manufactures.[58] Settler capitalists did not, however, rest content with this vision of an expanded local economy. This was only one component of a far more ambitious programme of eastern Cape colonial growth that was integrally connected to, but simultaneously in regional rivalry with, western Cape capital.[59]

In the first place an extension of roads and villages within the new province would be welcome.[60] Effective domination over the Gcaleka Xhosa to the east of the Kei River would also be desirable to 'tranquilize [*sic*] and promote the interests of this fine country'.[61] Beyond that, direct state support for settler penetration right through the Xhosa and Mpondo to Natal was not seen as being out of the question.[62] The commercial vision voiced by the *Graham's Town Journal* was certainly tempting enough for certain officials to look upon Xhosa territory with an anticipatory, possessive eye. The surgeon accompanying Smith's forces across the Kei reported: 'I really do not think there is a more healthy climate in the world than this, and the country at the same time extremely picturesque and beautiful . . . and the soil is evidently very fertile and well adapted to the rearing of cattle, sheep and horses'.[63]

Regardless of the strength of local opinion on the need for expansion, and of certain officials' attraction to such proposals, however, they were not to be fulfilled. As far as land grants were concerned, both D'Urban and Smith were inclined more towards British settler, rather than Afrikaner, expansion in the new province, seeing this as being most in line with the colony's general commercial 'improvement'. But there were differences between the two men. While Smith was recklessly expansionist, D'Urban was more cautious. When the expulsion of the Xhosa from the province was still being considered, Smith enthused that it offered 'every faculty on earth for emigration'.[64] He also tried to convince D'Urban that, if dispossessed Xhosa were to remain within the 'new and beautiful' province, they would 'render its occupation to settlers far less desirable'.[65] D'Urban's approach though, was more informed by security considerations. He envisaged the placing of settlers between the Xhosa locations and along the main communications routes primarily as a strategic guard against future Xhosa mobilisation. He also realised early on that, due to Colonial Office opposition, he was going to be constrained in his ability to accede to voluble settler land demands.[66] In the short term, settler pressure for land would have to be released only within the former 'ceded' territory between the Fish and Keiskamma Rivers, rather than within the new province itself, and even there it would have to compete with Mfengu, Khoesan and possibly 'friendly' Xhosa claims.

Some settlers were outraged once it was realised that the 'irreclaimable savages' were to have 'not only their old haunts and fastnesses, but nearly the whole of their territory back', but the *Graham's Town Journal* counselled patience, seeing in a confirmation of D'Urban's current plans the long term prospect of considerably more land grants.[67] In pursuit of more land, the most vocal of the settlers could be devious, often manipulating both official security concerns and even influential humanitarian discourse. The humanitarian Dr A. G. Campbell noted that:

> In a community like that which composes the Graham's Town population, it is difficult to obtain any thing like truth or impartial statements, more particularly at this present period of excitement , where one or all are moving heaven and earth to have the Governor's measures confirmed.[68]

Playing to the security concerns of the colonial state, the *GTJ* advised its readers that if they wished for land grants, they must consider their 'efficiency . . . as forming a line of defence against the common enemy'.[69] Godlonton warned that 'it must not be supposed . . . that our farmers crave the possession of this land for their own private purposes'. At the same time, he sought to head off large scale settlement of 'friendly' Xhosa and Khoesan within the 'ceded' territory by emphasising the opportunity that this would allow for plunder of the colonial margins. In stark contrast to the *Journal*'s frequent diatribes against Khoesan perfidy and unassimilability, Godlonton went on to argue that appropriation of the 'ceded' territory on behalf of the Khoesan would go against the grain of their benign integration with the colonists: 'any attempt to separate their interests cannot be entertained without danger to the whole . . . the whole community should be treated as one large family'. This resort to assimilationist rhetoric appears particularly cynical when it is contrasted with the argument developed in the previous week's issue of the same paper that, 'amidst such incongruous materials as we have here', amalgamation between colonists and the 'coloured classes' was unattainable.[70]

However, in the short term it was clear that any new land grants would be confined to the 'ceded' territory and tension mounted over who was entitled to such limited gains. Some settlers felt that those who had suffered most by the war and who would occupy and work these farms themselves should be favoured over absentee landlords and those who usually benefited from government patronage. Godlonton joined them in arguing specifically against the release of new lands purely for speculation, and in favour of their owner-occupation. In order to avoid the 'unfair' allocation of land according to patronage, he advocated strongly that systems for the distribution of land similar to those practised in the United States, New South Wales and Van Dieman's Land be adopted on the frontier.[71] These, he stated, gave all who had a stake in the colonial frontier community a greater chance of claiming properly surveyed and advertised new lands. In practice though, it was not these more impartial criteria which determined new land grants. To the frustration of many British settlers, leading families like the Southeys, who had established connections with Smith and D'Urban during the war, seem to have been given claims to most of the land that was allocated in the 'ceded' territory.[72] Land expansion was a pressing issue on the frontier then. But it was also a divisive issue. There was no one programme for colonial expansion agreed upon by the British settlers, let alone by officials and Afrikaners as well as those settlers.[73]

The same can be said of the two other critical and interrelated issues within frontier political discourse – those of labour and security. Accurately enough, a frustrated colonial labour demand is a constant in most materialist accounts of the frontier during this period, but the contradiction between labour demands and the more basic need for security of person and property – a contradiction which, as I suggested in the previous chapter, was closely bound up with the initial construction of settler identity – is often over-looked. Fear of violence from Khoesan farm servants, was still pervasive along the frontier after the mass desertions and rebellions of the late eighteenth century. Leaving their families exposed to the whims of their servants was often given as a reason why colonists refused to do commando duty.[74] J. C. Chase was not the only settler to express his concern that the Xhosa were also 'too addicted to marauding' to become suitable labourers.[75] While the *Graham's Town Journal* agitated at times for the undermining of the Xhosa chiefs, it also recognised that those Xhosa, Tswana and Thembu who had shaken off chiefly authority to work as servants in the colony, were responsible for further 'depredations'.[76] As patriotic Britons, settlers generally applauded the abolition of slavery, but they could not help feeling that in the specific circumstances of the frontier, it had regrettably loosened the grip on 'apprentices' who escaped from their masters and committed additional 'outrages'.[77]

However, it was neither Khoesan, Xhosa nor freed slaves, but the Mfengu who provided the greatest additional contribution both to colonial labour supplies, and to the associated anxieties, in the mid-1830s, and here the focus is on their representation. In settler accounts, established first by the Rev. John Ayliff (a settler turned Wesleyan missionary with the Gcaleka), and then disseminated by the colonial authorities, the Mfengu originated entirely as refugees from the widespread strife known as the 'Mfecane' to the north and east. They were accepted within Xhosa society as slaves before Smith 'rescued' them from their 'most degraded state of bondage' by escorting them into the colony during the Sixth Frontier War.[78] Their supposed condition as slaves has been decisively challenged by Peires, who draws upon oral evidence to explain the more benign nature of refugee client-ship that the Xhosa exercised towards them.[79] Recent revisionist accounts, however, have further questioned the origins of many of these 'refugees'. Julian Cobbing, Alan Webster and Timothy Stapleton have argued that many, if not most of the Mfengu who crossed from Gcaleka territory into the colony with Smith during the war, were actually captive Gcaleka Xhosa. These captives were 'rebranded' as willing Mfengu labour so that they could be legitimately allocated to settler and Afrikaner farmers.[80]

While it is likely that many of those who crossed into the colony during the war were indeed Xhosa seeking new opportunities as colonial allies rather than as enemies, I believe that few if any were captives. Some Xhosa may have been persuaded into becoming 'Mfengu' by the promised allocation of land to Mfengu when the colony was displaying its intention to strip it away from the Xhosa, by the prospect of some colonial assistance with agriculture (which will be investigated further below), or by the desire for personal reasons to escape Xhosa chiefly authority. Many would see acceptance of a Mfengu identity simply as a way to escape appalling destitution in the wake of the war.[81] Even if the mass of Mfengu had been imported as captives, the opportunities for them to cross back over a very permeable frontier were too great for them to have remained in that condition for long. In other words, they were not 'natally alienated' in the way that African slaves shipped to the Americas, or indeed Asian slaves shipped to the Cape had been.[82] Furthermore, the Mfengu's and Xhosa's enduring and mutual hostility, suggests that the Mfengu were not being prevented from returning to their Gcaleka homes simply by British coercion, but that they were seen by those Xhosa who remained as traitors. Some Mfengu assisted Smith with his invasion of Gcaleka territory and when the column of Mfengu and British troops left that territory to enter the new province and the colony, they took with them considerable numbers of 'plundered' Xhosa cattle. Thus a basis of animosity between them and certain Xhosa chiefdoms was firmly established during the war.[83] Finally, the retention of a captive labour force numbering some 10,000 to 19,000 individuals could not have escaped the notice of the Cape's humanitarians, with their numerous and observant informants on the Cape frontier. Humanitarians, who, as we have seen, consistently condemned settlers for their land hunger and their greed, never claimed that they were practising slavery. Given the hegemonic antislavery discourse of the time, to have done so would have been akin to playing a 'trump card'. The fact that they did not make such an allegation suggests that slavery was never practised by the British settlers on a large scale.[84]

Regardless of the proportion who were Xhosa clients, willing Xhosa or captive Xhosa, Mfengu origins were undoubtedly diverse, and perhaps the most useful contribution of recent work has been to indicate the great extent to which a coherent Mfengu identity was created not so much among the Xhosa and their clients, but subsequently, within colonial discourses.[85] D'Urban and Smith certainly constructed the Mfengu deliberately in contrast to the supposedly idle, savage and thieving Xhosa. Indeed the Mfengu were almost their antithesis: 'an industrious, gentle and well disposed tribe, good herdsmen, good agriculturalist [sic] and useful servants'.[86] Medical opinion supported the distinctions. The Army Doctor Murray obligingly reported that 'Our new allies and colonists the AmaFingos are a very healthy race of people – indeed they seem to have no diseases among them; and they appear to be of a mild, docile and industrious character, which is more than can be said either of the Caffres or Hottentots'.[87]

Once they had been moved into the colony, and in line with the thesis of Mfengu as captive labour, Stapleton argues that the Mfengu were located in 'labour camps' around Fort Thomson within the new province. From there, they were 'sent into the colony to work on European farms'.[88] However, the authorities did not necessarily force Mfengu to work across the old frontier. Indeed, as we shall see, there is plentiful evidence that too many were considered to be entering the colony in an uncontrolled fashion, threatening the security of the colonial margins and exacerbating existing concerns over 'internal' servant, 'apprentice' or 'vagrant' theft. There is actually no evidence of a systematic official channelling of labour from Queen Adelaide Province or the 'ceded' territory into the colony.[89]

Nevertheless, that the Mfengu were first perceived as a potential labour supply is indisputable. D'Urban admitted to Glenelg that the 'rescue' of the Mfengu would relieve a labour shortage brought about among frontier farmers by the recruitment of Khoesan labourers for the war, and he was congratulated on doing so by the leading inhabitants of George.[90] Henry Francis Fynn, appointed Superintendent of the new Mfengu subjects, was gratified that 'great numbers have . . . taken service in the colony'. He hoped that they would be particularly useful given their animosity towards the Xhosa. Whereas Xhosa labourers would often return across the frontier with their payment and themselves steal colonial stock, Mfengu men would stay to work longer and had their own interests in fighting off Xhosa cattle raiders. The Mfengu's establishment within official and settler discourse as almost synonymous with labour ultimately led even to the transhipment of some to the western Cape in order to relieve labour shortages there.[91]

Mfengu labour then, was very much in demand by colonists, but importantly, not at any price. It was simply not possible for settlers to create African labour as a commodity in the ways that they wished, nor to forcibly dovetail their broader capitalist commodity structure with the possibilities offered by Xhosa society.[92] The official endeavour to define the Mfengu as different in every respect from their Xhosa 'hosts' may have been part of such an attempt – a means of creating a new and distinct, commodified labouring group, but it did not prevent Mfengu immigrants developing agendas of their own within colonial space. Despite conspiracy theories about the wholesale capture and retention of Mfengu 'slaves' by British settlers on the frontier, the process of labour acquisition thus lay to a great extent outside of the eastern Cape's colonists' control.

The *Graham's Town Journal's* initial response on hearing of the Mfengu migration was far from welcoming. It expressed the hope that the news was unfounded since 'we are firmly convinced that no people of that class can or will, resist the temptation of plundering the colonists'.[93] A contributor to the journal's letters column reminded frontier colonists of the difficulty that the colonial authorities had experienced controlling labour admitted from across the frontier under Ordinance 49 of 1828, when a pass system had proved ineffectual. The Ordinance had had to be suspended the following year due to the number of stock thefts blamed almost universally by colonists on the labourers allowed into the colony. The conclusion was that 'much as we may want servants . . . the Kafirs [in this case, including Mfengu] cannot with safety be employed generally for many years to come'.[94]

Indeed, fears concerning the Mfengu's 'reliability' as labourers seem to have been widely realised along the frontier. As one colonist put it, 'The Fingoes having been allowed to enter the Colony and work for the inhabitants have had an opportunity (and one they have not failed to improve) of stealing from the farmers to a very considerable extent'.[95] Despite the officially constructed difference between Mfengu and Xhosa, vocal colonists soon perceived that 'there is not a shade of difference between the Kafir and the Fingoe, and . . . both of them will steal whenever there is a chance'.[96] A particularly thorny issue was the arming of Mfengu herds against possible raiders. For a start, the value of a gun was likely to exceed the amount that a servant would earn by remaining in service – a temptation to desert if ever there was one. But in addition, many settlers had qualms about putting 'weapons into the hands of those who may, very probably, turn them upon us'.[97]

The colonial authorities' ability to ensure that only docile labourers were admitted into the colony was evidently seen by colonists as being far too limited. Some suggestions envisaged a return to the type of vagrancy legislation which had been vetoed in London in 1834. Other proposals included a system whereby Mfengu (and Tswana) within the colony would have to carry certification that the cattle accompanying them had been paid in wages, and an annual hiring fair at which those to be employed on farms and those to be barred from the colony would be designated.[98] In the event none of the settler proposals was implemented. Official attempts to reconcile labour and security demands hinged on an attempted pass system which, as we shall see, created further colonial divisions.

Apart from a simple lack of policing resources along the frontier, there was another reason why colonists did not get the official control that they wanted over Mfengu labour. This was that officials themselves did not perceive the Mfengu exclusively in terms of their labouring function. They were also intended to serve a particular strategic function. It was realised in official circles that Mfengu men would act as a more effective buffer against future Xhosa incursions if at least some were established within the colonial margins as settled farmers, with a stake in colonial stability, rather than entirely as servile labourers.[99] Mfengu were located within the 'ceded' territory around Fort Thomson on the Tyhume River and at Peddie and Fort Beaufort. In Queen Adelaide Province, they were concentrated around King William's Town. Commissioners were to locate them in designated areas, as far as possible in 'tribes' and families, making sure to leave fertile ground between the locations for colonial farms. In the instructions given to Bowker, the Resident Agent for one of these Mfengu groups, it was made clear that the governor attached 'great importance to the security and improvement of these tribes and expects the settlement about to be formed to become of great political consequence to the Colony'.[100] All the Mfengu men on the locations were to assemble armed for the defence of the colony when required and to pass on intelligence concerning the Xhosa, but a particularly vital strategic role was to be played by the Mfengu located on the Tyhume River. They were to 'serve as a cordon or watch line' against Xhosa descending into the colony from the Amatolas.[101]

The idea of establishing a certain number of Mfengu as peasant farmers was thus critical to official plans, and it was for this reason that the designated Mfengu locations were not merely labour camps. While impoverished 'Mantatee' and 'Bechuana' refugees entering the colony to beg were to be expelled or put to work, Mfengu were initially to be sent to join those in the designated locations.[102] Within them, a significant minority of Mfengu seem to have flourished with colonial support. The Commissioners of Fort Beaufort reported that in the six months since the Mfengu had been located there, 'barren' land had been turned into 'large patches of Indian corn in a most luxurious state'. They felt assured that 'the first step towards their civilisation has been made'.[103] With colonial donations of food, goats, seed corn and agricultural implements and with what seemed to be stable tenure within the Mfengu locations, it is not surprising that some Xhosa, like the missionary Chalmers' acolyte 'John', switched to an Mfengu identity. John, noted Chalmers, 'has ambition to be a colony farmer and he finds he cannot go forward in improvement in the middle of such a people as [the Xhosa]'.[104] However, the establishment of Mfengu as landed colonial allies directly conflicted with settler claims to land, and was accordingly resented. Godlonton complained that while British settlers were denied land, 350 square miles of the 'ceded' territory was allocated to the 'friendly' Gqunukhwebe Xhosa (located in a wedge of coastal land extending either side of the Keiskamma River) and the Mfengu, 'a strange nation who had no claims upon us, but who plundered us'.[105]

If the Mfengu provided the colonial government with a co-opted and potentially assimilable strategic buffer and colonists with an ambivalent labour supply, they also served in a political role for D'Urban in his relations with the imperial government. When it came to the Mfengu, D'Urban was able to manipulate the potent discourse of emancipation. His 'liberation' of the Mfengu from their previous state of 'slavery' among the Xhosa cast him as a representative of benign British influence, a role that he believed that Lord Glenelg, the humanitarian Colonial Secretary, would appreciate.[106] Furthermore, the governor may have hoped that a demonstration of 'success' in the acculturation of the Mfengu would establish a good precedent for the attempted transformation of the Xhosa within Queen Adelaide Province.[107]

Regardless of D'Urban's strategic representations to England though, the Mfengu realised only partially each of the colonial hopes entertained of them. Some were able to farm successfully within the former ceded territory, but they did not assist greatly in the 'pacification' of the Xhosa. Neither, as we will see in the next chapter, did their 'emancipation' from Xhosa bondage enable D'Urban to persuade the Secretary of State of his generally benign intentions. Many did provide labour to frontier farmers and others further afield, but for every group of docile workers there was another of dispossessed raiders and 'beggars'. Theirs, then, was an ambiguous and differentiated kind of 'service', both to the colonial government and to settlers.

The limits of colonial power

If settlers did not find all of their projects pursued enthusiastically by the officials in charge of Queen Adelaide Province, those officials themselves did not find it easy to achieve their own governmental objectives of controlling and 'civilising' the Xhosa. Having already demonstrated how Xhosa military resistance resulted in a compromised kind of British occupation in the new province, in this section, I will highlight the relative weaknesses, rather than the strengths, of continuing colonial administrative power within that province. I will also consider the further effects of Xhosa resistance on official practice and discourse.

It was largely because of an earlier settler conviction that martial law was proving effective, and because of Smith's bluster and his and D'Urban's attempts to defend their actions, that 'settler historians' of the early twentieth century conveyed an impression of a new and draconian British power being introduced into Queen Adelaide Province.[108] More recently, the power exercised by Smith and his Resident Agents within the province has been represented varyingly according to the sources upon which historians have placed most reliance. At one extreme, Peires depends to a great extent on Stockenström for his assessment that the Xhosa chiefdoms within the province were on the verge of rebellion throughout the period in which Smith governed them.[109] But Stockenström, as we will see in the next chapter, had his own axe to grind. His defence of the alternative system that he himself devised after the British withdrawal from the province, was bolstered by repeated reference to Smith's prior inability to control the Xhosa. I would suggest that Peires thus underestimates the chiefs' cautious response to the British occupation.

If Peires sees the British presence in the province as perhaps too weak, Crais, who sometimes takes Smith's reports at their word, overestimates British power in his own Foucaultian interpretation. While the British occupation of 1834–5 could be considered as part of a wider colonial *attempt* to 'control the time, space and cultural practices of an "intimate enemy" and to seek to redefine the body of the African as a metonym of a dominated life',[110] such a description is far removed from the rather more balanced structure of power between coloniser and colonised which, I would argue, actually developed in the province. My own assessment is that the kind of authority that officials wielded during this brief exercise in colonialism, lay between the extremes of Smith's fantastic hyperbole of colonial power, and Stockenström's assertion that the province was perpetually on the verge of Xhosa revolt. In what follows, I argue that the presence that the British established within the territory was in many ways a 'forcibly negotiated' one.

In the wake of the war, wholesale Xhosa destitution was evident and widespread. Communities had not only been shattered by British invasion forces and had their crops destroyed, but were also plagued by locusts.[111] Such was their distress that the *GTJ* was able to report gleefully on 19 May 1836 that the Xhosa would now accept whatever traders were willing to offer them. The suffering continued later in some areas than others, where the occupying forces brought partial relief, but particularly to Mfengu groups.[112] Other than making do under their chiefs, there seem to have been three main Xhosa responses to their deprivation. Some went to seek assistance at mission stations, possibly claiming to be Mfengu. Many migrated to find work within the colony or beg there or among the Gcaleka to the east, and others, remaining with their chiefs, turned to raiding other Xhosa, colonists or Mfengu.[113] Without doubt, the numbers releasing themselves from direct chiefly authority after the war were unprecedented.[114]

As commander of the new province, Smith was determined to pursue this incipient displacement of chiefly authority with direct British influence. The intention was legitimated by an expressed concern for Xhosa commoners *vis-à-vis* their chiefs. Stretch, described by Laing as 'the philanthropic Commissioner', was genuinely concerned to counter the worst abuses of chiefly authority to which Xhosa commoners were subject, and the Xhosa chiefs themselves were worried by the possibility that the British would succeed in hiving their followers away from them.[115] They were initially extremely anxious about the presence of the military posts.[116] Responses to the early British presence varied though. Maqoma planned an abortive emigration and then threatened collaborators while Sarhili apparently bowed to British hegemony and used the British courts in the province, even though British jurisdiction did not technically extend to his Gcaleka territory.[117]

However, it soon proved that, although their autonomy was definitely restricted by the British presence, the Xhosa chiefs had less to fear than they had originally thought. In fact the British military and administrative presence seems to have been overstretched. Even after Smith's military grid had descended upon the Xhosa, the British force in Queen Adelaide Province consisted of only 1,300 men, scattered over the vast tract of country from the Keiskamma to the Kei. As one settler put it, 'Whatever use these troops may be . . . they certainly are of little avail as advanced posts.'[118] The forts that were built were too widely spaced to allow even the efficient patrolling of the old frontier line, let alone the securing of a new, expanded one. Indeed the problem of defending frontier colonists could even have been exacerbated by the annexation of the new province, since it dispersed the colonial forces over a far wider area.[119] Within the new province itself, many of the soldiers were ill, for much of the time Smith was distracted by the ongoing Court of Inquiry into Hintsa's death, where, as we will see in the next chapter, he was forced to fabricate a version of events which would enable him and certain settlers to escape direct censure, and the Resident Agents were burdened by administrative duties.[120]

Due to the weakness of the administrative infrastructure, none of the instructions for proceeding with the transformation of the Xhosa of which, as we have seen, Smith had boasted, seem to have been paid much attention by the Resident Agents.[121] In a rare moment of candour, Smith wrote to D'Urban 'everything at a standstill . . . no salaries for the magistrates, no anything done which ought to be'.[122] What seems to have developed in Queen Adelaide Province was thus not the exertion of British might usually portrayed by Smith and historians who draw upon him, but an unstable balance of power negotiated at a variety of scales.

At the largest scale, along a broad stretch of the frontier, the struggle was waged over pass regulations, with Charles Lennox Stretch and the Civil Commissioner Duncan Campbell at the forefront.[123] Campbell advocated the use of passes as a more effective control over both the Xhosa and the Mfengu and he was supported by Captain Armstrong, in command of the Kat River military post. Both men expressed widespread anger that Stretch was being seemingly duped by Xhosa men and women applying for entry into the colony under a variety of implausible pretexts.[124] In a prelude to a latter settler and official assault, their anger was also directed at the Khoesan inhabitants of the Kat River settlement and military expulsions from the settlement began at this time.[125] In the mid-1830s though, Stretch was the more realistic of the three men in recognising the relative weakness of his position. He was aware that the military was unable to police the frontier adequately and he knew that harsher implementation of the pass regulations would lead only to their being flouted more obviously. At least with a tolerant application of the regulations, they could retain an apparent integrity.[126]

As the example of the pass laws indicates, Smith and the Resident Agents within the province were forced into compromised and conciliatory positions not simply due to their own inadequate military and bureaucratic resources, but also because of persistent Xhosa exploitation of the weaknesses within their administration. Mhala, described as a 'clever man' even by the *Graham's Town Journal*, proved particularly adept at this and his story is illuminating.[127] The Resident Agent placed in charge of him, Henry Rawstorne, first tried to exert his authority over a cow that Mhala had confiscated from a subordinate.[128] When summoned though, Mhala informed the messenger that he was busy going to a dance. After further ignored summonses, Rawstorne had Mhala's cattle seized. Much to his frustration though, Mhala soon appeared with orders from Smith to release first some and then all of the livestock, the commander of the province having apparently realised that stiffer resistance would be encountered if the chief was not appeased. Shortly afterwards, Mhala unilaterally reclaimed the *lobola* (bridewealth) paid to a man whose daughter had subsequently refused to marry the chief.

He then bore patiently Rawstorne's official reprimand, before taking off the cattle anyway.[129]

Things did not always go Mhala's way. In his inability to force this nameless woman to marry him, he faced a curtailment of his former power. His frustration led to an angry but ineffective outburst at the Resident Agent followed by a scuffle with a sentry (after which he had to be pacified with a silk handkerchief and a sheep).[130] Nevertheless, Rawstorne concluded from all this that the power of the chiefs was 'still very extensive'. He continued, 'We must . . . guard against giving the chiefs *too much trouble* . . . at present they are losers by the change, whilst we still require of them assistance in administration of justice'.[131] On the one hand Rawstorne was facing up to the fact that his was not the transformative power heralded by Smith and on the other hand, Mhala was recognising that he no longer had the freedom of action which he formerly held. Both men were negotiating a fine and unstable balance of power.

And it was not only Mhala who was able to explore the limits of British power in the province. Resident Agent Bowker found that instead of punishing cattle thieves, he could only enforce the return of the stolen animals and even then many who were summoned on charges of theft sent the 'police' away contemptuously. Even when 'criminal' culprits could be caught, in his new official capacity as Resident Agent, John Mitford Bowker complained, 'The Kafirs are such a wild race should I commit one [to jail] I shall never catch another'.[132] The wartime collaborator Phatho himself restrained his followers from using Bowker's court and Bowker ended up relying on Phatho to secure for him accused Xhosa who did not appear voluntarily, thus giving the chief ample autonomy to decide who the British should and should not punish.[133] As in the case of Rawstorne and Mhala, Bowker and Phatho worked their way hesitantly towards a system in which each co-operated to a certain extent so that both could save face.

Not all the chiefs resented the British presence. Some profited, for example through trade with the occupying soldiers, and some needed protection from other chiefdoms after their collaboration in the war.[134] But as the British administration prepared to abandon the province towards the end of 1836, the majority of chiefs demonstrated that their residual power was now to be made manifest once more. During the gradual withdrawal, while still wary of the British response, some revenge was exacted on the Mfengu and, with increased fines and harsher punishments, the chiefly grip was drawn tighter around commoners who may have wavered.[135]

Missionary visions and the Xhosa

Military and civilian officials were not the only Britons within Queen Adelaide Province to find their projected goals diminished and redefined by the Xhosa. Missionaries shared the experience. Smith, as we have seen, intended the missionaries distributed among the Xhosa within and around the new province to be the key agents for their cultural transformation. The London Missionary Society (LMS) had Friedrich Kayser at Knapp's Hope and John Brownlee at King William's Town. The Glasgow Missionary Society (GMS) had William Chalmers and Robert Niven at the Tyhume, James Laing at Burnshill, John Ross at Pirie and John Bennie at Lovedale (the site of which was shortly to be moved). James Weir and Alexander McDiarmuid were further GMS missionary artisans. The Wesleyan Methodists (WMMS) in Xhosa territory included John Shepstone at Wesley-ville, William Boyce at Mount Coke and John Ayliff at Peddie.[136] Many of these men were accompanied by their wives, and by assistants, who ran Bible classes and, in the case of the missionary wives, classes specifically for Xhosa women and infants.[137] In all cases, the mission station locations had had to be approved by local chiefs and in all cases too, missionaries and their helpers were surrounded by a population that was largely indifferent to their preachings, even if it was aware of their political utility.

The LMS's Kayser, along with other Cape humanitarians, had objected vigorously to D'Urban and Smith's original intention, expressed in May 1835, of expelling the Xhosa entirely from Queen Adelaide Province. They were particularly offended by the assumption that Xhosa enemies were incapable of redemption – an assumption which apparently lay behind the plans for their expulsion. Kayser felt that the governor had made a 'grave error' in alienating the hostile Xhosa's lands 'in an unfair manner'.[138] Challenging D'Urban and Smith's description of the Xhosa as 'irreclaimable', he argued that, like Britain's own barbarian forefathers, they could ultimately be brought to civilisation if subjected to just policies.[139] The LMS Director, John Philip, also made his disagreement with D'Urban and Smith over the causes of the war and the May policy of expulsion evident.[140]

Things changed temporarily as a result of the policy elaborated in September of 'allowing' even the hostile Xhosa to remain within the province. Smith's early reports of tranquillity and progress with the benign trans-formation of the Xhosa were briefly believed by Philip and Fairbairn, bolstered as they were by the humanitarian Resident Agent Stretch's own accounts.[141] The objectives of the individual LMS missionaries now over-lapped significantly with officials' expressed intentions. Aware that they themselves lacked the power to install ideal disciplinary regimes among the Xhosa, the LMS and other missionaries looked forward to the effective exer-cise of a just and humane sovereign power on the part of a newly enlightened colonial government.[142] The LMS missionaries all requested to be allowed back into the new province immediately after the war to carry on enthusias-tically a work of conversion that was now the cornerstone of government policy. Reporting to Smith, most returned in December 1835.[143]

While Philip and Fairbairn themselves continued to hold that the annexation of Queen Adelaide Province had the potential to make Britain's 'dominion a blessing to this ill-fated continent', they both soon developed pragmatic reservations concerning Smith's attempts to undermine chiefly authority and the cost of establishing a proper administrative infra-structure.[144] As the nature of the transformative process envisaged under military occupation became clearer, Fairbairn expressed further reservations.[145] Philip's was soon to become the leading voice invoked against D'Urban's scheme in London.[146]

Like Philip had been, the GMS missionaries were willing to utilise the opportunity of Queen Adelaide Province for what they saw as the spiritual gain of the Xhosa. The government in London was informed by Philip that the GMS missionaries also believed that the Xhosa had been provoked to the recent war. However, most of the GMS men 'on the ground' seemed much less sympathetic to the Xhosa, and to Philip's interpretation of the war. Chalmers actually assisted Smith enthusiastically by providing intel-ligence and Laing, frustrated at the lack of progress with Xhosa conversion, certainly felt that the Xhosa were in the wrong to attack.[147] The GMS missionaries all agreed that the British conquest of the province had in fact opened the door to the Xhosa's widespread conversion, provided the province's subsequent occupation was handled properly. Chalmers in par-ticular had a utopian vision of the Xhosa 'transformed and saved and made happy' under more direct British influence, and he, Niven and Laing were impatient to employ converted Xhosa to fan out across the countryside and provide grassroots Christian training.[148] To assist in this long-term endeavour, Bennie of the GMS concentrated on a first Xhosa translation of the Bible.

Alongside the GMS missionaries' educational efforts were more immediate contributions. Notable among these was the construction of a model irriga-tion channel, reflecting Christianity's status as part of the entire package of Western material civilisation.[149] However, there were varying degrees of enthusiasm within the GMS over the mechanics of the British administration and in particular, over Smith's plans for the missionaries. Chalmers was most pleased with Smith and communicated his enthusiasm to a metropolitan GMS audience.[150] But even he had reservations about the formalised role envisaged for the missionaries as a whole, and he came into direct conflict with Smith over the appropriation of Xhosa land for a new mission station. Chalmers, like the other GMS missionaries, did not wish to be alienated from the Xhosa by too close an association with Smith's military state.[151] Other GMS missionaries went so far as to make representations on the chiefs' behalf for more land.[152] Laing ventured yet further in expressing his concern that the missionaries' endeavours, at least in the short term, might be actively undermined by Smith's unsubtle interventions. His initial approval for the military authority soon gave way to reservations about the quasi-official role that was being developed for the Wesleyans, and about the whole concept of 'forced civilisation'.[153] As a specific manifestation of his qualms concerning the whole project, Laing expressed himself most dis-appointed that the military in the new province were not leading by Christian example.[154]

The Wesleyan missionaries generally shared the LMS and GMS mission-aries' early perceptions of Queen Adelaide Province as an opportunity for state-sponsored evangelism, but they were willing and able to exploit much closer ties both to settlers and to the colonial authorities. Their inter-ventions became more controversial as a result. Shepstone and Ayliff had themselves been members of 1820 settler parties and, among the most vocal settlers, including Godlonton, membership of the Methodist church had pro-vided 'a school for the development of political and organisation skills' even before they left the British Isles.[155] Once in the Cape, the Wesleyanism of many settlers provided a network of mutual support within the broader net-works forged by the British settler community. Methodists were the leading proponents of the celebrations of the anniversary of the Albany settlement as a whole in 1844.[156]

Wesleyan missionaries thus tended to be closely attuned to settler interests, often reproducing settler discourse in specifically evangelical terms. But their ties to the colonial government were also strong. Unlike Philip, and far more clearly than most GMS missionaries, the Wesleyans agreed with Smith and D'Urban's interpretation of the origins of the recent war. For them, the Xhosa were the ruthlessly guilty party, and the settlers unoffending and unprovoking (aside that is, indirectly, from possibly having provoked God's wrath through their consumption of alcohol).[157] It was this coincidence of opinion, as well as Ayliff's role in securing Mfengu allies and labourers, that allowed Shepstone and him to secure official roles in the post-war administration.[158]

Wesleyans also tended to see eye-to-eye with settlers and, to some extent officials, on potentially favourable outcomes to the war. Shaw's scheme for the post-war treatment of the Xhosa, although harsh, was relatively moderate in the light of Shrewsbury's proposals. Like D'Urban and Smith, Shaw wished to expel the 'hostile' Xhosa and retain within the province only the 'friendly', in his case, so that they could defend the frontier on behalf of the colonists and be subjected to intensive state-funded and missionary-led education and evangelism.[159] Shrewsbury's measures, mentioned in chapter 3, were more draconian. They included the confiscation of all the offending Xhosa's property, and not just their land, the deposition of their chiefs, the prompt judicial execution of any who could be found to have killed British subjects during the war, and the 'merciful' sentence of hard labour for all offenders whose lives were spared. But this was not all. After the victory, every Xhosa man was to wear perpetually around his neck a tin plate bearing his name and that of his chief. Those found in the province without this 'passport' were immediately to be treated as enemies and presumably shot, while those with them could more easily be enumerated and detected in any crimes. Thus would the British empire 'subserve the great principles of justice and mercy'.[160] Shrewsbury had been associated with the humanitarian struggle against slavery in the West Indies prior to his posting to the Cape, and before the war he had contrasted the hospitality shown by the Xhosa with the 'tyranny' exercised by white men on the Caribbean slave plantations.[161] His more recent disillusionment at finding few willing converts, and the anger aroused in him by Xhosa attack on the colony, must have been profound.

It was not surprising to contemporaries that the Wesleyans developed a fond regard for Smith's administration in Queen Adelaide Province. Boyce, for example, compared the 'start' that had been made with the Xhosa, with the beginnings of the more successfully completed 'civilisation' of the Scottish Highlanders over the preceding hundred years.[162] Regardless of their attitude towards the provinces' authorities though, all the missionaries within it were to experience frustration. Much as they had done before the war, when most converts were in some way marginal to Xhosa society, the missionaries continued to despair at the Xhosa's resistance to the Christian message.[163]

Most missionaries in the new province had roughly 20 to 40 regular church attendees, unless it was a special occasion, when attendance could be much greater. But if other Xhosa did not seek to hide on their approach, they sometimes told them straight that they would not support the God of the men who had destroyed their gardens in the war. GMS missionaries who attempted to interrogate the Xhosa that they met on the road as to the meaning of the immortal soul or to interrupt their daily activities to sermonise, were frequently met with deserted kraals and the sight of Xhosa men, women and children fleeing in the distance.[164] Despite Smith's attempts publicly to discredit the sangomas, the missionaries continued to despair at the Xhosa's resistance to the Christian message. Many Xhosa commoners resented missionary favouritism of the Mfengu and most chiefs played a subtle game with the missionaries, attempting to manipulate them whilst avoiding the cultural surrender and the tedious rituals to which the missionaries wished to subject them.[165]

If missionaries found it difficult during this first British occupation of Xhosaland to earn expressions of outward respect, their attempts at the inner 'salvation' of their Xhosa charges were even more problematic. As Helen Ross, the wife of the GMS missionary John Ross wrote, 'The people . . . are far from being properly affected by the goodness of God. They do not hate and turn from their sin to God, nor cry to Him to be merciful to them . . . They are much given to feasting and dancing'.[166] Even those who did attend missionary services were not always well behaved. Stephen Kay, for instance reported that 'our public services were occasionally disturbed by whisperings, bursts of laughter, or jocular remarks amongst the hearers'.[167] Nevertheless, relations between missionaries and Xhosa in the province were by no means based on total rejection. Balances were often struck with, for instance, the Xhosa more or less co-operating in the construction of watercourses supervised by Stretch and the LMS and GMS missionaries.[168] Such schemes brought more reliable water supplies for the Xhosa while they brought signs of a willing transition towards 'civilisation' for the missionaries.

In the face of such pragmatic Xhosa responses to their 'civilising' and Christianising mission British representatives tried various tactics. In order to encourage mission school attendance, Stretch offered a cow to the best reader in the Burnshill mission school and 10s. to the most 'deserving' pupils. Smith suggested fining the kraals which did not send children to the schools and Ross proposed rewarding those kraals that did, but none of these schemes worked.[169] Ross believed that the problem did not lie entirely with the Xhosa and he pointed more than once to the bad example set by the white soldiers and settlers whom the Xhosa were supposed to be emulating.[170] In the longer term, the negotiations being made between the missionaries of Queen Adelaide Province and the local Xhosa were to have tremendous significance. If the construction of water courses manifested a selective Xhosa appropriation of 'useful' missionary endeavours, with the GMS translation of the Bible into Xhosa, further foundations were being laid. Despite the missionaries' continuing insistence that the Xhosa eventually jettison their culture, this very act of rendition into the vernacular presaged what Elphick calls a 'broader cultural translation'. It 'asserted first that any language could be made the bearer of the Word of God, and second, that any culture could become a Christian culture'.[171]

However, in 1836, the overwhelming majority of the Xhosa were not disposed to listen to the Christian message, regardless of its language. It would take further colonial assaults on Xhosa social and political structures, and more material support for missionary schools, buildings and materials, to set a widespread appropriation and reformulation of Christianity in motion. The essential integrity of Xhosa culture still remained in Queen Adelaide Province, rendering Christianity largely superfluous for most individuals. Typical is the resigned report of Laing: 'Failed to persuade boys to attend school as they were looking in the forest for herbs which they needed for their circumcision rites'.[172]

Neither the missionaries nor the Resident Agents nor Smith, then, were the representatives of a new and overwhelming imperial power. The latter in particular did exercise power, but of a compromised nature, and within limits prescribed by the need not to push the Xhosa chiefs and their followers too far. Smith himself, as administrator of the later British Kaffraria, admitted the lesson:

> When I administered the government of kaffirland in 1836, I opened the gates of a flood which I could not stem, by undermining the power of the chiefs. My error was soon apparent; and I was compelled to re-establish that which it had before been my purpose to weaken.[173]

As this chapter has sought to demonstrate, the initial British colonisation of Xhosa territory was not the outcome of a simple alliance between colonial officials and settler capitalists, as materialist historians have suggested. Aside from the continuing tensions between official and settler discourses, each colonising group had also to reformulate its objectives in the light of Xhosa resistance.

As we will see in the next chapter, D'Urban was as angered by the abandonment of Queen Adelaide Province as were most settlers, but this is not to say that in the annexation of the province, his colonial state was simply the willing tool of those settlers. With each of the most pressing settler demands, the governor complied only partially at this stage, his strategic concerns remaining paramount. Both settlers and officials wanted expulsion of the Xhosa from their land during the war, but the state was forced, by Maqoma and the other resisting chiefs and commoners, to recognise its military incapacity to achieve this. In the planning of the colonial land grants that would be allowed in the new province, D'Urban envisaged settlement along narrower belts and squeezed between larger Xhosa locations than the most vociferous settlers would have liked. Recognising imperial reluctance to go even this far, the governor limited the land to be made available to settlers by confining it within the 'ceded' territory. While this limitation was indirectly imposed from without by the imperial government, the strategic decision to locate 'friendly' chiefdoms and Mfengu locations rather than settlers in most of that territory was the colonial governor's own initiative, grounded in the militaristic thinking which informed official colonial discourse more generally.[174]

Again, settler labour demands were not entirely met by D'Urban's government in the mid-1830s. Officials' failure to prevent potential labour coming into the colony from becoming a more threatening presence was not the result of reluctance; it was due to simple incapacity. But the creation of a settled farming group of elite Mfengu was deliberate colonial government policy, again strategically informed and again resented by leading settlers. In fact, it was not to be until late in the next decade that a fuller coincidence of settler and state imperatives developed, particularly under Harry Smith's governorship. (D'Urban himself had become more closely aligned with the leading settlers only when he found in them valuable allies against the abandonment of the province, and shortly before his enforced resignation as governor).[175]

If the colonial government was not the tool of settler-capitalists at this stage, neither were missionaries the tools of the government. The missionaries in the new province and adjacent territories saw in the extension of British control the potential for genuine evangelical endeavour, but were divided over its practical implications. For the Wesleyans in particular, the imposition of colonial authority was *necessarily* compatible with their spiritual endeavours. But some LMS and GMS missionaries showed signs of doubt that the possible benefits of state support in the province would be realised in practice. They expressed anxieties that Smith's coercive military designs, couched though they were within an evangelical rhetoric, were neither the most effective nor moral method of stimulating conversion. These missionaries advocated in the short term the more 'organic' integration of Christian agency within an existing Xhosa society, and it was their concerns, as we will see in the next chapter, that were picked up, amplified and given political clout by humanitarian allies in Britain.

The first British thrust into Xhosa territory occurred during a transitional period in which defensive official security concerns stemming from an older rough equilibrium of power on the frontier were interacting in ambivalent ways with a swelling settler desire for aggressive capitalist expansion. The relative weakness of the mid-1830s colonial government is revealed in the administration of Queen Adelaide Province itself, where expressed official intention differed excessively from what colonial officials and missionaries 'on the ground' experienced.

Despite all of Smith's bluster and his and D'Urban's representations to London, no coherent attempts were made to culturally transform and discipline the Xhosa in the 1830s. Far from it. The relatively small and greatly stretched colonial presence could only maintain its authority by reaching accommodations with the Xhosa chiefs. While those chiefs resented colonial curtailment of their former autonomy, in the absence of effective force and facing an unprecedented problem of loss of patronage, they too could only compromise. In effect they became unwilling participants in an early, incoherent and untheorised version of indirect rule – a form of rule in which the failure to transform would ultimately be defined as the success of conservationism.[176] The first, brief episode in the colonisation of the Xhosa, marked by Queen Adelaide Province, then, was the outcome of contestation and compromise between multiple loci of power, both within and beyond the former colonial boundaries, rather than the achievement of any united colonising endeavour.

5 Obtaining the 'due observance of justice'

The apotheosis of the humanitarian imagination

> The situation of Great Britain brings her beyond any other power into communication with the uncivilized nations of the earth. We are in contact with them in so many parts of the globe, that it has become of deep importance to ascertain the results of our relations with them, and to fix the rules of our conduct towards them.
>
> (Report of the Select Committee on Aborigines
> (British Settlements), 1837)[1]

From 1835–7, Queen Adelaide Province became a battleground in the contests between settlers, officials and humanitarians, not just in the Cape, but in Britain as well. It was during the struggle over the fate of the province that the divergence between humanitarian and settler notions of a proper colonial order became most marked. These political struggles had very little to do with the compromised relationships that colonial officials and missionaries were able to carve out with Xhosa chiefs and commoners within the province itself. Rather, they were fought through the politics of representation across a discursive terrain connecting the Cape with Britain. In disputing the future of the Xhosa within the province, colonial and metropolitan participants found themselves discussing the processes of British colonisation *per se*. Their frame of reference expanded to incorporate all those diverse territories where Britons were 'encountering' non-European peoples. The contests waged over the colonisation of the Xhosa in the late 1830s, then, came to manifest many of the tensions that characterised nineteenth-century British colonialism as a whole.

In this chapter, I aim to examine these tensions through a close reading of the evidence collected, and the conclusions reached, by two humanitarian-inspired 'committees'. One of these was based in London and had the brief of investigating the relations between Britons and 'aborigines' in territories scattered across the globe. This committee's investigations represent the moment at which humanitarian power was at its peak in Britain. The other committee, or more properly, military court, was based on the Cape frontier and had the far more specific task of enquiring into the circumstances surrounding the killing of the Xhosa paramount, Hintsa, during the 1834–5

Cape frontier war. Despite their differences the two enquiries, taken together, established an exemplary humanitarian agenda for empire. In doing so, they attempted to demarcate humanitarian projects from those of settlers and unreformed officials more clearly than ever before. However, I will argue that, in refining humanitarian discourse, they also provided opportunities for its appropriation, assimilation and subversion by antithetical interests opposed to its ultimate temporal objectives.

The humanitarian imagination and the Aborigines Committee

Queen Adelaide Province and the Colonial Office

As well as being represented as an exercise in colonial state and settler capitalist power, Queen Adelaide Province has featured in the South African historiography as a pawn in an unusual, personal struggle between two imperial officials. The conflict over the province between Lord Glenelg, Secretary of State for the Colonies in London, and Sir Benjamin D'Urban, the Cape's Governor, is of interest though, not just because of what it indicates about the two men's personalities and their immediate political influences. It can also tell us a great deal about more systemic British debates over the purpose and morality of colonialism.

Glenelg's father, Charles Grant, had been a leading light of the abolitionist Clapham Sect, an organiser of the Church Missionary Society and a campaigner for the missionary-led reform of Indian colonial administration. Glenelg himself was raised within his father's circle of evangelical friends and allies. He was taught by John Venn, Rector of Clapham and one of the founders of the Clapham Sect. He had some personal experience of the Cape, having served there during 1806 as secretary to the acting governor. Glenelg's colleague as Under-Secretary at the Colonial Office, James Stephen, grew up within the same tradition. Venn was his father-in-law and his father was also a founder member of the Clapham Sect. Given the small size of the Colonial Office's staff, it could always prove susceptible to the particular interests of its personnel and, during the mid-1830s, it is not surprising that both Glenelg and Stephen were considered to be important allies by bourgeois humanitarian reformers.[2]

However, it was neither the personal background and character of Glenelg and his deputy, nor the malleability of their departmental practice alone, that shaped government thinking on colonial affairs. Glenelg and Stephen may have been exemplary in their reproduction of a humanitarian discourse, and in its deployment against older, more aristocratic notions of colonial govern-mentality, but they should by no means be thought of as isolated individuals swimming against antithetical currents of opinion. Indeed their personal influence was so pronounced precisely because they were located powerfully in relation to currently hegemonic strands of political thought. Glenelg and Stephen were as concerned to bring about a divinely inspired, just and stable order of government within colonial space as their more domestically minded associates in the Clapham Sect were to secure such an order in Britain itself. In the Cape, Fairbairn was aware of this when he welcomed the news that Glenelg had been appointed as Colonial Secretary. 'The People of England' (by which he meant the middle class), he wrote, 'will now bear with all its clearness, with all its nobleness, with all its wisdom, on every branch of our Colonial Policy'.[3]

Glenelg and Stephen's humanitarian concern over events in the Cape was profoundly reinforced by anxieties about expenditure which plagued the entire British governmental system. Highlighting these anxieties, Galbraith has argued that economic considerations were more important in Glenelg's ultimate decision to renounce British jurisdiction over Queen Adelaide Province than were humanitarian principles. For him, Glenelg's repudiation of D'Urban's annexation was 'humanitarianism "on the cheap", designed to please both God and mammon'.[4] Glenelg did indeed make it quite clear to D'Urban that 'the strongest necessity exists for carrying on an enlightened but strict economy into every part of the Publick [*sic*] service.'[5] However, this does not mean, as Keegan suggests, that 'it was the commitment to economy – the essential principle of the informal imperialism of free trade – that dictated policy', while 'the rage of humanitarians' merely 'provided the public rhetoric'.[6] To conceive of humanitarianism as a rhetorical smokescreen, or an ideological superstructure overlaying more profound economic considerations, is to revert to an unhelpful binary between ideology and materialism.

The humanitarian discourse reproduced by Glenelg and Stephen, as I argued in chapter 2, was materially grounded. It defined proper economic relations and practices, including the avoidance of wasteful expenditure, as part of a wider set of divinely sanctioned and 'just' individual and collective behaviours. As we will see in relation to the Select Committee on Aborigines below, 'economic issues' were morally framed by humanitarians in the same way as the other situated and contingent 'issues' which preoccupied them. Some economic practices could be considered legitimate and others not, and any explicit distinction that humanitarians drew between economic issues and issues of justice and morality, was made to appeal only to those antithetical audiences who insisted on writing and speaking about them within separate categories.[7]

During most of 1836, the only official communication that Glenelg had received from D'Urban on his post-war plans was that setting out the intention to expel all of the hostile Xhosa beyond the Kei River, reserving most of their land for white farmers. D'Urban's realisation that this would be impossible, and that the Xhosa would have to be accommodated in extensive locations within the conquered territory, was not known to Glenelg until his response to D'Urban's annexation had already been decided. D'Urban's initial anticipation that tracts of land in Queen Adelaide Province would be left open for colonial settlement prompted Glenelg to add a marginal note to the

governor's despatch, reading 'European speculations!'[8] The divergence
between the two men's deeper understanding of the colonial frontier and of
the Xhosa is apparent throughout their correspondence with, for example,
Glenelg employing a more universalist notion of human differentiation to
refer to the Xhosa as a 'nation', and D'Urban more problematically and consistently describing them as a 'race'.[9] Even this apparently trivial termino-
logical difference, I would suggest, indicates that a significant rift had
come about between metropolitan and colonial official understandings of
social relations on the Cape frontier.

We have seen in previous chapters how D'Urban's construction of the
frontier had been shaped by the experience of defending against Xhosa
attack and planning a post-war military regime. Glenelg's knowledge was
undoubtedly influenced by Thomas Fowell Buxton, and through him, by
Philip and his political allies in the Cape. At Buxton's request, his sister-
in-law, Anna Gurney, had compiled a digest of John Philip's letters from
the Cape to be presented before the Colonial Secretary. Buxton anticipated
that this evidence would be used 'to save a nation of 100,000 beings and
several flourishing missions from destruction'.[10] Buxton also made a series
of personal visits to Glenelg, who was an old debating club acquaintance.
In one of these meetings, Buxton introduced Glenelg to the Secretary of
the London Missionary Society and another crucial humanitarian witness to
colonial abuses, William Ellis. Meanwhile, Ellis was receiving his own
stream of letters from Philip and he used his introduction to Glenelg to
reinforce Buxton's points that the war in the Cape had been provoked by
commandos acting under the spoor law and by successive, unjust expulsions
of the Xhosa.

Buxton's purpose in arranging these meetings was made clear in one of
Philip's letters. He wrote that 'It will be of great importance to get the ear
of the Ministers before they shall have time to form an opinion on the
Governor's Despatches on this subject [the causes of the frontier war and
the annexation of Queen Adelaide Province], and one word from you in the
present state of England will be enough to prevent them taking the wrong
course.'[11] Buxton seems to have been quite satisfied of his powers in this
respect. He was pleased to report, after one of his meetings with Glenelg,
that he had been able to give 'our new Colonial Secretary a disquisition to
my heart's content on the treatment of savages . . . the atrocities of white
men, and above all, on the responsibilities of a Secretary of State'. He continued, 'I believe . . . that Lord Glenelg feels both soundly and warmly on
the subject.'[12]

While Buxton's personal and informal campaign was influential, however,
it was the formal evidence given before the Select Committee established by
him in London in 1835 that proved decisive. Buxton had first agitated for a
committee to enquire into the humanitarian allegations about Cape frontier
policy in 1834, before the outbreak of the war. He had written to Philip:
'It appears to me that we ought to fix and enforce certain regulations and

laws, with regard to the natives of all countries where we make settlements. Those laws must be based on the principles of justice.'[13] After delivering a speech to this effect in the House of Commons, Buxton had succeeded in getting a circular passed to all colonial governors which set out a humanitarian agenda for local policies, but he persisted in his endeavour to achieve something more effectual. He had asked Philip to 'furnish me with facts', so that he might institute an official enquiry into Cape frontier policy in particular.[14]

Once news of the December 1834 Xhosa attack on the colony had reached Britain in March 1835, Buxton realised that it provided an opportunity to bring the attention of metropolitan groups to bear directly on the provocations which had caused it. In May, he moved in Parliament for an enquiry into the Cape frontier system. On hearing news of his success, he wrote to Macauly: 'The events of the war, Hintza's death, and the clamours of the settlers for permission once more to spoil these "irreclaimable savages", have called attention of the Government to our evidence, and, coming at the very nick of time, I have reason to know it affected the decision of the question.'[15]

The Select Committee on Aborigines

Buxton's' Select Committee on Aborigines (British Settlements) soon became a rallying point for humanitarian discourse. In the same way that the 1831 Parliamentary Committee on the question of slavery had brought the activities of colonial planters under the gaze of a metropolitan population, so the Committee on Aborigines brought the relations between officials, settlers and indigenous peoples on the frontiers of colonial settlement to the very centre of the empire.[16] As the Committee's chair, Buxton instructed its members 'to consider what Measures ought to be adopted with regard to the native Inhabitants of Countries where British Settlements are made, and to the neighbouring Tribes, in order to secure to them the due observance of Justice, and the protection of their Rights; to promote the spread of Civilization among them, and to lead them to the peaceful and voluntary reception of the Christian Religion'.[17] The Committee was given powers to investigate colonial policy across southern Africa, the Canadas, Newfoundland, New South Wales and van Diemen's Land (Tasmania). It also received and published information on New Zealand and the South Sea Islands, 'which countries, though not British possessions, are continually visited by Subjects of Great Britain, and on which many of them reside'.[18]

As far as Buxton was concerned, the Select Committee would serve publicly to reinforce and substantiate the points that he and Ellis had already made to Glenelg in private. However, the Committee's final composition meant that his control was far from complete. Aside from Buxton himself, the Committee comprised fourteen other men, of whom at any one sitting usually about ten were present. Buxton could generally rely on the support of most of these men, and particularly of Charles Lushington, an influential evangelical ally and friend who took the chair in Buxton's absence. But he was occasionally challenged by the conservative Tory (and future Liberal prime minister) William Gladstone. Gladstone was brought onto the Committee in February 1836 in order to replace a departing member. Having recently defended his father in the House of Commons from abolitionist accusations that slaves had been worked to death on the family's West Indies plantation, he was far from a humanitarian ally. Indeed, Gladstone's maiden speech in parliament had been an attack on abolitionists who wanted emancipation immediately, and a plea for a more gradual introduction to freedom.[19] Gladstone was also at this time a proponent of more repressive measures in Ireland. Not surprisingly, he came into conflict with Buxton on a number of issues during the Committee's hearings, but especially over the settlers' and colonial government's project of instituting a vagrancy law.[20]

Buxton was also intermittently undermined during the Committee's hearings by Sir Rufane Donkin, former governor of the Cape. While Buxton generally asked the Committee's witnesses leading questions designed to prove humanitarian assertions, both Gladstone and Donkin insisted on asking questions which allowed witnesses greater scope to articulate settler and Cape official arguments. Both men also attempted to exclude the only Xhosa witness before the committee, the Christian convert and minor Gqunukhwebe chief, Dyani Tshatshu, whom, as we will see below, Philip had brought over from the Cape. Indeed, Donkin tried to have Philip himself excluded as a witness. Both motions were unsuccessful, as was Gladstone's attempt to make the wording of the Committee's final report less critical of current colonial policy.

Despite Gladstone and Donkin's endeavours, the Committee's final report supplies the definitive humanitarian analysis of the evils of settler-led colonialism and of unreconstructed colonial government. It lays before the reader the corrective moral vision that lay at the heart not just of a specifically colonial humanitarian sensibility, but of early nineteenth-century bourgeois reformist discourse as a whole. By the same token, however, it exposes those aspects of humanitarian discourse that were most vulnerable to settler and official appropriation in pursuit of decidedly non-humanitarian projects. Although the minutes of the Committee's evidence and its final report have been mined for empirical material by dozens of historians of the Cape and of other colonial territories, given its emblematic status, it is worthy of a far more detailed discursive analysis than it has yet received.

The Select Committee's discourse and its appropriation

An analysis of the Select Committee's discourse could begin at a number of significant points, but I will start with the ways in which the Committee, both in its questioning of witnesses and its final report, framed the intersection between morality and capitalist practice. The 'rules of conduct' that the Committee prescribed, like the broader reformist complex in Britain, advocated a profitable economics, but in such a way that a particular vision of justice was enshrined within material transactions. As had been the case during the long debate over slavery, a humanitarian conception of *legitimate* economic practice was defined in opposition to antithetical activities. In the Committee's case, these were the activities engaged in by colonial settlers across the globe, rather than by planters and slavers in the West Indies and West Africa alone. As had also been the case in anti-slavery discourse, there was a secondary consideration: the reform of illegitimate practices would actually result in long-term benefits of a *material* as well as a spiritual nature.

'In reviewing the general case before us', the Committee's report established, 'we have endeavoured to fix our attention rather on the requirements of justice and morality than on the motives of interest.' These requirements were always primary. However, motives of interest could provide a subsidiary rationale for pursuing a more humane colonial policy, since the present system of settler-led colonisation 'has not only incurred a vast load of crime, but a vast expenditure of money and amount of loss'.[21] The Cape provided a perfect example of the ways that rapacious economic practices, those which ignored the principle of justice, proved counterproductive in a material as well as a moral sense. The recent war had been provoked by the illegitimate practices of seizing Xhosa cattle under the pretext of the spoor law, and had resulted in the loss of a trade with the Xhosa amounting to £30,000 per annum. Furthermore, successive expulsions of the Xhosa from land adjoining the Cape Colony, carried out either because of misguided military planning or settler acquisitiveness, had caused 'the loss of thousands of good labourers to the colonists' and 'the checking of civilization and trade with the interior for a period of 12 years'. The committee estimated the total cost to the British government of various official and settler provocations as being £241,884.[22]

An alternative, humanitarian agenda for the colonies, founded on 'relations of peace and mutual good understanding', by contrast, 'would materially contribute to promote the civil and commercial interests of Great Britain'.[23] The widespread diffusion of Christianity would be a first step, leading to 'the adoption of salutary laws'. In turn, such laws would secure *'protection to the merchant and the mariner*, and the greatest *facilities for the extension of commerce'*. After all, 'where missionaries have introduced the Gospel, our vessels go with safety and confidence'.[24]

Aside from contributing to greater profitability for traders and settlers, humanitarian programmes for colonial government would bring strategic and military benefits to colonial officials. The Committee could not fail to point out that those Xhosa chiefs who had assisted the British in the recent war were those most under the influence of the colony's missionaries. The Gqunukhwebe chiefs such as Phatho and Dyani Tshatshu, whose missionaries had most successfully interceded with the colonial government to have confiscated land restored, had proved especially co-operative.[25]

Stockenström used his appearance before the Committee as a witness in order to emphasise such firmly practical, administrative reasons for a humanitarian policy. For him, 'justice' in the colony's dealings with the Xhosa was necessary if only to plug the gaps in colonial military power by securing Xhosa compliance: 'justice, trade and commerce must ultimately be your principal means for the preservation of peace; for . . . 5,000 military cannot protect that frontier effectually'.[26] Stockenström's comments were endorsed by Buxton: 'we must either adopt one of those systems, have an overwhelming military force, with all the expenses attendant upon it, or enter into amicable relations with the people, and treat them with justice'.[27]

Despite its concessions to economically and strategically minded thinkers, however, the Committee maintained that 'there is a class of motives of a higher order which conduce to the same conclusion'. It argued that:

> The British empire has been signally blessed by Providence, and her eminence, her strength, her wealth, her prosperity, her intellectual, her moral and her religious advantages, are so many reasons for peculiar obedience to the laws of Him who guides the destinies of nations. These were given for some higher purpose than commercial prosperity and military renown . . . Can we suppose otherwise than that it is our office to carry civilization and humanity, peace and good government, and, above all, the knowledge of the true God, to the uttermost ends of the earth?[28]

If settler activities could be condemned on economic grounds – a condemnation designed to counter the appeals of official and trading interests – they should be condemned far more vociferously on moral grounds. Whether in 'the south and west of Africa, Australia, the islands in the Pacific Ocean, a very extensive district of South America', or in the 'immense tract which constitutes the most northerly part of the American continent', it was felt that

> the intercourse of Europeans in general, without any exception in favour of the subjects of Great Britain, has been, unless when attended by missionary exertions, a source of many calamities to uncivilized nations. Too often their territory has been usurped; their property seized; their numbers diminished; their character debased; the spread of civilization impeded.[29]

The atonement that Britons had achieved through their exemplary act of abolishing slavery was jeopardised if such abuses were to continue in its expanding colonies of settlement. This was a consideration of a far higher order than mere economics.

Having thus established its principles and their order of significance, the Committee embarked upon a more detailed analysis of the problems created by settlers and unreconstructed officials, considering each of the colonial peripheries under its purview in turn. In this section of its report, it revealed the more specific grounds on which humanitarians condemned settler and official activities. However, reading between the lines of this section also tells us much about the ways that humanitarian discourse was capable of being repackaged by settler and official interests. It indicates how the rhetorical practices of humanitarianism, applied in specific instances, could effectively be assimilated into settler and official projects, even during this period of humanitarian discursive ascendancy. As we will see in the next chapter, such an appropriation and subversion would become far more widespread in the second half of the nineteenth century.

The main imperative established by the Committee was the necessity for greater, not less, colonial intervention. In the first instance, such intervention was needed simply to prevent the pursuit of indigenous genocide by uncontrolled settler interests. The precedent was the eradication of the Caribs. The Committee felt that it, 'need not speak' much of them, as 'little more remains than the tradition that they once existed'. In Australia, the same outcome could be predicted: 'intercourse with Europeans has cast over [the Aborigines'] original debasement a yet deeper shade of wretchedness. . . . The effects have consequently been dreadful beyond example, both in the diminution of their numbers and in their demoralization'. It was only 'through the influence of Christianity, brought to bear upon the natives by the zealous exertions of devoted missionaries, that the progress of extinction can be checked'.[30] In Newfoundland, 'as in other parts of North America', the Committee asserted that settlers 'accounted it a "meritorious act" to kill an Indian'. There was 'a proneness in the new occupants . . . to regard the natives as an irreclaimable race, and as inconvenient neighbours . . . If it had not been for the introduction of Christianity, they [too] would speedily have become extinct'.[31]

In Van Diemen's Land, the Committee regretted that 'such was the unfortunate nature of our [local] policy, and the circumstances into which it had brought us, that no better expedient could be devised than the catching and expatriating of the whole of the native population'. However, noting that the British government had desired only to 'protect and conciliate' the island's aborigines, the Committee was satisfied that those surviving 'Tasmans', who had been 'relocated' to Flinders Island (all of whom were ultimately to perish), were being treated humanely.[32] After all, the Archdeacon of New South Wales and Van Diemen's Land, Broughton had professed to be 'persuaded their happiness and every point in which we could wish them well, were increased by the removal'.[33] Such a construction, of course, suited those engaged in the forcible colonisation of Tasmania very well.

Even where active genocide was not in prospect, the moral corruption of native populations at the hands of uncontrolled British interests provided a further imperative for intervention, and one which could similarly be appropriated by local settler and official interests. Indigenous corruption could most effectively be countered not by the withdrawal of unruly Britons, but by the more effective imposition of a properly constituted governmental order. This was most clearly demonstrated in the case of New Zealand, where there were about 2,000 British subjects and several trading ships anchored in the Bay of Islands at any one time, and on the 'South Seas' islands, which were visited by hundreds of British trading vessels.[34] As far as the Maoris and the Pacific Islanders were concerned, the Committee felt that

> it will be hard . . . to find compensation . . . for the murders, the misery, the contamination which we have brought upon them. Our runaway con-victs are the pest of savage as well as civilized society; so are our runaway sailors; and the crews of our whaling vessels, and of the traders from New South Wales, too frequently act in the most reckless and immoral manner when at a distance from the restraints of justice.

Evidence of the degradation of which Britons were capable when un-constrained by proper authority included the horrifying assertion that 'Till lately the tattooed heads of New Zealanders were sold at Sydney as objects of curiosity'.[35]

It was in relation to this state of colonial anarchy that the Committee made its most explicit connection between the untutored barbarians of the colonies and the 'degraded' underclasses of Britain. As the Wesleyan Secretary Rev. Beecham noted in his evidence to the Committee, 'Our own country may perhaps be regarded as the best specimen that can be produced of a civilized nation; but there is a very considerable portion of the population even of this country which cannot be said, in the correct sense of the expression, to be thoroughly and properly civilized'.[36] And, tragically, it was representatives of this 'uncivilised' portion of Britain's population who were coming into 'first contact' with the Maori and South Seas islanders. As the most degraded representatives of the metropole, they had the greatest potential to introduce these indigenes to 'knowledge of depraved acts and licentious gratifications of the most debased inhabitants of our great cities', leading inevitably to both the decline and the corruption of the local population.[37] In parts of Australia too, of course, where British authority *was* provisionally established, aborigines were still subject to 'the contamination of the dregs of our countrymen'.[38]

The Committee's response to these examples of anarchic, uncontrolled colonisation – one that was to be seized upon in settlers' defence by the *Graham's Town Journal* – was to advocate a strengthened colonial inter-vention, rather than a withdrawal of British interference. The Committee endeavoured to ensure that further colonisation proceeded under humanely constituted governmental authorities. These authorities, in South Australia and New Zealand, would impose the kind of restraints on colonial Britons to which their metropolitan counterparts were being exposed under a reforming, bourgeois-dominated government. The Committee was satisfied that 'the preliminary measures for the formation of settlement' in South Australia made it 'likely to be undertaken in a better spirit than any such enterprises that have come before our notice' – a conclusion that was largely the result of a new governor, Sir James Stirling's more 'conciliatory measures towards the neighbouring tribes'.[39]

Imperial expansion was thus vital to the protection of indigenes – an argument that would later be deployed in the pursuit of confederation to allow the more effective exploitation of minerals in South Africa as well as countless other expansionist schemes elsewhere in the late nineteenth century. The Committee, however, did not stop at establishing the prevention of genocide and indigenous corruption as rationales for further colonial intervention. In British Guiana, for instance, the rapaciousness of settlers was less evident, but this did not mean that humanitarian programmes were being fulfilled. The native tribes 'have been almost wholly neglected, are retrograding, and are without provision for their moral or civil advancement . . . They are brought into acquaintance with civilized life not to partake its blessings, but only to feel the severity of its penal sanctions'.[40] The failure to effect the moral improvement of 'aborigines', then, was a crime almost on a par with their active destruction.

The corrective vision of colonialism upheld by the committee rested upon a notion of fair and equal exchange. The nature of this exchange becomes apparent in a question which Buxton asked of the Rev. William Shaw during one of the Committee's sittings:

> Is it your opinion, that we, having driven them [the Xhosa] from so large a space of country which they had previously occupied, are under an obligation to confer upon them all the benefits of knowledge, civilization, education and Christianity that it is in our power to bestow?[41]

Of course, Shaw answered in the affirmative. Colonialism, then, was to be a compact between coloniser and colonised, the loss of the latter's independence and the historic loss of some of their land being compensated by the benefits of civilisation in the here-and-now as well as salvation in the after-life.

Within this moral scheme, it was not the imperative for practical measures to constrain settler expansion which loomed largest. Far more significant in the Committee's deliberations was the question of which 'recompense' should come first: Christianity or civilisation. Virtually every witness before the Committee who had some connection with the church or with government in the colonies was asked this question and pages of evidence were collected on it.[42] Ultimately the Committee agreed with the evidence supplied by Ellis that Christianity was essential to the reformation of the individual character that, in time, brought true civilisation. This was a response reminiscent of Philip's earlier condemnation of Governor Somerset for his insistence on the use of cutlery as the only sign of civilised achievement. As Ellis stated:

> An inferior kind of civilization may precede Christianity, and prevail without it to a limited extent; such, for instance, as the adoption, by comparatively rude tribes, of the dress and modes of living of more cultivated society, a taste for their arts, manufactures and comforts. All this may occur without any change of character. This kind of civilization is only superficial; it may polish and smooth the exterior of human society, but it leaves the deep foundations of crime and wretchedness, the vices of human nature, which are the causes of all barbarism in every part of the world, untouched, and consequently supplies no sufficient remedy for the evils to be removed.

On the other hand, 'Christianity has never been introduced into any nation or tribe where civilization has not invariably followed'.[43] Beecham also testified that 'the savage . . . must be made to feel the importance of the truths of religion before he will discover anything desirable in the quietness and sobriety of civilized life, or will dare to break through his superstitions in order to subdue it', and William Williams, a Pacific islands missionary, asserted that 'There must be an impetus given to the mind before [indigenous peoples] will aspire to . . . improvements'.[44]

However unintended on the part of Philip and Buxton, from such observations flowed the inference that Christianity could have the effect of further undermining indigenous resistance to such colonisation. Given Methodism's role in the 'pacification' of the British working classes, it was perhaps no coincidence that it was Beecham, Secretary of the Wesleyan Missionary Society, who stated this most explicitly. For him, the native's 'superstitions are generally found opposed to any change in his accustomed course of life . . . It is only when the truths of the Gospel produce their powerful effect upon the minds of the heathen, and arouse them to a consideration of their higher destinies . . . that they will dare to break through the bondage of their superstitions, and forsake their paternal customs, which are generally bound up with the superstitions themselves'.[45] They would thus become more receptive to other 'civilising' endeavours. As Beecham continued, 'Christianity furnishes a complete moral machinery for carrying forward all the great processes which lie at the root of civilization'.[46]

Ellis looked to the experience of converts on the Pacific Islands as proof of the transformative effects of religion. There, it was the desire to acquire knowledge of Biblical passages that had given rise to literacy, and it was the appropriation of Christian principles which had led to the phasing out of indigenous practices of slavery. 'Christianity condemned indolence, *required industry*, and supplied inducements to labour; and the natives, since they embraced Christianity, have acquired a knowledge of a number of useful manual arts.'[47] Following from this assertion, Ellis was also able to be quite explicit about the inextricable ties between the missions' cultural endeavours and the penetration of a particularly moral kind of capitalism: *'now they have new wants*; a number of articles of clothing and commerce are necessary to their comfort, and they cultivate the soil to supply them'.[48]

Finally, Christianity was a first, vital step towards ensuring proper gender relations. As Beecham explained, 'it enforces that the husband shall be faithful to his one wife, it enjoins also that he love her as his own flesh; and thus it raises woman from that state to which heathenism invariably depresses her'.[49] The Rev. Stephen Kay referred to concrete examples in Xhosaland. There, before the missionaries brought Christian teachings, women were in 'the lowest possible state of degradation, in which they were doomed to the drudgery of building, digging, sowing, reaping, &c.' Around the missions though, 'numbers have been raised to the comforts of social life, having exchanged the field for the domestic circle, in which, as wives and as mothers, they are now found attending to household duties, almost exclusively; a change which nothing, I conceive, short of a powerful conviction of their being fellow immortals, could have induced the Caffre to allow'.[50]

This emphasis on the need for inner salvation before real civilisation could be achieved, led the Committee on to an explicit riposte of the settler construction of the 'irreclaimable savage'. The current, widespread failure to 'civilise' did not mean that the native was unicivilisable. The settlers of North America, for instance were wrong 'to banish the Indians from the neighbourhood of the white population, on the supposition that they are not capable of being reclaimed or elevated into a civilized or well ordered community'. It was just that the wrong kind of civilisation had thus far been pursued. A concentration on the secular goals of the adoption of European-style clothing, housing, agriculture and trade would have to wait until the inner self had been awakened and reformed. At the very least, 'the two objects [should] be pursued simultaneously'.[51]

In the committee's rationalisation of humanitarian discourse and of a humanitarian imagined geography of the world, then, Christianity was the most remarkable panacea to all colonial ills, temporal and spiritual. And with their global reach and their special place in God's favour, Britons of the right kind were the people most fitted to effect that panacea. However, the emphasis on heathens' need for reclamation and barbarians' need for civilisation at the hands of the British was, of course, one which could be deployed most effectively by the very settlers whose activities the Select Committee was most concerned to refute. In articulating the ways in which colonial expansion and interference could be considered legitimate, the Committee was unwittingly providing greater scope for colonial officials, settlers and traders across the empire to enframe all of their actions within a moral discourse. As we will see in the next chapter, the humanitarian attempt to counter settler notions of indigenous irreclaimability was to fail during the mid and late nineteenth century, largely because it was inadequately prepared to deal with the question of indigenous resistance to a British 'civilising' mission that was newly enframed in these moral terms.

Models of colonialism and humanitarian geographies

During the mid-1830s, though, before humanitarianism had succumbed to the material interests of settlers and the strategic planning of officials, rosy prospects of a forthcoming 'golden age' in colonial relations could be entertained. Exactly the kind of internal and exterior reformation which humanitarians sought could already be found in communities attached to missions across the globe.

In North America, the River Credit Mission was invoked as a model: 'About ten years ago' the people there 'had no houses, no fields nor horses, no cattle, no pigs, and no poultry . . . They are now occupying about 40 comfortable houses' containing furniture, crockery and cutlery. 'Some have clocks and watches.' Furthermore, and indicative of the necessary deeper reformation of manners, there had been a 'great amelioration of the condition of the women, who have been raised from the drudgery of beasts of burthen, and are now treated with consideration by their husbands'.[52] In Tahiti, acceptance of Christianity had similarly paved the way for an enduring system of order. An 'explicit and wholesome *code of laws* . . . is printed and circulated among them, understood by all, and acknowledged by all as the supreme rule of action for all classes in their civil and social relations'.[53]

In the Cape, of course, there was the exemplary Kat River settlement, whose genesis was examined in chapter 2. There, the Khoesan freed by Ordinance 50 had been told 'Show yourselves worthy of freedom, and your farther improvement is in your own power'.[54] Philip testified before the Committee not only that the Kat River Settlement's inhabitants had proved themselves worthy of their emancipation, but that their success could serve as a model for unreclaimed metropolitan groups as well.[55] Once they had been given the property that they had contended for, the Committee was gratified that the Kat River 'settlers' were now 'as covetous and litigious about land and water as any other set of colonists'.[56]

It was the Kat River's radical missionary, James Read, who did most to extol its success before the Committee in London. He neatly deployed the narrative of hard-won prosperity that was simultaneously being used by Godlonton in defence of the British settlers, on behalf of their 'coloured' counterparts.[57] For Read and, subsequently for the Committee, the most important lesson from the experience of the Kat River was that 'it took at its very commencement a religious character, to which . . . may be ascribed its subsequent well-doing'.[58] It was the influence of religion which had enabled the freed Khoesan there to become 'a more moral and a better conducted class than a very great number of the lower class of settlers residing in South Africa'. Even for the hard-bitten Stockenström, the improvement in manners, morality and productivity that had taken place in the settlement 'was almost like magic'.[59]

In the Committee's discourse, The Kat River, and other colonial locales where the missionary-led transformation of subjectivities had begun, would act as the models for a far broader, trans-imperial societal change revolving around the concepts of order, justice and economy. In order to effect such change at a more global scale, however, the more effective co-ordination of humanitarian networks remained a priority. This was an agenda most explicitly set out before the Committee in 1835 by another favoured witness, Saxe Bannister.

As we saw in chapter 2, in 1830 Bannister had already published his own book, *Humane Policy*, in an endeavour to mobilise metropolitan public opinion against official and settler practices in the Cape. Before the Committee, he advocated the construction of a more tightly knitted web of imperial communication in order to build upon the achievements of such publicity.[60] He declared,

> The documents and proceedings which show our relations with the Aborigines are not enough known, and unless from day to day, and from year to year, more is known in England of what passes in all the colonies, and more is known in each colony of what is passing in other colonies, it is extremely probable there will be a recurrence of mistakes leading to fatal consequences . . . I would say, that there should be a system of publicity, to a very extensive degree, immediately instituted'.[61]

In Bannister's scheme, the British parliament would be a more effective node at the centre of imperial communication, receiving published information on officials' and settlers' actions in each colony and disseminating it outwards again to the other colonies. The lessons of colonialism could thus be learnt more effectively at both metropolitan and colonial sites:

> The advantage of printing, and sending to each colony what is happening amongst its neighbours, would be, that each would be judged of by impartial people in other circumstances, and frequently would be adopted, so that they would have an interchange; but they all ought to come home.[62]

As well as using the flourishing colonial press to carry this flow of information, Bannister proposed that the political infrastructure connecting metropole and colony, which currently operated largely in the interests of settlers and officials, be deployed in favour of indigenes. 'An agency in London for the affairs of all aborigines is an essential part of this plan. The colonists have always found agents in London for their own affairs indispensable . . . The aborigines of all the colonies have greater need of this than the colonists.' Furthermore, the British metropole was to play a key role in cultivating 'civilised' and 'educated' 'natives' to return to the colonies and disseminate the learning that they had acquired in Britain. In other words, Britain, and London in particular, would act not only as a node of information exchange, but as the cosmopolitan centre of global instruction and the locus of humane imperial knowledge.[63] This would be the ultimate achievement of the humanitarian geographical imagination.

In the wake of the Committee's hearings, Bannister's objectives would continue to be pursued. While it had little immediate political impact outside of the Cape,[64] the Committee's report continued to be seen as a humanitarian manifesto and, as Andrew Porter has noted, it remained to influence Buxton's and other humanitarians' approaches to the post-abolition 'regeneration' of West Africa.[65] More immediately, after the Committee's dissolution, the Quaker ethnologist Dr Thomas Hodgkin, who had testified that even 'the slave trade and slavery was, with all its abominations, a smaller evil' than 'the influence of our colonization in Africa and in America', was galvanised to establish a permanent organisation in order to pursue the matters that the Committee had raised.[66] His British and Foreign Aborigines' Protection Society was instituted in 1837, with Buxton himself as its first president. The Society aimed 'to assist in protecting the defenceless and promoting the advancement of Uncivilized Tribes' by guiding colonial policy through the publication of materials and the mobilisation of 'popular opinion'.[67]

The Select Committee and the Cape

The Committee's humanitarian summation of colonising activities at the Cape in particular began with a brief history of the Dutch colonisation centring on the conquest and subordination of the Khoesan. This was based largely on Philip's *Researches* and other humanitarian treatises. The Bushmen were represented as being 'hunted down like wild beasts' while, for the Khoesan as a whole, 'the system of oppression . . . never slacked till the Hottentot nation were cut off, and the small remnant left were reduced to abject bondage'. The British colonial government, after making some 'feeble efforts' at the Khoesan's emancipation 'suffered the boors [*sic*] to retain them'. The Caledon Code in particular had done 'much towards riveting their chains'. It was only the crowning humanitarian achievement of Ordinance 50, 'a measure of admirable justice', which had secured their freedom and recognised their rights.[68] The Ordinance had 'operated as the removal of a weight which had kept down the spring of the people's energy'.[69]

The remainder of the Committee's history of the Cape pivoted on two specific instances of British injustice towards the Xhosa. First, there was the seizure of the ceded territory and the interference on Ngqika's behalf against Ndlambe in the late 1810s, and secondly, the successive, unjust expulsions of Maqoma from the Kat River area in 1829 and 1833. While the Committee had concluded that there was no effective colonial government in New Zealand, that on the Cape frontier, it seemed, had an 'appearance of caprice, and of a confusion' which rendered its workings 'perfectly unintelligible' to both colonist and Xhosa.[70] It was this deficiency of government, combined with settler acquisitiveness, which, the Committee concluded, had been the major cause of the 1834–5 war.

In constructing this history of British provocation on the Cape frontier, the Committee paid especial attention to the letters despatched by Philip, and to the testimony that he gave in person. At one point, Philip employed the same trope of vulnerable females in need of protection as he had earlier wielded in favour of the settlers (see p. 53), only now his intervention was on the side of the Xhosa. He appealed that it was

> truly heartrending to listen to their complaints, and the complaints of the men were almost forgotten in the distress of the women and children, who were literally perishing, being stricken through for want of the fruits of the field and the milk that had been the means of their support, their cows having been carried away by the [colonial] patrols.[71]

A further effective tactic, employed in Philip's written testimony was that of 'quoting' the words of Xhosa chiefs themselves. This involved 'translating' their protestations into English, but in particular accordance with those conventions of European rhetoric designed to affect the audience's sensibilities. Philip described a letter transcribed from Maqoma's speech, for instance, as exemplifying 'a beautiful simplicity, a touching pathos, a confiding magnanimity, a dignified remonstrance, which shows its author to be no common man, and to be worthy of the friendship and confidence of the British Government'.[72] Partly because of Philip's representations, whether or not the Xhosa were genuinely capable of expressing their experiences and feelings, unassisted, and in such a way that European sensibilities *could* be aroused by them, became an important issue of debate between humanitarians and settler-apologists during the Committee's hearings.[73]

Apart from making available the written translations of Xhosa chiefs' words in his testimony, Philip also brought 'authentic native' voices to bear more directly. He travelled from the Cape to attend the hearings in the company not only of his LMS colleague James Read, but also of Andries Stoeffels, a Christian Khoesan from the Kat River settlement, and Dyani Tshatshu, the converted Gqunukhwebe Xhosa chief. In bringing these two men forward as witnesses, as Elbourne has argued, Philip was trying to produce the Cape's black people, or at least these Christianised and literate representatives, as speaking 'native subjects', able to generate statements with a particular claim to truth. As well as testifying before the Committee, Stoeffels and Tshatshu travelled across England, being lionised at evangelical dinner parties, presented before the annual meeting of the LMS at Exeter Hall and represented on the frontispiece of the *Evangelical Magazine*, where Tshatshu was shown posing with a regal air in Western military garb and Stoeffels was portrayed as 'the honest worker'.[74] As Elbourne comments,

Philip showed off the Africans as 'occular proof' of the feasibility of remaking primitive man' in the image prescribed by humanitarian discourse. After Stoeffels and Tshatshu had impressed the assembled company at a London dinner party by singing hymns and making speeches, Philip exclaimed ironically, 'These are [D'Urban's] irreclaimable savages!'[75]

However, Elbourne also adverts to the ways that these representatives of reclaimed African humanity had to distance themselves from popular conceptions of African-ness if they were to have the desired political impact. After meeting them, a Mrs Upcher wrote to her friend,

Enter Dr Philip with his tail, *such* a tail – The Caffre chief a fine personable man – handsomely dressed in a military coat blue and gold, he has a good forehead & more – I will go no lower, lest I should affront you as I have affronted myself for fancying (I will just whisper in [your] ear) that his mouth caricatured a Negro's! Oh! For shame to breathe it especially as their champion protests there is *nothing African* in his countenance.[76]

The actual testimony supplied by Stoeffels and Tshatshu to the Committee was frequently drowned out by the existing preoccupations of a humanitarian discourse that had its own established agendas, both domestic and colonial. Thus Tshatshu's calls for metropolitan Britons to disown their brethren at the Cape – 'they are South Africans, they are not Englishmen' – were overshadowed by Philip's endeavours to prove that the chief had developed a good understanding of the Bible, and thus of literacy.[77] Tshatshu tried to point out the frustrations that Xhosa chiefs experienced in orientating missionaries to their own worldly concerns. He described how, in one of Philip's meetings with the chiefs, the missionary director had 'pressed upon Macomo [Maqoma] the necessity of having Sandile' and his own children educated in Kayser's missionary school. Tshatshu testified that Maqoma had responded: 'Yes, all that you have said is very good, but I am shot every day, my huts are set fire to, and I can only sleep with one eye open and the other shut. I do not know where my place is, and how can I get my children to be instructed'.[78] Even if most metropolitan humanitarians condemned the colonial aggression which had prompted Maqoma's outburst, the point that he, and Tshatshu in turn, were making about the missionaries' priorities was lost. When Buxton enquired whether the spread of Christianity would be some recompense for 'the injuries which Europeans have done to the natives of Africa', Tshatshu could reply only that 'I come here to complain'.[79]

When the Committee did consider the provocations to the Xhosa caused by the spoor law and the commandos that enforced it, it was the colonial administrator and frontiersman Stockenström's evidence, rather than that of the Xhosa chief Tshatshu, which proved decisive. The Committee's summation contained extensive extracts from the minutes of Stockenström's testimony.

Included within them was the critical assertion that when the Xhosa's cattle were taken, they 'have nothing else to live on; they consequently try to keep possession and defend themselves: this is "resistance;" we then use violence, they are shot, and at last comes war, and war without end. It is in vain to attempt to civilize and christianize, if people have nothing to eat'. If the prevailing system of provoking war and then punishing through the confiscation of land continued, argued Stockenström, 'We will go from one line to another, and we will take one slice of the country after another, and as long as you continue to take the people's cattle, so long will this take place, and you will go from river to river till you get to Delagoa Bay'.[80] Thus, injustice and expense were again conflated, and the necessity to challenge prevailing official and settler discourses of colonialism, on both grounds, confirmed.

In order to get the Committee's report accepted by the end of the 1837 parliamentary session, Buxton was forced to compromise on the most scathing criticisms that he had intended to make of the Cape's colonial authorities and the British settlers. Along with the other humanitarian committee members, he had to be content to name the cause of the constant insecurity along the frontier in general terms, as 'the systematic forgetfulness of the principles of justice in our treatment of the native possessors of the soil'.[81] Nevertheless, the hearings of the Select Committee influenced Glenelg directly during 1835 and informed his decision, made at the end of that year, to renounce Queen Adelaide Province. Philip's own view, that the province should now be retained provided that the Xhosa were subjected to humanitarian rather than settler influences within it, was made clear to the Select Committee in July 1836, too late to influence Glenelg's response.[82]

Although Glenelg remarked critically upon Stockenström's role in expelling Maqoma from the Kat River, it was his evidence that proved decisive with the Secretary of State as well as with the Select Committee. In his private notes on the minutes of Stockenström's testimony, Glenelg jotted entries such as: 'so long as the Caffre cattle are taken peace is impossible', and 'patroles [*sic*] are decidedly the main cause of the misfortunes of the frontier'.[83] In response to D'Urban's assertion that the Xhosa had invaded the colony without excuse, Glenelg wrote 'far from it'.[84] Further evidence of the influence of the Committee's hearings as a whole can be found in one of Glenelg's early despatches to D'Urban. The Secretary of State informed his governor that

> The cost of the war is the least of the causes of regret the continuation of the war would cause the people of Great Britain. Indeed, it is a melancholy and humiliating but an indisputable truth that the contiguity of the subjects of the nations of Christendom with uncivilised tribes has invariably produced wretchedness and decay and not seldom the utter extermination of the weaker party.[85]

The death of Hintsa and the Court of Enquiry

Despite the Gcaleka Xhosa's lack of direct involvement in the war, the Gcaleka paramount Hintsa had been killed during the 1834–5 campaign. As well as being lodged in the collective Xhosa memory as an instance of colonial treachery and barbarism, his death would serve further to define an ascendant humanitarian discourse in opposition to those of Cape officials and settlers, even if in a more roundabout fashion.[86]

Hintsa's death

During the late stages of the war, frustrated by his inability to clear Xhosa resisters out of the Amatola mountain range near the Cape's frontier, Harry Smith had led a column of Khoesan and British troops, backed by Afrikaner and British colonists, across the Kei River and into 'neutral' Gcaleka territory. There is no doubt that the Gcaleka had been assisting the frontier Rharhabe chiefdoms in their struggle against the British indirectly, particularly by sheltering their cattle. But Smith was determined to prove that the Xhosa's attack on the colony was a grand plan orchestrated by Hintsa himself, rather than the response of those frontier chiefs who had most directly experienced land loss and harassment at the hands of the colony. Smith's invasion force was intended both to punish the Gcaleka and to undermine the capacity of the frontier chiefdoms to continue resisting by seizing as many cattle as possible and returning with them to the colony. As we saw above, the column also brought Mfengu clients of the Gcaleka across into the colony where they would act as allies and labourers.

In his endeavours to round up the Gcaleka's cattle, Smith had had Hintsa taken captive when he had come to the British camp to negotiate terms. The chief was to instruct his followers to hand over their livestock and to lead the column towards them. When Hintsa, however, tried to escape on horseback, Smith, who had been riding alongside him at the front of the column, chased after him and tried to shoot him. His gun failed, so he threw it at the chief and unsaddled him. Despite being shot and wounded in the leg and torso by pursuing troops, Hintsa managed to limp into a gully and hide behind some rocks. Khoesan witnesses serving with the British force later described how a British settler, George Southey then shot and killed the chief as he was calling out for mercy. Southey himself maintained that Hintsa was about to throw a spear at him, and that his shot was fired in self-defence. After his death, Hintsa's ears were cut off and kept by colonists or soldiers as trophies, while others tried to dig out his teeth. Some witnesses suggested that soldiers even cut off his genitals as mementoes.[87]

Glenelg heard of the manner of Hintsa's death during the period in which he was weighing up the claims of humanitarians and Cape officials. In the Cape, Philip had collated information on the incident from the man who was to become Godlonton's rival newspaper editor in Graham's Town,

Dr Ambrose Campbell, and from the GMS missionary, Rev. John Ross. These men in turn had apparently heard the testimony of Khoesan soldiers and of a translator who had been accompanying Smith's column when Hintsa was killed. Philip passed the local reports on to Buxton and his associates in London, where Anna Gurney drew up a pamphlet to be submitted for the Colonial Office's consideration. It seems to have had a remarkable effect on both Glenelg and Stephen.

The Secretary of State was profoundly shocked and disappointed at the news, describing the killing and especially the mutilation as unbecoming of 'Englishmen' and a stain on the character of Britain's imperial mission. Buxton wrote to Gurney:

> You remember how cold used to be my reception at the Colonial Office when I talked about South Africa – Kaffirs – aborigines . . . I went there yesterday – saw Glenelg . . . and Stephen – I found the atmosphere changed to blood – almost to fever heat. They talked of Hintza – Southey – Philip . . . D'Urban with absolute familiarity – intimated that they would revoke D'Urban – restore the country to its owners – acknowledge error and national disgrace . . . Stephen said . . . 'I am lost in astonishment, indignation, shame, and repentance'.[88]

Glenelg became rapidly convinced of the reason why D'Urban and Smith had launched hostilities against Hintsa and his Gcaleka followers in the first place. He wrote to the governor informing him that he was well aware that there were many settlers who would be gratified by Hintsa's identification as a colonial enemy. After all, his fertile country was rich in cattle, 'offering a far more tempting prospect of indemnity, or of gain', than the lands of the frontier chiefs who had actually invaded the colony.[89] Glenelg also told D'Urban that he had irrefutable evidence that Hintsa, having been knocked off his horse and wounded in his bid for freedom, had cried for mercy. Although the Khoesan soldiers present had 'granted the boon', the settler Scout, George Southey, had disregarded his pleas, killing him in cold blood. As if that was not appalling enough, the king's body was then 'basely and inhumanly mutilated'.[90]

The repercussions

As Thomas Lacquer has argued, the humanitarian discourse of the late eighteenth and early nineteenth centuries was at its most compelling when it centred upon and publicised the details of cruelty inflicted on individual bodies.[91] Hintsa's death and his body's mutilation provided an extraordinarily powerful symbol that could stand for the much broader set of colonising processes against which humanitarians were campaigning. After reading of the particularities of the mutilation, Glenelg underlined the following section in one of the letters that Buxton had submitted to him:

'the Caffres have no prospect in view, unless some powerful exertion be made on their behalf, than extermination or rather death' in the manner of Hintsa himself; 'there is no chance of mercy being manifested towards them in this part of the Colony'.[92] What had happened to Hintsa – an unprovoked death followed by a savage mutilation – was thus emblematic of the entire process of colonialism in the Cape in its current form, and as we saw from the deliberations of the Select Committee, the Cape in turn was representative of colonial practices as a whole.

Hintsa's treatment was also symptomatic of D'Urban and the settlers' construction of the Xhosa as 'irreclaimable savages'. Glenelg was personally offended by this appellation. Finding it difficult 'to describe the pain with which I have read [this phrase] and laid [it] before His Majesty', he informed the governor that 'there is, I fear, little prospect of reconciling your estimate of the Kaffre character with mine'. Of the settlers, he noted, with Hintsa's fate in mind, that 'these claimants to the exclusive title of human beings have found little difficulty in defending, at least to their own satisfaction, whatever measures were necessary to the subjugation or destruction of the enemy'.[93]

Philip agitated for the institution of a Court of Enquiry so that the significance of Hintsa's death could be more forcefully driven home for the metropolitan public at large. Through a full enquiry, he felt that:

> You will teach even the men of our Colonies to call things by their proper names, cover such deeds with everlasting infamy and compel the English Government to introduce on the Frontier of our Colonies a system of international law and prevent the British name from being [handed] down to posterity like that of the Spanish loaded with the execrations of all Nations.[94]

In response, Buxton spoke privately with Glenelg and, in addition to establishing the Aborigines Committee in London, his government instructed D'Urban to institute a military enquiry into the killing of Hintsa.

On hearing of Hintsa's death and a version of its circumstances from Smith, D'Urban had already anticipated that such a reaction might occur. In a letter to his secretary in Cape Town, he wrote that although he considered Hintsa 'a most irreclaimable and treacherous villain, of the most villainous race that I have ever been acquainted with', he was sorry for his death 'in as much as it may serve as a handle of mischief to a certain Party at home'. His secretary had replied, 'I understand they [the humanitarians] are in Cape Town already making it out to be a most atrocious murder'.[95] And indeed, it was largely the humanitarians' construction of events that was shared by the British press, which first picked up on the news from Fairbairn's *South African Commercial Advertiser*. When D'Urban supplied an official version of events, the popular journal *John Bull*, mocked it:

In the present History, his Majesty King Hintza takes a ride with Colonel Smith . . . in order to make the English a present of 25 000 cows and 500 horses [the indemnity demanded by Smith of the Gcaleka for their support of the hostile chiefs]; but because his Majesty took it into his head to ride a little faster than the gallant Colonel liked, that gentleman snaps a pistol at him . . . and when he runs away, 'Southey the younger' shoots his Majesty first through the leg and then in the ribs. His Majesty hides himself under a rock, and Colonel Smith is half frantic, but 'Southey the younger' spies the King a minute or two after, and by way of an agreeable windup of the day, shoots his Majesty through the crown of the head, and, having thus exterminated the Monarch who was on the point of giving us 25 000 cows and 500 horses, 'Southey the younger' strips him of his girdle, his bracelets, and his red and white bead necklaces, and Sir Benjamin D'Urban announces that we have added 7 000 square miles to the Colony.[96]

The LMS's influential *Missionary Chronicle* published William Ellis's speech before the annual Exeter Hall meeting, which also adverted to the incident. Ellis said of the settlers in the Cape in general that 'They have mutilated and mangled the corpses of their enemies. They have cut off their ears and brought them away as trophies, and the individuals who have done this have been celebrated'.[97] More soberly, the Whig *Edinburgh Review* reported that, in his final moments, the wounded Hintsa, 'up to his waist in water, leaned against a rock for support, and begged for mercy; the Hottentots heard his prayer and spared him, but a British officer, climbing the rock above him, shot the unfortunate chief'.[98]

Against this backdrop of metropolitan distaste for colonial aggression in the Cape, the military Court of Enquiry into Hintsa's Death became in a sense a microcosm of contemporary imperial political interrelations: on the one hand, there was a diversity of colonial interests, with settlers defending the culpable colonial scouts, colonial officials and soldiers closing ranks behind both Harry Smith and George Southey, and local humanitarians appealing vociferously to both the Cape and metropolitan authorities for justice. And on the other hand, there was a liberal metropolitan concern prompted by the British humanitarians' condemnation of the settlers, and enormously resented by those settlers and their officials in the periphery.

Unlike the Aborigines Committee, however, the Court of Enquiry was held at Fort Wilshire, on the Cape frontier itself, and most of the witnesses were soldiers under Smith's command. This altered its dynamics considerably from those that had enabled humanitarians to dominate the Aborigines Committee.[99] Colonel Wade had appreciated the significance of the location of any enquiry when he had protested about the Select Committee hearings being held exclusively in London. He stated his wish to 'protest against the "representations" or "statements" in question being admitted as in any degree proving the correctness of the accusations with which [officials and settlers in the Cape] have been assailed, without a formal and public investigation *there*, where alone it can be instituted with any reasonable hope of the truth'.[100] Certainly, the truth established by the Court of Enquiry in the Cape itself would be a more ambiguous one.

The Court of Enquiry investigators consisted of a number of field officers led by the most senior military officer in the colony, Lt.-Col. John Hare. They were invested with the power to recommend a court martial if they found sufficient evidence of wrongdoing in the case of any individual soldier.[101] As the officer in command, and the man who had ordered that Hintsa be taken captive after his entry into the camp to negotiate, and fired upon in the event of his escape, Harry Smith had much to fear. This was why he tried, largely unsuccessfully, to get D'Urban to rig the court in his favour through the appointment of old friends. Apart from Smith himself, the man most likely to be condemned as the result of any enquiry was George Southey, who was widely known to have fired the fatal shot. However, he was a civilian settler who had been acting ostensibly as a guide, and the military court's only sanction as far as he was concerned was a potentially embarrassing loss of reputation.

During the hearings, Smith contradicted many of the assertions contained in the official reports that he had written soon after the incident. He clearly instructed his military subordinates to conform to a new, embellished description of events. Hintsa, it seemed, was not being held as a prisoner in the British camp; he had merely volunteered himself as a hostage until his followers had paid their war reparations in full. Treacherously, he had plotted to lead Smith into a gully in which hundreds, perhaps thousands of his warriors were positioned, ready to fall upon the small British column as soon as their King was free. After Smith had failed to halt his flight, however, George Southey had bravely pursued the king into the bush and, seeing Hintsa about to throw an assegai, shot him through the head in self-defence.[102]

In attempting to establish this version of events, Smith was privileged by a concession made before the court even began sitting. He would be allowed to take part in the examination of other witnesses even though he was himself a key witness. As Pretorius notes, this 'ensured that the witnesses, almost all of whom were soldiers or had taken part in the campaign and were his subordinates, would give the kind of information he desired'.[103] Leading questions from Smith certainly assisted them in doing so. Smith subjected one of the Khoesan witnesses, Nicolas, who had been the first to supply Philip, *via* Ross and Campbell, with the information that Hintsa had been shot while crying out for mercy, to an especially intensive interrogation. Faced with the question from his superior officer, 'You say [Hintsa] turned his head when he stood up [just before being shot by Southey]. Did he do so as a Kaffir does when he is about the throw an assegai', the subordinate Nicolas had little option but to answer 'yes'.[104]

Nevertheless, the Court saw through most of Smith's fabrications. In response to the claim that the gully into which Hintsa had attempted to escape was full of hostile Xhosa, and that the safety of the small column was in jeopardy, the presiding officers enquired why, rather than retiring, the troops had advanced a further 50 miles into Gcaleka territory the next day. The Court's conclusion was that there was 'no satisfactory proof of [Hintsa] having . . . meditated an attack upon, or any other act of treachery towards, the British force'. The findings concerning Hintsa's last moments also confirmed the allegations of the Khoesan troops and humanitarians that the chief had been seeking simply to elude his pursuers rather than leading them into a trap. The Court decided that 'there is no direct evidence . . . that the Chief either did attempt resistance, or that he could have offered any effectual resistance . . . so severely wounded as it is proved he then was'. However, the Court was deliberately ambiguous as to Southey's actions, stating that he had fired the fatal shot 'from the impulse of the moment and very possibly form a sense of personal danger also'. The issue of Hintsa's mutilation was also fudged. On the one hand, it was pronounced that Hintsa's ears had definitely been cut off, an act 'so barbarous, and so contrary to the uses of civilised warfare', that the Court could not 'but feel pain and indignation that it should have been perpetrated by any person or persons calling themselves Englishmen'. On the other hand, 'in the midst of so much conflicting and contradictory Evidence . . . they are unable to fix this foul act on any person in particular'.[105]

Smith's behind-the-scenes preparations, then, may not have convinced the Court of the truth of his testimony, but they allowed for the intimidation of the humanitarians' key witnesses and the renunciation of the evidence which they had given earlier to Campbell and Ross. This proved enough to prevent specific charges being levelled, and indeed to produce a statement from the Court exonerating Smith himself from any blame for the king's death.

The significance of the Court of Enquiry, however, lies not so much in its failure to censure specific individuals. Rather, as an investigation of one specific instance of colonial barbarism, it served to highlight the abominations of prevailing colonial projects, and the degradation of which British settlers were capable in the distant colonies. It thus reinforced the conclusions of the Select Committee on Aborigines. Like the later debate on the Morant Bay Revolt and Governor Eyre's reaction to it in Jamaica, at the heart of the struggle over Hintsa's death lay the issue of legitimate conduct at both collective and individual levels. Just as an arbitrary, personalised and often brutal, aristocratic mode of authority was being replaced by a humane, bourgeois-led order at home, so arbitrary acts of personal degradation like the killing and mutilation of an African king, would have to be prevented overseas through the construction of a more modern and systematic, philanthropic state of discipline.

Taken together, the Aborigines Committee, with its macro-scale interest in the broad affairs of empire and the Court of Enquiry into Hintsa's death, with its micro-scale focus on a single, symbolic and emotive instance of horror, defined the political programmes of bourgeois-led colonial humanitarianism at the peak of its power. Both enquiring bodies made it abundantly clear that there was a pressing need for 'fair dealing and . . . Christian instruction' in order to redress the wrongs inflicted by settler colonisation.[106] Both helped establish humanitarianism as a model of colonialism distinct from, and opposed to, alternative and existing governmental and settler models. The Aborigines Committee and the Court of Enquiry into Hintsa's death made it clear that if colonial governments and settlers were to fulfil their objectives in the remainder of the nineteenth century, they had to be able to convince the metropolitan government, and even the British public at large, that they were constructing an appropriately moralising and improving form of authority. However, the irony is that in crystallising humanitarian discourse, in defining and articulating various avenues of imperial intervention and expansion as morally legitimate within their terms of reference, these enquiries indicated the ways in which antithetical interests could provide just such legitimation for the projects of control, appropriation and subordination that humanitarians railed against.

Official and settler counter-mobilisation: the beginnings

Given that D'Urban's initial instructions had been to secure order through treaties that recognised the Xhosa chiefs as if they were independent national powers, he was well aware that his sanctioning of the occupation of Queen Adelaide Province, in accordance with local settler and official wishes, would have to be defended from Colonial Office critique. In his defence, he helped construct a representation of the province's administration that is very much at odds with those contained in my analysis in the previous chapter. In doing so, he was beginning a reformulation of official discourse in the Cape, enframing older military and strategic objectives within a newer humanitarian-influenced set of representations. This was a project which would be continued by his successors and, as we will see in the next chapter, refined in particular by Sir George Grey in the late 1850s.

The compromised, negotiated form of power that the British administration seems to have been capable of developing within Queen Adelaide Province contrasts sharply with the story told by D'Urban, Smith and most of the settlers, once it had become clear that the hostile Xhosa could not be expelled from the territory. Smith's rendition of the province's brief history, as I have mentioned, had not only an effective British transformative power installed, but a positive Xhosa appreciation of that power and a desire for its continuance. Indeed, the commander of the province tried to persuade the Xhosa themselves that the extension of British 'protection' had been their own initiative. He announced in his first general address to the assembled chiefs that 'whoever he was among you who first suggested the idea of your becoming British subjects, deserves to be marked by you as a man who has rendered you the most eminent service'.[107] It was such a version of the province's reception by the Xhosa that both Smith and D'Urban attempted to convey to the Colonial Office in London.

In Smith's reports to D'Urban, which the governor in turn belatedly passed on to Glenelg, the British administration is credited with significant success in sweeping away barbaric Xhosa customs and introducing the anticipated general improvement of the 'race' for which humanitarians themselves had longed.[108] Smith's portrayal of administrative progress in the province is summed up neatly in the contents heading of one of the chapters in his autobiography:

> witchcraft forbidden . . . a rebellious chief awed into submission, agriculture and commerce introduced, nakedness discountenanced, burial of the dead encouraged, buying of wives checked, hopes of a general conversion to Christianity.[109]

Once it became clear from Glenelg's communications that the future of the province was in doubt, Smith set about collecting testimonials from Xhosa chiefs proving that his new subjects were dismayed at the prospect of a British withdrawal. Depositions to this effect were drawn up mostly from those chiefs who had collaborated during the war.[110] Stockenström dismissed Smith's attempts to show that formerly hostile Xhosa chiefs were also in favour of the British remaining, as wholly contrived.[111] Finally, in his defence, Smith blamed the Afrikaner emigration from the frontier districts on the British abandonment of the province. Despite the fact that the exodus was underway well before news of the abandonment had reached the trekkers, Smith and then D'Urban claimed that the trekkers had decided to leave the colony in exasperation at Xhosa cattle raids, and due to the imminent withdrawal of the protective screen of British troops.[112]

From D'Urban's private comments on Smith's despatches, it is evident that the governor cringed at some of Smith's worst rhetorical excesses and at his crudely bullying behaviour (especially in respect of his attempts to defend himself before the Court of Enquiry into Hintsa's death), but it was expedient to accept Smith's representations and convey them to London.[113] D'Urban persisted through most of 1836 in trying to persuade Glenelg of Smith's successes in the province.[114] As part of his own campaign, designed to counter that of the humanitarians, he sent his aide-de-camp, Captain G. de la Poer Beresford, to London. The captain carried with him the governor's first despatch to Glenelg justifying the intention of expelling the hostile Xhosa from Queen Adelaide Province. He also carried a memorial drawn up by British settlers in Albany in support of the expulsion of the Xhosa, which was to be published in *The Times*.[115]

Soon after his arrival in London, Beresford was optimistic. Not only had he been assured of King William IV's support for D'Urban's scheme, he was also pleased with the response of London merchants who traded with the Cape.

They were willing to represent D'Urban's plan for the new province to Glenelg 'as the only means of effectually putting the question at rest, and placing the Eastern Provinces [*sic*] on a footing of security'.[116] One merchant, who traded in wool with the British settlers out of Port Elizabeth, wrote to the Colonial Office that D'Urban's measures for colonising the Xhosa were entirely necessary against 'such an enemy who is gifted with cunning, and faithlessness to a degree above all others of the coloured population in the world'.[117] Another trader, J. S. Christopher, pleaded with Glenelg that if the annexation of Queen Adelaide Province was not confirmed, 'then goodbye to the hopes and expectations of your humble servant'.[118] Appearing as a witness before the Select Committee itself, Beresford argued that 'if you put the Caffres on the right side, as suffering great injustice from us, and suppose us to have committed every injustice without provocation, then we are decidedly wrong; but I cannot suppose that case, when I know the contrary to have occurred'.[119]

Within the colony itself, the Albany settlers were also mobilising against humanitarian interference. Indeed, as I argued in chapter 3, this mobilisation was critical to their sense of a new collective identity. Graham's Town's Civil Commissioner, Captain Campbell, began by orchestrating affidavits to appear before the Select Committee, blaming the Kat River missionary and 'friend of the Khoesan', James Read, for initiating the war. By questioning his literacy, the affidavits were also intended to undermine Tshatshu's credibility as the sole Xhosa witness before the Committee.[120] Settlers also requested Colonel Wade to reappear before the Committee during its last sitting in 1837, in order specifically to refute certain claims made by Tshatshu and Philip.[121] The *Graham's Town Journal* serialised the evidence heard before the Committee in highly selective fashion, concluding that

> Witnesses, whose evidence would not for a moment be listened to in a court of law, such as persons laboring under mental aberration,[122] and others who state circumstances not within their own knowledge, but on the authority of somebody who told them so, are brought forward and listened to with all the gravity imaginable; – that is provided they give evidence of a particular character, and concur in those sentiments which are openly avowed in certain quarters to our great prejudice'.[123]

It was relatively easy for settlers to vent some of their anger at the Committee's proceedings by drawing attention to instances of humanitarian hypocrisy. While metropolitan humanitarians were so concerned to prevent the oppression of the cattle-raiding Xhosa, one settler complained, 'In England . . . the law awards *death* to a man who steals corn from a stack in the field'.[124] The humanitarians on the Committee seemed to be doing nothing in respect of such metropolitan abuses. Furthermore, as we saw above, settlers pointed out that influential humanitarians not only tolerated, but were actively involved in schemes for the colonisation of

South Australia and New Zealand.[125] Not only should such schemes of colonisation be halted if humanitarian principles were to be fully applied, but the Kat River settlement should be taken from the Khoesan and given back to the Xhosa, and so should Stockenström's own farm in the 'ceded' territory.[126]

Stockenström himself made many enemies among the settlers as a result of his influential testimony before the Select Committee. Through his criticisms of settler aggression, he was seen to be severing vital links between the Albany community and the metropole. The settler attacks on him were consequently wide ranging, but they too tended ultimately to converge around his perceived hypocrisy. Having been involved in some critical decisions of pre-war frontier policy, including the original expulsion of Maqoma from the Kat River area, he was far from immune from criticisms of harshness towards the Xhosa himself.[127] When he was subsequently appointed by Glenelg as Lieutenant Governor of the frontier zone, entrusted with the task of reversing the annexation of the new province, the settler response was vicious.[128] He was accused by a group of settlers of having shot a young Xhosa man in cold blood whilst on commando many years before. The allegations, testified in a number of sworn statements made by Afrikaners who were part of the commando in question, were orchestrated in particular by Duncan Campbell. He sent the statements to J. C. Chase in Cape Town so that he in turn could direct them to Colonel Wade, who was at that point trying to defend the settlers before the Aborigines Committee.[129] Although Stockenström was unsuccessful in his pursuit of Campbell for libel, he was officially exonerated of the charge of murder by an official inquiry in 1837.

It was not only Stockenström who made enemies on the frontier through his role before the Select Committee, though. Although they had defenders at the Committee's hearings, like Gladstone, Donkin, Major Dundas, Colonel Wade, Captain Beresford and Thomas Philipps, who testified that 'the British colonists in Albany are equally as undeserving of the slanders bestowed on them by a few casual travellers, as they are of the wanton cruelties inflicted on them by the misguided and unreflecting savages',[130] it was clear to the settlers that both Philip's evidence, and his behind-the-scenes information, were playing a decisive role in the metropole. Of course, Philip and his Cape allies were already despised for their role in securing the 'freedom' of the Khoesan, but, as a result of their evidence to the Committee, they became yet more generally loathed. D'Urban himself bemoaned the degree of influence that Philip wielded through Fairbairn's newspaper, blaming the *South African Commercial Advertiser* for 'many of the evils which have befallen' the colony.[131] Along with many settlers he went much further in trying to implicate the local humanitarians in the causes of the war.[132] In 1836, J. C. Chase published *Some Reasons for Our Opposing the Author of the 'South African Researches', Dr John Philip . . . By the British immigrants of 1820*. The pamphlet contained seventeen arguments against Philip's *Researches*, all designed to discredit his representation of the causes of the recent war and his advocation of a solution more favourable to the Xhosa.[133]

Before the Select Committee itself, Major Dundas similarly condemned Philip's work, declaring that, in the *Researches*, 'there are many statements and many assertions which an honest man ought not to have made, to serve his own purpose; to become important in the eyes of a certain sect in England, he has written that book, and he is disturbing the peace and quietness of that country [the eastern Cape] by having done so'.[134] Chase also forwarded to the *Graham's Town Journal* the *Edinburgh Review* article on Hintsa's death, cited above, as evidence of the 'inaccurate' reporting of the frontier prevailing in Britain.[135]

In his own reaction to the Aborigines committee, and to humanitarians' role upon it, Chase found an ally in a metropolitan-based travel writer, W. Cornwallis Harris, who, in 1838, published his *Narrative of an Expedition into Southern Africa*. Harris held that the settlers had been misrepresented by 'canting and designing men, to whose mischievous and gratuitous inter- ferences veiled under the cloak of philanthropy is principally to be attributed the desolated condition of the Eastern frontier'. He also claimed that the settlers were 'flanked by a population of . . . dire irreclaimable savages, naturally inimical, warlike and predatory, by whom the hearths of the . . . colonists [had] for years past been deluged with the blood of their nearest and dearest relatives'.[136] Quoting Harris in his *Natal Papers*, which were pub- lished in the conviction that enough public pressure would bring about a reversal of colonial policy, Chase reaffirmed his point that the metropolitan government had been deluded by 'a powerful anti-colonial party within the colony itself, led on by Dr John Philip and most ably championised [*sic*] by John Fairbairn'.[137]

The Select Committee was a distant and inaccessible target (settler attempts to bring the hearings to the Cape and to have an official local investigation of Glenelg's allegations proved unsuccessful), but a much nearer manifestation of humanitarian influence was the Court of Enquiry into Hintsa's death. For leading settlers, this too was being used by humani- tarians to 'most essentially prejudice [settlers'] most vital interests with the home government'.[138] During the presentation of evidence, vocal settler opinion rallied around those most obviously implicated in Hintsa's killing and subsequent mutilation. Smith and the two Southey brothers were defended vehemently against the insinuations and accusations of the humanitarians.[139]

The Albany settlers realised, though, that their best chance of countering humanitarian representations lay in forging connections with an oppositional Tory counter-discourse in Britain itself. *The Times* was the leading anti-Whig and anti-humanitarian organ within metropolitan politics, and, as we have seen, it also best represented the interests of the commercial enterprises trading with Cape Town and Port Elizabeth.[140] In it, the settlers found their most influential metropolitan voice. The paper warned that if reports of an intended withdrawal from the province 'be true, and the savage be permitted to triumph in his deeds of atrocity by any concessions, this signal of our weakness will not be lost upon him'. While withdrawal would certainly be 'destructive to a trade of considerable magnitude', the paper's stated main concern, like that of the Aborigines Committee, was of a more universal nature: 'when civilization and barbarism meet, a shock will be felt, and is the liberal cabinet of Downing – street to decree, in their excessive devotion to a mistaken philanthropy, that the former is to give way?'[141]

As we have seen, the settlers also had a sympathetic ear in the King himself. Indeed it was his intervention which prevented Glenelg from revoking D'Urban's measures sooner.[142] Finally, in June 1836, a group of Graham's Town settler men established a 'Representative Fund' to raise money to pay for an agent to counteract unfavourable publicity in Britain. Their model was derived from Canada where paid representatives of colonial interests sat in parliament.[143]

If organs such as *The Times* were the settlers' best access to the metropolitan public sphere, their only direct connection with government was through their governor. Although they had been frustrated by D'Urban's reluctance to accede to all of their demands during the early occupation of Queen Adelaide Province, settlers appreciated his attempts to secure compensation for their real or imagined material losses during the war.[144] As Kayser noted, a large proportion of the settlers 'defends and singles out the governor for praise'.[145] Reciprocally, finding himself censured by Glenelg, D'Urban came to see himself as a representative of settler interests to the metropolitan government. He wrote that he found it difficult to understand Glenelg's attitudes towards the settlers on the one hand and the Xhosa on the other. While the former were 'faithful, industrious and unoffending subjects', Glenelg portrayed them as rapacious warmongers. While the latter were 'a savage and treacherous enemy', Glenelg thought of them as a wronged and unoffending people.[146] How the Colonial Secretary could claim that any group of indigenes in the world could have 'a perfect right to hazard the experiment' of launching an attack on a British colony was beyond the D'Urban's comprehension.[147]

In objecting to the humanitarians' representations, D'Urban and the settlers received some support from the Wesleyan missionaries[148] As we saw in the previous chapter, the Wesleyans overtly identified themselves with the settler cause during the war, and Shrewsbury in particular had proposed draconian measures for dealing with the hostile Xhosa. Glenelg specifically denounced the Cape Wesleyans' role in the war, stating that he could not 'attach the slightest value to [Shrewsbury's] judgement'.[149] The metropolitan directors of the WMMS, who were far more in tune with prevailing British humanitarian sentiment than they were with the views of their settler-affiliated Cape missionaries, were placed in a difficult situation due to Shrewsbury's remarks. While John Beecham, the Society's Secretary, described the Cape missionary's epistle as 'the objectionable letter', he claimed that there was no real rift between the WMMS's metropolitan and colonial representatives, insisting that Shrewsbury had been misinterpreted.[150] Shrewsbury's own immediate defence was that the Xhosa, being wicked and depraved, would benefit from his suggestions. The argument was supported by the other WMMS missionaries, Shepstone and Boyce, as well as by Godlonton.[151]

But once the political influence of humanitarianism in the metropole and the stance taken by their Secretary in London had been fully appreciated, Shrewsbury and Boyce switched tactics. They adapted their original arguments to what they now appreciated was a very different audience. Thus, despite his earlier suggestion that the followers of hostile chiefs were to 'forfeit their lands', Shrewsbury held that he had never supported the Xhosa's expulsion from Queen Adelaide Province, while Boyce tried to persuade British readers that D'Urban himself had never envisaged such an expulsion.[152]

D'Urban's representations too, became more moderate as the debate over the future of Queen Adelaide Province was prolonged.[153] Despite expressing a personal sense of injustice about humanitarian condemnation, he became aware from the first metropolitan response to his May proposals for expulsion, and from Glenelg's reaction to his 'irreclaimable savage' tag, of the need to frame his intentions as far as possible within a hegemonic humanitarian rhetoric.[154] Rather than blustering like Smith or holding ever more firmly to an inverted humanitarian construction of the Xhosa and a programme of further colonisation, he emphasised those aspects of his actions which could be most effectively moulded into a humanitarian discourse. Notable among these, as we have seen, was the 'liberation' of the Mfengu from the 'bonds of slavery' in which they had been held by the Xhosa. D'Urban set about using abolitionist representations to his own ends, stating that his 'emancipation' of the Mfengu during the war was even more worthy than the empire's freeing of its own (better treated) slaves, since it was at the cost of a wartime enemy.[155] During the hearings of the Select Committee, Beresford had written to D'Urban, 'I have little doubt that in the main points your measures will be confirmed here. The emancipation of the Fingoes has had its effect.' The Cape colonist Henry Cloete, who was also in London during the hearings, similarly wrote to the governor that 'news of the 'liberation' of the Mfengu would 'go far in silencing the outcry raising [*sic*] by the Saints, and putting down effectually the sympathy they were endeavouring to create in favour of the Caffres'.[156]

The wider project of Queen Adelaide Province was also subjected to a humanitarian reconstruction. With the Xhosa now to be contained in locations within it, rather than expelled from it, the province was to become an arena for the benign civilisation of the unfortunate savage. Such a construction was supported by the official interpreter Shepstone, who, 'knowing the African mind', attempted to give extra credence to D'Urban's protestations of worthy intent.[157] At this time though, if not necessarily at a later date, such representations were already regarded with suspicion by metropolitan humanitarians. They had, for example, seen through the rhetoric deployed by British traders who wanted to begin the colonisation of Natal. While these entrepreneurs had also expressed themselves as being 'influenced by the wish to diffuse religious knowledge and principles amongst the natives', the Select Committee felt that 'It is impossible to contemplate without serious distrust' their attempt 'to combine European colonisation with plans for the conversion of the natives to Christianity'.[158]

Despite D'Urban, Smith and the settlers' best efforts, the Governor was notified by Stockenström, as the Lieutenant Governor designate of the frontier districts, of the inevitable withdrawal of troops from Queen Adelaide Province in September 1836. He issued the necessary order for its gradual abandonment the following month.[159] The Xhosa chiefs were handed back their autonomy under treaties devised by Stockenström at the end of the year, the Lieutenant Governor being careful to handle the withdrawal in such a way that the chiefs would not feel that they had scored any victory over the British authorities.[160]

When the abandonment of Queen Adelaide Province was formally announced in the Cape, the *Graham's Town Journal* opined that the imperial government seemed to have 'deliberately considered how public opinion in this part of the colony might be most outraged, defied and insulted'. It continued, 'we can scarcely persuade ourselves that . . . the subjects of a free, powerful, and enlightened country could thus be treated with such monstrous cruelty and injustice'.[161] The withdrawal raised the real prospect of an imperial abandonment of the settlers on the Cape's frontier. Such an abandonment would not only stifle any economic growth which the region might otherwise expect and undermine the value of current investments; it would also jeopardise the settlers' personal and collective security within a marginal and dangerous colonial space.[162] Settlers would have to resist, and that meant restitching the frayed political, military and cultural bonds that tied them to the metropolitan public and its government.

6 Imperial contests and the conquest of the frontier

The editor of *The Graham's Town Journal* . . . is . . . the representative of a class, alas both numerous and influential in the eastern province . . . whose motto is 'Bow down that we may pass over'.[1]

(William Thompson, LMS agent in Cape Town, March 1851)

In the face of opposition from humanitarians, settlers' representations proved insufficiently persuasive in the metropole during the mid-1830s. The abandonment of Queen Adelaide Province marked a defeat for both settlers' and Cape officials' colonial projects. However, in retrospect, the 1830s can be seen as the highpoint of humanitarianism's direct political influence. Thereafter, while the mobilisation of a humanitarian network continued in Britain and its colonies, its influence would be dispersed into more diverse and less cohesive projects. By the early 1840s, the key proponents of earlier humanitarian thinking had retired from active politics. Buxton had lost his seat in the House of Commons and the ageing Philip had withdrawn from contests with the colonial state and settlers. The Whigs, now dependent on Daniel O'Connell and other 'radicals' for parliamentary support, were a more marginal group within the House of Commons. But the malaise of liberal humanitarianism went far deeper than the loss of vigorous metropolitan and colonial adherents and the contingencies of electoral politics. It occurred within a broad context of disillusionment with the humanitarian notion that 'unreclaimed' human subjectivities could be rapidly transformed.

This disillusionment was especially profound in relation to the colonised 'others' of empire, even though, as we will see, it was not restricted to them. It was a discursive development that favoured settlers not just in the Cape but in all those places where the Aborigines Committee had noted increased incursions upon indigenous autonomy and resources. In order to comprehend the eclipse of humanitarians' discursive hegemony in the Cape, and, indeed, the conquest and subordination of the Rharhabe Xhosa against which humanitarians had struggled, we have to situate the Cape once more within a broader imperial terrain. Accordingly, like the preceding chapter, this chapter shifts back and forth between the Cape, Britain and other locales of colonial settlement.

Humanitarian disillusionment

Disillusionment with colonised people's capacity to learn the lessons of freedom and of civilisation began with the experience of the abolition of slavery itself, and its roots can be located within the very expectations upon which humanitarianism was based. As we saw in chapter 2, abolitionists and their supporters had assumed that, while some freed labourers in the West Indies would make a success of independent peasant agriculture, most would progress towards civilisation and 'culture' through continued work on the plantations.[2] Within a few years of emancipation, however, the majority of planters in Jamaica were in debt and capital was scarce. Despite the influence of more structural economic conditions, planters blamed their distress on the desertion of roughly half of their labour force as former slaves moved off the plantations to cultivate their own small plots of land in the hilly parts of the island. Sugar exports almost halved between 1838 and 1840.[3] In the aftermath of abolition, not only did freed slaves refuse to work in the ways prescribed by humanitarians, they also refused to assimilate their religious teachings, appropriating them instead to new and syncretic forms such as revivalism, obeahism and myalism. The disappointments engendered by the behaviour of freed slaves in the West Indies were a prelude to a broader disillusionment with emancipated slaves and the indigenous peoples of empire, and this disillusionment in turn, I would argue, helped secure the discursive conditions for the imperial hegemony of planter and settler, rather than humanitarian, representations.

The 'failure' of emancipation in the West Indies and the Cape

When the freed slaves in the West Indies asserted their autonomy, when they refused to conform to the humanitarians' expectations of economic and cultural behaviour, some explanation had to be provided, and it was bound to have profound political effects. As Thomas Holt points out, 'the answer to the question of what went wrong in Jamaica . . . had consequences beyond its particular boundaries and in domains other than the economic'. It seemed apparent to many humanitarians themselves that, 'released from the restraints of the plantation before new values and social aspirations took hold, the freed people had . . . moved into the Jamaican hills, beyond the reach of civilizing forces, and reverted to African barbarism'.[4]

In 1840, abolitionists endeavoured to maintain the momentum behind the antislavery campaign, and to extend it beyond Britain's empire, by organising the first World Anti-Slavery Convention in London. The tests applied to abolition in the West Indies, however, served only to confirm the failure of the humanitarian 'experiment' thus far. O'Connell pointed out that if global emancipation was to be secured, 'other governments needed to be assured that abolishing slavery was "safe", and the 'only proof that would be sufficiently convincing was the continued, and preferably expanded, production of sugar in the post-emancipation British Caribbean colonies'.[5] In stressing the continued productivity of the plantations, of course, humanitarian discourse was rendering its own claims about the reclaimability of the West Indian slave a hostage to fortune. Within five years of the Convention being held, even William Knibb, the Baptist missionary and prominent abolitionist admitted that 'The new Black subjects he had envisaged were less industrious and domesticated than he would have liked'.[6] Henry Taylor, one of the principal metropolitan abolitionists, concurred that 'negroes, like children, require a discipline which shall enforce upon them steadiness in their own conduct and consideration for the interests of others'.[7]

If humanitarians themselves expressed a certain disappointment at the results of emancipation in the West Indies, it is not surprising that planters and other interests sympathetic to them capitalised on the 'lesson'. Planters were certainly not loath to communicate the humanitarians' 'failure' to metropolitan audiences. 'Throughout the 1840s – in parliamentary hearings and debates, in memorials to the Queen, in the popular press – planters succeeded in drumming their particular construction of West Indian reality into British consciousness with little effective rebuttal'.[8] In this construction, it was the inherent laziness of the 'negro' which had caused sugar production to plummet. Given the parameters of their own colonial vision, humanitarians necessarily found it difficult to formulate a counter-argument.

The entry of the planters' explanation of post-emancipation developments into popular British discourse was assisted by a host of celebrated writers, perhaps the best known of which was Thomas Carlyle, to whom we will return below. But Carlyle was not alone in channelling planters' imagery to British audiences. In 1859 Anthony Trollope (who was later to urge the civilising necessity of work for blacks on South Africa's diamond mines) claimed in his popular *The West Indies and the Spanish Main*, that 'The negro's idea of emancipation was and is emancipation not from slavery but from work. To lie in the sun and eat breadfruits and yams is his idea of being free.'[9] His view was affirmed by the same journal which had earlier mocked official accounts of Hintsa's death, *John Bull*. It testified that experience had now shown that 'the negro is disinclined to labour, and has not the disposition towards self-improvement manifested by the white man'.[10] As Holt points out, since Jamaican blacks were 'incapable of self-direction and inner restraint', the planters seemed to have proved their point that 'they must be subjected to external controllers. Having failed to master themselves, they must have masters'.[11]

Despite a smoother economic transition, the dominant post-emancipation discourse in the Cape paralleled that in the West Indies.[12] This time the complaints were not only about the behaviour of the freed slaves themselves, but also that of the Khoesan who had been 'liberated' by Ordinance 50. Both groups – former slaves and Khoesan – could now be lumped together and described as the 'coloured classes', and their behaviour, within the terms established by humanitarian discourse, left much to be desired. Although, as we have seen, settlers had argued vociferously against Ordinance 50 since its inception, it was not only settlers who expressed their disappointment with the effects of abolition on the 'coloured' population as a whole. As Andrew Bank notes,

> By the late 1840s John Philip's Cape Town office was being flooded with missionary complaints about the immoral behaviour of the newly emancipated. In one particularly severe 'year of trial for our Brethren', the missionary at Paarl referred to the 'demoralising influence' of those 'sinks of iniquity', the canteens; the Graham's Town report lamented the 'scenes of dissipation daily presented in the streets'; that from Graaff Reinet complained of a 'fearful increase in drunkenness'.[13]

Even William Elliot, one of the LMS's leading campaigners, wrote that 'the authority of the missionary had been diminished' in the Cape since emancipation, because the freed slaves and Khoesan escaping their masters on the mission stations 'prefer abundant leisure and unrestrained freedom to those habits of industry and those salutary restraints, which must be sustained and submitted to in ordinary social life'.[14]

A dispute conducted in 1844 between the stalwart defender of the Kat River Khoesan, James Read snr, and the former LMS missionary-turned colonial administrator, Henry Calderwood, is indicative of the shift in dominant missionary discourse that took place in the Cape after emancipation. The argument was brought about because Read confided his qualms about other missionaries to a 'coloured' Kat River settler instead of 'properly' keeping them to himself or expressing them only to other white men. What Read confided to his 'coloured' friend was his bitterness at the racialised disillusionment of Calderwood and other 'Kaffrarian' missionaries including Kayser. Read was disgusted that his fellow missionaries were becoming concerned only with 'the danger and difficulty of bring[ing] the [Khoesan] to a state of equality!!' He commented sarcastically: 'Tis a thousand pities that by conversion Hottentots and others do not get white skins and long hair. I think wigs would be a good substitute for the last, but for the first there is no remedy. I think the Hottentots should get a number of peruke-makers out immediately.'[15]

Kayser intimated that most of the other Kaffrarian missionaries knew, or thought they knew, the kinds of things that Read would be saying to his Khoesan congregation behind their backs. He noted that

> it has been long known that the Reads are in the habit of representing themselves to the [Kat River] people as more than others the Friends of the natives, and that too in the most unscrupulous manner . . . both missionaries and the Society are to be denounced. For there is a covert attack even upon the Society – represented as ready to oppress the Hottentots, if the Reads did not stand in the way.[16]

Calderwood himself felt that 'Considering the circumstances and natural disposition of the Natives . . . a more serious offence against the souls of the
people and the comfort and influence of his Brethren could scarcely be committed than that which Mr Read had many a time committed on speaking
and writing to the Natives in [such a] manner'.[17] Calderwood formally
charged Read with 'dishonourable and unworthy conduct', 'clandestine and
most unchristian proceedings' and 'incalculable injuries done to the cause
of Christ'.[18] Philip concluded that 'Both parties would do the coloured
people good but in different ways. In order to raise the people James Read
would treat them as brethren and to this Mr Calderwood says, "We object".'[19]

While the dispute took on the appearance of a storm in a teacup to the
LMS's directors in Britain, Bank points to its broader discursive significance:
'The attacks by his fellow missionaries and the rising current of conservatism
within the London Missionary Society left unrepentant humanitarian liberals
like James Read ostracised and despairing . . . the ageing Read confided [in a
letter to a friend] "I am at present an outcast among my Brethren".'[20] As Read
was discovering, and as will become clearer below, by the mid-1840s, many of
the doctrines of 'proper' behaviour which the Cape's humanitarians had
employed during the 1830s to combat settler and official notions, had
been assimilated into and deployed within a more reactionary dominant
discourse.

The Niger expedition

If emancipation of the Cape's 'coloured' population had 'failed', subsequent
endeavours to pursue the recommendations of the Aborigines Committee
concerning other parts of Africa were also to prove disastrous within the
very terms of humanitarian discourse. This could only reinforce settler
claims about the intractability of the African character. In 1841, Buxton
helped to organise the Niger expedition 'to attack slavery at its source' by
introducing Christianity and 'legitimate commerce' to those parts of Africa
most blighted by the practice. The expedition's intention to establish oases
of Christian example in 'this kingdom of darkness', as Buxton put it, failed
miserably as most of the Europeans died of malaria and the expeditionary
party disintegrated. As a result of the expedition's failure, the Aborigines'
Protection Society was forced to conclude that it had 'not attained to that
magnitude and importance, or achieved those results, which doubtless [its]
early friends . . . might reasonably anticipate'.[21]

The lesson of the expedition for most British observers was more stark:
Europeans had no hope of bringing redemptive light to the denizens of a
'dark continent' which was more than capable of swallowing puny and
naïve humanitarian endeavours. For influential metropolitan sceptics such
as Charles Dickens, the expedition was 'the prime example of philanthropic
folly'.[22] In a piece entitled *The Niger Expedition*, Dickens wrote,

The history of this Expedition is the history of the Past in reference to the heated visions of philanthropists . . . to change the customs even of civilised men . . . is . . . a most difficult and slow proceeding; but to do this by ignorant and savage races, is a work which, like the progressive changes of the globe itself, requires a stretch of years that dazzles in the looking at.[23]

The Niger expedition thus served to convince a metropolitan public that if the emancipation of 'negroes' who had been under white 'supervision' for decades in the West Indies had failed, the task of reclaiming Africans in all their untutored 'savagery', within their own 'primeval' homelands, was a yet more ridiculous venture. 'News' from the settlers of the eastern Cape frontier during the 1840s would reinforce this conviction. It would contribute to a shift in the terms of imperial debate which facilitated not only the passage of Masters and Servants laws to re-establish controls over freed slaves, but also the renewed colonisation of the Xhosa.

The rejection of 'civilisation' in the eastern Cape

Disillusionment with the behaviour of freed slaves was accompanied from the 1840s by a resurgence of indigenous resistance to the extension of British imperialism at different sites across the globe. This resistance, which will be examined in more detail below, was generated through diverse local conditions, but it was discursively marshalled into a pattern of non-European people's behaviour by settlers and their metropolitan sympathisers. As Bank has argued, the Cape was among the first sites in which the 'lessons' of indigenous resistance became 'known'. Accordingly, Cape humanitarians, including John Fairbairn, lost their faith in the capacity of Britons to secure improvement among independent peoples like the Xhosa before most of their counterparts at other sites in the imperial network.[24] Following Bank, in this section, events in the Cape are considered not just in their own right, but according to the influence that they exerted across a wider imperial expanse.

With Queen Adelaide Province abandoned and humanitarian-inspired treaties regulating the relationships between chiefs and colonial officials in the late 1830s, the Albany settlers, and, predictably, the *Graham's Town Journal* in particular, took the lead in marshalling new representations of humanitarian failures among the Xhosa and conveying them to Britain and other colonies.[25] Well after the retrocession of the province, settlers continued to organise a series of petitions to the King and subsequently the Queen, to the House of Commons and to the Colonial Secretary, bemoaning missionary and humanitarian 'misrepresentations' of the settlers' cause.[26] Through the late 1830s and 1840s, the *Journal* published a litany of accounts of stock losses, robberies and murders committed by the Xhosa against unoffending colonists. The continuing 'plunder' of the colonial margins was represented as proof positive that humanitarian endeavours to deal with the Xhosa were not only misguided, but fundamentally dangerous.

If, as Michael Taussig argues, 'people delineate their world, including its large-scale as well as microscale politics, in stories and storylike creations', rather than through ideologies as they are conventionally understood, then the *GTJ* provided readers with meaningful stories of inherent Xhosa savagery in abundance. Through its steady stream of complaints about the lack of security under Stockenström's treaty system and its sensational reporting of specific incidents of danger to which colonists along the frontier were exposed on an apparently daily basis, this paper, more than any other vehicle, created 'the coils of rumour, gossip and chitchat' where racist ideas 'enter[ed] into active social circulation and meaningful existence'. Rather than the frontier being the space of British provocations as the Select Committee had imagined, settlers established through the Journal that *their* frontier was a 'space of terror' inflicted by the Xhosa.[27]

In conveying such representations to the metropole, however, the eastern Cape settlers had to tread a difficult path. On the one hand, they needed to convince metropolitan observers that they were living among dangerous and irreclaimable savages in order to argue for greater military protection and the eventual conquest of the Xhosa. On the other hand, if they were to attract further emigration and British investment to the region, and thus to secure their own material well being, they needed to provide assurances of its safety. In 1841, *The Frontier Times* attacked 'those who would lead by exaggeration or ill-grounded statements all distant persons to suppose that we are constantly in a state of danger and terror' on the grounds that such representations would deter 'capital and emigrants' from the Cape's shores.[28] The problem that settlers were creating for themselves was made clear in comparative guidebooks for intending British emigrants. Whereas the Australian Aborigines were represented in the *Colonial Magazine and East India Review* as 'fortunately for us . . . the greatest cowards on the face of the earth', the Xhosa would have to be met by a 'stern exterminating system', which few potential emigrants were likely to relish encountering upon their arrival in a new home.[29]

In the 1840s, however, most settlers' priority was to reverse the treaty system, reclaim Queen Adelaide Province and bring about a greater British military presence. If this could be done only at the expense of precluding further civilian immigration and deterring the extension of credit and investment from the western Cape, at least in the short term, then so be it. In any case, many settlers were well aware that a stronger military presence brought material benefits of its own that compensated any deferral of immigration. A number of settlers, as we have seen, had already made fortunes provisioning troops stationed permanently in the district. In 1848, Godlonton, himself hardly a reticent publicist of settler arguments, wrote to his friend Richard Southey, 'You have no idea what a desire there is here to keep up the War

Cry and what sturdy opposition I meet in my endeavours to discharge my Editorial duty with faithfulness to all parties.' The following year, he elaborated revealingly upon the more covert reasons why so many settlers demanded a local garrison:

> Fort Beaufort . . . since the withdrawal of the troops has gone to the dogs . . . numerous persons find themselves absolutely ruined . . . Grahamstown is also in a very bad plight in respect to business. Were [the governor] to make it his headquarters for a month or two it would infuse some spirit into it, and they might improve, but unless some alteration takes place a good many houses of trade must, I fear, close their business.[30]

The political effects of systematic settler propaganda were apparent within the Cape itself, if not quite yet in Britain, from the late 1830s. Fairbairn's defence of the Xhosa in the *South African Commercial Advertiser* during the 1834–5 war had provoked 'a petition by hundreds of outraged British frontier settlers demanding the suppression of his newspapers'. Under this pressure, George Greig, the Cape Town merchant and Fairbairn's erstwhile ally, withdrew from his established position as publisher of the paper in 1835. Fairbairn himself, however, continued to defend Stockenström's treaty system against the 'political liars' who denounced it until the mid-1840s.[31] Aside from Fairbairn, the settler community's propaganda assault continued to be directed against Stockenström himself during the late 1830s. Local officials on the frontier, many of them now recruited from the ranks of the 1820 settlers, simply refused to co-operate with him, Charles Lennox Stretch being a notable exception. Settler officials sent their own reports flagrantly contradicting Stockenström's, direct to the government in Cape Town.

Settlers' most frequent specific complaints centred on one particular clause in the treaties that Stockenström had negotiated with the chiefs to end the British occupation of Queen Adelaide Province. This was the clause shifting the onus on preventing stock theft to colonial farmers, who were now required to employ armed herds at all times. While the colonial authorities would negotiate the surrender of all other stolen livestock through the chiefs, beasts that were stolen through the farmer's negligence were not officially reclaimable. Godlonton was soon using the *Graham's Town Journal* to publicise a list of stolen, but 'not reclaimable' cattle, and local settler officials were helping to distribute it as an effective way of undermining Stockenström's treaties. Stretch described the list as 'a debt against Caffreland which increased according to the inclination of reporters for the press', but, together with the widespread non-compliance encountered by Stockenström, it nevertheless became an embarrassment for the metropolitan government.[32]

In 1838, *The Times* published 'information' received from the *Graham's Town Journal* on the disastrous effect that Stockenström's treaties were having on the trans-frontier trade, using the Cape to make a broader point about the 'supineness of the Ministry in all that relates to the trading interest of the Country'.[33] With London merchants who traded with frontier farmers joining in the clamour, Glenelg's successor as Colonial Secretary, Lord Normanby, was persuaded to suspend Stockenström from his post, citing his 'unpopularity' as the main reason. The following year, D'Urban's successor as Cape Governor, Sir George Napier, managed to persuade Stockenström to resign altogether, with a baronetcy in recognition of his services. Humanitarians such as John Herschel were outraged that 'the mere hostility of such a party [as the settlers] may have the power to outweigh the deliberate approbation of the Government itself . . . and without other cause assigned to assure his deprivation'.[34]

Although Stockenström's successor, Lieutenant Governor Hare, distrusted the Graham's Town settlers (he described them as 'longing after the lands of the Kaffirs'), Stockenström's treaties with the Xhosa were breached in 1840, when, after the clamour about the 'not reclaimable list', colonists were allowed once more to cross the frontier and retrieve 'stolen cattle'. Then, in 1844, and without consultation with the chiefs, Napier's own successor as governor, Sir Peregrine Maitland replaced the treaties with a scheme of his own.

From his despatches it seems that Maitland agreed with Godlonton that the settlers were living 'amidst a "sea of troubles"', with 'murder and robbery of frequent occurrence within the Colonial Border'.[35] The governor wrote to the Colonial Office that settler petitioners 'have some substantial grounds of complaint . . . it is an irritating and harassing thing to be liable to have their property driven over the border by nocturnal thieves to their inconvenience and loss, and the creation of an uncomfortable feeling of insecurity'. Moreover, Maitland reproduced the *Graham's Town Journal*'s discourse faithfully when he described the Xhosa as being 'greedy of cattle and equally unscrupulous as to the mode of obtaining them'.[36] Maitland's new, imposed 'treaties' allowed colonial forts to be built in the former ceded territory, commandos to resume their confiscations of cattle in lieu of stolen beasts, and Xhosa converts living on mission stations to be placed under colonial rather than chiefly jurisdiction.

Many of the frontier chiefs were already preparing for war again when, in 1846, a party of Xhosa men freed a friend who had been taken prisoner in the colony for stealing an axe, cutting off the hand of the fellow Khoesan prisoner to whom he was handcuffed. Urged on by the settlers, Maitland responded to the incident by formulating an ultimatum, and it was this which initiated the 1846–7 frontier war.[37] Maqoma and other veterans of the 1834–5 war including Nqeno, who had suffered much by it, stayed out of this latest attempt at the armed defence of Xhosa land and autonomy. Indeed, Maqoma actually asked and was refused permission to cross into the colony in order to avoid being embroiled in the fighting. But while colonial commanders were relieved at Maqoma's apparent passivity, and pleased to receive intelligence from the chief Mqhayi, they were disappointed that their former ally, Phatho, and even Philip's shining example of the Xhosa 'reclaimed man', Dyani Tshatshu, now turned against the colony.[38] Both chiefs joined in the war on the side of Sandile's Ngqika and Mhala's Ndlambe.

As far as this study is concerned, it is British discursive constructions of the war which are its most significant aspect. This time, the Xhosa had no British advocates, colonial or metropolitan, of any description. The war was almost universally seen as a manifestation of the humanitarians' naïvety in assuming that the Xhosa could be civilised, at least in the short term, and of the Xhosa's unwillingness, if not incapacity to 'learn'. Macmillan notes the lack of a defence of the Xhosa in the western Cape press. Humanitarian discourse in the colony was effectively suspended and even 'Fairbairn and the *Commercial Advertiser* supported Maitland's policy, not without some eyebrows being raised'.[39] It was in their transformed representations of the Xhosa and of a 'just' frontier policy after the war that the Cape humanitarians' loss of faith in an earlier model of interaction was most dramatically demonstrated. As Bank points out, 'The continued advocacy of diplomatic solutions to the frontier problem, albeit in more cautious terms, in the late 1830s gave way to a stridently imperialistic language of conquest, appropriation and punishment from the late 1840s'.[40] In Britain, Gladstone, who was now Colonial Secretary, felt that his oppositional role on the Aborigines Committee back in 1836 had been vindicated as a result of the renewed Xhosa resistance. As he put it, 'Philanthropy is at a discount' and 'very short work had been made with the Kaffirs'.[41] Godlonton's assertion that 'The British race was selected by God himself to colonize Kaffraria' now seemed to go unchallenged.[42]

Fairbairn's personal political transition, thought to be 'so very strange!' by Philip's daughter back in England, can be seen as indicative of the wider processes of empire.[43] Following the 1846–7 war, Fairbairn, as other humanitarians were beginning to do after the disappointments of emancipation, rejected his earlier 'idealism'. Influenced by Cape merchants, he formulated a less sympathetic and more utilitarian political economy. In this new scheme, the Xhosa's conquest should be effected for their own good, as they would never 'improve' without it. Describing the Xhosa's act of defiance in 1846–7 as a 'betrayal', Fairbairn insisted that 'The Caffres have forfeited all claim to forbearance'. It was now necessary to 'add Cafferland to the dependencies of the Cape . . . both chiefs and people have to learn that the effects of an unjust war are not to end with the termination of actual resistance in the field. They have forced the British government most reluctantly to declare, that not victory but conquest is to be the end of this outbreak'.[44] Fairbairn went on to claim that 'humanity without money, without troops, without magistrates, constables, prisons and other civilized apparatus will go a very short way to ensure the peaceable possession of their lands to the settlers'.[45]

In reassessing the Xhosa's aptitude for civilisation within a liberal frame of reference, Fairbairn carried out a manœuvre that, as we will see, was to become characteristic of a 'turn' in liberal thinking within the empire as a whole in the mid-nineteenth century. He connected the threat posed to colonial Britons by 'uncivilised barbarians' like the Xhosa with that posed to the metropolitan middle classes by the unruly, unassimilated elements in British society. Arguing effectively that the middle classes' accumulation of capital was 'the root of all that strengthens the state and adorns society', he vehemently condemned 'the Chartist rabble' in England.[46] This connection, between the middle classes' Others 'at home' and abroad, is one that I will explore further below.

With his powerful western Cape and metropolitan acquaintances, Fairbairn's transfigured discourse proved of great utility to the Albany settlers. It was referred to extensively in an open letter written on their behalf by Charles Grisbrook, and addressed to Earl Grey, Gladstone's successor as Colonial Secretary. The letter began by contrasting the passage printed by Fairbairn in the *South African Commercial Advertiser* which had so offended settlers in 1830 by referring to them as 'timid cockneys and pin makers who shrink from the bold eyes of a natural man', with a passage in the same newspaper of 1846. In contrast, this referred to the Xhosa destroying the progress which settlers had brought about, and which was 'rapidly assimilating [the Cape] to a section of the Mother Country'.[47] Grisbrook went on to claim that, 'For the first time, during a residence in this Colony of five-and-twenty years, [Fairbairn] has taken up the gauntlet in *defence* of the just and righteous claims of his hitherto calumniated fellow-colonists and, it is fervently hoped, has finally deserted the ranks of *mendacity and faction*'. The settlers, declared Grisbrook, 'In the spirit of Christian charity' were willing to 'forget and forgive' Fairbairn's 'past delinquencies'.[48]

Even Philip refrained from defending the Xhosa in 1846, also in part because of a sense of broader imperial disillusionment. He wrote that 'Many of our friends are dissatisfied with the smallness of our success . . . [and] begin to doubt whether our missions are not in a state of retrogression . . . Tahiti, Madagascar and South Africa are appealed to justify the surmise'. His pessimism was substantiated by Laing, another former defender of the Xhosa. During the war, he wrote that the Xhosa 'might have been a happy people, for they had a fertile country, and the gospel of peace . . . but alas they have . . . rejected the gospel and now they are to be called to account for their abuse of the mercies [of] God and for their rebellion against him'.[49]

In accepting the need for renewed colonial annexation up to the Kei River, the Colonial Office too, announced its despair of ever attaining peace on the frontier without renewed imperial domination of the Xhosa.[50] For the new Colonial Secretary, Earl Grey, 'experience had clearly demonstrated' that 'entering into treaties with the frontier Kafirs' was 'perfectly useless'. Instead, the colonial authorities needed 'to insist upon the obedience of these people within a certain district to British officers stationed among them, and supported by a military force'.[51] He elaborated in 1847:

I have no doubt that to subdue [the Xhosa's] savage nature a strict and even severe system of government is necessary . . . by such a system of government . . . [they] may be kept in order, and if peace is thus maintained, religion, education and commerce will gradually civilize them. It appears to me to be the duty of this country and a duty it is bound by the most sacred obligations not to shrink from performing, to endeavour to work out this result.[52]

Thus was a humanitarian discourse of Christian intervention appropriated and moulded into a settler and official discourse of active colonisation in the Cape.

A new Governor, Sir Henry Pottinger, was despatched to the Cape even before the 1846–7 war had ended.[53] His instructions were to carry into effect a revitalised scheme for the colonisation of the Rharhabe Xhosa. They would be prevented from gaining further access to the bush-covered areas, especially the Amatola Mountains, where their military resistance had been concentrated. In their remaining lands, they would be 'civilised' along the lines envisaged in 1835. Pottinger's problem, however, was that the war seemed to have ground to a halt without the necessary decisive victory. As his predecessor Maitland wrote, the Xhosa 'will not go from the country which we require them to evacuate nor will they fight for it. They will stay, and sow and reap and merely avoid us when we enter to eject them'. The missionary Richard Birk reported that 'if peace be made now . . . it is much to be feared that [the Xhosa] will not bear the yoke which will be attempted to be laid upon them'.[54]

Pottinger was thus obliged to resume the war with a fresh attack on Sandile's Ngqika within their Amatola stronghold. The army's chief medical officer summed up the new tactic. It comprised a 'system of cattle stealing and hut burning' which, given the Xhosa's continuing refusal to resist, he felt, was 'a disgrace to the age we live in'.[55] Nevertheless, the tactic resulted in a more decisive Xhosa surrender, and the re-annexation of the former Queen Adelaide Province in 1847. The territory was now renamed British Kaffraria. Rather than being subject to the laws of the colony, it was administered by the military, so as to ensure, as Grey put it, 'the despotic system of government which is necessary'.[56] With the annexation of British Kaffraria, Pottinger was quickly replaced as governor by the one man within the entire imperial network who was the most eager to implement such a 'despotic system', Harry Smith, Commander of the former Queen Adelaide Province, himself.

New experiments in colonial government

Following his 'glorious' extension of British conquest over the Sikhs in the Punjab (he was the self-proclaimed 'hero of Aliwal'), Smith was delighted to be asked to return to the Cape in the more elevated role of Governor and, indeed, High Commissioner. Upon his return to the colony, and no doubt much to his own surprise, he found himself, as Bank puts it, 'acclaimed

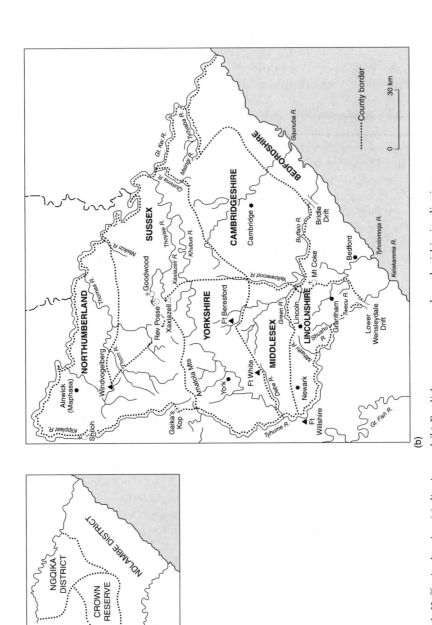

Figure 3 British Kaffraria showing (a) districts and (b) English county names adopted within its districts

Source: A. Lester, E. Nel and T. Binns, *South Africa Past, Present and Future: Gold at the End of the Rainbow?* Prentice Hall, London and New York, 2000, p. 84

by the disillusioned humanitarians, who offered to build a statue in his honour. The same ideologues who had denounced Smith's military expansionism when he served as commander . . . in the mid-1830s welcomed him as a political ally a decade later'.[57] Smith at once made his intentions regarding the Xhosa clear. He would return to the system of colonisation that he had envisaged all along for Queen Adelaide Province, back in the halcyon days of D'Urban's administration. Smith declared that he would 're-do what Lord Glenelg so ably did undo'.[58]

After the chiefs' surrender, Smith accordingly had them assembled at King William's Town, just as he had done in 1835. After having made them go through the ritual of choosing either a 'stave of war' (a pike) or a 'stave of peace' (a tent pole with a doorknob fastened on the end), Smith next made them kiss his boots as he sat astride his horse.[59] Two weeks later, on 7 January 1848, he held another 'great meeting'. After a supposedly intimidating display of fireworks, Smith warned the chiefs what would happen if they were not 'faithful' to his new regime. He pointed dramatically to a wagon that had been prepared with explosives, saying 'Look at that wagon and hear me give the word Fire!' When the wagon was promptly blown to pieces, he continued, 'That is what I will do to you if you do not behave yourselves'. Next, he took a symbolic sheet of paper in his hands and, ripping it in two, declared, 'Do you see this? There go the treaties! Do you hear? no more treaties'.[60] The chiefs then had to swear a series of oaths. They included loyalty to Queen Victoria, the banning of witchcraft, the halting of the further 'violation of women', the prevention of 'robbery' from the colony, the abolition of the 'sin of buying wives', the promise to pay attention to the words of the missionaries, and the annual payment of an ox in tribute to their new ruler.[61] The only recorded response to all of this from the chiefs was to ask for more land in the former 'ceded territory', which Smith had now formally added to the colony, and which would soon be granted to colonial land speculators and Mfengu allies.

While Smith was ostensibly in personal command in British Kaffraria, responsibility for its daily administration rested in the hands of his assistant, Chief Commissioner Colonel G. Mackinnon. Under Mackinnon, there were three Native Commissioners responsible for overseeing the chiefs' activities within their respective locations. As had been the case in 1835, these were surveyed and set out soon after the resumed occupation. Captain John Maclean would have oversight of Phatho from Fort Murray, W. M. Fynn would supervise Mhala from Fort Waterloo and Charles Brownlee would control the Ngqika under Sandile from Fort Cox. Charles Lennox Stretch, the humanitarian former Resident Agent in Queen Adelaide Province, had been removed from office partly due to a campaign against him led by Henry Calderwood (the same Calderwood who had contested the fate of the Khoesan with James Read). Each subdivision within British Kaffraria was given an English county name such as Sussex, Lincolnshire and Cambridgeshire (see Figure 3) – a cartographic fantasy that was simply ignored by the

Xhosa and, in practice, by most colonial administrators too. The 'Kafir police' were revived and Smith insisted that new 'sticks of office' be handed out to them.

Four villages of discharged military men and their families were settled in the former ceded territory to seal off the Xhosa locations from the main body of settlers in Albany. (Located on some of the Ngqika's best grazing ground and interfering with the mobility of Xhosa cattle, these were the first locations to be attacked when, as we will see below, British Kaffraria's Xhosa rose up again in armed resistance in 1850.) Smith intended to settle far broader swathes of British Kaffraria as well, informing Earl Grey in 1849 that 'we require good Trigonometrical Surveyors for the large tracts of Territory to be sold and disposed of'.[62] Collaborating Mfengu communities were also established on the colonial side of the territory, with annual prizes being awarded to 'the man, woman and child most respectfully clothed throughout the year, for the best and cleanest house, the best and largest area of cultivated ground, the best fenced area, the best waggon, best produce, best poultry'.[63]

As Smith's initial tirade had portended, the British Kafrrarian administration tried to experiment with a new form of colonial governmentality. Despite Smith's reluctant acceptance of the need to conciliate the chiefs in 1836, he still strove to effect a governmental system that would dispense with the need for their acquiescence. The native commissioners were encouraged to bypass chiefly authority and commoners were instructed to appeal direct to the British magistrates in civil cases. Despite Maclean's misgivings, Smith insisted that the chiefs' power to fine their subjects be whittled away. There were soon developments that British officials interpreted as signs of their success in divorcing commoners from chiefs. Henry Calderwood, Commissioner with the Ngqika, reported in April 1847 that many Xhosa were residing within one chief's location whilst professing allegiance to another – a sure sign of the breakdown of Xhosa political structures. Furthermore, a census indicated that in the two years following 1846, the number of Ngqika Xhosa, nominally under Sandile's authority, had diminished from 55,000 to 30,000. Many of these absentee Xhosa, however, far from abandoning their chiefs, were simply searching for food and land in other areas, including independent Gcaleka territory, less afflicted by post-war conditions of impoverishment and colonial control.[64]

Smith upheld the erosion of chiefly power within British Kaffraria as being simply the first step towards the Xhosa's 'civilisation'. Within a post-emancipation discourse of more forceful intervention, this was a more realisable prospect. Humanitarian endeavours had, of course, been directed at an individual reformation of the self, whereas the utilitarian techniques of reformation that were becoming 'common sense' among mid-century Victorians relied upon the necessity for some compulsion by the state. An example of the shift in practice that this twist in discourse entailed concerned the serious issue, as far as all colonial reformers were concerned, of the indigenous use of alcohol. In the humanitarian schemes which were dominant in the 1830s, the revision of the Xhosa subjectivity under Christianity would preclude the abuse of alcohol, without the need for legal restraint. In British Kaffraria though, the sale of wine or beer to 'natives' was simply prohibited, and with no humanitarian opposition.[65] If they could not be reformed from the inside as evangelicals had always hoped, the Xhosa would have to be reformed by external forces, and specifically, by colonial government regulations such as these.

The missionaries within British Kaffraria now seemed similarly reconciled to the need for forceful regulation if the inner salvation of their Xhosa charges was ever to be effected. In turn, their reformulated representations informed those of their metropolitan supporters. Harry Smith had no difficulty in gaining assistance from the Aborigines Protection Society in his attempts rapidly to 'civilise' the Xhosa. They willingly sent £80 worth of agricultural implements and clothing to assist with the government's propagation of the 'habit of industry' in British Kaffraria.[66] When Smith asked the British Kaffrarian missionaries themselves for suggestions in 1848, as Mostert notes, they 'seemed barely able to contain their excitement'. One of them wrote of his profound happiness 'that in a work in which we hitherto laboured alone and unassisted encouragement will be given us'.[67] Robert Niven felt that Smith had been called by Providence 'to initiate a transition state in the Caffre nation, which had been denied to . . . any of his honoured predecessors'. The missionaries as a whole shared a fantasy of 'irrigation, model farms, nurseries, schools, neat homes and everyone soberly dressed' in a transformed British Kaffraria.[68] By the late 1840s, there was none of that sense of unease about too close an association with a military state and with militaristic techniques which had so troubled the LMS and GMS missionaries and their allies in the previous decade.

One of Smith's favourite British Kaffrarian projects, and the one which has possibly received most attention from South African historians, was the export of its youth to service the labour demands of colonists within the Cape proper. Repealing Ordinance 49 of 1828, which had formerly prescribed the conditions on which Xhosa would be allowed to work in the colony, Smith established a system by which Xhosa 'apprentices' would be sent, via their local British Kaffrarian Magistrate, to the Civil Commissioners in those colonial districts requiring extra labour. There they were to be dispersed among 'kind and humane employers'. The scheme was approved of by the Colonial Office in London, as a means of introducing the rising generation of Xhosa to the civilising effects of work. While few Xhosa took up the scheme in Smith's period as High Commissioner, by the mid-1850s, landlessness, further defeat and punishment in war and, finally, drought, were encouraging hundreds of men, women and children to migrate for work.[69]

The continuing problem of resistance

Despite its ever more sophisticated schemes of utilitarian control during the late 1840s, however, the nascent British Kaffrarian state continued to find that supervision over the movements and behaviour of its Xhosa subjects, and indeed its settler citizens, perpetually slipped beyond its grasp. At any given time, there were far more Xhosa working informally for colonial farmers, without official permission, than there were being channelled through the recognised labour distribution networks.[70] Other Xhosa continued to circumvent colonial authority within British Kaffraria, in the same ways as they had done under the Queen Adelaide administration. Calderwood reported that Xhosa were ignoring the boundary of the territory and grazing their cattle, even establishing new kraals, across the old frontier within the colony proper. Maqoma persisted in moving with his followers in and out of colonial territory without bothering to apply for permission. Ultimately Mackinnon was forced to warn him that if he did not stay within his designated location in British Kaffraria, he would be sent to Robben Island.[71] The effect of the warning is unclear.

More seriously, however, as Stockenström pointed out in 1849,

> The Government organs . . . are beginning to discover that our 'children' [Smith's phrase] are preparing for another struggle with us by supplying themselves with firearms and ammunition. I know for certain that they are just as happy and contended as they *were* (not as they were represented to be) under the D'Urban system [in Queen Adelaide Province] . . . [although] their preparations and plans for war are certainly not as far advanced and matured as they were in the middle of 1836.[72]

It was only when he found himself besieged in Fort Cox due to a fresh outbreak of armed Rharhabe Xhosa resistance in 1850, that Harry Smith realised he had pushed the chiefs and their followers too far. His recent decision to depose Sandile altogether and govern the Ngqika directly had been merely the immediate spur for the Xhosa to resume their military struggle. Realising that this was the least fragmented and therefore most powerful and concerted Xhosa uprising that the frontier had yet seen, Smith suddenly panicked. 'Something must be done' he wrote, 'for the Kaffirs of 1851 are not the Kaffirs of 1835!' His directions 'that the Government would in future uphold [the chiefs'] authority and would no longer interfere with native laws and customs', however, came too late.[73]

The 'Eighth Frontier War' of 1850–2 was a testament to the remarkable tenacity of the most direct, 'primary' form of Xhosa resistance to British colonialism. It was to leave 16,000 Xhosa and 1,400 British, settler and Khoesan combatants dead. It has recently been constructed by historians as the last desperate attempt, not just by the Xhosa, but by all of the groups facing proletarianisation in the eastern Cape, to escape their forcible incorporation within a pervasive settler capitalist system.[74] The missionary Rev. Niven outlined the context for this materialist interpretation, noting the 'evil of depriving [the Xhosa] of so much land and giving the Europeans a position in the little that is left, which will, I fear, end in the Caffres becoming a nation of degraded servants on their own soil'.[75] Stockenström, however, alluded to the additional and more emotive concerns which had driven the majority of the Xhosa to rebel once again:

> I tell the government . . . once more that . . . [the Xhosa] are looking . . . upon . . . our gloriously working system *as a state of war of which they are tired*; and although we may by the bayonet and the cat, and by trying like good Christians to identify these with the Bible . . . succeed for a time in keeping up the appearance of tranquillity . . . we may be certain that unless human nature can be changed as well as degraded by foot kissing, a fearful reaction must naturally succeed as the night the day.[76]

When it came, that reaction was guided by the prophecies of Mlanjeni, a Xhosa who had worked in the colony and who promised protection against colonial bullets to those who rose up to overthrow colonial control. As Peires notes, Mlanjeni's influence was enhanced by a severe drought. Many Xhosa blamed it on the activities of witches who, in the light of Smith's ban on witchcraft accusations, had apparently enjoyed more freedom to practice. Even Smith, deploying the kind of imagery that connected distant parts of Britain's imperial periphery within an apparently continuous fabric, felt that 'This drought is much against us, and may enable this regenerated Mahomet to play upon the credulity of your Orientals'.[77]

The actual fighting was once again led by Maqoma, who had been personally goaded into renewed resistance not least by Smith's ritual humiliations. While Phatho remained neutral this time and Mqhayi and most of the minor Ndlambe chiefs sided with the colony, all the other chiefs were united against Smith and the British settlers. Out of the 400 'Kaffir police' appointed by Smith to patrol British Kaffraria, 365 deserted and joined in the rebellion. Even more worryingly for the High Commissioner, though, the Xhosa fighters were soon joined by unprecedented numbers of Khoesan 'rebels' from the colony, and, much to the embarrassment of former humanitarians, especially from the Kat River settlement, where 266 men rebelled.[78]

It is in this 'Kat River Rebellion' that historians have found their most persuasive argument for a class alliance among Khoesan and Xhosa. Both groups seem to have been waging the same struggles against incorporation within a capitalist colonial system, and they therefore seem to have joined forces against the colonial authorities which represented settler capitalist interests.[79] However, I would suggest that the tendency to conceive of the Xhosa 'uprising' and the simultaneous Kat River rebellion as a seamless venture in incipient class struggle can easily be pushed too far. An awareness of an ill-defined future as exploited wage labour was probably more of a galvanising force among the Kat River rebels, who tended to fight their own struggle in the war, than it was among the Xhosa. Certainly, the coincidence of colonial state and settler capitalist imperatives was clearer in the civilian administration of the Kat River settlement, where settlers themselves comprised the local government, than it was in the military governance of British Kaffraria, where resentment at the forcible intrusion of a state pursuing more immediate culturally disruptive and humiliating objectives was paramount. As had been the case in much earlier frontier conflicts, I would argue that most of the Khoesan facing renewed dispossession and servitude who rebelled in 1850 did so at a time when the Xhosa were preoccupying colonial military resources in order to have the best chance of success, rather than because of any nascent, ethnically transcendent class consciousness.

In any case, there is no dispute that it was settler control over the local state, granted from the late 1830s, that had impacted most severely on the Khoesan along the Kat River. The kind of local state imposition envisaged by the Albany settlers was apparent in Graham's Town, where settlers had been granted permission to establish a municipal authority in 1837. Almost immediately, its elected commissioners had begun to effect projects of black spatial containment, control and moral improvement, decreeing that 'Locations' were 'to be marked out' for the Mfengu and Khoesan inhabitants of the town. 'Their dwellings or huts [were] to be so constructed, as to form regular Street at right angle (if practicable) and to be of sufficient breadth, for the comfort and health of the residents.'[80] By the 1840s, the local commissioners were trying to implement dress codes for the inhabitants of the 'native locations' and, most significantly, clearing 'squatters' from government land around the town and forcing them into the official location.[81] It was such practices on a wider scale that led to the Kat River settlement being used as a 'dumping ground' for Khoesan 'squatters' across the frontier zone during the 1840s.[82]

Even in the mid-1830s, James Read had noted that official encroachment on the Kat River settlement itself, in the form of an appointed magistrate, had resulted in the imposition of new constraints. He had testified before the Aborigines Committee that

> things went on much better [in the early years of the settlement] than they have done since they were managed by a magistrate; it was more satisfactory to the Hottentots when all was managed by what might be called a jury; the parties might choose the persons to be their judges, with the field-cornet at their head; this system worked very well.[83]

The actions of local officials in the settlement were soon reinforced by those of a central administration disappointed with the results of emancipation in the Cape. Although General Berkley had reported that 900 out of 1,000 males in the Kat River settlement were already doing military service for the British during the 1846–7 war, Governor Pottinger had insisted that a further 400 men be recruited. At the same time, he had described the settlement, in a private letter to the Colonial Secretary, as 'a concourse of rebellious, idle paupers'.[84] As Kirk, demonstrates, Pottinger clearly based the entire policy of his government towards the Kat River on the representations of local settlers and the *Graham's Town Journal*. Indeed, in his private correspondence with the Colonial Secretary he even plagiarised Godlonton's editorials.[85] Godlonton himself drew upon a trans-imperial imagery for his characterisation of the Kat River valley's inhabitants, describing the settlement as 'the little Ireland of South Africa – a huge accumulation of pauperism'.[86] And indeed, largely because of the localised removal of 'squatters' from Crown land, the settlement was much poorer by the late 1840s than it had been in the mid-1830s.

In May 1847 Pottinger appointed a vocal settler critic of the settlement, T. J. Biddulph, as its superintendent. As du Toit puts it, rather mildly, 'he seems to have taken a violent dislike to his coloured charges and reported adversely on them'.[87] In fact, he described the foundation of the settlement as 'the most transparent piece of humbug ever practised upon the public to serve the purposes of unscrupulous, intriguing people'.[88] He told the Kat River 'settlers' that they must abandon their land and work for colonists; he sold supplies brought in for their relief after they had served with the colonial military in the 1846–7 war; and, when many Khoesan settlers began to cut timber to make a living in the aftermath of the war, he raised taxes on the commodity to the highest levels ever seen in the colony. After vehement complaints, directed by the Khoesan inhabitants through the auspices of James Read, Biddulph was removed, only to be replaced by the equally unsympathetic J. H. Bowker. Bowker's immediate governmental priority was to impound strayed livestock, fine their owners and, frequently, seize the livestock as well.[89]

As High Commissioner, Smith, too, was guided in his approach to the Kat River by local settler representations. These included the demand articulated in the *Graham's Town Journal* that 'nests' of 'coloured' people such as the Kat River settlement 'be broken up' so as to prevent 'the incursions of the brood'.[90] With Smith's approval, early in 1850, Bowker brought the police into the settlement to expel 'unauthorised' Xhosa. Not only were 'squatters' ejected, but a 'legitimately' settled group of Xhosa led by Hermanus Matroos, a former translator for the British army, and a number of 'loyal' Mfengu, had their houses burnt down.[91] If they had a complaint, they were told, they must report it at Fort Hare before possibly being allowed to return to their destroyed homes. The police also raided the district supervised by the loyal field cornet and military veteran Andries Botha, evicting families who had been established in the settlement since its foundation. Botha was to become the main rebel leader during the 1850–2 war.

In an example of the way that the objects of colonial discourse, in this case, the Khoesan of the Kat River, could gain access to that discourse and formulate a response, it is clear that many of the Kat River rebels had been further alienated from the central and local colonial authorities by reading the colonial press. Press coverage of the contemporaneous settler struggle for Representative Government, to which we will return below, had a particular impact within the settlement, since it denoted that the settlers intended using new-found powers of government to re-enact the vagrant laws against freed 'coloureds'. Khoesan soldiers in the Cape Mounted Rifles decided to desert the British forces and join the rebels when they read of such things in the *Graham's Town Journal*, and particularly when they encountered a call for the 'ultimate extinction of the worthless creatures [the Khoesan]' in the Afrikaans paper, *De Zuid Afrikaan*.[92]

As Elbourne comments, 'one of the main complaints of rebels . . . was that they were to be removed from the protection of "the Queen" and placed under direct settler jurisdiction under the new constitutional dispensation'. Their first response had been to utilise missionary networks, as they had been able to do in the 1820s and 1830s, in order to 'incite the British Empire into putting into practice self-proclaimed "English" political ideals, such as the rule of law, freedom of labour and rights without respect to persons'.[93] However, they were now appealing to a metropolitan government and populace that were no longer generally disposed to listen. If they did not seize the opportunity to rise up in arms in 1850, the rebels reasoned, their status as an independent peasantry would almost certainly be whittled away until they were reduced once more to the kind of servitude that had characterised Khoesan life in the Cape before the passage of Ordinance 50.[94]

Regardless of the 'real' reasons for the rebellion, as if such could ever be definitively established, as Bank argues,

> The uprising of the Kat River rebels was typically interpreted [within dominant colonial discourse] not as a last desperate stand by a community whose lands were being encroached upon by white settlers . . . but as the product of [Khoesan] and missionary delusion. For William Porter [the Cape's Attorney General and the humanitarian ally who had so vociferously condemned Shrewsbury's punitive scheme for the Xhosa after the 1834–5 war] . . . the treachery was inspired by a 'foolish notion of nationality' based on the Khoikhoi belief that they were the ancient owners of the land . . . and their envy at the prosperity and industry of the whites which contrasted with their own poverty, 'sloth and inactivity'.[95]

This was a far cry from the humanitarians' early endeavours to extol the Kat River community as a model of progress.

As a result of the 1850–2 war, a second Select Committee was appointed by the British government specifically to inquire into frontier policy in the Cape. Its conclusions could not have been more different from those of its 1836 predecessor. As du Toit notes, one of its keynotes was 'the general feeling of disappointment and scepticism as to the influence of the missionaries'.[96]

In the aftermath of the Kat River uprising and during the trial of the leader Andries Botha, The *Graham's Town Journal* could claim with confidence that 'the case of the Queen versus Andries Botha' was in reality the case of the 'colonists versus the Kat River Settlement', and that the verdict would favour the former.[97] Botha, who was charged with handing over Fort Armstrong to the Kat River rebels (once the Britons defending the fort had fled), was condemned to death after a lengthy trial. When pronouncing sentence the Chief Justice exclaimed, 'Prisoner, the bolt of the law strikes you down! . . . The trial here is at an end. The greater trial, where the thoughts and feelings of the heart are judged awaits you hereafter.'[98] The trial that those left behind in the Kat River were to face, both the 'innocent' and the 'guilty', consisted of more material punishments. They included the confiscation of 'rebel' land and its allocation to white settlers, followed by a series of local government edicts which made the earning of an independent income through firewood collection and other local pursuits illegal.

In Britain, *The Times* carried a series of editorials on the 1850–2 war. This metropolitan press coverage too, was markedly different from that of the 1834–5 war. While metropolitan commentators were still critical of the settlers, pointing to the profiteering in which frontier communities had engaged, they had discarded their concern for the Xhosa. What was of paramount concern now was to give settlers representative government so that the British exchequer would no longer have to pay the costs of seemingly continual warfare against the untamed and quite possibly untameable 'savages' of the Cape frontier zone. *The Times'* attacks on Smith for provoking the war and misleading the Colonial Office, and on Earl Grey for being misled, helped to bring about the fall of Russell's government in February 1852, but they also helped to establish that the 'handful of sheep farmers' on the frontiers of the British empire should be given control over their own 'native policy'.[99]

I will consider post-war developments in British Kaffraria in the ensuing, and final chapter. First, though, I want to examine the discursive effects of other outbreaks of resistance across a far broader terrain, with Britain at its centre, during the 1850s and 1860s. It was these effects, I suggest, that rendered the post-war administration of British Kaffraria feasible within a reformulated imperial system.

The discursive effects of global resistance

As I have mentioned, and as Bayly notes, there was a 'coincidence in the mid-nineteenth century of large-scale indigenous resistance in very diverse economic and cultural circumstances' in different parts of the globe.[100] Both formal and 'informal' components of Britain's empire were embroiled in contests associated with a more expansive imperial and capitalist phase. Each of these contests allowed for the further undermining of humanitarian representations, the more emphatic adoption of settler discourses by powerful metropolitan groups, and the more forceful operation of colonial governance. In a number of respects, as will become clearer in the next chapter, developments in the mid-century Cape cannot be conceived of in isolation from these more global transformations.

Commerce and civilisation in China

The first indications of a clearer coincidence between metropolitan and 'peripheral' expansive imperatives in the mid-nineteenth century came with respect to China. The Opium War was fought by Palmerston's government in 1840–2 to enforce a Treaty Port system in the interests of British traders who had long appealed against restrictions on their trade (notably in opium from India). The governor of Hong Kong, however, persisted in arguing for a more effectual British authority in the region and, in 1856–60, the 'Arrow War' was fought to overcome Chinese resistance to the further expansion of the opium trade.[101]

These wars on the periphery of Britain's 'informal empire' were framed discursively by a reversal of the relationship between Christianity and civilisation that had been decided upon by the Aborigines Committee. As we saw in the last chapter, the Committee had asserted firmly that the Christian reformation of the self must come before 'real' civilisation could be achieved. By the mid-century, though, after the apparent failure of the missions to generate sufficient numbers of freed, 'properly' Christianised black subjects, especially in the West Indies and in Africa, the sequence had been popularly re-evaluated. The 'renovation of the world' (as David Livingstone put it), was now to be achieved first with material civilisation in the form of trade. Palmerston himself stressed with particular conviction that 'Commerce is the best pioneer of civilization'. China became a test case, with Palmerston arguing that freer trade would 'lead civilization with one hand and peace with the other, to render mankind happier, wiser, better'.[102] It was Palmerston as well, who played a leading role in reinterpreting the earlier campaign against the slave trade, for the benefit of mid-century Britons. For him, the campaign had been launched not just to remove a 'foul and detestable crime', but to bring about a better global order, based on mutual prosperity. He argued that 'virtue carries its own reward . . . These slave trade treaties . . . are indirectly treaties for the encouragement of commerce'.[103]

The mid-century struggle in China was thus represented for metropolitan observers in very particular ways. From his position at the hub of empire, Palmerston presented a case for an aggressive war there on the grounds of a mutually beneficial and civilising free trade. But local British traders and officials were able to supplement his propagandistic endeavours by feeding a bellicose anti-Chinese rhetoric to the domestic press. In 1856, Palmerston picked up on these more racist representations, speaking in parliament of the 'kidnapping, murdering, poisoning, barbarian' Chinese who had refused to co-operate with local British merchants. Ultimately, the rhetoric was reflected in the indemnities that the Chinese were expected to pay for the war.[104]

If commercial ventures within parts of the 'informal' empire of commerce were being pursued more aggressively during the 1840s and 1850s, more formal settler colonization and/or imperial intervention was simultaneously impacting, unprecedentedly destructively on the populations of much of Australia, New Zealand, North America and India, as well as the eastern Cape. Technological improvements were simultaneously allowing the more effective transmission of visual and written representations from these colonies. Along with greater government assistance, they were also facilitating increased emigration.[105] The vastly increased numbers of Britons with relatives and friends in New Zealand, Australia, the Cape, Natal and India, helped ensure that settler communities would have a large and sympathetic audience 'at home'. Settlers within each colonial 'hot spot' were thus better able to influence metropolitan constructions of their particular 'crises'. And, invariably, these constructions involved concepts of indigenous irreclaimability.

The shock of resistance in India

Of these numerous mid-century colonial crises, the Indian 'Mutiny' of 1857 was the most shocking to local and metropolitan British observers, and possibly most critical in undermining humanitarian claims about indigenous reclaimability. Given India's prominence within the empire, its administrators and settlers had always enjoyed particularly well-developed connections with the metropolis. Apart from the financial relations between the government of India and the City of London, the empire depended to a great extent on the use of Indian troops, and private financial investment in India was considerable.[106] Furthermore, as Eric Stokes pointed out, many of the hegemonic ideas of the Victorian middle class had been worked out with reference to India. Free trade had been tested against the East India Company's monopolies, Charles Grant and John Shore (Lord Teignmouth) of the Clapham Sect had bolstered their Christian militancy in the Indian service, and middle-class evangelicalism as a whole owed 'much of its impetus' to intervention among Indians. All this is not to mention James Mill's Indian experiments in the application of utilitarian doctrine.[107]

Given the enormous pride that Britons had in their governance of India, the 'Mutiny' proved a tremendous trauma to liberals as well as to the interested British public. As Hyam points out,

> over 500 books appeared about the Mutiny between 1857 and 1862. In later memoirs, all possible superlatives abound. The Mutiny was always the most calamitous, the most tremendous catastrophe, the most serious life-and-death struggle, the most hideous occurrence of the century.[108]

With its most frequently represented characteristic being irrational, demonic violence, the revolt generated a 'fever of race hatred' in the British newspapers.[109]

While some humanitarians continued to claim that the revolt was due to a failure to proselytise Christianity sufficiently rigorously in the face of entrenched 'superstitions', as James Walvin argues, the more general effect of the rebellion was to undermine 'British confidence that they might be able to recast the subcontinent in their own image'. Queen Victoria's reactive proclamation once the revolt had been suppressed, announced that the British renounced 'the right and desire to impose Our convictions on any of Our subjects'. The subtext was that such a desirable outcome could no longer be considered feasible because of the demonstrable 'irreclaimability' of the Indian.[110] As the dominant stereotype of the mild and tractable Hindu was displaced by that of the incomprehensibly scheming and treacherous Oriental in the aftermath of the revolt, Indians too, came to be widely described as 'niggers'.[111]

From his perspective as commissioner with the Ngqika within British Kaffraria, Charles Brownlee felt that the Xhosa could at least claim not to have harmed colonial women and children during the recent frontier wars. After the massacre at Lucknow, he posed the question, 'Will the highly civilized inhabitants of India bear comparison with this?'[112]

Indigenous 'recalcitrance' in New Zealand

During the early 1860s, metropolitan notions of indigenous irreclaimability were consolidated by the New Zealand colonial government's wars against certain Maori chiefdoms. These were fought not simply to appease the land hunger of settlers, but to extend British governmentality in line with utilitarian projects of the kind that I will describe in the Cape in the concluding chapter. As James Belich argues, the wars were primarily the result of British governors' desires to 'convert nominal sovereignty into substantive sovereignty'.[113] In much the same way that successive wars against the Xhosa had consolidated irredeemable representations among settlers and officials in the Cape, the New Zealand Wars allowed for the construction of a new hostility towards New Zealand's indigenes.

The relative success of Maori resistance also raised new doubts in the minds of their former defenders, including those who had testified before the Aborigines Committee itself. As Belich points out, since the well-publicised humanitarian cause of 'salvageability' in New Zealand had come to be 'based partly on [the Maoris'] readiness selectively to adopt European ways in commerce, agriculture, literacy and religion . . . resistance was seen as a reversal of this trend; evidence that the civilising mission had failed, or even that it had always been doomed to failure'. Accordingly, 'Many who had fearlessly argued the justice of the Maori case in the Taranaki War of 1860 felt that the

Waikato War of 1863 was the "sharp lesson" which, sadly, the Maoris both needed and deserved.'[114]

The parallels between experiences with 'indigenes' in the Cape and New Zealand, and the 'lessons' to be learned from them, were not missed by contemporaries. If only the word 'Maori' were replaced with 'Kaffir', the following extract from the New *Zealand Southern Cross* could easily have come from the *Graham's Town Journal*:

> We have dealt with the natives of this country upon a principle radically wrong. We have conceded them rights and privileges which nature has refused to ratify . . . and we now experience their hatred of intelligence and order . . . The Maori is now known to us as what he is, and not as missionaries and philanthropists were willing to believe him . . . a man ignorant and savage, loving darkness and anarchy; hating light and order; a man of fierce, and ungoverned passions, bloodthirsty, cruel, ungrateful, treacherous.[115]

In 1861, Merrivale argued that 'The Caffre or the Maori may be rendered equal in legal rights with the settler, but he is not really equal in the power of enjoying or enforcing those rights, nor can he become so until civilization has rendered him equal in knowledge and mental power'.[116]

Humanitarianism overawed: Jamaica and the Morant Bay revolt

In the 1850s and early 1860s, then, communities of settlers on the empire's most remote fringes were orchestrating representations of resistant indigenous peoples that were far removed from those of the earlier humanitarians, and these representations were carrying more weight 'at home' in Britain. But it was the locus of the original anti-slavery debates, the West Indies, which supplied the images that really consolidated settler discursive influence. In Jamaica, the Morant Bay rebellion broke out in 1865, part of its context being freed blacks' frustrated appeals for land. The island's Governor, Edward Eyre, a former explorer of Australia and humanitarian Protector of the Aborigines, crushed the uprising and had 439 of its participants, as well as a scapegoated 'mixed-race' member of the House of Assembly hanged.[117] As Christine Bolt has argued, the events 'crystallized Victorian thinking' about racial difference.[118]

Eyre found his reaction to the revolt condemned by metropolitan humanitarians, prominent liberals and radicals. His severest critics included John Stuart Mill, John Bright, and Charles Darwin. These men sought to have Eyre prosecuted for the arbitrary brutality with which he had put down the uprising. However, Eyre was successfully defended both by the island's planters and by such leading metropolitan figures as Charles Dickens, Alfred Tennyson and Thomas Carlyle, to whom we will return below, who formed a Defence Committee on his behalf.[119] As Catherine Hall has pointed out, though, what is most significant about the whole controversy is not so much the fate of Eyre himself as the discursive terms on which it was conducted. Mill himself maintained that 'The question was, whether the British dependencies, and eventually, perhaps, Great Britain itself, were to be under the government of law, or of military licence.'[120] For Mill and his liberal allies, 'The great advance in the world was not the abandonment of force in society but its more efficient regulation.'[121] Eyre was therefore attacked 'because it was felt he represented conservatism . . . [and] indifference to the rule of law'.[122] It was thus in the sense of a considered utilitarian exercise in state power on the one hand, as opposed to the 'heroic' and individual exercise of force on the other, that the Eyre controversy became, as Leonard Huxley put it, 'the touchstone of ultimate political convictions'.[123]

Given this preoccupation, whether or not the revolt of Jamaica's blacks was a justifiable, or even an understandable action, did not generally feature in the metropolitan discussions surrounding Morant Bay and its aftermath. Given the prior disappointment of humanitarians with the outcome of abolition, even Mill had to agree with speaker after speaker in Parliament that the refusal of blacks to labour productively in Jamaica was an obstacle to their political defence. Jamaica's blacks were 'unfit to exercise political power', as Grey put it, because they had failed to discipline themselves in accordance with the contract that abolitionists themselves had sought to impose.[124] Indeed, far from inducing greater sympathy with Jamaica's freed black population, the revolt confirmed the British press's worst fears about freed slaves. *The Times* claimed that Morant Bay was even more of a disappointment than the Indian 'Mutiny' because 'its inhabitants are our spoilt children . . . It seemed to be proved in Jamaica that the negro could become fit for self-government . . . Jamaica herself gainsays the fact and belies herself'. The reason for the failure was also alluded to in the paper:

> It seems . . . impossible to eradicate the original savageness of the African blood. As long as the black man has a strong white Government and a numerous white population to control him he is capable of living as a respectable member of society. He can be made quiet and even industrious by the fear of the supreme power, and by the example of those to whom he necessarily looks up. But wherever he attains to a certain degree of independence there is the fear that he will resume the barbarous life and fierce habits of his African ancestors.[125]

As Thomas Holt argues then, with 'British sympathy for coloured peoples' already 'dulled by the Indian Mutiny . . . and the ongoing Maori War', the relieved Eyre discovered upon his recall to Britain 'that racist fears found a receptive public'.[126]

In the wake of the rebellion, Jamaica's planters relinquished their representative government – a government that had included many blacks and that was soon going to include many more. No one in Britain argued that black Jamaicans should retain their claim to citizenship, and its loss in Jamaica was soon extended throughout most of the West Indies. This was a significant manoeuvre: 'At a time when America was trying to implement human equality in the South, and agitation for suffrage reform and white colonial self-determination was moving forward successfully in Britain, the latter was deciding in favour of semi-despotic government over millions of [black] colonial subjects.'[127]

Lessons from America

As the New Zealand Wars and Morant Bay were being discussed in Britain, further racialised representations were being communicated to the British reading public from outside the imperial network. Robert Young notes that 'the debates about slavery that preceded and accompanied the American Civil War were undoubtedly significant in changing the terms of debate about race even in Britain'.[128] Already, British sympathy for the North's cause of slave emancipation had been rendered problematic due to the 'failure' of abolition in the West Indies.[129] As Lorimer points out, 'British newspapers friendly to the Union remained in a minority throughout the war; Lincoln's administration was ridiculed until his death; while Southern Independence societies flourished.'[130]

With the assistance of propagandists from the Southern states, the events of the Civil War itself helped British observers to refine their hardening racial discourse, associating the 'proper' place of the 'Negro' in the US South with that of the freed slave and the African in the British colonies.[131] In both the USA and the British empire, according to papers like *The Times*, an inherent incapacity of blacks to work, unless forced, had been demonstrated by premature acts of emancipation.[132] Even humanitarians, who continued to protest during the war against representations of the American slaves 'as a highly endowed species of ape', could only exhort British popular opinion to acknowledge that it would still 'be cruel to let them perish when the war is no fault of theirs'.[133] As Philip Curtin notes, then, 'In the trans-Atlantic exchange of ideas, Britain gave the anti-slavery crusade to America in the 1830s and received back the American racism of the 1850s.'[134]

Images of unreclaimed Southern US slaves thus converged with an established flow of representations of racial 'others' from within the empire itself during the 1860s. As we have seen in previous chapters, similar representations had been transmitted along imperial networks by colonial settlers and officials like those in the Cape since the early nineteenth century. Powerfully assisted by the expansion of the medium of print, and by the popularity of 'Romantic and dreadful stories of alien depravity', which progressively supplanted missionary tracts as popular reading material, settler images from across the colonised world had been carried to British audiences through potent books and articles, through parliamentary debates, and through published memorials like Godlonton's, as well as thorough more personal forms of correspondence.[135] The flow of propagandistic imagery, however, became a torrent during the period of fiercest indigenous resistance to imperial encroachment in the 1850s and 1860s. Former slave-owners and colonists managed more successfully than ever before to convince those in the metropole of the dangers they faced in living among 'irreclaimable savages', and indeed, of their heroism in doing so. In the context of Morant Bay, for instance, *The Times* urged its readers 'to visualize the terrors facing a minority threatened by a numerous and barbarous enemy'.[136]

In Belich's phraseology, 'Victorian attitudes to race were a web spun from many starting points . . . literate Victorians were caught at the intersections; the junctions where many otherwise diverse strands overlapped'.[137] However, the points of origin of many of these diverse strands was indicated, again in the context of Morant Bay, by the *Saturday Review*. The paper claimed, 'There is too much disposition in English society so far to share . . . Colonial prejudice'.[138] The particular racialised 'other' which featured most prominently in metropolitan imaginations at any one time was contingent on the course of events in peripheries ranging from New Zealand to India. However, the aggregate effect of 'news' from these marginal spaces of British authority was to consolidate distinctions between Britons and more backward or downright dangerous colonial subjects. All of these subjects were now popularly constructed as possibly irreclaimable, and at the very least, dangerously backward.[139] Thus, due to the revived influence of Britain's colonial settlers, the behaviour of colonised subjects in one part of the world could be seen in Britain as much like that of colonised subjects in another. As Rear Admiral J. L. Stokes wrote to *The Times* in 1865, the Morant Bay revolt in Jamaica, Fenianism in Ireland and the New Zealand War all demonstrated 'the risk, failure, and subsequent expense often attending conciliatory measures' in Britain's imperial peripheries.[140]

Metropolitan and colonial discourses of difference

The mid-nineteenth-century triumph of settler over humanitarian imagery was by no means due solely to the flow of representations from sites of conflict in the colonies to sites of consumption in the metropole. Colonial representations became more potent within Britain because they intersected with and helped to reformulate domestic discourses of class, ethnic and gender difference. At the imperial centre, as Holt points out, 'much of the British middle class . . . connected the need to repel class challenges from below with support for racism and empire'.[141] Thus, 'the debate about the "condition of the native" cross cut, time and time again, with the debate about the condition of the British poor' and other marginalised metropolitan groups.[142] In turn, domestically refashioned discourses, not just of class, but of ethnicity and gender, helped underpin practices of racial domination in the colonies. In this final section of the chapter, I intend to indicate the ways in which they did so in a more general sense, before I return to the Cape frontier to examine some of the local effects of metropolitan and colonial interaction in the mid-nineteenth century.

Respected spokesmen for the British bourgeoisie were becoming frustrated by the 1840s with humanitarian liberalism, in so far as it pertained to Britain itself. The reformist drive at Westminster, with which colonial humanitarians had been able so effectually to connect in the 1830s, ground to a halt during the following decade. Through the reforms that had already taken place, the wealthiest and most 'respectable' of Britain's middle classes had been effectively incorporated within the governing elite. As Evans argues, 'government based on property [had] not only survived but was strengthened thereby'.[143] It was now felt by many reformers that the imperative for national atonement identified in the early decades of the century had been met and that Britain was indisputably the most free, the most enlightened and the most blessed country in the world. At the same time, the propertied classes feared that further reform might give 'proletarian hordes' the opportunity of exploiting 'bourgeois democracy to make socialism', a spectre that loomed especially large during the unsettling years of Chartist activity in the late 1830s and 1840s.[144] As Davidoff and Hall put it, 'class distance took solid form as the more prosperous watched the night skies flare with burning ricks or saw Chartist crowds sweep past their comfortable parlour windows'.[145]

There were a number of indications of a shift in dominant ideas of proper moral and governmental authority associated with this new middle-class orientation in Britain. By the late 1830s, for instance, Whig journals such as the *Edinburgh Review* 'were already showing a marked decline in their reforming attitudes, above all through an unquestioned acceptance of the dogmas of political economy'. When presented with the massive Chartist petition of 1842, the reformer Macaulay responded, 'Civilization rests upon the security of property, and to give the vote to those without property would be destructive of the whole of society'.[146] The economic crisis and the events of the Famine in Ireland in 1847, the revolutionary turmoil on the European continent in 1848, and the later association between Fenianism and English radicalism served only to harden alliances within the propertied middle classes, and to reinforce demands for the more effective policing of politically radical working-class elements.[147]

Such metropolitan bourgeois anxieties could only generate new sympathies with those colonial emigrants who faced the dangers of similarly unregenerate groups in the imperial periphery. In the 1860s, just as the divide between 'civilised' colonists and 'irreclaimable' indigenes seemed to have widened, so the gap between the propertied classes and the non-propertied in Britain was increasing. In the early 1800s, the wealthiest 10 per cent of Britain's population had controlled 40 per cent of its national income; by 1867, they had 51 per cent. Perhaps the most salient marker of middle-class achievement was the rise in servant-keeping. By the late 1860s, this had become a '*sine qua non* for middle class respectability and was even a feasible goal for established artisans and well-paid manual workers'.[148] The practice not only reflected the material achievement of these groups, however; it also served to mark them off more clearly from the 'residuum' who were unable to aspire to such a goal. As Lorimer asserts, 'mid-Victorian householders did not require the visible distinctions of race to assign a marked place to their servants, nor did they need servants with black skins to ensure that domestics stayed in that assigned place'.[149]

In the face of continued working-class mobilisation, the Liberal Party first attempted to draw a further distinction between those workers who had realisable ambitions of achieving 'respectability', and who were thus deserving of the vote, and the remainder, who were not, in the mid-1860s. As Gladstone expressed it, the intention was to make the change appear as a 'boon granted' rather than a 'fortress stormed'.[150] When it seemed that a more reactionary Tory Party would again be elected into office, demonstrations were organised by the Reform League, involving trade unionists, members of friendly societies and republicans, the most spectacular of which took place in Hyde Park in London. It was the fear of demonstrators' capacity to destabilise the fragile social order which surrounded subsequent debates over the 1867 Reform Act. In the event, the franchise was extended by the Tories themselves to 'registered and Respectable' working men. As had been the case with the 1832 Reform Act, the concession had the effect of separating those men among the 'lower orders' who could most safely be absorbed into the politics of the ruling classes from women and from the 'residuum', the roughly one third of the male population who were still considered to be unfit to exercise citizenship.

Catherine Hall has pointed out that the metropolitan contest over the franchise in the late 1860s was closely tied in with discussion of colonial conditions, and especially with the debate over the Morant Bay revolt.[151] On the one hand, the radical demonstrators meeting Eyre on his return to Southampton 'linked [his] brutal repression of Jamaican blacks with the newly inaugurated Tory government's repression of the Hyde Park demonstration in July 1866'.[152] On the other hand, arrayed against the liberals and radicals who condemned Eyre, were men who sought to consolidate and protect male bourgeois power. For these men, the connections between colonial and metropolitan politics were just as important, but they drew very different conclusions form them. The Morant Bay revolt had taught them, as the *Pall Mall Gazette* put it, that 'securing civil rights to a people is one thing, and conferring on them political privileges is another; that all races and all classes are entitled to justice , but that all are not fit or ready for self-government; that to many, and notably to the West Indian negroes, giving them to themselves, as we have done, is simply the cruellest and laziest neglect'. The implication, of course, was that not all Britons either could be expected to exercise political privileges safely. For conservatives, descriptions of the Morant Bay rebels in Jamaica thus shaded into those of the threatening lower classes at home. Elements of both groups could be described as 'fanatical democrats of the socialist type'.[153] When Mill admitted defeat in the Eyre controversy, he ascribed it 'to the sympathy with authority and power, generated in our higher and upper middle classes by the feeling of being especially privileged to exercise them, and by living in a constant dread of the encroachment of the class beneath, which makes it one of their strongest feelings that resistance to authority must be put down'.[154]

Those working men who were enfranchised in 1867 were accordingly the ones who were 'increasingly marked off from the unhealthy residuum through the Poor Law and sanitary reform, through the differentiation between sober and drunkard'. As Beales, one of the leaders of the Reform League argued, it was safe to enfranchise such men, for they 'are deeply interested in the preservation of law and order, of the rights of capital and property; of the honour and power and wealth of our country'.[155] Their very demarcation from the 'residuum' served to reinforce the notion that those who had not thus far striven for their own improvement were social outcasts, morally incapable of inclusion within the body politic.[156] Through the new property qualifications, not only poorer casual labourers in Britain, but groups such as women, gypsies, criminals and the transient Irish, continued to be defined as part of this 'residuum'.[157] All of these groups could be described, in Jeremy Bentham's terms, as 'a sort of forward children – a set of persons not altogether sound in mind – not altogether possessed of that moral sanity without which a man can not in justice to himself any more than to the community be intrusted with the uncontrolled management of his own conduct and affairs'.[158] Just in the way that colonised groups like the Maori and the Xhosa stood in relation to colonial settlers, many of these domestic categories could be referred to as a 'gigantic evil' which 'threatens the civilization to which it is a reproach, is a standing danger to the middle and upper classes, and tends to the deterioration of the race'.[159]

If dominant political discourse in Britain was coming to reflect exclusive colonial settler, rather than universalist humanitarian constructions of human difference and legal entitlement in the 1850s and 1860s, so too was metropolitan scientific discourse.[160] Indeed, the preoccupation of physical anthropologists with biological differences between the races can be seen as an appropriation of the representations of immutable difference that planters and settlers had been propagating for decades. One of the colonial settlers' greatest metropolitan allies in the struggle to define racial difference was Robert Knox, the pioneering scientific racist and author of *The Races of Men*, who had served as army surgeon in the 1819 Cape frontier war against Ndlambe, collecting 'specimens' of Khoesan and Xhosa skulls in between performing his duties.[161] Together with James Hunt, Knox's scientific work represented a crusade against humanitarian 'interference', both in Britain and the colonies. Following Knox, Hunt ridiculed all those who made 'the gigantic assumption of absolute human equality', describing them as being afflicted by 'rights-of-man mania'. Their 'defective reasoning power', he felt, should be exposed as a 'sham and a delusion' through the presentation of scientific evidence.[162] These scientists effectively strengthened the connections between settler-originated constructions of race and metropolitan middle-class constructions of other kinds of 'internal' social difference. In Hunt's view, the brain of the 'Negro' was much like that of the European woman or child, and in the view of many contemporaries, both shared certain characteristics with those of criminals, Celts and the labouring poor.[163]

By the late 1860s, then, the racial differences represented by settlers were intersecting powerfully in Britain not only with dominant representations of class, but with reformulated notions of gender, ethnicity and criminality. Settlers in the Cape and elsewhere were no longer marginalised by hegemonic metropolitan discourses as they had been in the 1830s. They were not only deriving legitimation from these more reactive discourses; they were actively contributing to the debates surrounding them, and thus to their refinement.[164]

Thomas Carlyle, Matthew Arnold and colonial settlers

If metropolitan scientific racists like Hunt were concerned indirectly with the political struggles of groups of colonial settlers, two other extremely influential mid-century intellectuals were involved directly. Thomas Carlyle and Matthew Arnold each played crucial roles in effecting a broad discursive shift across the spaces of empire. Both men can be conceived as mediators of a transition in dominant notions of liberalism and liberty. They helped translate the humanitarianism of the 1830s into the more utilitarian classism and racism of the mid to late nineteenth century. Furthermore, their work indicates quite explicitly the ways in which a reactionary bourgeois movement in Britain was linked to racialised representations from the frontiers of the empire. Through their broader discursive refinements, both men in a sense helped to create the climate within which the Rharhabe Xhosa among others would ultimately be colonised.

Carlyle in particular, who opposed the extension of the franchise in Britain in 1867, nevertheless played an influential role in formulating and voicing concepts that were becoming culturally normative among the Victorian middle classes. They included a 'critique of democracy', an 'insistence on leadership and strong government' and a 'preoccupation with Empire and with racial difference'.[165] Over the preceding twenty years, while his writings had shifted their emphasis and sometimes contradicted each other, his main endeavour had been to reformulate humanitarian liberalism in such a way that it could accommodate ideas of 'natural' difference between properly governing classes and their 'others'. His political philosophy thus allowed quite legitimate exclusions from political privilege. Carlyle's diatribe on the inherent limitations of freed Jamaican slaves, prompted by his personal connections with Jamaican planters, was an important part of this reformulation.

In his *Discourses on the Negro* (subsequently *Nigger*) *Question*, first published in 1849, Carlyle channelled the Jamaican planters' imagery of former slaves 'sitting . . . with their beautiful muzzles up to their ears in pumpkins . . . grinders and incisor teeth ready for ever new work . . . while the sugar crops rot around them uncut because labour cannot be hired', to metropolitan audiences. He addressed the freed labour force directly on behalf of their former masters: 'You are not "slaves" now; nor do I wish, if it can be avoided, to see you slaves again; but decidedly you have to be servants to those that are born *wiser* than you, that are born the lords of you; servants to the whites, if they *are* (as what mortal can doubt they are?) born wiser than you.' As Thomas Holt puts it, 'here was the slaveholder's propaganda in the mouth of one of Britain's most prominent men of letters'.[166]

The lesson of emancipation in Jamaica was one which Carlyle felt had a direct relevance 'at home'. His views were also shaped very much with Ireland in mind, and it was here that he qualified the racism which was so prevalent in *Discourses on the Nigger Question*. It was his travels in Ireland that persuaded him of the proper treatment of subordinated classes in general. As the 'noisy, turbulent, irreclaimable savagery' of the Irish proved, it was 'not the colour of the skin that determines the savagery of the man'. Rather, it was wilful rebellion against 'the laws of Nature'. As Holt maintains, blacks were merely Carlyle's 'emblem of degradation, of the level to which whites could sink'. To be 'forced to found the right path, and to walk thereon, to learn, or to be taught what work he actually is able for, and then, by permission, persuasion, and even compulsion, to set about doing the same', Carlyle argued, was the only 'true liberty' for those afflicted by such a condition of savagery, be they black or white, Jamaican, Irish or even English. The free labourer in any of these spaces had only 'the indisputable and perpetual *right* to be compelled, by the real proprietors of . . . the land, to do competent work for his living. This is the everlasting duty of all men, black or white, who are born into this world'.[167]

For Carlyle, even 'the enfranchisement of respectable [British] working class men was [therefore] a disaster'.[168] Like settlers in the Cape and other colonies, he identified the 'cancer at the heart of [the] crisis' in both metropolitan and colonial affairs as being the notion of equality, only he did so more effectively, and in terms more appealing to metropolitan audiences than settler communities were capable of achieving on their own. As Hall points out, he made it seem

> ludicrous to talk of the equality of the uneducated with educated, female with male, black with white. It was the 'Nigger-Philanthropists' as he described them, the critics of Eyre, the abolitionists, the supporters of the North in the American Civil War, who were the real enemy within, sapping the vital energies of English men with their crazy comparisons of 'Quashee Nigger' with Socrates or Shakespeare.[169]

In his *Shooting Niagara*, the dangers posed by colonial humanitarians (whom he also referred to as 'Exeter Hall philanthropists' with their 'dismal science'), and of metropolitan democracy, were represented as being one and the same. In each case, Carlyle asserted, the humanitarian concept of 'Liberty requires new definitions'.[170]

Carlyle served further to undermine the evangelical humanitarianism that had attained such power in the 1830s through his assault on the sentimentalism, naïvety and other-worldliness of missionaries and liberal reformers. Indeed the risible picture that he painted of missionaries concerned with the sufferings of distant savages, while English men and women starved through misgovernment, was perhaps his most powerful appeal. It was largely through the ridicule of humanitarians by eminent figures such as Carlyle and Charles Dickens, with his *Bleak House* character Mrs Jellyby, and her overwhelming concern for the savages of a fictitious African kingdom, that the meaning of words such as 'sentiment' and 'sentimentalist' shifted during the mid-nineteenth century. Having been 'a positive sense of a strong emotion which prompted the individual into action' in the 1830s, the concept of sentiment 'became tinged with hypocrisy, a mere self-indulgence of the emotions; and a sentimentalist became a weak-kneed, impractical individual who, in the words of Carlyle, was particularly associated with the . . . "spoutings, anti-spoutings, and interminable jangle and babble of Exeter Hall"', by the 1860s.[171]

The utility of Carlyle's arguments, not just for West Indies planters, but for settlers in places like the Cape, and the fact of their trans-imperial deployment, is testified by John Mitford Bowker. Among all the Cape's colonists, he drew most explicitly upon Carlyle's work to articulate notions which had long been held less systematically within the settler community. Bowker was particularly fond of quoting from Carlyle's *Past and Present*, a book published in 1843 in an endeavour to promote a sense of white racial kinship transcending dangerous social tensions in Britain.[172] In this book, Carlyle emphasised the humanitarians' failure to change the stereotyped freed slave figure of 'Quashee', who, 'it must be remembered', wrote Carlyle, 'is a kind of blockhead'. 'The Hayti King', Carlyle continued, 'educated now *for half a century*, seems to have no sense in him. Why, in one of our weavers dying of hunger, there is more thought, heart – a greater arithmetical amount of desperation in him – than in the whole gang of Quashees'.[173] Carlyle's work seemed to suggest to Bowker, at least, that 'the savages' in South Africa 'will [also] baffle the [missionaries'] scheme, and the scale must fall from philanthropy's eyes, for they repel every attempt on our part towards conciliation or amelioration'.[174]

It was the secure knowledge of Carlyle's influence in Britain that enabled Bowker to state with confidence that

> Aborigines' protection societies, Anti-slavery societies, mission institutions, as at present conducted, are things of naught. Savage nations

must be taught to fear and respect, to *stand in awe* of a nation whose manners and customs, whose religion, it is beneficial and desirable for them to adopt . . . we must prove to these people that we are their superiors before we can ever hope for much good to be done among them, by conquering them if no milder means are effectual . . . Could the missionaries persuade the Kafirs to become a nation of cotton growers . . . conquering them would perhaps be unnecessary.[175]

While Carlyle was presenting not only the Jamaican planters but communities such as the Cape settlers with a new and especially influential mouthpiece in Britain, and a means by which their racial discourse could inflect dominant metropolitan notions, Matthew Arnold was heaping further scorn on the settlers' enemies.

Like Carlyle, Arnold was opposed to working-class enfranchisement in Britain. Although he differed from Carlyle in his critique of wealth and industrialism and although he never advocated the same degree of authoritarian leadership, he too attacked 'naïve' and downright dangerous humanitarian notions of individual rights. Believing that 'great and pregnant elements of difference . . . lie in race', Arnold insisted on the English race's need for discipline and on the rejection of humanitarian reformist 'sentiment'.[176] He was particularly well placed to become a protagonist in the controversy over the Bishop of Natal, John Colenso's published analysis of parts of the Old Testament in 1862. As Jeff Guy notes, this controversy, taking place at a time when 'scientific discoveries in geology, history and biology appeared to undermine the basic tenets of conventional Christian belief', was to develop into 'one of the sensational public debates of the mid nineteenth century'.[177]

By the late 1850s, Colenso had already raised the hackles of many other missionaries and most settlers in Natal and the Cape, first because of his resistance to the missionary tactic of threatening everlasting punishment in order to terrorise potential converts, and secondly because of his tolerance of polygamy on the part of converts. In the early 1860s though, he was encouraged by his Zulu translator, William Ngidi, to ask more fundamental questions about spiritual belief and conversion. As well as advising Colenso on Zulu linguistics, Ngidi insisted on interrogating certain biblical passages, pointing out their contradictions and absurdities, and presenting Colenso with insoluble difficulties in their interpretation. In Colenso's published analysis of the first six chapters of the Old Testament, Ngidi's influence was acknowledged alongside that of European scientists who had similarly destabilised the notion of the bible as objective historical truth. Following his experience with Ngidi's questioning, Colenso looked forward to the day when 'we shall be able . . . to meet the Mahomedan and Brahmin and Buddhist, as well as the untutored savage of South Africa and the South Pacific, on other and better terms than we now do, – being no longer obliged to maintain every part of the bible as an infallible record of past history, and every word as the sacred utterance of the Spirit of God'.[178]

Colenso's 'heresy' of relativism, ultimately confirmed when he was excommunicated by the Bishop of Cape Town, prompted a settler newspaper, *The Natal Witness*, to pen the ditty:

> A Bishop there was of Natal,
> Who had a Zulu for a pal,
> Said the native 'Look here,
> 'Ain't the Pentateuch queer?'
> Which converted my Lord of Natal.

But more damaging to Colenso's reputation than local settler satire was the profound metropolitan debate over religious belief and culture that his writings prompted. The 'Colenso affair' became a political controversy waged across the spaces of the empire, because, as Guy points out, 'the laughter at the story of the Zulu who converted the Bishop was not just derisive – it was also nervous. It was laughter at a disturbing reversal of the idea of coloniser and colonised which switched dominated for dominant, unlearned for learned, heathen for christian, savage for civilized, the self and other'.[179]

Matthew Arnold took it upon himself to demolish Colenso's pretensions to be a biblical scholar, or indeed, a respected intellectual in any sense. For Arnold, 'literary criticism has to try the book of the Bishop of Natal, which all England is now reading. It has to try it in respect of the influence which it is naturally calculated to exercise on the culture of England or Europe'.[180] Arnold found Colenso's attempts to render the bible intelligible to Africans and others not only ridiculous, but dangerous, and he did so on similar grounds to Carlyle's critique of humanitarianism. 'The highly instructed few, and not the scantily instructed many', he wrote, 'will ever be the organ to the human race of knowledge and truth. Knowledge and truth, in the full sense of the words, are not attainable by the great mass of the human race at all'.[181] Thus, as Guy suggests, what lay behind Arnold's well-publicised attack on Colenso was not only 'a smirk at a Christian bishop who takes seriously the beliefs of the other – and a snigger at the religions of the colonised, at the people of empire', but also a reaction to the democratic demands of Britain's own poor, but increasingly assertive, labouring classes.[182] It was Arnold's dogged pursuit of the logical flaws and pedantic preoccupations in Colenso's account which did most to reduce the former Bishop to a laughing stock within polite metropolitan circles. Much to the satisfaction of the majority of Natal's and the Cape's settlers, Colenso was quite literally shut out from these circles and ostracised.

Long-held settler representations, such as those that were reformulated for metropolitan consumption by Carlyle and Arnold, became more powerful in the hub of the mid-nineteenth-century empire because they articulated a language of inherent difference in which domestic class and gender relations could now be more conveniently framed. They helped establish, as Ann Stoler puts it, 'a "mobile" discourse of empire that designated eligibility for citizenship, class membership, and gendered assignments to race'. Both settlers' constructions of the colonised and domestic bourgeois constructions of the uneducated and unreconstructed labouring classes 'captured in one sustained image internal threats to the health and well-being of a social body where those deemed a threat lacked an ethics of "how to live" and thus the ability to govern themselves'.[183]

7   Epilogue and conclusion

> In England a large and influential class believe that the natives of this country are an inoffensive race and oppressed by Europeans. There is also another class, consisting specially of those who have suffered from the natives, who believe that in them nothing but evil is to be found. The opinions of both are equally wide of the truth.
>
> (Charles Brownlee, Commissioner with the Ngqika, 1867)[1]

In this final chapter, I want briefly to examine those governmental structures of control that finally came into existence within the mid-nineteenth-century discursive atmosphere described in the last chapter, along what had been the eastern Cape frontier zone. I will suggest that, although the colonial government was able to implement schemes of governance that were unprecedentedly sophisticated and impressive during the late 1850s and 1860s, it still experienced a perpetual deferral of objectives. This ongoing deferral was due to the effects of more mundane forms of Xhosa resistance than those that had resulted in the preceding 'frontier wars', combined with the sheer material costs of fulfilling colonial state projects. Finally, I will conclude the book as a whole by drawing attention once again to the ways in which the compromised colonisation of the eastern Cape was the result of the region's constitution through its connections with other places within an imperial network.

Epilogue: The eastern Cape and British Kaffraria in the mid-nineteenth century

In 1850, the outbreak of yet another war on the eastern Cape frontier had been seized upon by the advocates of representative colonial government and free trade in Britain. As Richard Cobden put it:

> The proper cure for these recurring wars is to let the Colonists bear the brunt of them. This must be done by first giving them the powers of

self-government, and then throwing on them the responsibility of their own policy. . . . At present it is the interest of the Colonists to provoke the natives into war, because it leads to a most profitable expenditure of British money.[2]

If metropolitan interests were becoming concerned about the Cape's settlers' tendency to embroil imperial troops in repeated frontier warfare, many colonists were becoming just as wary of metropolitan interference in other matters, and therefore just as keen to secure self-government. The most significant of these other matters was the British government's attempt during the late 1840s to bring convicts out to the Cape, establishing it as a penal colony. This proposal met with such a furore that it became the most emotive local rallying cry for settler political representation. As Ross points out, such was the burning nature of the convict issue to the Western Cape elite that even respectable women were permitted to join the campaign.[3] This was the first instance of a mass political mobilisation on the part of the western Cape's citizenry, using techniques similar to those that had been deployed in Britain against the slave trade, including petitions, public meetings, printed propaganda and newspaper interventions.[4]

With representative government on both imperial and local elite agendas, the major struggle being waged was over the property qualification needed to exercise the vote. The Albany settlers were generally in favour of a high qualification to exclude 'coloured' voters, while western Cape Afrikaners and English-speaking merchants favoured a lower qualification, the former so that poorer Afrikaner colonists could be enfranchised, and the latter so that the 'coloured' peasants with whom they traded could be privileged.[5] While the eastern Cape settlers had enjoyed Harry Smith's support, the convict crisis and his unrestrained and costly expansionism put paid to his career as governor, leaving them isolated from local state power. A lower franchise qualification was ultimately adopted when Representative government was granted in 1853. What is most significant about the struggle for Representative government here, however, is that, as Stanley Trapido has indicated, 'the Cape would not have been granted [it] if James Stephen's anxieties regarding white domination in the early 1830s were still taken seriously. Colonial Office support for low franchise qualifications was based rather on the necessity of securing a wider class of white collaborators for the effective administration of informal empire'.[6]

Self-government and self-confidence

As we have seen, official and settler discourses had always converged around certain points (most notably those concerning security) and diverged on other issues (most notably settler land acquisition). Settlers and governors would continue to pursue projects of their own, and ones that would by no means always coincide, during the 1850s and 1860s. But after the granting of self-government and the dispersal of metropolitan humanitarian programmes, there was far greater potential to consolidate the common ground between them within a formal political arena.

It was soon after the establishment of representative government that the governor, in close liaison with the western Cape merchant elite, set about improving the colony's infrastructural networks. Such improvement would benefit the state by enhancing its capacity for government in both near and remote parts of the colony. It would favour settlers by facilitating commercial growth and social communication. Together, the governor and elected settler representatives swiftly passed a Tariff Act implementing free trade, but raising the duty on imported goods by 50 per cent. Along with the growth in woollen production and continued imperial military expenditure, this greatly increased the government's revenue enabling it to raise credit of £500,000 in London, so that the Cape's first railway line could be constructed.[7] Governor Sir George Grey himself raised a further £200,000 for improvements in Table Bay and began an ambitious scheme of governmental works throughout the colony involving the construction of court houses, schools, prisons, hospitals and roads.

These schemes of improvement were of particular benefit to the British settlers on the eastern frontier. The improvement of roads connecting them to the markets of the west and to the harbour at Port Elizabeth gave a further boost to the local production and transportation of wool, enabling vastly increased profits. While, in 1834, the Cape had exported 114,000 lb. of wool, by 1851, it was exporting 5,500,00 lb., worth £286,000. From 1846 to 1866, wool exports increased in value tenfold with western Cape merchants and bankers continuing to finance the expansion. While, as Kirk notes, 'the local "gentry"' of the eastern Cape still 'lacked the social rank of the western merchants . . . those living at Port Elizabeth certainly matched them for riches'. One visitor wrote: 'I don't think I ever saw in any other town so large a proportion of rich men's houses.'[8] And these merchants were increasingly able to maintain powerful metropolitan connections. They frequently forged partnerships with London merchants who had themselves lived in the colony for a time, but who had returned 'home' once they had successfully established commercial links between the Cape and London financiers. These men exported a whole range of metropolitan produce to the Cape, and brought back its wool, wine, hides and ivory to supply British markets.

Not only did infrastructural improvements more effectually connect Albany's British settlers with mercantile contacts in the western Cape and beyond; they also facilitated greater regional and trans-continental, cultural and political integration – a kind of integration that would continue long after Grey had exhausted the colony's credit in London. Communication of this less overtly material kind linking the eastern Cape and Britain was promoted in particular by the innovation of a monthly steamship, sailing between Cape Town and Plymouth in 1851. This cut journey times to

43 days and allowed the Cape reading market to be flooded with more up-to-date metropolitan newspapers, magazines and books. It was from about this time that the eastern Cape settlers began to cut the time-lag between the introduction of new fashions in clothing and décor in Britain and their adoption in the eastern Cape.[9] Such consolidated connections were essential to the increasingly confident assertion of Britishness that was traced in chapter 3, even while political connections with the metropole were being reformulated to give the settlers greater autonomy. In turn, the more confident assertion of a British-derived identity had material effects, as new immigrants and their capital were attracted to a colony in which the importation of Britain in the miniature had apparently been achieved.

The eastern Cape settlers' social and cultural articulation with the rest of the Cape Colony was similarly facilitated by communications improvements from the late 1840s. Just as, in Britain itself at mid-century, the connection of places through stage and mail coaches were 'forces incorporating the middle ranks in a wider culture',[10] so the construction of roads linking Cape Town via its surrounding passes to the eastern Cape from the mid-1840s, the creation of a twice-weekly postal service in 1846, and the maintenance of telegraph connections from 1860, enabled the settlers to feel in touch with a more self-confident colonial culture.[11]

By the early 1850s, journey times between Algoa Bay and Cape Town had been cut to 48 hours, facilitating new intellectual and institutional endeavours which united western and eastern Cape interests around collective aims. Institutions founded in the western Cape during the early and mid-nineteenth century, such as the South African Library, the South African Museum, the South African Literary and Scientific Institution and the Commercial Exchange had already given educated men there, acting in association, 'the right to speak for their communities', preparing the way for self-government.[12] The Graham's Town elite now strove to catch up with Cape Town's 'progress', founding a botanical garden as evidence of their scientific prowess in 1850, establishing St Andrew's College in the mould of a British public school in 1855 and shortly thereafter creating the Albany Museum, a Literary, Scientific and Medical Society and a new magazine, the *Eastern Province Monthly Magazine*. Such institutions enabled colonists to achieve what the eastern Cape settlers had been striving for since the 1820s: a demonstration 'of European civilisation in Africa as well as of the importance of Africa to the civilised world'.[13]

Grey's governmentality

Within this framework of tighter integration between the western and eastern parts of the colony, and between the colony and the metropole, the Cape's mid-century governors were able to concentrate on ambitiously revised schemes of governmentality. Governors such as Grey were assisted by the growth in government bureaucracy in both the colonies and the metropole.

Official lines of communication were now so complex and multifaceted that ministers in London simply had no time to listen to the protestations of individuals who opposed governmental colonial schemes, unless those individuals were able to mobilise massive public opposition. Grey himself, described by Keegan as 'the archetypal utilitarian liberal of his age', has become notorious for his governmental innovation, but also for his success in monopolising communications between the Cape and the British government, to the exclusion of dissonant voices.[14]

Grey has received a fair amount of attention from historians as perhaps the most remarkable governor of the Cape. He was a friend of Thomas Carlyle among other metropolitan luminaries of the day, a noted explorer of north-west Australia and governor of South Australia at the age of twenty-five, as well as a later governor of New Zealand. His leisure interests centred around ethnology (he was a member of the London Ethnological Society), philology and natural science, but in addition to these unofficial pursuits, he fostered a number of far-reaching schemes of colonial expansion, each of which equated metropolitan utilitarianism with colonial despotism.[15] It is his governmental scheme for British Kaffraria which is the issue here. But before addressing this issue, we need briefly to revisit the frontier scheme which Grey inherited in 1854, and its relations to settler interests.

In the late 1840s, while military 'pacification' was the colonial government's first priority, settlers were not allowed into British Kaffraria other than to trade. However, after the 1850–2 war, Maclean persistently advocated larger land grants within the territory and the promotion of colonial immigration. Smith's successor, Governor Cathcart, had remained opposed to the idea for fear that it would provoke another war. While, in the wake of the war, Cathcart had the Amatola mountains seized from the Ngqika for strategic reasons, much to the disgust of the *Graham's Town Journal* and the more recently established *Cape Frontier Times*, the region was not to be filled with settlers. As Cathcart had told the Colonial Secretary, 'military control, not colonisation, is the principle of policy which has induced me to advise the retention of Kaffraria as a separate government . . . therefore the greediness of land speculators must be resisted'.[16]

Nevertheless, in denying the Xhosa further access to the Amatolas, Cathcart had probably done more than any other governor to bring an end to the Rharhabe Xhosa's lengthy period of 'primary' armed resistance. Without access to the protection afforded by the Amatola mountains and bush, and with the Fish River bush and the Waterkloof already confiscated, in any future campaign Xhosa warriors could simply be hunted down across relatively open grasslands.[17] As Cathcart's successor from 1854, Grey was determined to make yet more profound changes to the spaces of British control in British Kaffraria, both consolidating the colonial authorities' strategic gains and providing more opportunities for settler accumulation. But he also had more far-reaching plans for the civil reformation of Xhosa society.

While governor of New Zealand in 1852, and before he had even conceived of becoming the Cape's governor, Grey had sent a description of the Industrial Schools system which he had devised to 'civilise' the Maoris to his Cape counterpart. He proposed it as a model for the 'civilisation' of the Xhosa. After describing two schools in which agriculture and practical training were taught, he advised,

> I ought . . . to add that I by no means regard these schools as the only means that should be employed to civilize the natives . . . I regard the employment of the natives at fair rates of wages upon the main roads for the purpose of opening up the country; the establishment of simple Courts of Judicature for the settlement of disputes amongst themselves, or between themselves and Europeans; the construction of hospitals . . . and other similar means, as essential and necessary adjuncts to such a plan as I propose.[18]

This outline was a fair summation of the hegemonic ambitions that Grey formulated when he was subsequently appointed to the Cape.

Despite the emphasis in some neo-Marxist accounts, colonial expansion under Grey was as much, if not more, about an expanded notion of governmentality – about the sovereignty of the state – as it was about fulfilling the desires of settler capitalists. For Grey, British Kaffraria was an exercise in a novel technology of government, one in which settlers could incidentally revel, but in which, more fundamentally, government would at last fulfil its own longstanding objectives.

Grey felt that he knew not only how to combat the kind of frustrations that the Xhosa had long engendered within governmental schemes, but that he alone among the Cape's governors had the means to counter them successfully. He shared the universalism of the humanitarians and this is where he departed most dramatically from Carlyle's racial discourse. But he qualified this universalism by situating non-European individuals within baneful social frameworks out of which they would not willingly emerge. Like many contemporary liberals in India, Grey was thus situated at the confluence of evangelical and utilitarian conceptions, identifying the necessity for broad social structures to be altered in order to facilitate individual reformation. If evangelicals had failed to bring about a change in indigenous subjectivities through missionary work alone, then the colonial state would have to intervene, if necessary, forcefully. As Stokes puts it, evangelical failure meant that 'the human legislator must assist men to avoid harmful acts by artificially weighting such acts with the pain of punishment'.[19]

While the enlarged bureaucracy which such a comprehensive governmental scheme would entail had aroused opposition on financial as well as moral grounds in Britain during the 1830s, by the 1850s, the social and political tensions in the metropole itself had rendered the dominant classes more amenable to a proliferating governmental machinery, as well as to a revised set of utilitarian doctrines.[20] Exercises in colonial government of the kind that Grey envisaged were thus assured of greater metropolitan support. Administrators like Grey, not just in the Cape but in the recently conquered Punjab and in New Zealand as well, were admired more emphatically than their predecessors had been, by reconstructed romantics like Carlyle, but also by metropolitan officials, for their 'strong aggressive logic with which a man of affairs could approach specific political issues'.[21]

Grey argued that the fatal weakness of the Kaffrarian administration as he found it was that 'no general plan is in operation to produce or better a state of things for the future or to clear off the difficulties which threaten us'.[22] Of these difficulties, of course, the most significant was the unreformed Xhosa 'character'. Following what he considered to be, and what he had effectively publicised as being, his 'successful experiments' among the Maori, Grey intended fundamentally to alter it.[23] This would be achieved by

> employing them upon the public works which will open up their country, by establishing institutions for the education of their children and the relief of their sick, by introducing among them institutions of a civil character suited to their present condition, and by these and other means to attempt gradually to win them to civilization and Christianity, and thus to change by degrees our at present unconquered and apparently unconquerable foes, into friends who may have common interest with ourselves.[24]

Grey envisaged British Kaffraria being transformed into

> A fertile and populous country, filled with a large population, partly European, partly native . . . the natives, won by our exertions to Christianity, trained by us in agriculture and in simple arts, possessing property of their own and a stake in the country, accustomed to our ways and aware of their advantages, attached to us from a sense of benefits received, respecting us for our strength and generosity.[25]

In order to effect this vision, Grey made a case to the Colonial Office for an annual grant of £40,000. This was to be spent solely on 'civilising' British Kaffraria. He persuaded the metropolitan government that such expenditure was more than worthwhile 'considering that the experiments of the last thirty-four years had all ignominiously failed'.[26] Merrivale concurred: 'We must remember . . . that we have entrusted these affairs to a man of singular and proved ability in dealing with savage races If he succeeds in this experiment, he will have accomplished what none of his predecessors ever dreamt of.'[27]

One of the first components of Grey's plan to be realised, from 1854, was the opening up of British Kaffraria to settler expansion. At first 'enrolled pensioners' and their families would be sent out to plots around King

William's Town. In the event it was German mercenaries and other German settlers who were attracted to the scheme rather than the anticipated British veterans. More comprehensive colonial settlement would have to wait until the Xhosa had been more effectively subdued. And this would not occur until after the Great Xhosa Cattle Killing.

Thanks to the work of Jeff Peires and rejoinders by his critics, it is now widely accepted as of vital historical significance that, in 1856–7, many of the Xhosa in British Kaffraria were exposed to yet another catastrophe besides the more effective imposition of colonial state authority – a lungsickness epidemic that was destroying their cattle. Thousands of them turned in desperation to the spiritual assistance of their ancestors. Despite the exhortations of local colonial officials, and of other Xhosas who did not believe, or who were wary of commitment, a majority placed their faith in the prophecies of a young Xhosa woman, Nongqawuse. These believers slaughtered their remaining cattle and destroyed their crops as sacrifices to the ancestral spirits and as a sign of willingness to accept a new purity of existence, if only an idealised precolonial order was restored. Whereas the Xhosa population of British Kaffraria had been recorded as 105,000 in January 1857, it was 37,000 by December of the same year. Within British Kaffraria, some 15,000 died of starvation and associated diseases, while the total number of deaths caused directly by the Cattle Killing movement, including the Gcaleka, is estimated at 40,000–60,000. Some 150,000 were displaced and beyond chiefly control.[28]

Although the British authorities did not encourage the Cattle Killing movement and local officials, seeing it as a chiefs' conspiracy against the colony, endeavoured to stop it, Grey was determined to 'draw very great permanent advantages from the circumstance', making it a 'stepping stone for the future settlement of the country'.[29] Servitude or 'public work' was made a condition for Xhosa famine relief. Even the former humanitarian Attorney General, William Porter, declared that

> He had once mistakenly thought that Kaffir relief was a fit object for private charity, like famine in his native Ireland. But he had come to realise that the Xhosa were a 'very difficult people to deal with' and that 'it is impossible in British Kaffraria to separate private charity from public policy'. The problem was that the Xhosa wanted to 'be supported in idleness, for he has no desire for work, and we know that idleness is their besetting sin'.[30]

During the worst months of the Cattle Killing, 29,000 Xhosa registered as workers in the colony, in an attempt to claim relief. Grey commented that 'A restless nation, who for years have harassed the frontier, may now, to a great extent be changed into useful labourers . . . I think that a transference to the Colony . . . of a considerable number of destitute persons from Kaffraria, as labourers, will prove highly advantageous to this country.'[31]

Aside from those who 'negotiated' their own 'contracts', others were directed into the colony on government-supervised schemes. For instance, 39 Xhosas ranging from 7 to 14 years old were 'apprenticed' to citizens in Cape Town through 'the good offices' of the newly appointed Superintendent of Kaffirs. These children were indentured for five years in order to learn a trade, during which period they would receive lodging and food from their masters, but no wages. Twelve were sent to work in the naval dockyards at Simonstown, of whom six eventually returned to British Kaffraria and one died. The only trade that the remainder learnt was that of domestic service in white households.[32]

In addition to undertaking privately negotiated and government-supervised work within the colony, up to 2,000 Xhosa were obliged after the destitution of the Cattle Killing to accept work on colonial road building schemes within British Kaffraria itself. Grey was able to declare that 'the Kaffirs are themselves conquering their country by opening up, through their fastnesses [especially the Amatolas], available roads, which will be of equal use to us either in peace or in war. They are acquiring habits of industry (formerly the men never worked) and a taste for the commodities of life'. As Du Toit notes, 'The officials in Downing Street were at first frankly incredulous but eventually Grey's continued success made such an impression that copies of his despatches were sent to the Queen and circulated to the Cabinet.'[33]

From 1857, further white settlement in the partially depopulated territory of British Kaffraria, and specifically in lands confiscated from the pro-Cattle Killing chiefs Maqoma, Mhala and Bhotomane, extended and consolidated a segregated 'patchwork of African and colonial agriculture'.[34] Some 300 further farms, each of 1,500 acres, were granted to settlers on the condition that they were able to defend them. Grey outlined the new system of land-holding:

> The territories occupied by the Kaffirs and termed locations, the chiefs are said to hold as a conquered people . . . that is, their lands are held only during pleasure. The Crown takes whatever tracts of country it requires . . . and requires the people on such tracts to move . . . Thus throughout British Kaffraria the native has no recognised right or interest in the soil.[35]

This legal innovation, confirming that the Rharhabe Xhosa had been converted in official discourse from an independent 'nation' with whom treaties had to be made to a 'conquered people' with no right in the land, would be directly copied the following year, with due acknowledgement by James Douglas, Governor of British Columbia.[36]

Along with colonial land seizure came more intensive efforts at administrative and judicial control and labour extraction. British magistrates were able to administer a hybridised and static version of 'native law' more effectively once 'troublesome' chiefs like Maqoma, Mhala and Phatho were imprisoned on Robben Island. They were arrested on charges ranging from murder and fomenting unrest to horse stealing. At the same time, Sarhili was expelled across the Bashee River, while the more co-operative chiefs were absorbed into the governmental system as salaried bureaucrats. As Grey crowed,

> The influence hitherto possessed by the Chiefs continues in the present state of general destitution rapidly to decline . . . The power of these Chiefs had already received a severe blow from their having been compelled to derive their Revenues from the Government . . . and I feel quite satisfied that their late conduct has irretrievably destroyed that portion of their influence which was still left to them, and that henceforth we may govern the country ourselves, the Chiefs being mere dependants upon us.[37]

The Xhosa's access to colonial space would be more efficiently regulated through a coherent implementation of the pass laws. First, strict segregationist safeguards were needed to protect the settlers within the Cape Colony proper, until such time as a favourable reformation of Xhosa subjectivity could be achieved. As Fairbairn now declared, 'the introduction of large numbers of [Xhosa] people into the colony' would have to be resisted:

> They would form a savage element in the population . . . the armed savage was even less to be dreaded than the domestic savage. It is contrary to all principle, to all precedent, to all experience to attempt to civilize a savage continent by directing the flood of barbarism down upon a single spot where a feeble civilization has but recently taken root.[38]

With more sympathetic resident agents like Stretch gone, it proved possible to formulate a more consistent governmental approach to the issuing of passes after the Cattle Killing, so that those Xhosa entering the colony were more efficiently restricted to a labouring function. But Xhosa mobility within their own 'locations' was also more closely policed. Indeed, this was a major priority for the military government of British Kaffraria, since such mobility had been intensely frustrating during each previous episode of armed conflict. It was partly the removal of livestock from the frontier chiefdoms into Gcaleka territory across the Kei that had frustrated colonial attempts to attack Rharhabe food supplies in the 1834–5 and 1846–7 wars, and during the latter conflict, resisting chiefs like Phatho had been able to avoid capture by crossing to and fro across the same Rharhabe–Gcaleka boundary.[39] Now that their colonisation was at last being effected 'properly', however, the Xhosa in British Kaffraria would be subjected to a new spatial regime of power which would prevent such transgressive movement.

Grey implemented a scheme of 'concentrated settlement' that had first been proposed by the Rev. Impey before the 1850 war. He had felt that those

'principles of good government and civil liberty', which could most effectually 'raise the natives in the scale of civilization' could best be propagated
if the Xhosa were concentrated in villages of about 100 families.[40] Impey
had elaborated on the relationship between space and colonial power in a
way that Grey found compelling:

> There are multitudes of localities [in British Kaffraria] where at present
> within a radius of 2 miles, or even less, there are numerous kraals consist-
> ing of from six to eight houses each; the whole of which could be
> collected to a central position from which the cattle might graze over
> the very same pasturage, the people obtain the same supply of water,
> and cultivate the same lands as they do at present, whilst they would
> be living in a village or Township of 100 families, get-atable for the
> purposes of instruction, and placed under the immediate government
> of a headman or local magistrate, who would be responsible to the Com-
> missioner of the District. The hold which the Government would thus,
> from the concentration of persons and property, have over the population
> would be vastly increased; the way for the introduction of municipal and
> fiscal regulations would be opened up. The people thus concentrated
> would soon acquire an interest in the soil and have a much greater
> stake in the peace and welfare of the country at large, and sedition
> could the more easily at once be nipped in the bud.[41]

In 1858, Grey drew up new regulations instructing magistrates to fix the
sites of villages of not more than 200 huts, each of them to be placed under
the care of an appointed headman. Within this settlement pattern, each hut
could be more effectively taxed at an annual rate of 10s. Their closer settlement, Grey also hoped, would bring the Xhosa more effectively under the
surveillance of the reconstructed Kaffrarian police force, rendering it 'practi-
cally impossible for anyone to commit theft without being immediately
apprehended'.[42]

More micro-scale schemes for spatial containment, control and individual
moral reformation were also pursued in post-Cattle Killing British Kaffraria,
largely through the establishment of specific institutions such as schools and a
hospital. Upon visiting the missionary school at Lovedale, Grey found the
tuition too 'bookish' and recommended more practical training, in mech-
anical arts for boys and needlework and knitting for girls. His government
supplied funds for the extra buildings necessary to teach the boys masonry,
carpentry, wagon-making and blacksmithing, and, much to their satisfaction,
finance was supplied to the Wesleyan Missionary Society for similar institutions at Healdtown, Salem, Lesseyton and D'Urban near Peddie, and to the
Moravians for their institution at Shiloh. The Anglican Church also set up
four industrial schools for the conquered Xhosa and the sons of some chiefs
were to sent to a new 'Kaffir College' well away from the 'corruptions' of
indigenous life and in the heart of colonial 'civilisation', in Cape Town.

Governmental and church funds enabled the college to be completed in 1860.[43]

In New Zealand, Grey had been determined to persuade the Maori of the superiority of European medicine, and thus of European culture in general, through the establishment of a native hospital. He promoted a similar scheme in British Kaffraria. The military helped erect the Grey hospital outside King William's Town and Dr J. P. Fitzgerald, formerly in charge of the Maori hospital at Wellington, was appointed its superintendent in 1856. Operations to remove cataracts were felt to have a particularly beneficial effect in convincing Xhosa patients of the 'miracles' that British science was capable of performing. Indeed, a letter of thanks written by one Xhosa cataract patient was sent to Queen Victoria as proof of Grey's broader success in securing Xhosa acquiescence for a revitalised programme of civilisation.[44] Grey's indignation that Fitzgerald continued to recognise the Xhosa amagqirha (healers) as fellow practitioners, and the ways in which these healers forged their own accommodations with FitzGerald, were less well publicised.[45]

The perpetual deferral of colonial projects

William Irons, Secretary of the Cape Town Mechanics Institute, published his *Settler's Guide to the Cape of Good Hope* after the Cattle Killing in 1858, in an endeavour to attract more British emigrants to the region. He now felt confident in explicitly contradicting the metropolitan population's 'vague notion' that the Cape attracted only 'foolhardy men' undeterred at being 'exposed to all the rude hazards of a frontier life'. On the contrary, he asserted, recent advances in British Kaffraria had secured 'order' on the frontier, while Grey's novel system of administration was more effectively than ever before introducing 'civilisation'.[46] However, even after the Cattle Killing had effectively ended the Rharhabe Xhosa's remarkably persistent phase of 'primary', armed resistance, the extension of colonial governmentality in British Kaffraria remained a perpetually incomplete project, as did the fulfilment of settler goals. Xhosa individuals continued to interrupt both settler and government narratives of success and to preclude the fulfilment of their programmes. Drawing attention to the lack of 'closure' in colonial schemes seems as good a way as any of ending the substantial narrative of this book.

That Grey's governmental vision was always a fantasy was pointed out by Fairbairn. He felt that 'while sketching a picture of the colony, its smiling present and glowing future', Grey 'was unconsciously drawing a portrait of his own mind, holding everything possible that is desirable, and ready to undertake any good work without encumbering his faculties or troubling his nerves with "difficulties"'.[47] While the early successes in undercutting chiefly authority, for instance, were being publicised, the failures of local colonial officials, mirroring those of Queen Adelaide Province before them, were kept hidden from metropolitan correspondents. Maqoma and Bhotomane's success in simply ignoring their new government agent, and Mhala's insistence on his agent waiting two months before he would be received in the chief's kraal were overlooked in official reports while Anta's grateful reception of a magistrate (a colonial recognition of status which he lacked by birth) was made much of.[48]

Even after the Cattle Killing, in 1860, Maclean was still writing that 'The Amaxosa [sic] Nation is not yet thoroughly conquered or subdued and any sudden attempt to interfere with or set aside many of the existing laws and customs will only meet with disappointment and in all probability end in rebellion.'[49] Where chiefs believed that they could not prevent the British law from interfering, it was side-stepped. In 1867, for instance Brownlee reported how the diviners who smelt out witches got around prohibitions on the casting of accusations by referring to 'culprits' more subtly, but 'in such a manner that there can be no mistake as to his identity, and thus while the accused may have no action at law, he is shunned and despised as if actually named'.[50] In the early 1860s, the most obvious forms of 'passive resistance' from chiefs may have been overcome by suspending their stipends until such time as they co-operated, but the taxes on commoners' cattle and sheep had to be withdrawn due to non-payment and the threat of violence to collectors. In 1867, Brownlee wrote that the chiefs 'now again see and feel their strength, and are using every effort to increase their adherents and strengthen their influence over them'.[51]

The villages which were eventually created under Grey's scheme of concentrated settlement were more dispersed and smaller in size than those which had been planned, and thus represented a compromised form of the precolonial pattern rather than a straightforward colonial imposition. In 1860, Maclean himself proposed a revised plan of controlling not only the size, but also the morphology of each village, but this too proved unrealisable.[52] While, by 1861, about two thirds of the tax that the Xhosa were supposed to be paying, was being collected, only 1,500 Xhosa children were attending the industrial and other schools. Furthermore, as thousands of impoverished Xhosa surprised Grey by returning from their places of refuge among the Gcaleka or further afield to their pre-Cattle Killing locations, settlers in British Kaffraria and along the old frontier continued to complain loudly of constant insecurity and 'depredations'. Brownlee admitted that even after the Xhosa's conquest and decades of missionary and state exertion, 'the process of elevation and enlightenment is slow and hard'.[53] Recognising the failure of colonial hegemony, he continued, 'we have no bond of common sympathy with the Kaffirs. We possess over the heathen [only] the influence due to our superiority in physical force; we have also a powerful money influence, through the subsidies paid to chiefs and headmen, which they would be loth to forfeit'.[54]

Aside from Xhosa resistance, the Foucaultian schemes of governmentality and the Gramscian models of hegemony which Grey envisaged for British Kaffraria quite simply came at a cost which made their fulfilment prohibitive.

Grey's expenditure on roads, schools, hospitals, subsidised immigration and military supervision launched the Cape's economy into a severe depression during the 1860s – one that forestalled further schemes of colonial expansion and led to the closure of all of Grey's 'native' schools except Lovedale, until the mineral discoveries at the end of that decade. It was thus both the Xhosa's cultural resilience and material conditions that led Brownlee to lament, as he gave his farewell speech to his Ngqika 'charges', that 'here, in a British possession, and under British protection, you still live as if you had never heard of a better way, nor seen a better example'.[55]

Concluding remarks: Imperial networks and colonial discourse

The utterances of some of the key personalities who figure in this account – Governors Somerset, D'Urban, Smith and Grey, humanitarian missionary director Philip, and settler spokesman Godlonton, for instance – were situated within systems of thought that traversed a diverse and dynamic, but interconnected imperial terrain. In the 1830s, Philip reproduced a discourse of humanitarian concern that had been constructed through connections with the bourgeois reform movement in Britain, but also with abolitionists in the West Indies and with early utilitarians in India. Somerset had previously considered himself the epitome of an aristocratic governing culture that held colonies and metropole together within an ordered and properly hierarchical system of rule. By virtue of their personal experience in other colonies, their alignments with other imperial officials and their correspondence with the Colonial Office, D'Urban and Smith in turn contributed to, and learned from, reformulated discourses of government incorporating Britain, Australia, New Zealand, India and Canada. And vocal eastern Cape settlers like Godlonton both communicated with, and devised strategy alongside, counterparts engaged in the redefinition of Britishness, the material production of commodities and the control of black labourers in the West Indies, New Zealand and Australia.

In the nineteenth century, then, the eastern Cape was one among other imperial sites in which contests were being waged over relationships between the propertied and propertyless, whites and blacks, and men and women. It was connected to each of these sites, both materially and discursively. During moments of imperial crisis in particular, colonial representations of the Xhosa were considered in the light of Australian settlers' images of the Aborigine, New Zealand colonists' constructions of the Maori, Indian officials' notions of the 'Hindoo', West Indian planters' portrayals of former slaves and not least, British bourgeois ideas of the labouring classes and other domestic 'subaltern' groups. As far as most colonial Britons were concerned, this mutual consideration of the empire's subordinated peoples in itself helped generate a collective consciousness of being part of a British diaspora.

In the 1830s, a consideration of metropolitan and colonial conditions within a single frame of reference had held out positive agendas for reform at both kinds of site. The newly ascendant and reforming propertied classes in Britain could conceive of rosy prospects for the inner salvation of slaves and indigenes in the colonies on the one hand, and of the lower classes in Britain on the other. From the mid-nineteenth century, however, the same intersection of colonial and metropolitan concerns created the basis for a more reactionary dominant imperial discourse. The entrenched propertied classes 'at home' now agreed more forcefully with settler capitalists in places like the Cape that there were certain natural distinctions between social groups, defined by race, class and gender – distinctions that rendered their own political dominance and their own economic privilege a requirement which had to be defended by force if necessary.[56]

Paradoxically, it was the resistance encountered by those pursuing settler and governmental projects in the colonies that consolidated their own particular racial imageries within metropolitan discourses. The mid-nineteenth-century dominance of settler representations was contingent partly upon humanitarianism's internal contradictions, the progressive disillusionment of its colonial proponents, and changes in the nature of bourgeois liberalism in the metropole. But active settler political representations also played their part in reformulating dominant imperial discourse. Through metropolitan intermediaries like Carlyle and Arnold, settlers pointed out the humanitarians' hypocrisy; they continually publicised their failure to transform the 'character' of indigenous peoples, and they successfully associated resistance to the British civilising mission with resistance to civilisation *per se*.

Settler representations, based on inherent difference rather than universalism, were successful partly because they seemed more robust and coherent within the very terms of humanitarian ontology, itself based, of course, on the notion that European, and especially British, civilisation was civilisation by any definition. The premise of a universal human nature, allowing global assimilation into a Christian brotherhood, was always going to be contradicted within such an ethnocentric framework of assumption, when freed slaves followed other agendas and when indigenous peoples fought tenaciously to preserve their difference. Far from being conceptually undermined by resistance to British power, however, settlers' constructions of irremediable racial difference, were strengthened by it. As Catherine Hall writes, for liberals of the mid-nineteenth century, even abolitionism could be seen as 'a dream necessarily unfulfilled, since the full measure of the difference between the races had not been recognised' by its proponents.[57]

If the arguments of this book concerning the operation of imperial networks are to be better substantiated, more research needs to be conducted on the forging of British and other colonial discourses in a variety of imperial locales. First, empirical work is needed on the ways that representations from other colonial peripheries were conveyed and reinterpreted in various media, and refracted through the prisms of class and gender in the metropolis, as well as vice versa. Studies of such interactions across the spaces of empire are required especially for the critical mid-nineteenth century, when colonial settler and metropolitan bourgeois discourses intersected so potently. Only with the proliferation of such empirically grounded studies can Anne McClintock's appealing notion of imperial power emerging 'from a constellation of processes' and 'taking haphazard shape from myriad encounters with alternative forms of authority, knowledge and power', be fleshed out.[58]

The pursuit of such a research agenda also depends upon a more 'grounded' notion of colonial discourse than that which informs many foundational postcolonial texts. Certainly, in the writing of this book, I have found it unhelpful to imagine a single, ahistorical and aspatial colonial discourse, regardless of how internally fractured and ambivalent that discourse may be.[59] Rather, I have been led to conceive of multiple, intersecting, and often competing discourses of colonialism.[60] Such a conception, I would argue, allows for accounts of colonialism, and indeed of postcolonialism, that are more politically, spatially and temporally sensitive. It also helps make it possible to avoid some of the more obfuscatory, abstract statements that are often generated by postcolonial critics – statements that have done so much to alienate materially orientated (and other) historians.[61]

I have sought to avoid an excessive degree of abstraction in this book by suggesting that tensions within colonial culture were the outcome of contestation between contingent constellations of colonial and metropolitan interests, each of which was competing to establish the dominance of its own representations, its own particular discourse. These constellations have certainly been conceptualised in theoretical terms, but their contingencies have necessarily been tracked empirically. Furthermore, I have posited that the power of the particular discourses that these constellations of interest generated 'derive[d] not so much from the abstract ideas they represent[ed] as from their material basis in institutions and practices that [made] up the . . . political realm'.[62] Finally, instead of using rather vacuous spatial metaphors such as 'thirdspace', which are currently popular with a number of postcolonial theorists, I have tried in this account to address the 'actual' spaces across which colonial discourses operated.[63]

While one of my main aims has been to generate a more differentiated and spatialised conception of British colonial discourses, however, I hope also to have demonstrated the limits of these discourses. The proponents of various colonial projects may have struggled for a realisable dominance in the shaping of colonial and metropolitan understandings and actions, but as numerous postcolonial and more traditional scholars have emphasised, they were by no means automatically capable of shaping the practices and imaginations of the colonised.[64] The mid-nineteenth-century development of a revised dominant discourse of empire, even one that sanctioned the Xhosa's, among others', dispossession and forceful subjection to a gamut of hegemonically inclined colonial devices, did not necessarily translate into the fulfilment of colonial programmes. The conversion of colonial discourse into material life was always a frustratingly incomplete project.

In common with colonised peoples elsewhere, I hope to have shown that most Xhosa were capable, as Gayan Prakash puts it, of shifting 'the terrain of engagement by occupying and carving out positions placed in between the powerful command of authority and the powerless silence of the victim'.[65] Each and every response, and each and every pro-active measure taken by Xhosa subjects, complicated colonial visions and further inflected colonial discourses. Whether or not they actually fought against British colonialism, collectively the Xhosa ensured that its nature failed to conform to any of the scenarios held out by various colonial interests. After the 1850s, British colonists', missionaries' and officials' endeavours entrapped more Xhosa than ever before in the cultural and discursive webs forged by imperialism, but they never resulted in the total abandonment of those practices and those 'patterns of discourse alive for many centuries' which had circulated in precolonial Xhosaland.[66] Given this resilience, as John Comaroff writes, the colonial state, and indeed I would add British colonialism as a whole, 'was always an aspiration, a work-in progress, an intention, a phantasm-to-be-made-real. Rarely was it ever a fully actualised accomplishment.'[67]

Notes

Preface

1 J. Comaroff, 'Images of Empire, Contests of Conscience: Models of Colonial Domination in South Afrca', in F. Cooper and A. L. Stoler (eds) *Tensions of Empire: Colonial Cultures in a Bourgeois World*, University of California Press, Berkeley and London, 1997, 192.

2 As Robert Ross points out, during the nineteenth century it was these British cultures and practices against which other identities in southern Africa had to define themselves, and which, above all, 'determined what was right and acceptable in the political life of the Cape Colony': R. Ross, *Status and Respectability in the Cape Colony, 1750–1870: A Tragedy of Manners*, Cambridge University Press, Cambridge, 1999, 43.

3 For metropolitan notions of Britishness, see L. Colley, 'Britishness and Otherness: An Argument', *Journal of British Studies*, 31, 1992, 309–29, and *Britons: Forging the Nation, 1707–1837*, Pimlico, London 1992. Philip Morgan, however, notes of colonial emigrants, such as those studied here, that 'Britishness became a reality abroad in ways it never did at home': P. D. Morgan, 'Encounters Between British and "Indigenous" Peoples, c. 1500–c. 1800', in M. Daunton and R. Halpern (eds) *Empire and Others: British Encounters with Indigenous Peoples, 1600–1850*, UCL Press, London 1999, 45.

4 My use of postcolonial theory is particularly selective in that I refer only very occasionally and briefly to the work of two of its major 'stars', Homi Bhabha and Gayatri Spivak. This is so for two main reasons: first because I am sceptical of their assumption that speculative and historically Western psychoanalytical tools are useful in the explanation of broad social and historical phenomena such as colonialism; secondly, because I find many of their passages obtuse, ahistorical and aspatial. For what I find to be useful critiques of Bhabha and Spivak's work, see B. Moore-Gilbert, *Postcolonial Theory: Contexts, Practices, Politics*, Verso, London and New York, 1996, 114–51; N. Thomas, *Colonialism's Culture: Anthropology, Travel and Government*, Polity, Cambridge, 1994, 42–9 and L. Gandhi, *Postcolonial Theory: A Critical Introduction*, Edinburgh University Press, Edinburgh, 1998, 156–60.

1 Introduction

1 M. Legassick, 'The Frontier Tradition in South African Historiography', in S. Marks and S. Trapido (eds), *Economy and Society in Pre-Industrial South Africa*, Longman, Harlow, 1980; B.A. Le Cordeur, *Eastern Cape Separatism, 1820–1854*, Oxford University Press, Oxford, 1981; J. Peires, *The House of Phalo: A History of the Xhosa People in the Days of Their Independence*, University of California Press, Berkeley, 1981 and 'The British and the Cape, 1814–1834', in R. Elphick and H. Giliomee (eds), *The Shaping of South African Society, 1652–1840*, Wesleyan University Press, Middletown, 1989. For the materialist dominance of South African historiography as a whole, see

C. Crais, 'South Africa and the Pitfalls of Postmodernism', *South African Historical Journal*, 31, 1994, 274–9, especially 274–5.

2 For a concise overview of settler and liberal narratives of the colonial Cape, see T. Keegan, *Colonial South Africa and the Origins of the Racial Order*, Leicester University Press, London, 1996, Introduction.

3 Legassick, 'Frontier Tradition'.

4 Peires, 'The British and the Cape', 472.

5 Le Cordeur, *Eastern Cape Separatism*, 71–9; Peires, *The House of Phalo*, 112–15.

6 M. Legassick, 'The State, Racism and the Rise of Capitalism in the Nineteenth-Century Cape Colony' *South African Historical Journal*, 28, 1993, 330.

7 N. Mostert, *Frontiers: The Epic of South Africa's Creation and the Tragedy of the Xhosa People*, Jonathan Cape, London, 1992. Crais' account diverges from the mainstream historiography in that it attempts to build a Foucaultian perspective into the dominant materialist account. This allows for a discussion of more subtle technologies of power on the frontier: C. Crais, *White Supremacy and Black Resistance in Pre-Industrial South Africa: The Making of the Colonial Order in the Eastern Cape, 1770–1865*, Cambridge University Press, Cambridge, 1992.

8 Keegan, *Colonial South Africa*, 131. In another recent history of the frontier zone, the early nineteenth-century conquest of the Xhosa is dealt with more cursorily as an outcome of colonial state policy rather than of settler capitalism *per se*: L. Switzer, *Power and Resistance in an African Society: The Ciskei Xhosa and the Making of South Africa*, University of Wisconsin Press, Madison, 1993, 52.

9 See for example Keegan, *Colonial South Africa*, 5, 36, 74, 129, 140–5; Crais, *White Supremacy and Black Resistance*, 117–18.

10 Keegan, *Colonial South Africa*, 14.

11 For a sampling of debates among historians, sociologists, anthropologists and geographers, see B. Bozzoli, 'The Discourses of Myth and the Myth of Discourse', *South African Historical Journal* 26, 1992, 191–7; J. Crush, 'The Discomforts of Distance: Post-Colonialism and South African Geography', *South African Geographical Journal*, 75, 2, 1993, 60–8; L. de Kock, 'For and Against the Comaroffs: Postmodernist Puffery and Competing Conceptions of the Colonial Archive', *South African Historical Journal*, 31, 1994, 280–9; M. Vaughan, 'Colonial Discourse Theory and African History, or Has Postmodernism Passed Us By?', *Social Dynamics* 20, 2, 1994, 1–23; J. Robinson, '(Dis)locating Historical Narrative: Writing, Space and Gender in South African Social History', *South African Historical Journal* 30, 1994, 144–57; F. Cooper, 'Conflict and Connection: Rethinking Colonial African History', *American Sociological Review*, 99, 1994, 1516–45; A. Norval, *Deconstructing Apartheid Discourse*, Verso, London, 1996; J. L. Comaroff, 'Reflections on the Colonial State in South Africa and Elsewhere: Factions, Fragments, Facts and Fictions' *Social Identities*, 4, 3, 1998, 321–61; D. Howarth and A. J. Norval, 'Introduction: Changing Paradigms and the Politics of Transition in South Africa', in D. Howarth and A. J. Norval (eds), *South Africa in Transition: New Theoretical Perspectives*, Macmillan, Basingstoke, 1998. My own views are expanded in 'Global Capitalism, Social Dislocation and Cultural Discourse in South African History: A Review Article': *South African Historical Journal*, 42, 2000, 277–89.

12 C. Crais, 'Representation and the Politics of Identity in South Africa: An Eastern Cape Example', *International Journal of African Historical Studies*, 25, 1, 1992, 100.

13 C. Crais, 'South Africa and the Pitfalls of Postmodernism', 275.

14 N. B. Dirks, 'Introduction: Colonialism and Culture', in N. B. Dirks (ed.) *Colonialism and Culture*, University of Michigan Press, Ann Arbor, 1992, 2.

15 L. C. Johnson, 'Text-ured Brick: Speculations on the Cultural Production of Domestic Space', *Australian Geographical Studies*, 31, 2, 1993, 202, citing D. Cosgrove and P. Jackson, 'New Directions in Cultural Geography', *Area*, 1987, 95–101.

16 G. Prakash, 'Writing Post-Orientalist Histories of the Third World: Indian Historiography Is Good to Think', in N. B. Dirks (ed.) *Colonialism and Culture*, University of Michigan Press, Ann Arbor, 1992, 369.

17 On ethnicity and race as social constructs in South African history, see for example, L. Vail (ed.), *The Creation of Tribalism in Southern Africa*, University of California Press, Berkeley and Los Angeles, 1989; Crais, *White Supremacy*; P. Bonner, P. Delius and D. Posel (eds), *Apartheid's Genesis, 1935–1962*, Ravan Press and Witwatersrand University Press, Johannesburg, 1993; Keegan, *Colonial South Africa*. On gender, see C. Walker (ed.) *Women and Gender in Southern Africa to 1945*, David Philip, Cape Town and London, 1990; E. Unterhalter, 'Constructing Race, Class, Gender and Ethnicity: State and Opposition Strategies in South Africa', in D. Stasiulis and N. Yuval-Davis (eds), *Unsettling Settler Societies: Articulations of Gender, Race, Ethnicity and Class*, Sage, London, 1995; H. Bradford, 'Women, Gender and Colonialism: Rethinking the History of the British Cape Colony and its Frontier Zones, c. 1806–70', *Journal of African History*, 37, 3, 1996, 351–70; P. Scully, *Liberating the Family? Gender and British Slave Emancipation in the Rural Western Cape, South Africa, 1823–1853*, Heinemann, Portsmouth N.H., James Currey, Oxford and David Philip, Cape Town, 1997; A. K. Mager, *Gender and the Making of a South African Bantustan: A Social History of the Ciskei, 1945–1959*, Heinemann, Portsmouth N.H., James Currey, Oxford and David Philip, Cape Town, 1999. On colonial India and the failures of capitalism, see R. O'Hanlon, 'Recovering the Subject: Subaltern Studies and Histories of Resistance in Colonial South Asia', *Modern Asian Studies*, 22, 1988, 189–223; R. O'Hanlon and D. Washbrook, 'After Orientalism: Culture, Criticism and Politics in the Third World', *Comparative Studies in Society and History*, 34, 1992, 141–67; Prakash, 'Writing Post-Orientalist Histories'. In the South African context, see D. Posel, *The Making of Apartheid, 1948–1961: Conflict and Compromise*, Clarendon Press, Oxford, 1991.

18 See A. Bank, *Liberals and Their Enemies: Racial Ideology at the Cape of Good Hope, 1820–1850*, unpublished Ph.D. thesis, Cambridge University, 1995; S. Dubow, *Scientific Racism in Modern South Africa*, Cambridge University Press, Cambridge, 1995; Keegan, *Colonial South Africa*. Foucault critiques the Marxist notion of ideology for its 'opposition to something like truth' and its 'secondary position in relation to something which must function as the infra-structure or economic or material determinant for it': M. Foucault, 'Truth and Power: An Interview with Alessandro Fontano and Pasquale Pasquino', in M. Morris and P. Patton (eds) *Michel Foucault: Power/Truth/Strategy*, Feral Publications, Sydney, 36. In contrast, a Foucaultian definition of discourse would make no claims about its relationship to 'truth'. It would claim only a relationship with power and 'knowledge'.

19 Saul Dubow's work is notable in this regard. See his *Racial Segregation and the Origins of Apartheid in South Africa, 1919–36*, Macmillan, London, 1989, and *Scientific Racism in Modern South Africa*, Cambridge University Press, Cambridge, 1995.

20 S. Mills, *Discourse*, Routledge, London and New York, 1998, 32. Similarly, recent work on Cape slavery and on highveld sharecropping has shown how material relations were constructed and regulated through flexible notions and practices of patriarchy and paternalism, even while the description of these notions and practices as 'discourse' is avoided: N. Worden and C. Crais (eds), *Breaking the Chains: Slavery and its Legacy in the Nineteenth-Century Cape Colony*, Witwatersrand University Press, Johannesburg, 1994; T. Keegan, *Rural Transformations in Industrialising South Africa: The Southern Highveld to 1914*, Ravan Press, Johannesburg, 1986; C. van Onselen, *The Seed is Mine: The Life of Kas Maine, a South African Sharecropper, 1894–1985*, James Currey, Oxford, 1996 and 'Paternalism and Violence on the Maize Farms of the South-western Transvaal, 1900–1950', in A. H. Jeeves and J. Crush (eds) *White Farms, Black Labour: The State and Agrarian Change in Southern Africa,*

1910–1950, Heinemann, Portsmouth, N.H., University of Natal Press, Pietermaritz-
burg and James Currey, Oxford, 1997. Only a few historians of nineteenth-century
South Africa have been willing to employ Foucaultian concepts of discourse explicitly.
See, for example, Crais, *White Supremacy* and Scully, *Liberating the Family*.

21 See E. Laclau and C. Mouffe, *Hegemony and Socialist Strategy: Towards a Radical
Democratic Politics*, Verso, London, 1985, 108.

22 M. Foucault, 'Politics and the Study of Discourse', in G. Burchell, C. Gordon and
P. Miller (eds) *The Foucault Effect: Studies in Governmentality*, Harvester Wheatsheaf,
London, 1991, 69.

23 I derive the term 'colonial project' from Nicholas Thomas, for whom it is 'a socially
transformative endeavour that is localised, politicised and partial, yet also engendered
by longer historical developments and ways of narrating them': N. Thomas,
Colonialism's Culture: Anthropology, Travel and Government, Polity, Cambridge, 1994,
105. Thomas goes on to note that colonial projects are both eminently practical
and discursive: 'the actors no doubt have intentions, aims and aspirations, but these
presuppose a particular imagination of the social situation, with its history and projected future, a diagnosis of what is lacking, that can be rectified by intervention, by
conservation, by bullets or by welfare. This imagination exists in relation to something to be acted upon – an indigenous population, a subordinate class, a topographic
space – and in tension with competing colonial projects, yet it is also a self-fashioning
exercise, that makes the maker as much as it does the made': 106.

24 C. Hall, 'William Knibb and the Constitution of the New Black Subject', in
M. Daunton and R. Halpern (eds) *Empire and Others: British Encounters with Indigenous
Peoples, 1600–1850*, UCL Press, London, 1999, 312.

25 L. Blake, 'Pastoral Power, Governmentality and Cultures of Order in Nineteenth-
Century British Columbia', *Transactions of the Institute of British Geographers*, 24,
1993, 89.

26 Keegan, *Colonial South Africa*; Bank, *Liberals and Their Enemies*; Crais, *White Supremacy*;
R. Ross, *Status and Respectability in the Cape Colony, 1750–1870: A Tragedy of Manners*,
Cambridge University Press, Cambridge, 1999. The phrasing here is derived from
Miles Ogborn's discussion of modernity in his *Spaces of Modernity: London's Geographies,
1680–1780*, The Guilford Press, New York and London, 1998, 19. For a South
African study which takes as its central theme the cultural and political connections
between the Cape and Britain, see E. Elbourne, *'To Colonize the Mind': Evangelical
Missionaries in Britain and the Eastern Cape, 1790–1837*, unpublished D.Phil. thesis,
University of Oxford, 1991.

27 C. A. Bayly, 'The British and Indigenous Peoples, 1760–1860: Power, Perception and
Identity', in M. Daunton and R. Halpern (eds) *Empire and Others: British Encounters
with Indigenous Peoples, 1600–1850*, UCL Press, London, 1999, 21. See also
H. V. Bowen, 'British Conceptions of Global Empire, 1756–83', *Journal of Imperial
and Commonwealth History*, 26, 3, 1998, 1–27.

28 S. Thorne, '"The Conversion of Englishmen and the Conversion of the World Inseparable": Missionary Imperialism and the Language of Class In Early Industrial Britain',
in F. Cooper and A. L. Stoler, *Tensions of Empire: Colonial Cultures in a Bourgeois World*,
University of California Press, Berkeley, 1997, 254.

29 M. Ogborn, 'Historical Geographies of Globalisation, 1500–1800', in B. Graham and
C. Nash (eds) *Modern Historical Geographies*, Prentice Hall, London, 1999, 43. For sug-
gestive comments on the ways in which language, economy, religion and material
forms such as the plantation also transgressed previously insurmountable spatial
boundaries during the eighteenth century, see S. Feierman, 'Africa in History: The
End of Universal Narratives', in G. Prakash (ed.) *After Colonialism: Imperial Histories
and Postcolonial Predicaments*, Princeton University Press, Princeton NJ. 1995, 42–3.

30 E. Said, *Culture and Imperialism*, Chatto and Windus, London, 1993, 60.

31 Feierman, 'Africa in History', 53.

32 Thus English representations of Irish and Scots were templates for images of 'savage' and 'wild' Others even during the earliest period of English colonisation in the Americas: P. D. Morgan, 'Encounters Between British and "Indigenous" Peoples, c. 1500–c. 1800' in Daunton and Halpern, *Empire and Others*, 56–8.

33 C. A. Bayly, 'The British and Indigenous peoples, 1760–1860: Power, Perception and Identity', in Daunton and Halpern, *Empire and Others*, 21.

34 R. Hyam, *Britain's Imperial Century, 1815–1914: A Study of Empire and Expansion*, 2nd edition, Macmillan, Basingstoke, 1993, 280.

35 Mary Louise Pratt was among the first postcolonial analysts to criticise the tendency 'to see European culture emanating out to the colonial periphery from a self-generating center' – a tendency which 'has obscured the constant movement of people and ideas in the other direction': M. L. Pratt, *Imperial Eyes: Travel Writing and Transculturation*, Routledge, London, 1992, 90.

36 S. Marks, 'History, the Nation and Empire: Sniping From the Periphery', *History Workshop Journal*, 29, 1990, 115.

37 A. Stoler and F. Cooper, 'Between Metropole and Colony: Rethinking a Research Agenda', in Cooper and Stoler, *Tensions of Empire*, 3. See also A. L. Stoler, 'Rethinking Colonial Categories: European Communities and the Boundaries of Rule' *Comparative Studies in Society and History* 1, 13, 1989, 134–61; *Race and the Education of Desire: Foucault's History of Sexuality and the Colonial Order of Things*, Duke University Press, Durham, N.C., 1995.

38 C. Hall, 'Histories, Empires and the Post-Colonial Moment', in I. Chambers and L. Curti (eds) *The Post-Colonial Question: Common Skies, Divided Horizons*, Routledge, London and New York, 1996, 76; C. Hall, *White, Male and Middle Class: Explorations in Feminism and History*, Polity, Cambridge, 1992. See also L. Colley, 'Britishness and Otherness: an Argument', *Journal of British Studies*, 31, 1992, 309–29.

39 Stoler and Cooper, 'Between Metropole and Colony', 14. A framework of analysis founded on the notion of an imperial network may help us to transcend some of the debates in which imperial historians have occasionally become bogged down. First, it brings metropole and colony into a single frame. This enables it to overcome what D. K. Fieldhouse has described as the Humpty-Dumpty syndrome in British imperial history – that is, the way in which studies of metropolitan and peripheral experiences have become disarticulated: D. K. Fieldhouse, 'Can Humpty-Dumpty Be Put Back Together Again? Imperial History in the 1980s', *Journal of Imperial and Commonwealth History*, 12, 2, 1984, 9–23. See also G. Martin, 'Was There a British Empire?', *Historical Journal*, xv, 3, 1972, 562–9. Secondly, as well as rearticulating the metropolitan and colonial circuits of empire, the concept of an imperial network enables connections between different 'core' and 'peripheral' regions to be envisaged. It thus addresses the central problem for the imperial historian identified by Feierman: 'how to capture all different levels at the same time, how to do justice to the local, the regional, and the international in a single description or a single framework of analysis': Feierman, 'Africa in History', 53. Finally, it suggests, if not a resolution, then at least a side-stepping of the issue of competing models of imperial expansion such as those of Robinson and Gallagher's 'official mind', or Cain and Hopkins' 'gentlemanly capitalism'. The concept of a network of multiple and 'located' colonial projects, intersecting and colliding contingently through particular circuits of empire, may enable us to avoid the contest between prescriptive models altogether. See R. Robinson and J. Gallagher, *Africa and the Victorians: The Official Mind of Imperialism*, Macmillan, second edition, 1981; P. Cain and A. G. Hopkins, *British Imperialism: Innovation and Expansion, 1688–1914*, Longman, London, 1993. For a discussion of these and other models of imperial history that allow insufficient space for

contingency, see J. Darwin, 'Imperialism and the Victorians: The Dynamics of Territorial Expansion', *English Historical Review*, June 1997, 614–42.

2 Colonial projects and the eastern Cape

1 Quoted in D. Turley, *The Culture of English Antislavery, 1780–1860*, Routledge, London and New York, 1991, 8.
2 R. Elphick and H. Giliomee (eds) *The Shaping of South African Society, 1652–1840*, Wesleyan University Press, Middletown, Conn., 1988; T. Keegan, *Colonial South Africa and the Origins of the Racial Order*, Leicester University Press, London, 1996; R. Shell, *Children of Bondage: A Social History of the Slave Society at the Cape of Good Hope, 1652–1838*, Witwatersrand University Press, Johannesburg, 1994. 'Khoesan' is an umbrella term used by historians to refer to pastoral kinship groups known to Europeans as 'Hottentots' and to themselves as 'Khoekhoe' ('men of men'), on the one hand, and small, dispersed communities of hunter-gatherers whom the Khoekhoe called 'San' and Europeans labelled as 'Bushmen', on the other. Since the latter did not have a generic name for themselves, or at least one that is now identifiable, they still tend to be referred to by one of these two appellations (both of which are derogatory). The relative permeability of the boundaries between Khoekhoe and San communities is still in dispute.
3 L. Guelke and R. Shell, 'An Early Colonial Landed Gentry: Land and Wealth in the Cape Colony, 1682–1731', *Journal of Historical Geography*, 9, 1983, 265–86.
4 L. Guelke, 'The Origin of White Supremacy in South Africa: An Interpretation, *Social Dynamics*, 15, 1989, 40–45.
5 Newton-King suggests that arable produce was too expensive to transport to Cape Town from outside a radius of about 110 km: S. Newton-King, *Masters and Servants on the Cape Eastern Frontier*, Cambridge University Press, Cambridge, 1999, 18.
6 L. Guelke, and R. Shell, 'Landscape of Conquest: Frontier Water Alienation and Khoikhoi Strategies of Survival, 1652–1780', *Journal of Southern African Studies*, 18, 1992, 803–24; P. J. van der Merwe, *The Migrant Farmer in the History of the Cape Colony, 1657–1842*, translated by Roger Beck, Ohio University Press, Athens, 1995; S. Marks, 'Khoisan Resistance to the Dutch in the Seventeenth and Eighteenth Centuries', *Journal of African History*, 13, 1972, 55–80.
7 S. Newton-King, 'The Enemy Within', in Worden, N. and Crais, C. (eds) *Breaking the Chains: Slavery and Its Legacy in the Nineteenth-Century Cape Colony*, Witwatersrand University Press, Johannesburg, 1994.
8 Quoted in Newton-King, *Masters and Servants*, 22.
9 J. B. Peires, *The House of Phalo: A History of the Xhosa People in the Days of Their Independence*, University of California Press, Berkeley, 1982, 13–19; R. Elphick, *Kraal and Castle: Khoikhoi and the Founding of White South Africa*, Yale University Press, New Haven and London, 1977, 50; G. Harinck, 'Interaction Between Xhosa and Khoi Emphasis on the Period 1620–1750', in L. Thompson (ed.) *African Societies in Southern Africa*, Heinemann, London, 1969; Newton-King, *Masters and Servants*, 29.
10 The Gcaleka paramount chiefs, located to the east of the Kei (Transkei) are still generally recognised by the Xhosa as having superior status over the Rharhabe chiefs to the west (Ciskei).
11 Peires, *House of Phalo*, 50.
12 M. L. Pratt, *Imperial Eyes: Travel Writing and Transculturation*, Routledge, London, 1992, 6–7.
13 See C. Crais, *White Supremacy and Black Resistance in Pre-Industrial South Africa: The Making of the Colonial Order in the Eastern Cape, 1770–1865*, Cambridge University Press, Cambridge, 1992, 42–3.

14 Peires, *House of Phalo*, 45–53.

15 See Newton-King, *Masters and Servants*.

16 On colonial farms, Khoesan subordinates were suspended outside of the colonists' moral community, through the religious notion of heathen exceptionalism. As Newton-King remarks, 'heathenness' 'seems to have been equated with a lack of moral faculties and an inability to discipline oneself or submit voluntarily to a higher authority, which put one "almost on a par with the animals"' (Newton-King, *Masters and Servants*, 309, fn. 244, quoting Alberti). In 1801, some frontier burghers rebelled when Khoesan were admitted, under the instructions of the landdrost, to their church. They demanded that the pews be washed and the pulpit be covered in black cloth in mourning: *ibid*, 228. For the metropolitan origins of colonists' religious exclusions, see also S. Trapido, 'The Cape Dutch and Problems of Colonial Identity', paper presented to the Societies of Southern Africa in the Nineteenth and Twentieth Centuries Seminar, Institute of Commonwealth Studies, London, Feb. 1994, 7.

17 Newton-King, *Masters and Servants*, 9, 115. The fact that some colonists tried initially to seize Xhosa as captive labour indicates that they too were thought to be 'ethnically qualified' for forced servitude when, of course, whites were not: *ibid*, 59.

18 C. A. Bayly, *Imperial Meridian: The British Empire and the World, 1780–1830*, Longman, Harlow, 1989; L. Colley, *Britons: Forging the Nation, 1707–1837*, Pimlico, London, 1992.

19 Bayly, *Imperial Meridian*, 135. For a wealth of detail on governors' military backgrounds and their experiences in the Peninsular campaign, see N. Mostert, *Frontiers: The Epic of South Africa's Creation and the Tragedy of the Xhosa People*, Jonathan Cape, London, 1992.

20 Bayly, *Imperial Meridian*, 202; Mostert, *Frontiers*, 410–11.

21 *Ibid.*, 209.

22 G. Martin, 'Was There a British Empire?', *Historical Journal*, xv, 3, 1972, 566.

23 A fair proportion of the relatively select band of colonial administrators was inter-related. Bayly, for instance, draws attention to the extent of involvement in colonial administration of particular families such as the Beauforts (including Lord Charles Somerset in the Cape and six other governors), the Maitlands and the Macartneys (which families also provided Cape governors): Bayly, *Imperial Meridian*, 134.

24 Bayly estimates that during the early nineteenth century, the empire sustained some 10,000 official positions worth over £500 per annum: *ibid.*, 214.

25 J. W. Cell, *British Colonial Administration in the Mid-Nineteenth Century: The Policy-Making Process*, Yale University Press, New Haven and London, 1970, 60.

26 B. Hilton, *The Age of Atonement: The Influence of Evangelicalism on Social and Economic Thought, 1795–1865*, Clarendon Press, Oxford, 1988, 205.

27 J. Black, *The Politics of Britain, 1688–1800*, Manchester University Press, Manchester, 1993.

28 Bayly, *Imperial Meridian*, 193.

29 W. M. Macmillan, *The Cape Colour Question: A Historical Survey*, Faber and Gwyer, London, 1927; A. Atmore and S. Marks, 'The Imperial Factor in South Africa in the Nineteenth Century: Towards a Reassessment', *Journal of Imperial and Commonwealth History*, 3, 1974, 105–39.

30 C. A. Bayly, 'The British and Indigenous Peoples, 1760–1860: Power, Perception and Identity' in M. Daunton and R. Halpern (eds) *Empire and Others: British Encounters with Indigenous Peoples, 1600–1850*, UCL Press, London, 1999, 26.

31 Bayly, *Imperial Meridian*, 10.

32 Trapido describes the western Cape Dutch elite as becoming 'liberal, monarchical and inclusive' under early British rule, while many poorer and more marginal

frontier farmers became 'conservative, republican and exclusive': Trapido, 'The Cape Dutch and Problems of Colonial Identity', 20.

33 See *ibid.*

34 S. Marks and S. Trapido, ' "Full of Enterprise and Bent on Conquest" Or Two Cheers for the Enlightenment: British Settler Identities in South Africa in the First Half of the Nineteenth Century', unpublished paper given at the ASEN conference, 1996.

35 R. Percival, *An Account of the Cape of Good Hope*, 1806, quoted in Bayly, *Imperial Meridian*, 203.

36 R. Ross, *Status and Respectability in the Cape Colony, 1750–1870: A Tragedy of Manners*, Cambridge University Press, Cambridge, 1999, 43.

37 Literal and metaphorical distance from 'civilization' was also a trope applied to convict settlers who became stockmen in the interior of Australia during the early nineteenth century. See *British Parliamentary Papers: Report from the Select Committee on Aborigines (British Settlements)*, reprinted Irish University Press, Shannon, 1968, *Minutes of Evidence*, evidence of D. Coates, Rev. John Beecham and Rev. William Ellis, 505–6.

38 Newton-King, *Masters and Servants*, 206. It was not just the new British governing class that condemned Afrikaners. Metropolitan Dutch visitors did as well, prompting colonists to form a more defensive and close-knit sense of colonial identity. See Trapido, 'The Cape Dutch and Problems of Colonial Identity'.

39 S. Dubow, *Knowledge and the Politics of Colonial Identity*, unpublished MS, 2000, no pagination. My thanks to Saul Dubow for letting me see this prior to publication.

40 See G. Fredrickson, *White Supremacy: A Comparative Study in American and South African History*, Oxford University Press, Oxford and New York, 1981; Crais, *White Supremacy*; Worden and Crais, *Breaking the Chains*.

41 Percival, quoted in Bayly, *Imperial Meridian*, 203.

42 See Bayly, *Imperial Meridian*, 202; W. M. Freund, 'The Cape Under the Transitional Governments, 1795–1814', in R. Elphick and H. Giliomee (eds) *The Shaping of South African Society, 1652–1840*, Wesleyan University Press, Middletown, Conn., 1988, 338.

43 Henry Ellis, Deputy to the Cape Colonial Secretary, quoted by Philipps and cited in Marks and Trapido, 'Full of Enterprise and Bent on Conquest', 1.

44 See M. Foucault, 'On Governmentality', in G. Burchell, C. Gordon and P. Miller (eds) *The Foucault Effect: Studies in Governmentality*, University of Chicago Press, Chicago, 1991, 87–104; *Discipline and Punish: The Birth of the Prison*, Penguin, London, 1977, 168; M. Mann, 'The Autonomous Power of the State: Its Origins, Mechanisms and Results', *Archives Européenes de Sociologie*, 25, 1984, 185–213.

45 Cape Town State Archives (hereafter CA) GH 28/4, Cradock to Graham, 6 Oct. 1811.

46 W. M. Macmillan, *Bantu, Boer and Briton: The Making of the South African Native Problem*, Clarendon Press, Oxford, 1963, 45.

47 For such responses in India, see B. Cohn, *An Anthropologist Among the Historians and Other Essays*, Oxford University Press, New Delhi, 1987.

48 Col. Collins, 'Supplement to the Relation of a Journey into the Country of the Bosjeman and Caffre People', 1809, in D. Moodie (ed.) *The Record: Or a Series of Official Papers Relative to the Condition and Treatment of the Native Tribes of South Africa*, 1838, reprinted by A. A. Balkema, Cape Town, 1960.

49 *Ibid.*, 17. Collins' adherence to a respectable evangelical discourse becomes questionable at a later point in his report, when his appreciation of African women is expressed. Collins was much enamoured of one of Hintsa's wives whom he witnessed breastfeeding, an activity which rendered 'her handsome appearance [all the] more interesting': 41.

50 *Ibid.*, 17.

51 Bayly, *Imperial Meridian*, 147.

52 Collins, 'Supplement', 17. In order to foster such colonial development, Collins was the first to suggest a settlement of Britons along the frontier, the implication being that they would generate more rapid civilisation than that of which Dutch-speaking colonists were capable. Specifically, Collins recommended that the frontier be settled with Highland Scots. Having just made the transition themselves from a clan-based system of retributive raiding, to a more 'civilised' and commercialised society, it was thought that they would be particularly well-equipped to lead the Xhosa through the same transition. Despite official disapproval, there were already hundreds of Xhosa men working for colonists, many of them aspiring to earn enough cattle to pay bridewealth upon their return across the frontier.

53 Extract of a letter from Stockenström to Caledon, in Moodie, *The Record*, V, 57.

54 CA, GH 23/2, Calderwood to Castlereagh, 18 Sept. 1809.

55 CA, GH 23/4, Cradock to Liverpool, 10 June 1812.

56 CA, CO 5807, Government Proclamation, 21 Aug. 1810.

57 J. S. Galbraith, *Reluctant Empire: British Policy on the South African Frontier, 1834–1854*, University of California Press, Berkeley, 1963, 50.

58 CA, GH 23/4, Cradock to Graham, 6 Oct. 1811. As future frontier wars would demonstrate, Cradock was wrong. Xhosa warriors were able to exploit the thick bush along the Fish River valley to approach colonial settlements undetected.

59 CA, GH 23/4, Cradock to Liverpool, 7 March 1812.

60 *Ibid.*

61 Quoted in B. Maclennan, *A Proper Degree of Terror: John Graham and the Cape's Eastern Frontier*, Ravan Press, Johannesburg, 1986, 136.

62 Freund, 'The Cape Under the Transitional Governments', 332.

63 Macmillan, *Bantu, Boer and Briton*, 48. Despite the continuance of retaliatory raids against the colony, Peires suggests that the experience of the 1812 expulsion was sufficiently traumatic to bring about a shift in the frontier chiefs' stance towards the colonial frontier: 'Whereas they had formerly resisted suggestions that they should keep to their own side of the boundary, they now began to see in a firmly sealed border their only hope of survival as an independent nation': J. B. Peires, 'The British and the Cape, 1814–1834', in R. Elphick and H. Giliomee (eds) *The Shaping of South African Society, 1652–1840*, Wesleyan University Press, Middletown, Conn., 1988, 481.

64 Bayly, *Imperial Meridian*, 12.

65 *Ibid.*, 194–5.

66 A. Millar, *Plantagenet in South Africa: Lord Charles Somerset*, Balkema, Cape Town, 1965, inside cover.

67 CA, GH 23/5, Somerset to Bathurst, 24 Apr. 1817.

68 *Ibid.*

69 CA, CO 5816, Government Advertisement, 18 Apr. 1817.

70 CA, GH 1/20, Goulbourn to Somerset, 22 Oct. 1816.

71 Ngqika's son Maqoma later raided the mission station – an indication of the extent of its local popularity: Mostert, *Frontiers*, 558–9.

72 CA, GH 23/5, Somerset to Bathurst, 24 Apr. 1817. Ngqika's status in this scheme could hardly be described as that of a colonial ally. In response to Maqoma's raid on the Tyhumie mission, Somerset ordered that the chief be seized and held captive. Humiliatingly, Ngqika reputedly escaped from the colonial patrol only by dressing as a woman.

73 For an account of the syncretic religious doctrines developed at this time by Nxele, and by Ngqika's rival wardoctor, Ntsikana, see Peires, *House of Phalo*, 69–74.

74 See Peires, *House of Phalo*, 143–5 and Mostert, *Frontiers*, 472–9.

75 Quoted in Macmillan, *Bantu, Boer and Briton*, 83.

76 Macmillan, *Bantu, Boer and Briton*, 71–83; Galbraith, *Reluctant Empire*, 33–4; Peires, 'The British and the Cape', 483–4.

77 Public Record Office, London (hereafter PRO) CO 48/165, 'Paper Prepared by Mr Beecham for the Use of Mr Buxton: The Cape of Good Hope', n.d. Not all Xhosa raids were launched in specific retribution for colonial acts. As Giliomee points out, 'peace-time cattle raids were generally the work of small groups evidently attempting to build up stock and power': H. Giliomee, 'The Eastern Frontier, 1770–1812', in R. Elphick and H. Giliomee (eds) *The Shaping of South African Society, 1652–1840*, Wesleyan University Press, Middletown, Conn., 1988, 449.

78 Freund, 'The Cape Under the Transitional Governments', 339, 344.

79 See F. Driver, *Power and Pauperism: The Workhouse System, 1834–84*, Cambridge University Press, Cambridge, 1993, 15.

80 J. Jorge Klor de Alva, 'The Postcolonization of the (Latin) American Experience: A Reconsideration of "Colonialism", "Postcolonialism" and the "Mestizaje"', in Prakash, *After Colonialism*, 243.

81 *Report from the Select Committee on Aborigines: Minutes of Evidence*, evidence of Andries Stockenström, 49–50.

82 Cory Library, Rhodes University (hereafter CL), *British Parliamentary Papers Relative to the Condition and Treatment of Native Inhabitants of the Cape of Good Hope*, part 2, 1835, 42, Sir Lowry Cole to Sir George Murray, 14 June 1829.

83 *Report from the Select Committee: Minutes of Evidence*, 90.

84 A. Stoler and F. Cooper, 'Between Metropole and Colony: Rethinking a Research Agenda', in F. Cooper and A. L. Stoler (eds) *Tensions of Empire: Colonial Cultures in a Bourgeois World*, University of California Press, Berkeley and London, 1997, 3.

85 L. Davidoff and C. Hall, *Family Fortunes: Men and Women of the English Middle Class, 1780–1850*, Routledge, London, 1987, 23.

86 *Ibid.*, 25.

87 *Ibid.*, 73.

88 E. P. Thompson, *The Making of the English Working Class*, Pelican, London, 1980, 385–440.

89 Quoted in E. Elbourne, *'To Colonize the Mind': Evangelical Missionaries in Britain and the Eastern Cape, 1790–1837*, unpublished D.Phil. thesis, Oxford University, 1991, 83.

90 Valenze, quoted in *Ibid.*, 14.

91 S. Thorne, '"The Conversion of Englishmen and the Conversion of the World Inseparable": Missionary Imperialism and the Language of Class In Early Industrial Britain', in F. Cooper and A. L. Stoler (eds) *Tensions of Empire: Colonial Cultures in a Bourgeois World*, University of California Press, Berkeley and London, 1997, 244. See also Colley, *Britons*.

92 C. Bolt and S. Drescher (eds) *Anti-Slavery, Religion and Reform*, Dawson, Folkestone, 1980.

93 T. W. Lacquer, 'Bodies, Details, and the Humanitarian Narrative', in L. Hunt (ed.) *The New Cultural History*, University of California Press, Berkeley and London, 1989.

94 *Ibid.*, 176–7; T. L. Haskell, 'Capitalism and the Origins of the Humanitarian Sensibility', part 1, *American Historical Review*, 90, 2, 1985, 339–61. A new humanitarian sensibility did not mean that it was middle-class reformers alone who brought about the abolition of slavery. If we were to understand that, we would also need to look at what slaves in the colonies were doing to bring about their own freedom. See R. Blackburn, *The Overthrow of Colonial Slavery, 1776–1848*, Verso, London and New York, 1988.

95 Stoler and Cooper, 'Between Metropole and Colony', 30. See also Colley, *Britons*, 351; D. Brion Davis, *The Problem of Slavery in the Age of Revolution, 1770–1823*, Cornell University Press, Ithaca, 1975, and J. R. Oldfield, *Popular Politics and British*

Anti-Slavery: The Mobilisation of Public Opinion Against the Slave Trade, 1787–1807, Cass, London.

96 Oldfield, *Popular Politics*, 117–8; Colley, *Britons*, 353.

97 J. Walvin, 'Freedom and Slavery and the Shaping of Victorian Britain', *Slavery and Abolition*, 15, 1994, 254.

98 Turley, *The Culture of English Antislavery*, 5; Oldfield, *Popular Politics*, 3; J. Habermass, *The Structural Transformation of the Public Sphere: An Inquiry into a Category of Bourgeois Society*, Polity Press, Cambridge, 1989.

99 See E. M. Howse, *Saints in Politics: The 'Clapham Sect' and the Growth of Freedom*, George Allen and Unwin, London, 1953.

100 J. Saville, *The Consolidation of the Capitalist State, 1800–1850*, Pluto Press, London, Boulder, Col., 1994, 61.

101 Davidoff and Hall, *Family Fortunes*, 20.

102 *Ibid.*, 18; Bayly, *Imperial Meridian*, 251.

103 Hilton, *The Age of Atonement*, 220–1.

104 *Ibid.*, 221.

105 *Ibid.*, Bayly, *Imperial Meridian*, 193–216.

106 Millar, *Plantagenet in South Africa.*.

107 For the overthrow of Somerset's regime see T. Keegan, *Colonial South Africa and the Origins of the Racial Order*, Leicester University Press, London, 1996, 95–100.

108 F. M. L. Thompson, *The Rise of Respectable Society: A Social History of Victorian Britain, 1830–1900*, Fontana, London, 1988, 16. Macaulay described the process as 'reform that you may preserve'. Quoted in Saville, *The Consolidation of the Capitalist State*, 46.

109 Bayly, *Imperial Meridian*, 12. See also Cain and Hopkins, *British Imperialism*.

110 Davidoff and Hall, *Family Fortunes*, 28; Turley, *The Culture of English Antislavery*, 110–11, 141.

111 Driver, *Power and Pauperism*, 18.

112 A majority of antislavery MPs either supported the New Poor Law or abstained. Those who opposed it were the more radical O'Connell and his Irish allies: Eltis, cited in Turley, *The Culture of English Antislavery*, 148.

113 Turley, *The Culture of English Antislavery*, 53. Most of the early nineteenth-century missionaries were drawn from those classes which were most rapidly becoming literate. Having worked their way up from working-class backgrounds to a middling status 'their own biographies, built on an unremitting commitment to self-improvement, were the very embodiment of the spirit of [bourgeois] capitalism, a living testimonial to its ethical and material workings' (Comaroff, 'Images of Empire, Contests of Conscience', 169). On missionary backgrounds, see also A. Ross, *John Philip (1775–1851): Missions, Race and Politics in South Africa*, Aberdeen University Press, Aberdeen, 1986, 38, 80; Elbourne, *To Colonize the Mind*, 42–4. One of the most effective of the mission societies' propaganda tools, devised to raise funds, reassure existing donors and establish the utility of particular denominations, was the evangelical periodical. In 1803, an obituarist of John Eyre, founder of the *Evangelical Magazine*, noted that such 'a periodical publication exhibits a mode of instruction, with which the world was formerly unacquainted; but since it has been adopted, has produced a surprising revolution in sentiments and manners. Thousands read a magazine who have neither money to purchase, nor leisure to peruse larger volumes' (quoted in Elbourne, *To Colonize the Mind*, 63).

114 C. Hall, 'William Knibb and the Constitution of the New Black Subject', in M. Daunton and R. Halpern (eds) *Empire and Others: British Encounters with Indigenous Peoples, 1600–1850*, UCL Press, London, 1999, 304–5, 309, 312.

115 Colley, *Britons*, 355.

116 For the crisis of authority in rural England which preceded poor law reform, see Hobsbawm and Rudé, *Captain Swing*, Pimlico, London, 1993, and for the

significance of slave revolts in inducing the abolition of slavery see Blackburn, *The Overthrow of Colonial Slavery*, 428–34 and Hall, 'William Knibb', 307.

117 Driver, *Power and Pauperism*, 18–19.

118 See T. Holt, *The Problem of Freedom: Race, Labor, and Politics in Jamaica and Britain, 1832–1938*, Johns Hopkins University Press, Baltimore and London, 1992 for apprenticeship in Jamaica and Worden and Crais, *Breaking the Chains* for the Cape.

119 M. Daunton and R. Halpern, 'Introduction: British Identities, Indigenous Peoples and the Empire', in M. Daunton and R. Halpern (eds) *Empire and Others: British Encounters with Indigenous Peoples, 1600–1850*, UCL Press, London, 1999, 4.

120 See P. D. Curtin, *The Image of Africa: British Ideas and Action, 1780–1850*, University of Wisconsin Press, Madison, Wis. and London, 1964; R. A. Austen and W. D. Smith, 'Images of Africa and British Slave Trade Abolition: The Transition to an Imperialist Ideology, 1787–1807', *African Historical Studies*, II, 1, 1969, 69–83. Curtin argues that 'for Britain itself the early nineteenth century image of Africa was, in fact, the image of West Africa', xii. As we will see below, though, this did not mean that representations of Africans to the south were unavailable to the British reading public. Aside from African travellers' tales, Edward Long's notoriously racist, pro-planter and polygenetic *History of Jamaica* (1774) was a particularly formidable obstacle to humanitarian representations of Africans, since it was respected among the educated classes for its detailed 'information': M. J. Turner, 'The Limits of Abolition: Government, Saints and the "African Question", c. 1780–1820', *English Historical Review*, Apr. 1997, 323.

121 Curtin, *Images of Africa*, 23–4.

122 This was a portrayal most famously encapsulated by Josiah Wedgwood in a popular ceramic badge showing 'a black man crying out, "Am I not a man and a brother?"', but doing so, as Colley notes, 'from the safe position of his knees' (Colley, *Britons*, 355). For the story of this badge and its origins in the commercialised print and artefact political culture of the late eighteenth century, see Oldfield, *Popular Politics*, 155–9.

123 Hall, 'William Knibb', 312. The humanitarian representation was reinforced by prevailing scientific and religious theories which challenged the planters' polygenetic assumptions. Racial theorists tended increasingly in the early nineteenth century 'to subscribe to the Biblically sanctioned theory of monogenesis and ascribed the physical signifiers of racial difference to the effects of climate and the environment': R. Young, *Colonial Desire: Hybridity in Theory, Culture and Race*, Routledge, London and New York, 1995, 118.

124 E. Stokes, *The English Utilitarians in India*, Oxford University Press, Delhi, 1959, 31; Bayly, 'The British and Indigenous Peoples', 33.

125 For the characteristics of this instruction in the Cape, increasingly identified as a powerful force in the shaping of nineteenth-century South African history as a whole, see Keegan, *Colonial South Africa*, 75–128; Worden and Crais, *Breaking the Chains*; M. Legassick, 'The State, Racism and the Rise of Capitalism in the Nineteenth Century Cape Colony', *South African Historical Journal*, 28, 1993, 329–68; S. Trapido, 'From Paternalism to Liberalism: The Cape Colony, 1800–1834 *The International History Review*, 12, 1990, 76–104.

126 Lacquer elaborates: 'Rousseau argues that the displacement of concern from oneself to others, to the love of the whole, is accomplished through the abolition of property, that selfishness is a product of ownership. The narratives with which I am concerned worked in precisely the opposite way. They created a sense of property in the objects of compassion, they appropriated them to the consciousness of would-be benefactors: 'Bodies, Details', 179. Quote from 180.

127 T. Todorov, *The Conquest of America: The Question of the Other*, Harper and Row, New York, 1985, 106–7.

128 Thomas, *Colonialism's Culture*, 61. Many postcolonial theorists have taken the tension between notions of freedom and social constraint to be indicative of the colonial enterprise as a whole. In focusing on the qualifications manifest in Western liberal humanism, they seek to characterise an entire colonial psyche (see for example, E. Said, *Culture and Imperialism*, Chatto and Windus, London, 1993; L. Gandhi, *Postcolonial Theory: A Critical Introduction*, Edinburgh University Press, Edinburgh, 1998, 27; B. Parekh, 'Liberalism and Colonialism: A Critique of Locke and Mill', in J. N. Pieterse and B. Parekh (eds) *The Decolonization of Imagination: Culture, Knowledge and Power*, Zed Books, London and New Jersey, 1995). Thomas Babington Macaulay's *Minute* of 1835 establishing the intrinsic superiority of European over Indian literature is often used by postcolonial scholars to reinforce the point about an apparently 'universal' humanism being a Eurocentric and therefore inherently qualified production (E. Said, *The World, the Text and the Critic*, Harvard University Press, Cambridge, Mass., 1983, 12; H. Bhabha, 'Signs Taken for Wonders: Questions of Ambivalence and Authority under a Tree outside Delhi, May 1817', *Critical Inquiry*, 12, 1, 1985, 144–65; G. Viswanathan, *Masks of Conquest: Literary Studies and British Rule in India*, Faber and Faber, London, 1989. Macaulay's *Minute* is reproduced in B. Ashcroft, G. Griffiths and H. Tiffin (eds) *The Postcolonial Studies Reader*, Routledge, London and New York, 1995). However, I would suggest that we need to be careful not to interpret the nuances within a specifically humanitarian system of thought as being indicative of colonising culture *per se*. The humanitarian tension between freedom and constraint was itself generated in opposition to other powerful ideas about how both metropolitan and colonial societies should be ordered. As Turley writes, Liberal 'reformers seem to have begun their engagement with victims, subject to harsh and brutal treatment and regarded as less than fully human by those who exercised power over them. This was equally true of slaves in the Middle Passage and on the plantations, prisoners in the unreformed gaols, the insane in madhouses, poor children in the hovels and workplaces or the sick poor. In each case a necessary step to improvement was the recognition of the essential humanity of these victims rather than their animality, an animality which required the equation of control with physical restraint or brutalisation' (Turley, *The Culture of English Antislavery*, 135). Humanitarianism was defined as much by its political opposition to these alternative discourses of animality or inherent inferiority, as it was by the more general notions of human-ness propagated within the European Enlightenment. We therefore need to historicise an ambivalent early nineteenth-century notion of universalism, to say who produced it, against what opposition, in what contexts and forms and when, rather than to assume that it captures the 'essence' of European colonialism as a whole. Indeed, given that postcolonial scholars have sought consistently to particularise apparently universal notions such as 'rationality', to show that they are 'historical constructions and therefore subject to historical investments and limitations', they should also distinguish the groups that produced the tensions between freedom and constraint from those against whom they had to struggle (quote from Gandhi, *Postcolonial Theory*, 27).

129 Holt, *The Problem of Freedom*, 53; Comaroff, 'Images of Empire, Contests of Conscience', 181–4.

130 Hyam, *Britain's Imperial Century*, 96.

131 *The Times*, August, 1819, quoted M. D. Nash, *Bailie's Party of 1820 Settlers: A Collective Experience in Emigration*, A. A. Balkema, Cape Town, 1982, 17. This description was generated after news had been received of the Ndlambe's attack on Graham's Town.

132 Justus (Beverley Mackenzie), *The Wrongs of the Caffre Nation*, James Duncan, London, 1837, 59.

133 *Ibid.*, 60.

134 LMS First Report, quoted in Elbourne, *To Colonize the Mind*, 74. Andrew Porter traces the transnational channels of communication subsequently established when William Ellis was the LMS's foreign secretary. Ellis began his missionary career in Tahiti, but accompanied an LMS delegation to, and ended up joining, an American mission in Hawaii. He forged friendships with reformers in the USA and upon his return home, was considered an expert on the progress of colonial missions in general. As we will see in chapter 5, in 1836–7 he was able to demonstrate this expertise before a House of Commons Select Committee which enquired into frontier relations in the Cape, Australasia, Canada and the Pacific. Ellis's continuing personal links with American reformers, and his participation in the publication and dissemination of trans-Atlantic humanitarian propaganda, was a microcosm of the wider network of knowledge and propaganda exchange within the LMS as a whole: A. Porter, 'North American Experience and British Missionary Encounters in Africa and the Pacific, c. 1800–50', in M. Daunton and R. Halpern (eds) *Empire and Others: British Encounters with Indigenous Peoples, 1600–1850*, UCL Press, London, 1999, 348–50.

135 It also established a mission on the eastern frontier, with the Xhosa chief Dyani Tshatshu, in 1815. This had obtained the governor's approval because it could be used to counter the influence of rebel colonists living among the frontier Xhosa: Ross, *John Philip*, 48.

136 Freund, 'The Cape Under the Transitional Governments', 340.

137 Ross, *John Philip*, 67.

138 Quoted in Porter, 'North American Experience', 352, 354.

139 H. Botha, *John Fairbairn in South Africa*, Historical Publication Society, Cape Town, 1984.

140 *South African Commercial Advertiser*, 19 April 1826, quoted in Marks and Trapido, '"Full of Enterprise"', 10.

141 *South African Commercial Advertiser*, 27 June 1829, quoted in A. Bank, 'Losing Faith in the Civilising Mission: The Premature Decline of Humanitarian Liberalism at the Cape, 1840–60', in M. Daunton and R. Halpern (eds) *Empire and Others: British Encounters with Indigenous Peoples, 1600–1850*, UCL Press, London, 1999, 367.

142 Quoted in Ross, *John Philip*, 95.

143 Fairbairn used the *South African Commercial Advertiser* to popularise Philip's account within the Cape itself, propagating 'an image of Philip as an altruistic humanitarian campaigner': A. Bank, 'The Politics of Mythology: The Genealogy of the Philip Myth', *Journal of Southern African Studies*, 25, 3, 1999, 463–4.

144 *Report from the Select Committee, Minutes of Evidence*, Major Dundas, 141.

145 J. Philip, *Researches in South Africa*, James Duncan, London, 1828, vol. 1, 2.

146 *Ibid.*, vol. 1, 2. For comments on the raced, classed and gendered nature of such nineteenth-century claims to veracity and authority, see S. Mills, *Discourses of Difference: An Analysis of Women's Travel Writing and Colonialism*, Routledge, London and New York, 1994; R. Mitcham, 'Geographies of Global Humanitarianism', unpublished Ph.D. thesis, Royal Holloway and Bedford New College, University of London, in progress.

147 A. Bank, 'The Great Debate and the Origins of South African Historiography', *Journal of African History*, 38, 1997, 263.

148 Comaroff, 'Images of Empire', 164–5. The LMS itself retained a detached stance with regard to Philip's book, not wanting to be seen to be engaging too directly in a radical colonial politics: Porter 'North American Experience', 354.

149 Philip, quoted in Bank, 'The Great Debate', 263–4.

150 For Bannister's diverse colonial experience, see *Report from the Select Committee: Minutes of Evidence*, S. Bannister, 174.

151 S. Bannister, *Humane Policy; or Justice to the Aborigines of New Settlements*, London, 1830, reprinted by Dawsons, London. Bannister made it quite clear that he was aware of the controversy that Philip's book had aroused, and that he would therefore be drawing on evidence which could in no way be construed as partial: 220.

152 *Ibid.*, frontispiece.

153 *Ibid.*, 6.

154 Philip, *Researches*, vol. 1, ix–x.

155 *Ibid.*, 212–13.

156 Bannister, *Humane Policy*, 31.

157 *Ibid.*, iv.

158 *Report from the Select Committee on Aborigines: Minutes of Evidence*, evidence of Colonel Wade, quoting Philip, 318.

159 Macmillan, *The Cape Colour Question*; Ross, *John Philip*, 77–115.

160 Philip, *Researches* vol. 2, 388.

161 Hyam, *Britain's Imperial Century*, 94.

162 Justus, *The Wrongs of the Caffre Nation*, 239–41.

163 Bannister, *Humane Policy*, 159.

164 For the aftermath of Ordinance 50, see Worden and Crais, *Breaking the Chains*; R. Ross, *Beyond the Pale: Essays on the History of Colonial South Africa*, Witwatersrand University Press, Johannesburg, 1994; P. Scully, *Liberating the Family? Gender and British Slave Emancipation in the Rural Western Cape, South Africa, 1823–1853*, Heinemann, Portsmouth N.H., James Currey, Oxford and David Philip, Cape Town, 1997; Keegan, *Colonial South Africa*; R. Elphick and H. Giliomee, 'The Origins and Entrenchment of European Dominance at the Cape, 1652–c.1840', in R. Elphick and H. Giliomee (eds) *The Shaping of South African Society, 1652–1840*, Wesleyan University Press, Middletown, Conn., 1988.

165 See A. Stockenström, *The Autobiography of the Late Sir Andries Stockenström, Bart, Sometime Lieutenant Governor of the Eastern Province of the Colony of the Cape of Good Hope*, C. W. Hutton (ed.), Juta and Co., Cape Town, 1887, vols 1 and 2.

166 The settler 'spokesman' J. C. Chase paid Stockenström the tribute of referring to his many 'amiable qualities' and suggested that he could have rendered 'great service to his co-Colonists', but regretted that he had 'identified himself, in an evil hour of no common temptation, with their detractors . . . Never in this Colony has fallen a man who could have achieved more good for his native land than himself; but unhappily he missed his way': M. J. McGinn, 'J. C. Chase – 1820 Settler and Servant of the Colony', unpublished MA thesis, Rhodes University, 1975, 171.

167 Quoted in Elbourne, *To Colonize the Mind*, 285.

168 Bannister, *Humane Policy*, 93.

169 Stockenström, *Autobiography*, vol. 1, 347.

170 Quoted in Elbourne, *To Colonize the Mind*, 286, fn. 20.

171 Rose Innes, quoted in Elbourne, *To Colonize the Mind*, 290.

172 Keegan, *Colonial South Africa*, 118–19.

173 Quoted in Elbourne, *To Colonize the Mind*, 293. For a similar emotive outpouring, see Pringle, *Narrative of a Residence in South Africa*, London, 1834, reprinted Struik, Cape Town, 1966, 279–80. For more on the foundations of the Kat River Settlement and its deployment within networks of humanitarian propaganda, see T. Kirk, 'Progress and Decline in the Kat River Settlement, 1829–1854, *Journal of African History*, XIV, 3, 1973, 411–28; Elbourne, *To Colonize the Mind*, 282–300; Mostert, *Frontiers*, 621–5; Ross, *Status and Respectability*, 150–3; Crais, *White Supremacy*, 79–82, 159–72.

174 Quoted in Elbourne, *To Colonize the Mind*, 294.

175 *Ibid.*, 294.

176 Philip to Anderson, 13 Dec. 1833, quoted in Porter, 'North American Experience', 353.

177 Bannister, *Humane Policy*, 42.
178 Curtin, *The Image of Africa*.
179 Turner, 'The Limits of Abolition', 319–57.
180 Bannister, *Humane Policy*, 82.
181 Ross, *John Philip*, 96.
182 Justus, *The Wrongs of the Caffre Nation*, vi.
183 *Ibid.*, xii–xiii.
184 Quoted in Ross, *John Philip*, 96.
185 *Ibid.*, 129.
186 Wilberforce, quoted in Austen and Smith, 'Images of Africa', 79.
187 Bannister, *Humane Policy*, v.
188 *Ibid.*, 1; Pringle, *Narrative of a Residence*; Justus, *The Wrongs of the Caffre Nation*; Public Record Office, London (hereafter PRO) CO 48/165, 'Paper Prepared by Mr Beecham for the Use of Mr Buxton: The Cape of Good Hope', n.d.
189 Justus, *The Wrongs of the Caffre Nation*, 129–30.
190 J. Philip, 'A Narrative Written for Buxton', quoted in Ross, *Status and Respectability*, 117.
191 Bannister, *Humane Policy*, 48–9, 82, 104.
192 *Ibid.*, 85.
193 Bayly, *Imperial Meridian*, 162.
194 For the labour shortages and Ordinance 49's attempts to resolve them, see S. Newton-King 'The Labour Market of the Cape Colony 1807–1828' in S. Marks and A. Atmore (eds) *Economy and Society in Pre-industrial South Africa*, Longman, London, 1980, 171–207.
195 CL, MS968.033 (7) GRE, British Parliamentary Papers Relative to the Condition and Treatment of Native Inhabitants of the Cape of Good Hope, Bourke to Bathurst, 30 June 1827.
196 Quoted in C. Hamilton, '"The Character and Objects of Chaka": A Reconsideration of the Making of Shaka as Mfecane Motor', in C. Hamilton (ed.) *The Mfecane Aftermath: Reconstructive Debates in Southern African History*, Witwatersrand University Press and University of Natal Press, Johannesburg and Pietermaritzburg, 1995, 200.
197 See T. Stapleton, *Maqoma: Xhosa Resistance to Colonial Advance, 1798–1873*, Jonathan Ball, Johannesburg, 1994, 63–99; Mostert, *Frontiers*, 625–65 and Peires, *House of Phalo*, 89–94.
198 For the disputes surrounding the term *Mfecane*, and over the processes involved, see J. D. Omer-Cooper, *The Zulu Aftermath: A Nineteenth Century Revolution in Bantu Africa*, Longman, London, 1969; J. Cobbing, 'The Mfecane as Alibi: Thoughts on Dithakong and Mbolompo', *Journal of African History*, 29, 1988, 487–519; J. Peires, 'Paradigm Deleted: The Materialist Interpretation of the Mfecane', *Journal of Southern African Studies*, 19, 2, 1993, 295–313; Hamilton *The Mfecane Aftermath*, and Keegan, *Colonial South Africa*, 337, n. 27.
199 PRO, CO 58/165, 'Paper Prepared by Mr Beecham'.
200 CL, Cory Transcript MS 17042, 52, Somerset papers, 5 Feb. 1828.
201 *South African Commercial Advertiser*, 18 July 1826, quoted in J.G. Pretorius, *The British Humanitarians and the Cape Eastern Frontier, 1834–1836*, Archives Year Book, Government Printer, Pretoria 1988, 16.
202 For the generation of these fears, and the ambivalent roles played in their production by British traders at Port Natal, see Hamilton, '"The Character and Objects of Chaka"'.
203 Julian Cobbing has construed the whole battle as a deliberate exercise in the capture of slave labour, but this version is disputed by other historians. See Cobbing 'The Mfecane as Alibi' and J. Peires, 'Matiwane's Road to Mbolompo: A Reprieve for the Mfecane?' in C. Hamilton (ed.) *The Mfecane Aftermath: Reconstructive Debates in*

Southern African History, Witwatersrand University Press and University of Natal Press, Johannesburg and Pietermaritzburg, 1995. As far as Cape officials themselves were concerned, the most horrific aspect of the tragic episode concerned the actions of their African allies. According the British reports, the Gcaleka and Thembu warriors set about killing the women and children survivors of the British attack. Thus, further evidence was supplied to military men of the tremendous gulf between the Xhosa's present 'temperament' and what humanitarians expected of them: CL, Cory Transcript MS 17042, 59–61, Somerset papers, 29 Aug. 1828.

204 Bannister, *Humane Policy*, 158.

205 British Parliamentary Papers, 146–7, Commissioners of Inquiry to Col. Somerset, 27 Jan. 1826. When called to account by Bigge and Colebrooke for sending in misguided patrols in pursuit of stolen cattle, Colonel Somerset had maintained that those most 'clamorous in their complaints' were not the Xhosa themselves, but colonial traders annoyed that the patrols had 'interrupted their trade for a short period': Parliamentary Papers, 149, Col. Somerset to Commissioners of Inquiry, 6 Feb. 1826. For the commissioners' discussion of charges brought against military officials concerning specific incidents in which innocent Xhosa were killed, see pp. 146–57.

206 Justus, *The Wrongs of the Caffre Nation*, 138, vi.

207 *Ibid.*, 171–2, 179. See also Bannister, *Humane Policy*; PRO, CO 48/165, 'Paper Prepared by Mr Beecham and Pretorius', *The British Humanitarians*.

208 Foucault outlines the genesis of this more fundamental discursive contest when he contrasts the Romantic notion of an ideal society, which informed abolitionism and colonial humanitarianism, on the one hand, with the military notion of order, which informed colonial governance, on the other. While a 'military dream of society' had as its fundamental reference a set of 'permanent coercions', humanitarians believed in 'the primal social contract'; while military officers placed their faith in 'indefinitely progressive forms of training', humanitarians looked 'to fundamental rights'; and while colonial officials sought 'automatic docility', humanitarians wished to reconstruct 'the general will': Foucault, *Discipline and Punish*, 168–9.

209 Justus, *The Wrongs of the Caffre Nation* 129–30.

210 Ross, *John Philip*, 122.

211 Bannister, *Humane Policy*, 7.

212 Hilton, *The Age of Atonement*, 13.

213 Bannister, *Humane Policy*, vi.

214 Quoted Ross, *John Philip*, 141.

3 British settlers and the colonisation of the Xhosa

1 In R. Godlonton (ed.) *Memorials of the British settlers of South Africa*, Godlonton, Graham's Town, 1844, 117.

2 T. Kirk, 'The Cape Economy and the Expropriation of the Kat River Settlement, 1846–53, in S. Marks and A. Atmore (eds) *Economy and Society in Pre-industrial South Africa*, Longman, London, 1980; B. A. Le Cordeur, *Eastern Cape Separatism, 1820–54*, Oxford University Press, Cape Town, 1981; J. B. Peires, *The House of Phalo: A History of the Xhosa People in the Days of Their Independence*, University of California Press, Berkeley, 1982, and 'The British and the Cape, 1814–34, in R. Elphick and H. Giliomee (eds) *The Shaping of South African Society, 1652–1840*, Wesleyan University Press, Middletown, Conn., 1988.

3 C. Crais, *White Supremacy and Black Resistance in Pre-Industrial South Africa: The Making of the Colonial Order in the Eastern Cape, 1770–1865*, Cambridge University Press, Cambridge, 1992; T. Keegan, *Colonial South Africa and the Origins of the Racial Order*, Leicester University Press, London, 1996; M. Legassick, 'The State, Racism

and the Rise of Capitalism in the Nineteenth Century Cape Colony', *South African Historical Journal*, 28, 1993, 329–68; Peires, 'The British and the Cape'.

4 Crais, *White Supremacy*, 94–5, 138; Keegan, *Colonial South Africa*, 72.

5 A. L. Stoler, 'Rethinking Colonial Categories: European Communities and the Boundaries of Rule *Comparative Studies in Society and History*, 13, 1989, 134–61; J. P. Greene, 'Changing Identity in the British Caribbean: Barbados as a Case Study', in N. Canny and A. Pagden (eds) *Colonial Identity in the Atlantic World, 1500–1800*, University of Princeton Press, Princeton, 1987.

6 CA, CO 5816, Government Advertisement, 18 Apr. 1817.

7 C. A. Bayly, *Imperial Meridian: The British Empire and the World, 1780–1830*, Longman, Harlow, 1989, 158; M. Harper, 'British Migration and the Peopling of Empire', in A. Porter (ed.) *The Oxford History of the British Empire, Vol. III, The Nineteenth Century*, Oxford University Press, Oxford and New York, 1999, 76.

8 M. Nash, *Bailie's Party of 1820 Settlers* Balkema, Cape Town, 1982, chapter 1; L. Bryer and K. Hunt, *The 1820 Settlers*, Nelson, Cape Town, 1984, 15; H. Johnston, *British Emigration Policy, 1815–30: 'Shovelling Out Paupers'* Oxford University Press, Oxford, 1972, 2–6, 12–14.

9 Cruikshank was satirising the empty promises made to pauper emigrants by a British government desperate to get them off its hands. In another cartoon on the emigration scheme, he presented the choices facing British paupers as being starved to death in England or eaten alive by cannibals and wild animals in the Cape. The cartoons are reproduced in Bryer and Hunt, *1820 Settlers*, 18–19.

10 Bryer and Hunt, *1820 Settlers*, 17–20.

11 G. Thompson, *Travels and Adventures in Southern Africa* Colburn, London, 1827, vol. 2, 135–6.

12 Some historians have suggested that the British were predisposed to keep sexual relations within the colonising group. Unlike other European colonisers, they tended to refrain from engaging in intercourse with colonised populations, whether formally recognised in marriage or not. However, there is plentiful evidence that where gender ratios among colonists were particularly unbalanced as, for example, in parts of North America, India and the Pacific islands, Britons engaged in such relations as frequently and as openly as any other set of European colonists. Where they avoided such relations, as on the Cape frontier, it was not because they were British, but because they were able to maintain heterosexual relations within the social boundaries that they had imported. For a good comparative overview, see P. D. Morgan, 'Encounters Between British and "Indigenous" Peoples, c. 1500–c. 1800' in M. Daunton and R. Halpern (eds) *Empire and Others: British Encounters with Indigenous Peoples, 1600–1850*, UCL Press, London, 1999, 63–7.

13 *British Parliamentary Papers: Report from the Select Committee on Aborigines (British Settlements)*, reprinted Irish University Press, Shannon, 1968, Minutes of Evidence, 37.

14 Quoted in Nash, *Bailie's Party*, 13.

15 *Ibid.*, 7.

16 Quoted in G. Butler (ed.) *The 1820 Settlers: An Illustrated History* Balkema, Cape Town, 1974, 66–7.

17 Quoted in Nash, *Bailie's Party*, 25–6, 31.

18 I. Edwards, *The 1820 Settlers in South Africa*, Green, London, 1934, 61, 64; G. Dickason, *Irish Settlers to the Cape*, A. A. Balkema, Cape Town, 1973.

19 See for example, A. Giffard (ed.) *The Reminiscences of John Montgomery*, A. A. Balkema, Cape Town, 1981.

20 A. Keppel-Jones (ed.) *Philipps, 1820 Settler*, Shuter and Shooter, Pietermaritzburg, 1960, 84–5; F. van der Riet and L. Hewson (eds) *Reminiscences of an Albany Settler* Grocott and Sherry, Grahamstown, 1958, 42.

21 The Wesleyan missionary William Shaw estimated that 107 Methodists were attending classes on the frontier in 1820: W. Hammond-Tooke (ed.) *The Journal of William Shaw*, A. A. Balkema, Cape Town, 1972, 40.

22 C. Hill, *Reformation to Industrial Revolution*, Penguin, Harmondsworth, 1969; E. Hobsbawm and G. Rudé, *Captain Swing*, Pimlico, London, 1993; E. P. Thompson, *The Making of the English Working Class*, Penguin, Harmondsworth, 1988; J. R. Walton, 'Agriculture and Rural Society 1730–1914', in R. A. Dodgshon and R. A. Butlin (eds) *An Historical Geography of England and Wales*, 2nd edition, Academic Press, London.

23 Quoted in Butler, *The 1820 Settlers*, 175–6.

24 *Ibid.*

25 Keppel-Jones, *Philipps*, 24.

26 T. Pringle, *Narrative of a Residence in South Africa*, London, 1934, 12–13, 205.

27 Quoted in Nash, *Bailie's Party*, 40.

28 Quoted in Edwards, *The 1820 Settlers*, 71–2.

29 Struggles over entitlement to relief were a part of the construction of 'citizenship' in other colonies too, including Upper Canada and Australia. See M. Daunton and R. Halpern, 'Introduction: British Identities, Indigenous Peoples and the Empire', in M. Daunton and R. Halpern (eds) *Empire and Others: British Encounters with Indigenous Peoples, 1600–1850*, UCL Press, London, 1999, 6–7.

30 S. Marks and S. Trapido, ' "Full of Enterprise and Bent on Conquest" Or Two Cheers for the Enlightenment: British Settler Identities in South Africa in the First Half of the Nineteenth Century', unpublished paper presented at the ASEN conference, 1996, 16.

31 Pringle, *Narrative of a Residence*; Nash, *Bailie's Party*.

32 W. Moodie, *Ten Years in South Africa*, Bentley, London, 1835, vol. 1, 52; Keppel-Jones, *Philipps*, 127.

33 S. Newton King, 'The Labour Market of the Cape Colony, 1807–28'. in S. Marks and A. Atmore (eds) *Economy and Society in Pre-industrial South Africa* Longman, London, 1980.

34 Keppel-Jones, *Philipps*, 54.

35 *Ibid.*, 126.

36 B. Le Cordeur, *Eastern Cape Separatism, 1820–54*, Oxford University Press, Cape Town, 1981, 3.

37 T. Pringle, *Some Account of the Present State of the English Settlers in Albany, South Africa* Underwood, London, 1824, 31, 33–4.

38 S. Frosh, 'Time, Space and Otherness', in S. Pile and N. Thrift (eds) *Mapping the Subject: Geographies of Cultural Transformation*, Routledge, London, 1995, 293. See also A. McClintock, *Imperial Leather: Race, Gender and Sexuality in the Colonial Contest*, Routledge, London and New York, 1995, 24–5.

39 Quoted in Nash, *Bailie's Party*, 63.

40 M. Rainer (ed.), *The Journals of Sophia Pigot*, A. A. Balkema, Cape Town, 1974, 93; Pringle, *Some Account*, 105–6.

41 Van der Riet and Hewson, *Reminiscences of an Albany Settler*, 23–4.

42 Nash, *Bailie's Party*, 64, 68.

43 Although Dagut is primarily referring to later emigrants who would have had a greater fund of advice literature at their disposal, there were guides for the 1820 settlers too, although mostly official ones which dwelt on the opportunities rather than the perils of emigration: S. Dagut, 'The Migrant Voyage as Initiation School: Sailing From Britain to South Africa, 1850s-1890s', paper presented at the International Conference on New African Perspectives: Africa, Australasia and the Wider World at the End of the Twentieth Century, University of Western

Australia, Nov. 1999. My thanks to Simon Dagut for sending me a copy of this paper.

44 The interpretation of the processes that are adopted here owes much to the work of Ann Stoler. She describes colonial racism as being 'more than an aspect of how people classify each other, how they fix and naturalise the differences between We and They. It is also, less clearly perhaps, part of how people identify the affinities that they share and how they define themselves in contexts where discrepant interests, ethnic differences, and class might otherwise weaken consensus': 'Rethinking Colonial Categories', 137–8, citing Lévi-Strauss.

45 Keppel-Jones, *Philipps*, 109.

46 'Paper Prepared by Mr Beecham'; Mostert, *Frontiers*, 559.

47 Keppel-Jones, *Philipps*, 131–4.

48 W. Maxwell and R. McGeogh (eds) *The Reminiscences of Thomas Stubbs*, A. A. Balkema, Cape Town, 1978, 81; Le Cordeur, *Eastern Cape Separatism*, 11.

49 Quoted in N. Mostert, *Frontiers: The Epic of South Africa's Creation and the Tragedy of the Xhosa People*, Jonathan Cape, London, 578.

50 CA, A602/2 Journal of S. H. Hudson, Bathurst, 1821 (no precise date).

51 Keppel-Jones, *Philipps* 152. For an excellent analysis of Philipps' intriguing approach to frontier life, see Marks and Trapido, '"Full of Enterprise and Bent on Conquest"', 21–4.

52 Thompson, *Travels and Adventures*, vol. 1, 169; Pringle, *Narrative of a Residence*, 289.

53 Keppel-Jones, *Philipps*, 149.

54 For example *ibid.*, 289; Moodie, *Ten Years*, vol. 2, 274, 328, 336–7.

55 See D. Sibley, *Geographies of Exclusion*, Routledge, London, 1995, 19.

56 Le Cordeur, *Eastern Cape Separatism*, 40, 58. See also Moodie, *Ten Years*, vol. 2, 304–5.

57 N. Erlank, '"Thinking it Wrong to Remain Unemployed in the Pressing Times": The Experiences of Two English Settler Wives', *South African Historical Journal*, 33, 1995, 64.

58 Pringle, *Narrative of a Residence*, 312–3 fn; CL MS 17042, Cory transcript, Somerset Correspondence, 17.

59 Maxwell and McGeogh, *The Reminiscences of Thomas Stubbs*; van der Riet and Hewson, *Reminiscences*, 30.

60 See N. Rapport, 'Migrant Selves and Stereotypes: Personal Context in a Postmodern World', in S. Pile and N. Thrift (eds) *Mapping the Subject: Geographies of Cultural Transformation*, Routledge, London, 1995.

61 Keppel-Jones, *Philipps*, 257.

62 *Ibid.*, 252; Le Cordeur, *Eastern Cape Separatism*, 65.

63 Thompson, *Travels and Adventures*, vol. 1, 124; commission quoted Edwards, *The 1820 Settlers*, 101.

64 Keppel-Jones, *Philipps*, 77–8, 96–7, 254; Pringle, *Narrative of a Residence*, 108–10; Giffard, *The Reminiscences of John Montgomery*, 92; Moodie, *Ten Years*, vol. 1, 328–9.

65 Thompson, *Travels and Adventures*, vol. 1, 124.

66 Justus, *Wrongs of the Caffre Nation*, 239–41; Maxwell and McGeogh, *The Reminiscences of Thomas Stubbs*, 71.

67 Quoted in M. J. McGinn, 'J. C. Chase – 1820 Settler and Servant of the Colony', unpublished MA thesis, Rhodes University, 1975, 8.

68 Quoted in Erlank, '"Thinking it Wrong to Remain Unemployed"', 71.

69 See Keegan, *Colonial South Africa*, 119–22 and Crais, *White Supremacy*, 130.

70 *Report from the Select Committee: Minutes of Evidence*, evidence of Major Dundas, 128.

71 *Report from the Select Committee: Minutes of Evidence*, evidence of Colonel Wade, 290.

72 *Report from the Select Committee: Minutes of Evidence*, evidence of Major Dundas, 128.

73 Quoted in McGinn, 'J. C. Chase', 19–20.

74 *Graham's Town Journal*, 12 Jan. 1837, 1 Dec. 1836, 19 Jan. 1837. See also R. God-lonton, *Sketches of the Eastern Districts of the Cape of Good Hope as They Are in 1842*, Godlonton, Graham's Town, 1842, 13. The resurrection of Dutch laws is adverted to by Dundas in *Report from the Select Committee: Minutes of Evidence*, 128.

75 Pringle, *Narrative of a Residence*, 250.

76 Quoted in Mostert, *Frontiers*, 1149.

77 See, for example, W. M. Macmillan, *Bantu, Boer and Briton: The Making of the South African Native Problem*, Clarendon Press, Oxford, 1963, and J. Cell, *The Highest Stage of White Supremacy: The Origins of Segregation in South Africa and the American South*, Cambridge University Press, Cambridge, 1982.

78 Crais, *White Supremacy*; S. Dagut, 'Paternalism and Social Distance: British Settlers' Racial Attitudes, 1850s–1890s', *South African Historical Journal*, 37, 1997, 3–20.

79 See. E. Genovese, *Roll, Jordan, Roll: The World the Slaves Made*, Vintage Books, New York, 1976; W. Dooling, '"The Good Opinion of Others": Law, Slavery and Com-munity in the Cape Colony, *c.*1760–1830', in N. Worden and C. Crais (eds) *Breaking the Chains: Slavery and its Legacy in the Nineteenth-Century Cape Colony*, Witwatersrand University Press, Johannesburg, 1994.

80 S. Trapido, 'The Cape Dutch and Problems of Colonial Identity', paper presented to the Societies of Southern Africa in the Nineteenth and Twentieth Centuries Seminar, Institute of Commonwealth Studies, London, Feb. 1994, 17.

81 Dagut, 'Paternalism and Social Distance'.

82 *Ibid.*, 18.

83 See also S. Dagut, *Racial Attitudes among British Settlers in South Africa, c.1850–c.1895*, unpublished Ph.D. thesis, Cambridge University, 1997.

84 Crais, *White Supremacy*, M. Foucault, *Discipline and Punish: The Birth of the Prison*, Penguin, London, 1977.

85 Crais, *White Supremacy*, 95.

86 Thompson, *The Making of the English Working Class*, 233–58; C. Hill, *Reformation to Industrial Revolution*, Penguin, Harmondsworth, 1969, 61–71, 268–74; J. Barrell, *The Dark Side of the Landscape: The Rural Poor in English Landscape Painting, 1730–1840*, Cambridge University Press, Cambridge, 1980; J. Yelling, 'Agriculture, 1500–1730' and J. R. Walton, 'Agriculture and Rural Society, 1730–1914', both in R. A. Dodgshon and R. A. Butlin (eds) *An Historical Geography of England and Wales*, Academic Press, London, 1990.

87 L. Davidoff and C. Hall, *Family Fortunes: Men and Women of the English Middle Class, 1780–1850*, Routledge, London, 1987, 21.

88 *Ibid.*, 113, quoting the Rev. John James Angell.

89 See *ibid.*, 390.

90 *Ibid.*, 195. Further parallels between the settlers' treatment of Khoesan dependants and metropolitan bourgeois practices towards domestic servants can be identified in respect of the supervision of tasks, misunderstandings over the purport of instruc-tions and an employers' rhetorical tendency to infantilise dependants. See *ibid.*, 392 for the metropolitan context, and Dagut, 'Paternalism and Social Distance' for colonial practices.

91 Kirk, 'The Cape Economy', 227–9.

92 Godlonton, *Memorials*, 15; Le Cordeur, *Eastern Cape Separatism*, 42–3.

93 McGinn, 'J. C. Chase', 22.

94 Nash, *Bailie's Party*, 86; Keegan, *Colonial South Africa*, 71–2, 115–6; M. Rayner, *Wine and Slaves: The Failure of an Export Economy and the Ending of Slavery in the Cape Colony, South Africa, 1806–34*, unpublished Ph.D., Duke University, 1986; L. Meltzer, 'Emancipation, Commerce and the Role of John Fairbairn's *Advertiser*, in N. Worden and C. Crais (eds) *Breaking the Chains: Slavery and Its Legacy in the Nineteenth-Century Cape Colony*, Witwatersrand University Press, Johannesburg, 1994.

95 Erlank, '"Thinking It Wrong to Remain Unemployed"', 64.

96 Included among these developments were expeditions into the Albany settlement's African hinterland, notably those led by Dr Andrew Smith, who had regular reports published in the *GTJ*. Such expeditions both sought out new and lucrative trading contacts in the interior and maintained a flow of knowledge between the colony and the metropole, as artefacts gathered to the north were taken to London for display. See numerous issues of *GTJ*, 1836, and McGinn, 'J. C. Chase', 32.

97 A. Bank, *Liberals and Their Enemies: Racial Ideology at the Cape of Good Hope, 1820–1850*, unpublished Ph.D. thesis, University of Cambridge, 1995, 191.

98 A. L. Harrington, *The Graham's Town Journal and the Great Trek, 1834–1843*, Government Printer, Pretoria, 1973, 18.

99 Settlers like J. C. Chase also broadcast their grievances, against both the Xhosa and the humanitarians, through Dutch language periodicals, notably the *Zuid Afrikaan*, which often allied itself politically with the *GTJ*. See McGinn, 'J. C. Chase', 17–19.

100 *GTJ*, various issues, 1831–4. The connection between the extension of private land-holding and progress was one which had by now become established in metropolitan discourse. If Blackstone and Bentham had condemned communal landholding on moral grounds in England, how much more was the 'freedom' to buy, sell and transfer land an imperative of both political economy and progressive law in the 'waste-lands' of the colonies? See Bayly, *Imperial Meridian*, 158 and C. Crais, 'The Vacant Land: The Mythology of British Expansion in the Eastern Cape, South Africa', *Journal of Social History*, 25, 1991, 255–74.

101 For the settler press's similar role in other colonies, see Greene, 'Changing Identity', 241 and Bank, *Liberals and Their Enemies*, 21.

102 The best account of the Xhosa attack is Mostert, *Frontiers*, 664–82.

103 Le Cordeur, *Eastern Cape Separatism*, 72.

104 J. M. Bowker, *Speeches, Letters and Selection From Important Papers*, Godlonton and Richards, Grahamstown, 1864, 137.

105 Hammond-Tooke, *The Journal of William Shaw*, 14; Smith quoted Le Cordeur, *Eastern Cape Separatism*, 76.

106 *Graham's Town Journal* (hereafter *GTJ*), 23 Jan. 1835.

107 CA, GH 12/1, Memorial of Traders, 24 Feb. 1835. Traders definitely became specific targets for some Xhosa warriors, many of them having been accused of exploiting their Xhosa customers. Certainly in the wake of the war, they were delighted that the terms of trade had turned so markedly in their favour due to the Xhosa's utter deprivation and desperation: *GTJ*, 19 May 1836.

108 While some mission stations were undoubtedly destroyed by Xhosa resentful of any manifestation of colonial influence, others were wrecked by the occupation and plunder of colonial troops, who ordered those mission Xhosa who had been defending the stations to depart: CL, GMS Reports (uncatalogued), report from Chalmers for 1837.

109 See Bank, *Liberals and Their Enemies*, 217–23 and A. Bank, 'Of "Native Skulls" and "Noble Caucasians": Phrenology in Colonial South Africa', *Journal of Southern African Studies*, 22, 3, 1996, 387–404.

110 *GTJ*, 12 Nov. 1835, 'Affairs of the Frontier'; 1 Dec. 1836, letter from 'A Kafir Doctor'.

111 *GTJ*, 15 Oct. 1835, letter from 'A.'.

112 Anonymous letter, *GTJ*, 21 Apr 1836.

113 *Ibid.* 12 Nov. 1835 and 10 Dec 1835. See also Bank, 'Of Native Skulls' and 'Noble Caucasians'.

114 As Andrew Bank points out, the 'science' of phrenology held little attraction for established Dutch-speaking colonists 'whose world view was shaped by institutions of slavery and servitude rather than frontier violence', and was ridiculed by humanitarians like Fairbairn. But it had 'greater appeal for those with experience of frontier

conflict and an associated antipathy towards a "savage" enemy': Bank, 'Of "Native Skulls" and "Noble Caucasians" '. Bank also refers to the similar popularity of phrenology among British agrarian capitalists in Australia and New Zealand, in the latter, particularly after the Maori wars of the 1850s and 1860s (402–3). On phrenology's late eighteenth-century origins, and its later metropolitan deployment, see N. L. Stepan, *The Idea of Race in Science: Great Britain, 1800–1960*, Macmillan, London, 1982, 21–8.

115 Fawcett's comparison of the 'enlightened' company administration in India with the prevailing virulence of racial thought in Grahamstown can be found in *GTJ*, 4 Feb. 1836. The howls of outraged denunciation of Fawcett's contributions can be traced through many of the issues thereafter.

116 Bowker, *Speeches, Letters*, 125. The humanitarian Attorney General of the Cape, William Porter, declared that Bowker's tirade contained 'within it the concentrated essence and active principle of all the tyranny and oppression which white has ever exercised over black': 176–7.

117 H. Fast (ed.), *The Journal and Selected Letters of Rev. William J. Shrewsbury, 1826–35*, Witwatersrand University Press, Johannesburg, 1994, 128–31, 173–7, 215–6. See also W. Boyce, *Notes on South African Affairs from 1834 to 1838*, Aldum and Harvey, Grahamstown, 1838.

118 Greene, 'Changing Identity', 9.

119 Bowker, *Speeches, Letters*, 125.

120 Bowker, *Speeches, Letters*, 141.

121 P. Silva (ed.), *The Albany Journals of Thomas Shone*, Maskew Miller Longman, Grahamstown, 1992, 56; Maxwell and McGeogh, *The Reminiscences of Thomas Stubbs*, 71, 112.

122 Bowker, *Speeches, Letters*, 2, 7.

123 Quoted in A. Bank, 'The Great Debate and the Origins of South African Historiography', *Journal of African History*, 38, 1997, 74.

124 *Ibid.*, 74–5.

125 *Ibid.*, 76. Moodie's compilation was published in Cape Town in instalments between 1838 and 1841 and entitled *The Record; Or a Series of Official Papers Relative to the Condition and Treatment of the Native Tribes of South Africa*. For more on the conditions of its creation and its historiographical significance, see *ibid.* and R. Ross, 'Donald Moodie and the Origins of South African Historiography', in R. Ross, *Beyond the Pale: Essays on the History of Colonial South Africa*, Witwatersrand University Press, Johannesburg, 1994.

126 Bowker, *Speeches, Letters*,119; *GTJ*, 7 April and 19 May 1836.

127 I do not intend to enter into the causes and consequences of the subsequently named 'Great Trek' here. I will suggest, however, that concerns that Afrikaner colonists shared with British settlers over the future effects of humanitarian influence on a racialised colonial hierarchy were, perhaps, more significant than recent revisionism has allowed. Recent explanations of the colonists' emigration tend to underplay the loss of their autonomy and capability in dealing with 'vagrant' and Xhosa threats after the abolition of slavery and during the frontier war. They do so for two main reasons. First there is the well-founded desire to stress commercial aspects of the colonists' expansion into the interior. A current tendency is to situate the trekkers, like settlers in other expanding colonial societies, as the vanguard of a capitalist expansion, which the British authorities themselves were constrained from promoting (see Keegan, *Colonial South Africa*, 184–96; N. Etherington, 'Old Wine in New Bottles: The Persistence of Narrative Structures in the Historiography of the Mfecane and the Great Trek', in C. Hamilton (ed.) *The Mfecane Aftermath: Reconstructive Debates in Southern African History*, Witwatersrand University Press, Johannesburg, 1995, 44–9). Secondly, there is the seeming paradox of a migration

ostensibly motivated by the desire for greater security, which involved outright conflict with independent Africans in the interior – a paradox noted at the time by Fairbairn (*South African Commercial Advertiser*, 3 Sept. 1836). Nevertheless, being subject to the raids of 'independent' Xhosa and the 'stealing' of mixed Xhosa, Khoesan, Mfengu and Thembu, and being bereft of autonomy in dealing with each of these threats, may well have made the construction of alternative arrangements with interior Africans seem preferable to many trekkers. See A. du Toit and H. Giliomee, *Afrikaner Political Thought: Analysis and Documents*, vol. 1, David Philip, Cape Town and Johannesburg, 1983, 17; H. Giliomee, 'Processes in Development of the Southern African Frontier', in H. Lamar and L. Thompson (eds) *The Frontier in History: North America and Southern Africa Compared*, Yale University Press, New Haven, Conn., 1981; C. Crais, 'Slavery and Freedom Along a Frontier: The Eastern Cape, South Africa, 1770–1838', *Slavery and Abolition*, 11, 2, 1990, 190–215.

128 R. Godlonton, *A Narrative of the Irruption of the Kafir Hordes into the Eastern Province of the Cape of Good Hope, 1834–5*, Meurant and Godlonton, 1836, Grahamstown.

129 For the same trait among European settlers in Sumatra, see Stoler, 'Rethinking Colonial Categories', 140.

130 Godlonton, *Narrative*, 9–10, 12–13.

131 Van der Riet and Hewson, *Reminiscences*, 20–1. See also Pringle, *Narrative of a Residence*, 24.

132 Bowker, *Speeches, Letters*, 4, 195.

133 M. Tausig, 'Culture of Terror – Space of Death: Roger Casement's Putumayo Report and the Explanation of Torture', in N. B. Dirks (ed.) *Colonialism and Culture*, University of Michigan Press, Ann Arbor, 1992, 152.

134 Godlonton, *Narrative*, 119, 129–30; Bowker, *Speeches, Letters*, 202.

135 Davidoff and Hall, *Family Fortunes*, 370.

136 D. Bunn, 'Our Wattled Cott': Mercantile and Domestic Space in Thomas Pringle's African Landscapes', in W. Mitchell (ed.), *Landscape and Power* University of Chicago Press, Chicago, 1994, 143.

137 The phrase comes from Mary Louise Pratt's analysis of male travellers' tendency to survey 'empty' landscapes from a dominant perspective, and with their future possession in mind: M. L. Pratt, *Imperial Eyes: Travel Writing and Transculturation*, Routledge, London and New York, 1992.

138 Quoted in H. Dampier, 'Settler Women's Experiences of Fear, Illness and Isolation on the East Cape Frontier, 1820–1890', unpublished MA thesis, Rhodes University, 2000.

139 M. Winer and J. Deetz, 'The Transformation of British Culture in the Eastern Cape, 1820–1860', *Social Dynamics*, 16, 1, 1990, 59.

140 Fast, *The Journal and Selected Letters of Rev. William J. Shrewsbury*, 27.

141 J. Elliott, 'Introduction: Colonial Identity in the Atlantic World', in Canny and Pagden, *Colonial Identity*, 11.

142 Keppel-Jones, *Philipps*, 98; Thompson, *Travels and Adventures*, vol. 1, 20.

143 Bowker, *Speeches, Letters*, 203; Keppel-Jones, *Philipps*, 69. Emphasis in original.

144 Godlonton, *Narrative*, 7–8, 212–15.

145 See Pile and Thrift, 'Introduction', 5.

146 CL, MS 3563/3, H. Halse, Transcript of an autobiographical manuscript of Henry James Halse (1817–80).

147 U. Long (ed.), *The Chronicle of Jeremiah Goldswain, Albany Settler of 1820*, van Riebeeck Society, Cape Town, 1948, vol. 2, xxix.

148 Maxwell and McGeogh, *The Reminiscences of Thomas Stubbs*, 50. For reproduction of the *Narrative*'s general structure, see van der Riet and Hewson, *Reminiscences*.

149 J. Ayliff, *The Journal of Harry Hastings*, A. A. Balkema, reprinted 1963, 4.

150 See Davidoff and Hall, *Family Fortunes*, 416–19.

151 McGinn, 'J. C. Chase', 56. See also Keegan, *Colonial South Africa*, 332 fn.; R. Ross, *Status and Respectability in the Cape Colony, 1750–1870: A Tragedy of Manners*, Cambridge University Press, Cambridge, 1999, 62–6.

152 Stoler, 'Rethinking Colonial Categories', 140–1.

153 Moodie, *Ten Years*, vol. 2, 50.

154 Godlonton, *Memorials*, 83. See also 9, xxxiv, and Shaw's speech, 4–33.

155 Dampier, 'Settler Women's Experiences', 17.

156 Godlonton, *Memorials*, 58–9. Chase concluded: 'Gentleman, I cannot help believing but that the Settlers of 1820 were destined by Providence to found in South Africa a new State. Many years may roll over, but the time will come, as predicted by Professor Balbi, that there shall be in the Eastern Hemisphere an Indian, and Australian, and a South African Empire': 59.

157 Maxwell and McGeogh, *Reminiscences*, 117–18; Godlonton, *Memorials*, 116.

158 Silva, *The Albany Journals*, 56. Shone was engaged in an extra-marital affair which would have been shocking to his contemporaries. References to illicit sex seem to have been substituted with an unexplained symbol in the published version of his diary: Robert Ross, personal correspondence, 17 Nov. 1997.

159 G. Revill, 'Reading Rosehill: Community Identity and Inner City Derby', in M. Keith and S. Pile (eds), *Place and the Politics of Identity*, Routledge, London, 1993, 129 (citing Cohen).

160 Harré quoted in Pile and Thrift, 'Mapping the Subject', 35.

161 See M. B. Formes, 'Beyond Complicity Versus Resistance: Recent Work on Gender and European Imperialism', *Journal of Social History*, 28, 3, 1995, 629–42. See also J. Buzzard, 'Victorian Women and the Implications of Empire', *Victorian Studies*, 36, 4, 1993, 443–53. Ambiguous feminine roles, of course, were a feature of metropolitan as much as colonial life. As Davidoff and Hall point out with regard to the British middle class, 'It was clear that women were subordinate, yet they had influence; it was evident that the home and children were their sphere, yet sometimes they had to engage in male pursuits and help support, or indeed entirely support, a family. It was this ambiguity on the finer points of detail that made the precise delineation of woman's role a matter of negotiation, rather than a fixed code': *Family Fortunes*, 117.

162 A. Blunt and G. Rose, 'Introduction: Women's Colonial and Postcolonial Geographies', in A. Blunt and G. Rose (eds) *Writing Women and Space: Colonial and Postcolonial Geographies*, Guilford Press, New York and London, 1994, 13.

163 M. Strobel, *European Women and the Second British Empire*, University of Indian Press, Bloomington, 1991, xiii.

164 Davidoff and Hall, *Family Fortunes*, 313, 25, 319. Davidoff and Hall trace the ways in which women were progressively excluded not just from public political activities, but from active participation in spectacles such fox hunting, racing, the fairground and certain parts of the marketplace: 408. See also C. Hall, *White, Male and Middle Class: Explorations in Feminism and History*, Verso, Cambridge, 1992.

165 S. Mills, 'Gender and Colonial Space', *Gender, Place and Culture*, 3, 2, 1996, 130.

166 This is admitted in another of Mills' analyses, 'Knowledge, Gender, and Empire', in A. Blunt and G. Rose (eds) *Writing Women and Space: Colonial and Postcolonial Geographies*, The Guilford Press, New York and London, 1994, 38. Here she writes: 'A distinction should be made between women settlers and travelers, since there seems to be quite a fundamental difference between the two groups. Women settlers . . . were subject to even stricter class and hierarchy rules than those that operated on them within Britain; this occurred partly because of the need to assert a strong cultural identity as a community in the face of overwhelming different communities – the maintenance of this structure fell largely to women.

Travelers, however, were not seen as necessarily a part of these communities and could behave in a slightly eccentric way'.

167   P. Pels, 'The Anthropology of Colonialism: Culture, History, and the Emergence of Western Governmentality', *Annual Review of Anthropology*, 26, 1997, 173, citing A. L. Stoler, 'Carnal Knowledge and Imperial Power: Gender, Race, and Morality in Colonial Asia', in J. Wallach Scott (ed.) *Feminism and History*, Oxford University Press, Oxford, 1996, and *Race and the Education of Desire: Foucault's History of Sexuality and the Colonial Order of Things*, Duke University Press, Durham, N.C. See also M. Norton, 'The Evolution of White Women's Experience in Early America', *The American Historical Review*, 89, 3, 1984, 595. Stoler's work is part of a broader conceptualisation of the ways that gender (defined as embracing both masculinities and femininities) intersected with race and class within recent studies of imperialism. See J. Haggis, 'Recent Women's Studies Approaches to White Women and the History of British Colonialism', *Women's Studies International Forum*, 13, 1/2, 1990, 105–15.

168   Rainer, *The Journals of Sophia Pigot*, 67–8; Thompson, *Travels and Adventures*, vol. 2, 124 and Bunn, 'Our Wattled Cott', 146–7, 152.

169   Erlank, '"Thinking it Wrong to Remain Unemployed"', 65.

170   *Ibid.*, 68.

171   I. Mitford-Barberton (ed.), *Comdt. Holden Bowker*, Human and Rousseau, Cape Town, 1970, 230–4; A. Cohen, 'Mary Elizabeth Barber: South Africa's First Lady Natural Historian', *Archives of Natural History*, 27, 2, 2000, 200–21.

172   Dampier, 'Settler Women's Experiences'. Dampier argues that settler women's frequent bouts of sickness were partly a survival mechanism: a way of withdrawing temporarily from the stresses and strains of life, and from gendered domestic responsibilities, on the frontier. At the same time, 'If a function of white women settlers was to instil the cultural values and social systems of their homeland, then playing the part of the sensitive, sickly, refined lady', which was well established in British feminine discourse, reinforced such connections: 128–9.

173   Quoted in Mills, 'Knowledge, Gender, and Empire', 32.

174   Dagut, 'Paternalism and Social Distance', 12; Davidoff and Hall, *Family Fortunes*, 25. See also Strobel, *European Women*.

175   Sibley, *Geographies of Exclusion*, 10, 92–3.

176   Davidoff and Hall, *Family Fortunes*, 320.

177   See Rainer, *The Journals of Sophia Pigot*. Settler women were also more successfully reproducing the clothing styles of the metropolitan middle class by the late 1830s, since they were by then able to import items direct from Britain: Bryer and Hunt, *The 1820 Settlers*, 39; E. Bradlow, 'Women at the Cape in the Mid-Nineteenth Century', *South African Historical Journal*, 19, 1987, 59–60. Although settler women reproduced contemporary British furnishing, they did so within an interior floor plan which was often antiquated by British standards. In the hostile Cape environment, interior architecture was premised upon 'communal living and the importance of corporate life' rather than the rigid and privatised space of the urban Georgian home that was by then the norm in Britain. Settler housing has been seen as developing in three fairly distinct phases. The first (1820–c.1823) consisted of the temporary and expedient adoption of local Dutch and Khoesan styles and materials, the second (c.1823–c.1834) of a vernacular form modelled on, but departing from, metropolitan styles and the third, prompted by the 1834–5 war, of the addition of fortified farmhouses, physically symbolising settler anxiety. Many houses manifested a greater 'hybridity' than their occupants were consciously willing to express in social terms, with the addition, for example, of the Dutch stoep: Winer and Deetz, 'The Transformation of British Culture', 60–4.

178 For the significance which settler women attached to maintaining a regular correspondence with 'home', see Dampier, 'Settler Women's Experiences'. For requests for British materials see Rainer, *The Journals of Sophia Pigot*.

179 As Margot Winer demonstrates, they were also able to acquire expensive tea-drinking apparatus from England, the importance of which will be made clear below. See M. Winer, 'The Indulgence of the Good Wife's Cravings' – Gender, Commodities and Domestic Space in a Nineteenth-Century Colonial Settlement, unpublished paper presented at the Gender and Colonialism Conference, University of the Western Cape, 1997. By the 1870s, British pottery manufacturers were designing items specifically for the Cape market, demonstrating the economic significance of colonial taste: Winer and Deetz, 'The Transformation of British Culture', 71.

180 Keppel-Jones, *Philipps 1820 Settler*, 98. For the men's attempts at British architecture, see also Rainer *The Journals of Sophia Pigot*, 67–8; Crais, *White Supremacy*, 136–7; Thompson, *Travels and Adventures*, vol. 1, 20 and Ross, *Status and Respectability*, 78–85.

181 Godlonton, *Memorials*, 109, 122.

182 Davidoff and Hall, *Family Fortunes*, 400.

183 Anti-slavery, with its appeal to feminine sentiment was another issue in which women could become involved, even if at a local rather than a national level: *ibid.*, 433–4; Hall, *White, Male and Middle Class*, M. Ferguson, *Subject to Others: British Women Writers and Colonial Slavery, 1670–1834*, Routledge, New York and London, 1992; C. Midgley, *Women Against Slavery: The British Campaigns, 1780–1870*, Routledge, London and New York, 1992.

184 As in the Cape, the women involved were largely excluded from the public celebrations marking the ultimate success of the Birmingham campaign: Hall, *White, Male and Middle Class*, 162–3. See also Winer, 'The Indulgence of the Good Wife'.

185 Winer, 'The Indulgence of the Good Wife', 8.

186 Rapport, 'Migrant Selves', 268.

187 Erlank, '"Thinking it Wrong to Remain Unemployed"'.

188 W. Beinart, 'Men, Science, Travel and Nature in the Eighteenth and Nineteenth-Century Cape', *Journal of Southern African Studies*, 24, 4, 1998, 798.

189 See Davidoff and Hall, *Family Fortunes*, 388–96.

190 E. van Heyningen, 'The Diary as Historical Source: A Response', *Historia*, 38, 1, 1993, 21. See also K. McKenzie, '"My Own Mind Dying Within Me": Eliza Fairbairn and the Reinvention of Colonial Middle Class Domesticity in Cape Town', *South African Historical Journal*, 36, 1997, 10; Bradlow, 'Women at the Cape', 61–2; S. Dagut, 'Gender, Colonial "Women's History" and the Construction of Social Distance: Middle-Class British Women in Later Nineteenth Century South Africa', *Journal of Southern African Studies*, 26, 3, 555–72.

191 Keppel-Jones, *Philipps 1820 Settler*, 331–2. Again, see Winer, 'The Indulgence of the Good Wife', and for another metropolitan parallel, Hall, *White, Male and Middle Class*, 164.

192 See Davidoff and Hall, *Family Fortunes*, 32.

193 Davidoff and Hall, *Family Fortunes*, 30, quoting Mary Ryan.

194 Bowker, *Speeches, Letters*, 195.

195 Giffard, *The Reminiscences of John Montgomery*,169. Chase used the same phrase about the British flag in the late 1840s: McGinn, 'J. C. Chase', 101. In fact the Union Jack was devised only in 1801.

196 Giffard, *The Reminiscences of John Montgomery*, 160.

197 Revill, 'Reading Rosehill', 128.

4 Queen Adelaide Province and the limits of colonial power

1   CA, GH 28/12/3, enclosure no. 10, Smith to D'Urban, 17 April 1836.
2   The phrase comes from B. Anderson, *Imagined Communities: Reflections on the Origins and Spread of Nationalism*, Verso, London and New York, 1991.
3   A. Cobley, 'Forgotten Connections, Unconsidered Parallels: A New Agenda for Comparative Research in Southern Africa and the Caribbean', *African Studies*, 58, 2, 1999, 152.
4   W. M. Macmillan, *Bantu, Boer and Briton: The Making of the South African Native Problem*, Clarendon Press, Oxford, 1963, 106–28.
5   CA, GH 23/11, D'Urban to Spring Rice, 21 Jan. 1835.
6   CA, GH 28/12/3, Smith to D'Urban, 17 Apr. 1836, enclosure no. 10.
7   J. G. Pretorius, *The British Humanitarians and the Cape Frontier, 1834–1836*, The Government Printer, Pretoria, 1988, 75, 107–8; H. Smith, *Autobiography of the Lieutenant General Sir Harry Smith*, BART. GCB, John Murray, London, 1901, vol. 2, 62.
8   CA, GH 19/4, Shepstone to D'Urban, 13 Jan. 1835.
9   *Ibid.*; Dugmore to D'Urban, 19 June 1835; C. Hummel (ed.) *F.G. Kayser: Journal and Letters*, Maskew Miller Longman, Cape Town, 1990, 117.
10 CA, GH 19/4, Hudson to D'Urban, 26 Aug. 1835. See also J. B. Peires, *The House of Phalo: A History of the Xhosa People in the Days of Their Independence*, University of California Press, Berkeley, 1982, 163–4. Phatho had successfully persuaded the Wesleyan missionary attached to him, William Shaw, to agitate for the partial return of the land of which he had been deprived when the colonial authorities seized the 'ceded territory'. He had assisted in the return of cattle raided from the colony since the early 1820s: *British Parliamentary Papers: Report from the Select Committee on Aborigines (British Settlements)*, reprinted Irish University Press, Shannon, 1968, *Minutes of Evidence*, William Shaw's evidence, 53, 56.
11 CA, GH 28/12/1, Memorandum, 12 May 1835, enclosure no. 16.
12 CA, GH 28/12/1, Proclamation, 10 May 1835, enclosure no. 12.
13 CA, GH 28/12/1, Notice, 19 May 1835, enclosure no. 19. This was much to the annoyance of the London Missionary Society (LMS) missionary, Kayser, on whose former station the new town was to be built: Hummel, *F. G. Kayser*, 117.
14 Pretorius, *British Humanitarians*, 125; CA, GH 23/11, D'Urban to Glenelg, 16 March 1836. We will examine what became of Hintsa in the next chapter.
15 Smith, *Autobiography*, vol. 2, 65.
16 CA, A 32, Chalmers to Balderston, 12 March 1836; Hummel, *F.G. Kayser*, 116; J. Milton, *The Edges of War: A History of Frontier Wars (1702–1878)*, Juta, Cape Town, 1983, 125–9.
17 CL, MS 17042, vol. 1593, Cory transcript, Governor to Macomo, Tyali and the tribe of Gaika, 20 Aug. 1835. B. A. Le Cordeur (ed.) *The Journal of Charles Lennox Stretch*, Maskew Miller Longman, Grahamstown, 1988, 120. Stretch was even more concerned about Smith's insistence that the chiefs must literally 'cry Mercy! Mercy! Mercy!' to him before their surrender would be accepted. Stretch personally apologised to Maqoma for his commander's behaviour (*ibid.*). The metropolitan Methodist magazine, *The Watchman*, influenced no doubt by Smith's exaggerated claims of military success, reported on 6 June 1836, that Maqoma, Tyhali and their followers had been re-admitted into the province on Smith's personal sufferance, having previously been expelled across the Kei River. In fact they had maintained their foothold in the Amatolas throughout the war.
18 Pretorius, *British Humanitarians*, 103–4.
19 *GTJ*, 3 Nov. 1836; Pretorius, *British Humanitarians*, 120 and 270; A. Webster, 'Unmasking the Fingo: The War of 1835 Revisited', in C. Hamilton (ed.), *The Mfecane Aftermath: Reconstructive Debates in Southern African History* Witwatersrand

University Press, Johannesburg, 1995, 259; *South African Commercial Advertiser*, 3 Feb. 1836.

20 CL, MS 17042, Cory transcript, vol. 1589, Smith to D'Urban, 1 Sept. 1835.

21 Milton, *Edges of War*, 128; N. Mostert, *Frontiers: The Epic of South Africa's Creation and the Tragedy of the Xhosa People*, Jonathan Cape, London, 772. See J. S. Bergh and J. C. Visagie, *The Eastern Cape Frontier Zone, 1660–1980: A Cartographic Guide for Historical Research*, Butterworths, Durban, 1985, 44.

22 CA, A 519, vol. 4, Smith to D'Urban, 10 June 1836, *GTJ*, 11 Feb. 1836.

23 CA, A 519, vol. 5, D'Urban to Smith, 30 Sept. 1835.

24 CA, A 519, vol. 5, D'Urban to Smith, 17 Sept. 1835.

25 CA, CO 4907, additional instructions to Resident Agents, 15 Jan. 1836; *Government Gazette*, Treaty of 17 Sept. 1835.

26 CA, A 519, vol. 5, D'Urban to Smith, 17 Sept. 1835.

27 CA, GH 23/11, D'Urban to Glenelg, 7 Nov. 1835.

28 CA, GH 28/12/3, enclosure no. 10, Smith to D'Urban, 17 April 1836; CL, MS 17042, vol. 1589, Cory transcript, Smith to D'Urban, 17 Sept. 1835.

29 CA, A 519, vol. 4, address given by Smith to Xhosa chiefs, 7 Jan. 1836.

30 *Ibid.*, Smith's delusions of grandeur reach dizzying heights in this prepared speech, including the self-application of biblical terminology ('after I came amongst you').

31 *Ibid.* and Smith to D'Urban, 29 March 1836, same volume. In the Wesleyan missionary, W. B. Boyce's account, the salaries were granted as a gesture of benevolence (W. B. Boyce, *Notes on South African Affairs From 1834 to 1838 With Reference to the Civil, Political and Religious Condition of the Colonists and Aborigines*, Aldum and Harvey, Grahamstown, 1838). In fact they were more a recognition of the limits of British power in the province.

32 Smith, *Autobiography*, 79.

33 CA, CO 4907, confidential instructions to Resident Agents, 15 Jan. 1836. *Government Gazette*, 26 Feb. 1836 and CA, CO 4907, additional instructions to Resident Agents, 26 Feb. 1836.

34 Smith, *Autobiography*, 78.

35 CL, MS 17042, vol. 1589, Cory transcript, Smith to D'Urban, 22 Sept. 1835. Read was a particular *bête noire* of Smith's, having been accused during the war of hiding arms destined for the hostile Xhosa: *Ibid.*, Smith to D'Urban, 21 July, 1835.

36 CA, A 519, address given by Smith. See also L. De Kock, *Civilising Barbarians: Missionary Narrative and African Textual Response in Nineteenth-Century South Africa*, University of Witwatersrand Press and Lovedale Press, Johannesburg, 1996, 49.

37 *Ibid.* For Smith's retrospective, whimsical evocation of what could have been achieved through schooling had he been given the opportunity, see his *Autobiography*, 89–90.

38 Col. Collins, 'Supplement to the Relation of a Journey into the Country of the Bosjeman and Caffre People', 1809, in D. Moodie (ed.) *The Record: Or a Series of Official Papers Relative to the Condition and Treatment of the Native Tribes of South Africa*, 1838, reprinted by A. A. Balkema, Cape Town, 1960, 58.

39 N. Erlank, 'Missionary Wives and Perceptions of Race and Gender in the Early Nineteenth Century Cape Colony', paper presented to the Gender in Empire and Commonwealth Seminar Series, Institute of Commonwealth Studies, University of London, 22 Feb. 1996, 3.

40 CA, A 519, address given by Smith.

41 Smith, *Autobiography*, 90.

42 CA, A 519, address given by Smith. Even these numerous spheres of transformation were not enough for Smith. He intended further to alter patterns of burial: CA, A 519, address given by Smith; mourning: *GTJ*, 26 Nov. 1835 and music: Smith, *Autobiography*, 93.

43 Mostert, *Frontiers*, 772. Mostert sets Smith in a wider context as the first of South Africa's social engineers – a predecessor to Grey, Milner and Verwoerd (762). Smith's personal impact was to be greater within the later British Kaffraria, but the compromised nature of his regime at this stage will become clear below.

44 Pretorius, *British Humanitarians*, 121.

45 T. Keegan, *Colonial South Africa and the Origins of the Racial Order*, Leicester University Press, London, 1996, 5, 36, 74, 129, 140–5. See also C. Crais, *White Supremacy and Black Resistance in Pre-Industrial South Africa: The Making of the Colonial Order in the Eastern Cape, 1770–1865*, Cambridge University Press, Cambridge, 1992, 117–8.

46 See for one among many examples the letter from 'A Ruined Farmer', *GTJ*, 1 Oct. 1835.

47 As one Xhosa sympathiser worked out, if all Xhosa reparations were to be paid after the war on the terms demanded by the settler press, the colony would have gained a net total of over 19,000 cattle and horses (letter from 'A. P. T.', *GTJ*, 12 Nov. 1835). A figure less than this was ultimately recovered and much of the livestock that was recaptured was used up by the army commissariat rather than returned to its settler owners. See A. C. M. Webb, 'The Immediate Consequences of the Sixth Frontier War on the Farming Community of Albany', *South African Historical Journal*, 10, 1978, 33–48; B. Le Cordeur, *Eastern Cape Separatism, 1820–54*, Oxford University Press, Cape Town, 1981, 72–3 and Peires, *The House of Phalo*, 122.

48 W. A. Maxwell and R. T. McGeogh (eds), *The Reminiscences of Thomas Stubbs*, Cape Town, 1978, 115 and 112. Stockenström estimated that local expenditure in the war amounted to half a million pounds (See W. Hutton (ed.), *The Autobiography of the Late Sir Andries Stockenström, Bart, Sometime Lieutenant Governor of the Eastern Province of the Colony of the Cape of Good Hope*, Juta and Co., Cape Town, 1887, vol. 2, 98), although Peires puts the figure at £154,000 (*The House of Phalo*, 124).

49 Le Cordeur, *The Journal of Charles Lennox Stretch*, fn. 141 (emphasis in the original). Stretch also reported suspicions that Robert Godlonton 'has his finger in the public chest "secret service money"', a fund administered by Smith to gain influence over the Xhosa chiefs (141). Stockenström was convinced that some of the loathing which he later encountered from Graham's Town's settlers derived from their fear that he would put an end to their illicit accumulation (Stockenström, *Autobiography*, 98). See also Pretorius, *British Humanitarians*, 70–1.

50 Peires, *The House of Phalo*, 124.

51 Letter from 'An English Settler', *GTJ*, 27 Oct 1836. While, as Keegan among others has suggested, such threats could conceivably have been inserted in the pages of the *Graham's Town Journal* to provoke the government into further military support and expenditure on the frontier, the underlying insecurity that the Xhosa attack brought united both victims and profiteers in constructing the Xhosa more coherently than ever before as incorrigibly savage.

52 *GTJ*, 24 Dec. 1835.

53 *Ibid.*

54 *GTJ*, 28 Apr., 6 Oct. and 1 Dec. 1836. For the eastern Cape traders' vital connections with Cape Town-based commercial interests, see Keegan, *Colonial South Africa*, 68–9.

55 *GTJ*, 11 and 18 Aug. 1836.

56 Le Cordeur, *Eastern Cape Separatism*, 71.

57 D'Urban had initially indicated that certain established British settler families would receive priority in the granting of any lands within the new province (J. S. Galbraith, *Reluctant Empire: British Policy on the South African Frontier, 1834–1854*, University of California Press, Berkeley, 1963, 122). Ross, *Beyond the Pale*, 41. For land applications, see CA, LG 545.

58 *GTJ*, 12 May 1836.
59 Le Cordeur, *Eastern Cape Separatism*, 65. For the promotion of a clear programme of state intervention in the provision of land, labour and capital in the eastern Cape, see *GTJ*, 2 June 1836. For a report of the Cape Trade Society's backing of expansion to the east, see *GTJ*, 21 Jan. 1836.
60 *GTJ*, 3 Dec. 1835.
61 *GTJ*, 30 June 1836. However, such expansion, as Stretch recognised, would require further conflict, the absence of which he thought proved disappointing to the expansionists (CA, LG 405, Stretch to Hudson, 11 Oct. 1836).
62 *GTJ*, 1 Dec. 1836.
63 Murray also reported that across the Keiskamma, in the new province and beyond, the water was better and the soldiers suffered from fewer bowel complaints (CA, CO 444, Dr. Murray to D'Urban, 13 Apr. 1835). Even in his account to D'Urban of Hintsa's recent killing and mutilation, to which we will return in the next chapter, Smith could not restrain himself from adding that the former paramount's territory was 'beautiful . . . rich in pasturage' (CA, GH 28/12/1, D'Urban to Glenelg, 19 June 1835, enclosure no. 18).
64 Pretorius, *British Humanitarians*, 79.
65 *Ibid.*, 107.
66 *Ibid.*, 116–20, 159. While Peires assumes that it was the census's revelation of a larger than expected Xhosa population which precluded D'Urban's anticipated grants, during the preceding month, D'Urban had already resolved to make no such grants in the new province. It was then that he became fully aware of the Colonial Office's opposition to any such expansionist scheme (Peires, *House of Phalo*, 114; Pretorius, *British Humanitarians*, 159).
67 *GTJ*, 19 Nov. 1835, letter from 'A Frontier Farmer'; 1 Oct. 1835, letter from 'A Ruined Farmer' and editorial response.
68 Quoted in *GTJ*, 13 Oct. 1836.
69 *GTJ*, 15 Oct. 1835, 'Affairs of the Frontier'.
70 *GTJ*, 17 and 10 March 1836. The *Journal* later admitted that there may be 'a few shallow persons who are craving to enlarge the colonial possessions, and to appropriate to themselves a share of the additional land', but insisted that they were a small minority: 2 June 1836.
71 *GTJ*, 29 Oct. 1835, letter from 'Kent'; 5 Nov. 1835, letter from 'A Frontier Farmer', 22 Oct and 5 Nov. 1835, editorials.
72 CA, LG 616, Stockenström to D'Urban, 28 Oct. 1836.
73 Before leaving the issue of land, it is worth noting settler responses to the 'Great Trek'. Keegan has suggested that British settler interests, expressed through the *Graham's Town Journal*, encouraged the trek so as to free up land formerly belonging to the trekkers: *Colonial South Africa*, 194–5, 197. But Keegan's main source, Harington, and my own reading of the journal would suggest that most settlers were more concerned in the early stages to retain valuable Dutch-speaking allies, both militarily against the Xhosa and politically, against the British humanitarians: A. L. Harington, *The Graham's Town Journal and the Great Trek, 1834–43*, Government Printer, Pretoria, 1973, 28, 63.
74 CL, MS 17042, vol. 770, Cory transcript, Pieter Uys memorial, 4 Aug. 1835.
75 Quoted in M. J. McGinn, 'J. C. Chase – 1820 Settler and Servant of the Colony', unpublished MA thesis, Rhodes University, 1975, 39.
76 *GTJ*, 30 June, 1836.
77 *GTJ*, 13 Oct. 1836.
78 CA, CO 5831, 3 May 1835, Notice, H. Smith, Headquarters. Despite doubting much that he heard from frontier sources, the Colonial Secretary in London, Lord Glenelg, accepted implicitly that the Mfengu were the Xhosa's inhumanely treated

slaves (CA, GH 1/107, Glenelg to D'Urban, 26 Dec. 1835). Most involved in frontier affairs also did not question Ayliff's construction, although Kayser demonstrated
implicit doubt when he discussed the difference between the Xhosa word 'Fingo',
apparently meaning 'vagabond', and that for a slave, 'ikoboka', meaning 'one who
is burnt' (C. Hummel, *F.G. Kayser*, 122).

79 Peires, *House of Phalo*, 88–9 and fn. 65, 224–5.
80 J. Cobbing, 'The Mfecane as Alibi: Thoughts on Dithakong and Mbolompo',
Journal of African History, 29, 1988, 487–519, and Webster, 'Unmasking the
Fingo'; T. J. Stapleton, *Maqoma: Xhosa Resistance to Colonial Advance 1798–1873*,
Jonathan Ball, Johannesburg, 1994, 101, 102. For a summary of the debates over
Mfengu origins, see Keegan, *Colonial South Africa*, 146 and fn. 85, 330–1.
81 The desperation of many Xhosa in the final stages of the war is described well by
Stretch: Le Cordeur, *Journal of Charles Lennox Stretch*, 130.
82 See O. Paterson, *Slavery and Social Death: A Comparative Study*, Harvard University
Press, Cambridge, Mass., 1982. As Newton-King points out, it was this very lack
of natal alienation that had made Afrikaner farmers' control of local Khoesan
labour so problematic in the late eighteenth century: S. Newton-King, *Masters
and Servants on the Cape Eastern Frontier*, Cambridge University Press, Cambridge,
1999. Although such a control had been established, if not securely, by the early
nineteenth century, the repetition of such an exercise in the enslavement of locals
was not only now illegal, it was much more widely seen as unwise.
83 CA, CO 4382, Bowker to Smith, 26 July 1836; Pretorius, *British Humanitarians*, 89;
Webster, 'Unmasking the Fingo', 256. For Ayliff's role in planning the Mfengu
move into the new province, see Pretorius, *British Humanitarians*, 83–9.
84 There is evidence, however, of its being practised on a small scale, with small groups
of women and children being seized opportunistically. Thomas Stubbs, for instance,
records that in 1822 some Xhosa women who had been given permission by the
authorities to collect clay were taken prisoner by local farmers (he does not say
whether they were British or Afrikaans). 'They were taken to Grahamstown and
we were given to understand were hired out to farmers'. Significantly, however,
Stubbs continues, 'This we learned some time afterwards from one of them who
had run away and got safe back to Kaffirland . . . This was the first piece of injustice
done to the natives by the Government, and this we had to suffer for afterwards':
Maxwell and McGeogh, *Reminiscences of Thomas Stubbs*, 162.
85 See T. Stapleton, 'The Expansion of a Pseudo-Ethnicity in the Eastern Cape: Recon-
sidering the Fingo "Exodus" of 1865', *International Journal of African Historical
Studies*, 29, 2, 1996, 41–58.; Webster, 'Unmasking the Fingo', 253–72.
86 CA, CO 5831, Notice, Headquarters, 3 May 1835.
87 CA, CO 444, Health Report, Murray to D'Urban, 25 May 1835.
88 Stapleton, *Maqoma*, 101, 102.
89 Webster provides evidence that Mfengu were forced by colonial officials to work in
various places, but in general he overestimates the capacity of the colonial state to
control and channel large scale Mfengu movements outside the locations: 'Unmasking the Fingo', 264–6.
90 CA, GH 23/11, D'Urban to Glenelg, 19 June 1835. *GTJ*, 7 Jan. 1836, address by
Dr Murray to Governor D'Urban.
91 CA, LG 420, Fynn to (Stockenström?), 1 Oct. 1836; GH 30/1, D'Urban to
Stockenström, 15 Sept. 1837.
92 For comparison, see M. Taussig, 'Culture of Terror – Space of Death: Roger Casement's Putumayo Report and the Explanation of Torture', in N. B. Dirks (ed.)
Colonialism and Culture, University of Michigan Press, Ann Arbor, 1992, 164.
93 *GTJ*, 8 May 1835.

94 *GTJ*, 7 April 1836, letter from 'A. B.' See also CA, LG 420, Bradshaw to Campbell, 21 Sept. 1836; CA, LG 616, Stockenström to D'Urban, 7 Oct. 1836.
95 CA LG 493, Collett to Stockenström, 17 Sept. 1836. See also *GTJ*, 24 March 1836.
96 *GTJ*, 16 June 1836. Many of these fears were exaggerated. For example, it took a letter to the *Graham's Town Journal* from J. Dugmore, who was perfectly satisfied with his Mfengu labourers, to dispel the impression created in the journal that they had run off with his stock: 25 Aug. and 1 Sept. 1836.
97 *GTJ*, 19 Jan. 1837, letter from Thomas Robson.
98 *GTJ*, 12 Jan. 1837, 1 Dec. 1836, letter from 'A Colonist', 19 Jan. 1837, letter from Thomas Robson.
99 See CA, GH 23/11, D'Urban to Glenelg, 19 Aug. 1837 and CL, MS 17042, vol. 1593, Campbell to Bowker, 21 May 1835.
100 CL, MS 17042, vol. 1593, Campbell to Bowker, 21 May 1835.
101 CA, LG 54, Instructions to Fingo Commissioners, 13 July 1835; CA, LG 54, confidential instructions to the Fingo Commissioners on the banks of the Chumie, 6 Aug. 1835. Once it had resigned itself to the Mfengu presence, the *Graham's Town Journal* suggested that the Mfengu not only serve as a military buffer, but also form a frontier police force, suitable for hunting down cattle thieves: 22 Sept. 1836.
102 CL, MS 17042, vol. 759, Cory transcript, van Ryneveld to D'Urban, 24 Nov. 1835.
103 CA, A 519, vol. 4, Fingo Commissioners to D'Urban, 2 Feb. 1836.
104 CA, A 32, Chalmers to Balderston, 12 March 1836. Boyce complained that many of the missionaries' most successful Xhosa followers left their stations to practise agriculture within the colony: W. B. Boyce, *Notes on South African Affairs From 1834 to 1838 With Reference to the Civil, Political and Religious Condition of the Colonists and Aborigines*, Aldum and Harvey, Grahamstown, 1838, 63–4. Bowker stated that at Peddie, the Mfengu, unlike the Xhosa, had learnt to prepare lands for sowing long before the sowing season: CA, GH 19/4, Bowker to D'Urban, 25 July 1836. For colonial agricultural assistance, see Webster, 'Unmasking the Fingo', 269. For Bowker's distribution of extra pumpkin seeds to Mfengu and Gqunukhwebe, see J. M. Bowker, *Speeches, Letters and Selection From Important Papers*, Godlonton and Richards, Grahamstown, 1864, 25.
105 *GTJ*, 5 Nov. 1835. See Bergh and Visagie, *The Eastern Cape Frontier Zone*, 45. In one sense, Godlonton's fears were well-founded. It quickly became evident that the majority of Mfengu, who were not favoured with land and colonial assistance, were being driven by distress to ignore the pass regulations and enter the colony or move back into Queen Adelaide Province around King William's Town. Some returned to seek a humiliating reinstatement of their former status as clients of the Xhosa. While others sought work, as had been intended, many, as we have seen, threatened the colonists' herds: GTJ, 8 Oct. 1835; CA, LG 420, Fynn to (Stockenström?), 1 Nov. 1836. After Queen Adelaide Province's retrocession, those Mfengu who had stayed on the locations were left there with the equivocal promise of British protection against Xhosa reprisals: Pretorius, *British Humanitarians*, 93.
106 See Pretorius, *British Humanitarians*, 83.
107 Pretorius, *British Humanitarians*, 83; Crais, *White Supremacy*, 117.
108 Smith's wish-fulfilling, supremely arrogant and downright dishonest assessments of his 'reign' within Queen Adelaide Province have long obscured the kind of compromised and negotiated power upon which the British occupation depended. In his descriptions, intention becomes reality and, as Mostert puts it, Xhosa culture is rapidly turned 'upside down and inside out', as a direct result of Smith's own personal interventions (Mostert, *Frontiers*, 766). Until recently, generations of South African historians went no further than Smith's representations to reach their assessment of this first exercise in British colonial control beyond the Cape.

One of the founding fathers of South African historiography, George Cory, wrote in his notes on Smith's correspondence with D'Urban: 'Do not these extracts give a picture of the man [Smith] – bold, determined, active, impatient, capable – and at the same time show his confidential relations with Sir Benjamin [D'Urban], and the difficulties he had to contend against?' (CL, MS 17042, 1589). The author of these letters would have been delighted with such an assessment.

109 Peires, *House of Phalo*, 114–15.

110 C. Crais, *White Supremacy*, 121. See also 117–18.

111 CL, GMS Reports (uncatalogued), reports of Bennie and Ross for 1836; Journal of Chalmers, 16 Oct. 1835 and letter from McDiarmuid, 3 Oct. 1836; MS 16579 Journal of Rev. Laing, 10 Dec. 1835; Le Cordeur, *Journal of Charles Lennox Stretch*, 135.

112 CA, LG 13, Superintendent of Fingoes to Hudson, 29 Oct. 1835.

113 CL, GMS Reports, Journal of Chalmers, 24 Sept. 1836, Extract from Laing's journal, 25 Nov. 1835; CA, LG 396, Campbell to Stockenström, 5 Oct. 1836; CL, MS 16579, Journal of Rev. Laing, 10 Dec. 1835; Hummel, *F.G. Kayser*, 127; CA, LG 405, Bowker to Hudson, 8 Nov. 1836; Bowker, *Speeches, Letters*, 25.

114 These responses to destitution were not mutually exclusive. Individuals for instance, could well both work on, and steal from, colonial farms. Correspondingly, colonial complaints of stock theft were persistent, although they were not uniform, during the lifetime of the province. They were concentrated at first in those areas to the north of the frontier line less closely administered by British officials, where Afrikaners themselves were raiding Xhosa and Thembu kraals for cattle and labour. Later it was these parts of the frontier which became particular source areas for the trekkers (CA, LG 396, Stretch to Smith, 16 and 22 June 1836; Le Cordeur, *Journal of Charles Lennox Stretch*, 139; CA, LG 420, Hartley to Campbell, 1 July 1836; CA, LG 396, Stretch to Smith, 22 June 1836; CA, LG 420, Hartley to Campbell, 1 July 1836 and CA, A 2564, vol. 1, C. L. Stretch, 'Queries Proposed With a View to Ascertain the Working of the System Introduced by Lord Glenelg . . .'). Raids emanating from the province into the rest of the colonial margins were initially not remarkable, but there was a general increase as the British grip on the province loosened and as another drought hit parts of the province in late 1836. Albany in particular had been subject to few Xhosa raids just after the province's annexation, but even military posts were being raided just before its abandonment, and the road to King William's Town was no longer safe for colonial wagons (CA, LG 420, Return of Cattle and Horses Stolen, Albany and Somerset, 1 Jan. to 17 March 1836; and Thompson to (un-named), 1 June 1836, CA, LG 405 and Stretch to England, 1 Oct. 1836; CA, A 50, Stockenström to Fairbairn, 1 Oct. 1836; Bowker, *Speeches, Letters*, 22). Many tales of Xhosa plunder were no doubt exaggerated or even fabricated in the interests of restoring a tighter military grip. Stretch certainly saw political motives even in earlier reports: CA, LG 396, Stretch to Hudson, 30 June 1836. See also CA, A 50, vol. 4, Stretch to Fairbairn, 4 Oct. 1836 and CL, MS 16579, Journal of Rev. Laing, 18 June 1836. For one instance of the *Graham's Town Journal's* exaggerations, see its report of the raid on Fort Wellington, 22 Sept. 1836, and compare with the official report condemning the rash actions of the military (CA, LG 408, Rawstorne to Stockenström, 19 Sept. 1836).

115 GMS Reports (uncatalogued), Extract from Laing's journal, 27 Nov. 1836. For Stretch's condemnation of Tyhali's and Anta's 'tyranny' over their followers, see CA, A 50, vol. 4, Stretch to Fairbairn, 4 Oct. 1836. See also Pretorius, *British Humanitarians*, 326. Ayliff alleged that Gcaleka commoner victims of 'smelling out' or witch-detection would cross the Kei to seek protection from the chiefs under Smith (CA, A 80, Ayliff's diary, 22 Aug. 1836).

116 CL, MS 16579, Journal of Rev. Laing, 18 Feb. 1836; CA, GH 28/12/1, Stretch to D'Urban, 27 July 1836; CA, LG 405, Bowker to Hudson, 10 May 1836; Stockenström, *Autobiography*, p. 68; CA, A 32, Chalmers to Balderston, 12 March 1836 and GMS Reports (uncatalogued), Journal of Chalmers, 12 Oct. 1835.

117 For Maqoma's plotted emigration, see CA, LG 405, Stretch to Hudson, 12 Apr. 1836, Smith, *Autobiography*, 89 and Stapleton, *Maqoma*, 103. For his threats to collaborators see CA, A 50, vol. 4, Stretch to Fairbairn, 4 Oct. 1836. For Sarhili see CA, LG 405, Returns of Cases Brought Before Resident Agent at Fort Murray From 1–31 March. For Sarhili's apparent request to be taken under British authority, see Smith, *Autobiography*, 76; *GTJ*, 14 Jan. 1836. This request was quite possibly fabricated; certainly Smith, who reported it, was simultaneously lying to other branches of British imperial authority about other aspects of the province's administration: Pretorius, *British Humanitarians*, chapter 6. Even the *Graham's Town Journal* questioned Smith's eagerness to extend British sovereignty further over the Gcaleka, taking on tens of thousands more subjects and a far larger area than had originally been intended. In the event, the Gcaleka were left outside of British control.

118 *GTJ*, 7 July 1836, letter from 'Selim'.

119 Pretorius, *British Humanitarians*, 276. For a colonist's fear of renewed Xhosa attack after the war, see CA, LG 493, Collett to Stockenström, 17 Sept. 1836.

120 *GTJ*, 10 Nov. 1836; CA, A 519, vol. 4, Smith to D'Urban, 4 July and 1 and 11 August, 1836; CA, LG 405, Bowker's diary for 1836; CA, LG 408, return of cases tried before Resident Agent Rawstorne.

121 Note the lack of directives in CA, CO 4908. See also Bowker, *Speeches, Letters*, 22–3. For the Xhosa chiefs' sense of their own residual strength see Peires, *House of Phalo*, 113.

122 CA, A 519, vol. 4, Smith to D'Urban, 30 May 1836.

123 Campbell had been one of the first of the settlers to call for violent retribution against the Xhosa for raids on the British settlement. As early as 1825 he had written to Philip that only a commando would 'teach them' not to raid his property, claiming that 'Powder and Ball, by G-d is the only means of civilising them'. Quoted in W. M. Macmillan, *The Cape Colour Question: A Historical Survey*, Faber and Gwyer, London, 1927, 121. As Civil Commissioner, he also colluded with settlers in claiming compensation from the British government for inflated claims of stock losses during the Xhosa attack: Webb, 'The Immediate Consequences of the Sixth Frontier War'.

124 CA, LG 396, Armstrong to Stretch, 13 June, Civil Commissioners to Stretch, 5 Oct. and Stretch to Hudson, 17 Oct. 1836; CA, LG 420, Campbell to Hudson, 16 Apr. 1836.

125 CA, LG 405, Stretch to Hudson, 29 Sept. 1836. See T. Kirk, 'The Cape Economy and the Expropriation of the Kat River Settlement, 1846–53', in S. Marks and A. Atmore (eds) *Economy and Society in Pre-Industrial South Africa*, Longman, London, 1980, 226–43.

126 CA, LG 396, Stretch to Hudson, 12 Oct. 1836. For Bowker's attempts to implement the pass regulations more stringently, LG 405, Bowker's journal, 12 March 1836. For his failure, LG 405, Bowker to Hudson, 5 Apr. 1836.

127 *GTJ*, 24 March 1836. Smith also showed reluctant respect (*Autobiography*, 72–3 and 83).

128 As we have seen, the fining of cattle ('eating up') was now supposed to be the preserve of the British authorities.

129 CA, LG 408, Rawstorne's journal, 19 and 20 March and 1 Apr. 1836. See also *GTJ*, 17 Dec. 1835 and Mostert, *Frontiers*, 773–4.

130 CA, LG 408, Rawstorne's journal, 2 Apr. 1836.

131 CA, LG 408, Rawstorne to Hudson, 5 May 1836. Emphasis in the original.
132 CA, LG 405, Bowker to Hudson, 27 Sept. 1836.
133 CA, LG 405, Bowker's journal, 12 March and 3 and 4 April 1836, Bowker to Hudson, 21 June 1836.
134 See Smith, *Autobiography*, 89; CL, MS 16579, Journal of Rev. Laing, 31 March 1836; CA, LG 405, Southey to Stockenström, 3 Oct. 1836.
135 CL, GMS Reports, Niven's report, 10 Oct. and Journal of Chalmers, 18 Sept. 1836; CA, LG 405, Index to letters received from resident Agent Southey, Oct. 1836; CL, MS 16579, Journal of Rev. Laing, 24 Oct. 1836; Stapleton, *Maqoma*, 107.
136 Pretorius, *British Humanitarians*, p. 120; CL, GMS Reports, annual report for 1837.
137 See N. Erlank, 'Missionary Wives'.
138 Hummel, *F. G. Kayser*, 117.
139 *Ibid.* 117–18.
140 A. Ross, *John Philip (1775–1851): Missions, Race and Politics in South Africa*, Aberdeen University Press, Aberdeen, 1986, 138. Philip also resented D'Urban and Smith's apparent favouritism towards the WMS missionaries, CA, A 50, vol. 4, Philip to LMS Directors, 9 Dec. 1835.
141 *South African Commercial Advertiser*, 3 Aug. 1836; H. C. Botha, *John Fairbairn in South Africa*, Historical Publication Society, Cape Town, 1984, 116; Hummel, *F. G. Kayser*, 134.
142 For a similar missionary response in Canada, see L. A. Blake, 'Pastoral Power, Governmentality and Cultures of Order in Nineteenth-Century British Columbia', *Transactions of the Institute of British Geographers*, 24, 1999, 79–93.
143 CA, CO 443, Kayser to D'Urban, 23 Nov. 1835; CL, GMS Reports, Annual Report of 7 June 1836; Hummel, *F. G. Kayser*, 124.
144 Pretorius, *British Humanitarians*, 158.
145 *South African Commercial Advertiser*, 11 July 1835, 3 Aug. 1836; Botha, *John Fairbairn*, 116.
146 Ross, *John Philip*, 141; Pretorius, *British Humanitarians*, 265. Even as his metropolitan allies were agitating for the province's retrocession, Philip himself nevertheless actually remained in favour of retaining British control over the territory, only in a less coercive form.
147 CA, GH 1/107, Glenelg to D'Urban, 26 Dec. 1835; CA GH 28/12/3, D'Urban to Glenelg, 9 June 1835, enclosure 7. See also CA, A 32, Chalmers to Balderston, 12 March 1836 and CL, GMS Reports (uncatalogued), Quarterly Paper, 20 Feb. 1836. Laing's frustration at the Xhosa's reluctance to listen to the word of God found a vent when a Xhosa man, who had blasphemously taken upon himself the name of 'Jesus' in order to mock the missionary, was struck dead by lightning whilst performing a 'heathen' dance. In beautiful symmetry is the story of Charles Brownlee, Commissioner to the Ngqika in the late 1850s who, 'to prove the absurdity of the witchdoctor's pretensions', deliberately swallowed some *muti* (magic substances) found in the home of a man accused of witchcraft. Shortly afterwards he fell ill with fever, confirming even waverers' belief in the power of the diviner (CL, MS 16579, Journal of Rev. Laing, 26 Feb. 1836; C. Brownlee, *Reminiscences of Kafir Life and History*, Lovedale, 1896, 10).
148 CA, A 32, Chalmers to Balderston, 12 March 1836; CA, CO 4382, Prayer said at General Meeting, 7 Jan. 1836; CA, CO 443, Laing to D'Urban, 19 Oct. 1835.
149 CL, GMS Reports, Quarterly Paper, 27 Feb. 1837, Report of Weir, 6 Oct. 1836.
150 *Ibid.* Reports of Chalmers, 29 Sept. 1835 and 7 June 1836.
151 CA, CO 454, Chalmers to Bell, 7 July 1836; CA, CO 443, Ross, McDiarmuid and Laing to D'Urban, 12 Aug. 1835.
152 CA, CO 443, Ross, McDiarmuid and Laing to D'Urban, 12 Aug. 1835.

153 CL, GMS Reports, Extract from Laing's Journal, 30 Nov. 1835; CL, MS 16579, Journal of Rev. Laing, 23 Jan., 14 March 1836. As William Elliss, Secretary of the LMS in London pointed out, 'Christianity itself has never been introduced to heathen countries by Government. Governments cannot advantageously attempt to propagate it; they can serve it best by protecting the missionaries sent out by our religious institutions': *Report from the Select Committee: Minutes of Evidence*, evidence of D. Coates, Rev. John Beecham and Rev. William Ellis, 517.

154 *Ibid.* 14 March 1836.

155 S. Marks and S. Trapido, '"Full of Enterprise and Bent on Conquest" Or Two Cheers for the Enlightenment: British Settler Identities in South Africa in the First Half of the Nineteenth Century', unpublished paper given at the ASEN conference, 1996, 29.

156 The association between the Wesleyans and the settlers stemmed from the Methodists' complex and dynamic role among the classes from which many settlers were drawn in industrialising Britain. See Le Cordeur, *Eastern Cape Separatism*, 68; Keegan, *Colonial South Africa*, 65–7; E. P. Thompson, *The Making of the English Working Class*, Penguin, London, 1988, chapters 2 and 11.

157 For Shaw's defence of the settlers and Cape officials in the war, see *GTJ*, 12 Nov. 1835, published letter from Shaw to Aberdeen. Boyce's sympathy for both settlers and officials is evident in his attack on the hypocrisy of London humanitarians (Boyce, *Notes on South African Affairs*, 48). The Wesleyans' formal memorandum in support of the colonial state's conduct of the war is in CA, GH 28/12/1, D'Urban to Glenelg, 19 June 1835, enclosure no. 21.

158 Boyce, *Notes on South African Affairs*, 48, 50, 168–73; CA, GH 28/12/1, D'Urban to Glenelg, 19 June 1835, enclosure no. 21.

159 *GTJ*, 5 Nov. 1835, published letter from Shaw to Aberdeen.

160 CA, GH 28/12/1, D'Urban to Glenelg, 19 June 1835, enclosure no. 14, Shrewsbury's 'Thoughts on the Principles to be Adopted in Reference to the Kafir Tribes', 10 Jan. 1835. The vengeful nuances within Shrewsbury's proposals were not solely present within Wesleyan rhetoric. They also appeared in Moravian and other responses (see *ibid*, enclosure no. 7, Rev. Bonalz to Armstrong, 3 March 1835 and Boyce, *Notes on South African Affairs*, appendix, vi–x). However, the particular intolerance of Wesleyan discourse as a whole has been discussed by Thompson, *Making of the English Working Class*, 918.

161 Soon after his arrival in the Cape, Shrewsbury had written, 'It would be very instructive for a high-handed [West Indies] planter to be necessitated to live in the heart of Kaffir-land for one year. If it did not cure him of that supercilious scorn he feels towards every man whose skin is black, it would at least humble him, by constraining him to feel his dependence on men of the same shade of colour with those who have been taught to his own lordly sway'. Shrewsbury had married a Barbadian woman and went on to thank God for delivering them both from the cursed West Indies: Cobley, 'Forgotten Connections', 139.

162 Boyce, *Notes of South African Affairs*, 52.

163 See J. Hodgson, 'Do We Hear You Nyengana? Dr. J. T. Vanderkemp and the First Mission to the Xhosa', *Religion in Southern Africa*, 5, 1, 1984, 3–47; H. Fast, '"In at One Ear and Out at the Other": African Response to the Wesleyan Message in Xhosaland, 1825–35', *Journal of Religion in Africa*, 33, 1993, 147–74; Peires, *The House of Phalo*, 74–8; E. Elbourne, 'Early Khoesan Uses of Mission Christianity', in H. Bredekamp and R. Ross (eds), *Missions and Christianity in South African History*, Witwatersrand University Press, Johannesburg, 1995, 81–2.

164 CL, GMS Reports, Journal of Chalmers, 9 July and 18 Oct. 1836 and Ross's report for 1837; Journal of Chalmers, 17 July and 4 Sept. 1836, Journal of Ross, 2 June 1836; Niven's report for 1837.

165 Smith, *Autobiography*, 81–2, 89–90; CL, GMS Reports, Journal of Chalmers, 9 July 1836, 7 Aug. 1836. Maqoma attempted to procure medicine from his missionary and learn literacy, but avoided appearing in church when possible: Hummel, *F. G. Kayser*, 132–4.
166 Quoted in Erlank, 'Missionary Wives', 8.
167 *Report from the Select Committee, Minutes of Evidence*, evidence of Rev. Stephen Kay (1837), 80.
168 CL, GMS Reports, extract of letter from McDiarmuid, 3 Oct. 1836, report of Laing and McDiarmuid for 1837; CL, MS 16579, Journal of Rev. Laing, 24 June, 12 and 25 July and 2 Aug. 1836. In general Stretch concerned himself far more with the Xhosa's agricultural and educational 'improvement' than did the other officials of the province. As well as personally funding missionary programmes, he ran an evening school at his own house. Hummel, *F.G. Kayser*, 134.
169 CL, GMS Reports (uncatalogued), reports of Chalmers and Laing and McDiarmuid for 1837; GMS Reports, journal of Ross, 16 June 1836.
170 For Ross's explanation, see *ibid.* 10 July and 26 June 1836.
171 R. Elphick, 'Writing Religion into History: The Case of South African Christianity', in H. Bredekamp and R. Ross (eds.), *Missions and Christianity in South African History*, Witwatersrand University Press, Johannesburg, 1995, 20.
172 CL, MS 16579, Journal of Rev. Laing, 30 June 1836. See also D. Williams, *The Missionaries on the Eastern Frontier of the Cape Colony, 1799–1853*, unpublished Ph.D., University of the Witwatersrand, 1959, 173, and for comparison, E. Elbourne, 'Early Khoesan Uses of Mission Christianity', 65, 80.
173 Pretorius, *British Humanitarians*, 115.
174 However, the fact that a number of settlers, most notably, John Mitford Bowker, had recently *become* officials and were able to exercise authority (however compromised and localised) directly over the Xhosa during this first, experimental episode of colonisation, would be of tremendous long-term significance, as we will see in chapter 6.
175 Harington, *The Graham's Town Journal and the Great Trek*, 34.
176 Macmillan hints at this, but goes no further (*Bantu, Boer and Briton*, 169). See also Stockenström, *Autobiography*, 100–1. Laing suggested that a form of indirect rule should be applied if the province was to be retained (CA, CO 4382, Laing to Smith, 6 Aug. 1836). For indirect rule being the translation of failure into success, see F. Cooper, 'Colonizing Time: Work Rhythms and Labor Conflict in Colonial Mombasa', in N. B. Dirks (ed.) *Colonialism and Culture*, University of Michigan Press, Ann Arbor, 1992, 223.

5 Obtaining the 'due observance of justice': the apotheosis of the humanitarian imagination

1 *British Parliamentary Papers: Report from the Select Committee on Aborigines (British Settlements)*, reprinted Irish University Press, Shannon, 1968, 3.
2 E. Elbourne, *'To Colonize the Mind': Evangelical Missionaries in Britain and the Eastern Cape, 1790–1837*, unpublished D.Phil. thesis, Oxford University, 1991, 307–8; J. G. Pretorius, *The British Humanitarians and the Cape Frontier, 1834–1836*, The Government Printer, Pretoria, 1988, 319.
3 *South African Commercial Advertiser*, 5 Sept. 1835, quoted in Pretorius, *British Humanitarians*, 9.
4 J. S. Galbraith, *Reluctant Empire: British Policy on the South African Frontier, 1834–1854*, University of California Press, Berkeley, 1963, 128. See also T. Keegan, *Colonial South Africa and the Origins of the Racial Order*, Leicester University Press, London, 1996, 148–9.

5 CA, GH 1/107, Glenelg to D'Urban, 26 Dec. 1835. For the simultaneous concerns over the expense of other parts of the empire, see Galbraith, *Reluctant Empire*, 128.

6 Keegan, *Colonial South Africa*, 148.

7 See D. Turley, *The Culture of English Antislavery, 1780–1860*, Routledge, London and New York, 1991; J. R. Oldfield, *Popular Politics and British Anti-Slavery: The Mobilisation of Public Opinion Against the Slave Trade, 1787–1807*, Cass, London, and L. Colley, *Britons: Forging the Nation, 1707–1837*, Pimlico, London, 1992, for the ways in which 'economic' and other considerations were inseparable within antislavery thinking. For the same point in regard to domestic reform, see A. Briggs, *The Age of Improvement, 1783–1867*, Longman, London and New York, 1979, 274–5. In relation to the Cape frontier, see Pretorius, *British Humanitarians*, 259.

8 As W. M. Macmillan wrote when noticing the same annotations, D'Urban's rendition of his intentions 'could hardly have been more nicely calculated to touch a sore spot in the conscience of Lord Glenelg and his permanent advisers': W. M. Macmillan, *Bantu, Boer and Briton: The Making of the South African Native Problem*, Clarendon Press, Oxford, 1963, 157. See also Pretorius, *British Humanitarians*, 158, 263 and 316. In phrasing his despatch, D'Urban was unaware that it would be received by Glenelg, not having heard at the time of its writing that Aberdeen's ministry had fallen: Pretorius, *British Humanitarians*, 77.

9 For Glenelg's specific criticisms of D'Urban's policies and his proposal of an alternative vision of Christian colonisation, see CA, GH 1/107, no. 1588, Glenelg to D'Urban, 26 Dec. 1835. For different terminology regarding the Xhosa, see that despatch plus CA, GH 23/11, D'Urban to Glenelg, 9 and 19 June 1835.

10 Quoted in Pretorius, *British Humanitarians*, 127.

11 *Ibid.*, 127–8.

12 Quoted in *ibid.*, 129.

13 Quoted in Pretorius, *British Humanitarians*, 12.

14 *Ibid.*

15 *Ibid.*, 13. Elbourne argues that there were contingent circumstances explaining why Buxton was granted his Committee. Three days earlier, Buxton had argued for the suspension of compensation payments to former slave owners in the West Indies, on the grounds that they continued to inflict abuse on their newly freed labourers. He was thus about to mobilise abolitionist networks against the government once again, and ministers hoped that the Committee would divert him into less harmful activities: E. Elbourne, *'To Colonize the Mind'*, 304–5.

16 For the 1831 Committee, see C. Hall, 'William Knibb and the Constitution of the New Black Subject', in M. Daunton and R. Halpern (eds) *Empire and Others: British Encounters with Indigenous Peoples, 1600–1850*, UCL Press, London, 1999, 312–14.

17 *Report from the Select Committee*, 2.

18 *Report from the Select Committee: Minutes of Evidence*, iii.

19 Gladstone compared British philanthropy towards the slaves of British Guiana, employed on the plantation for only seven and a half hours per day and thereafter hiring their labour for four shillings a day, with the disregard that humanitarians showed for children, handloom weavers and Irish peasants 'at home', who worked for twelve to fourteen hours a day and earned only four shillings a week. Speech quoted in M. Kale, ' "When the Saints Came Marching In": The Anti-Slavery Society and Indian Indentured Migration to the British Caribbean', in M. Daunton and R. Halpern (eds) *Empire and Others: British Encounters with Indigenous Peoples, 1600–1850*, UCL Press, London, 1999, 325.

20 See *Report from the Select Committee: Minutes of Evidence*, evidence of Lieutenant-Colonel Cox, 342–5. It was Cox who supplied the Committee with the information that the colonial forces had been unable to drive the hostile Xhosa out of Queen Adelaide

province, and that their colonisation would accordingly proceed within it, in April 1836: 349–52.

21 *Report from the Select Committee*, 44.

22 *Ibid.*, 73, 31, 44.

23 *Ibid.*, 5.

24 *Ibid.*, 5, 51. Emphasis in original.

25 *Ibid.*, 71.

26 *Report from the Select Committee: Minutes of Evidence*, evidence of Andries Stockenström, 243.

27 *Ibid.*, 249.

28 *Report from the Select Committee*, 76, quoting Rev. Whewell's sermon before the Trinity Board.

29 *Ibid.*, 5.

30 *Ibid.*, 10–11.

31 *Ibid.*, 9, 6–7.

32 *Ibid.*, 13.

33 *Report of the Select Committee, Minutes of Evidence*, evidence of Archdeacon Broughton, 23.

34 *Ibid.*, 57.

35 *Ibid.*, 14–15.

36 *Report from the Select Committee: Minutes of Evidence*, evidence of D. Coates, Rev. John Beecham and Rev. William Ellis, 539.

37 *Ibid.*, 17. Whereas Pagden argues that in reformist discourse, 'The same routes that had carried the colonist out would also allow his vices, his "tyrannies and his cruelties" to seep back into the motherland', one does not get this sense from the Committee's report. Their preoccupation is firmly with the 'worst' elements of metropolitan 'civilised' society corrupting those overseas who have not yet had a chance at 'reclamation', rather than with any reverse flow of degradation from colony to metropole. See A. Pagden, 'The Effacement of Difference: Colonialism and the Origins of Nationalism in Diderot and Herder', in G. Prakash (ed.) *After Colonialism*, Princeton University Press, Princeton, 1995, 139.

38 *Report from the Select Committee*, 10–11.

39 *Ibid.*, 12.

40 *Ibid.*, 9–10.

41 *Report from the Select Committee: Minutes of Evidence*, evidence of Rev. William Shaw 57.

42 For a discussion of this question in a wider context, see Porter, 'Commerce and Christianity', and '"Cultural Imperialism" and Protestant Missionary Enterprise, 1780–1914', *Journal of Imperial and Commonwealth History*, 25, 3, 1997, 367–9.

43 *Report from the Select Committee*, 45.

44 *Ibid.*, 45, 56. The anomaly of the ancient Greeks and Romans being civilised and yet pagan was addressed in the evidence given by Rev. William Shaw. He argued that, 'when carefully examined, their civilization will be found to have originated in the light of early revelation': *ibid., Minutes of Evidence*, 124.

45 *Report from the Select Committee: Minutes of Evidence*, evidence of D. Coates, Rev. John Beecham and Rev. William Ellis, 526.

46 *Ibid.*, 541.

47 *Report from the Select Committee*, 50. Emphasis in original.

48 *Ibid.*, Emphasis in original. Broughton stated that the greatest problem he encountered in dealing with Aborigines was that 'they have no wants; you find it impossible to excite any want in them which you can gratify, and therefore they have no inducement to remain under a state of restraint, nor are they willing to leave their children It is an awful, it is even an appalling consideration, that after an intercourse of nearly half a century with a Christian people, these hapless human beings continue to this

day in their original benighted and degraded state': *Report of the Select Committee: Minutes of Evidence*, 14–15.

49 *Report from the Select Committee: Minutes of Evidence*, evidence of D. Coates, Rev. John Beecham and Rev. William Ellis, 539.

50 *Report from the Select Committee: Minutes of Evidence*, evidence of Rev. Stephen Kay (1837), 76.

51 *Report from the Select Committee*, 46.

52 *Ibid.*, 47–8.

53 *Ibid.*, 51. Emphasis in the original.

54 *Report from the Select Committee: Minutes of Evidence*, evidence of D. Coates, Rev. John Beecham and Rev. William Ellis.

55 Infant schools of the kind that missionaries had helped establish among the Kat River Khoesan, he argued, should be employed among the 'population of the crowded districts of this metropolis [London]': *Report from the Select Committee: Minutes of Evidence*, evidence of Rev. John Philip, 645.

56 *Ibid.*, 62.

57 *Report from the Select Committee: Minutes of Evidence*, evidence of Rev. James Read, 599–601.

58 *Ibid.*, 63. The Griqua on the Cape's northern frontier were upheld as a further example of what missionary-led Christianisation could achieve by way of civilisation: 64–6.

59 *Report from the Select Committee: Minutes of Evidence*, evidence Captain of Bradford, 171 and of Andries Stockenström, 245.

60 S. Bannister, *Humane Policy; or Justice to the Aborigines of New Settlements*, London, 1830, reprinted by Dawsons, London.

61 *Report from the Select Committee: Minutes of Evidence*, evidence of S. Bannister, 175.

62 *Ibid.*

63 *Report from the Select Committee: Minutes of Evidence*, evidence of S. Bannister (1837 session), 16–17.

64 The Committee's report did result in the appointment of Protectors of the Aborigines in Australia and New Zealand. Their duties were not only to prevent settler encroachment and oppression, but also to endeavour to persuade their 'charges' to adopt settled, Christian, European lifestyles. See G. R. Mellor, *British Imperial Trusteeship, 1783–1850*, Faber and Faber, London, 1951, 290–2, 332–7.

65 A. Porter, 'Commerce and Christianity: The Rise and Fall of a Nineteenth-Century Missionary Slogan', *The Historical Journal*, 28, 3, 1985, 614.

66 *Report from the Select Committee: Minutes of Evidence*, evidence of T. Hodgkin, 455.

67 Quoted in R. Rainger, 'Philanthropy and Science in the 1830's: The British and Foreign Aborigines' Protection Society', *Man*, 15, 1980, 707–8. For the Society's later history and its contingently developing geographical imagination, see R. Mitcham, *Geographies of Global Humanitarianism*, unpublished Ph.D. thesis, Royal Holloway, University of London, 2001.

68 *Report from the Select Committee*, 26–7.

69 *Ibid.*, 61.

70 *Ibid.*, 39.

71 *Report from the Select Committee: Minutes of Evidence*, evidence of Rev. John Philip, 550.

72 *Ibid.*, 555. See also Philip's florid representation of Bhotomane's complaints about colonial commandos, and Captain Bradford's endeavours to represent Maqoma before the Committee: *Minutes of Evidence*: 42, 160,.

73 *Ibid.*, 560–3.

74 Elbourne, *'To Colonize the Mind'*, 310.

75 *Ibid.*, 309–10.

76 Quoted in *ibid.*, 310. In a similar denial of African particularities, a woodcut printed by the *Evangelical Magazine* as part of the humanitarian publicity campaign portrayed a Xhosa dressed in the style of the ancient Romans – a similarly heathen and yet virtuous people – rescuing a white child during the 1834–5 war: *ibid.*

77 See *ibid.*, 311–3. Tshatshu's literacy was questioned during the Committee's hearings by the settler apologist Colonel Wade. He suggested that what were claimed to have been Tshatshu's writings, published by LMS missionaries in the Cape, had in fact been written by those missionaries: *Report from the Select Committee: Minutes of Evidence*, evidence of Col. Wade, 417.

78 *Report from the Select Committee: Minutes of Evidence*, evidence of John Tzatzoe, 571.

79 *Ibid.*, 579. Despite, or perhaps because of, his visit to Britain, Tshatshu would renounce his alliance with the colony and his obedience to missionary prescriptions in order to fight for Xhosa independence once again in the 1846–7 and 1850–2 wars.

80 *Report from the Select Committee*, 34, extracted from *Minutes of Evidence*, 87.

81 *Ibid.*, 43.

82 *Report from the Select Committee: Minutes of Evidence*, evidence of Rev. John Philip, 625. Philip saw the Xhosa in a retained Queen Adelaide Province as fulfilling the same role as the Christianised Griqua on the Cape's northern frontier. Both groups would be a friendly, civilised buffer protecting the colony from as yet unreclaimed groups beyond the frontier. Implicitly, it was, of course their difference from white colonists which meant that the Griqua to the north and Rharhabe Xhosa to the east could legitimately be exposed in this way as a buffer, while white colonists themselves enjoyed the protection that they offered. 'Racial' difference thus continued to be intrinsic to Philip's plan for the frontier.

83 Quoted in Pretorius, *British Humanitarians*, 147.

84 *Ibid.*, 148.

85 Quoted in R. Vigne, '"*Die Man Wat Die Groot Trek Veroorsaak het*": Glenelg's Personal Contribution to the Cancellation of D'Urban's Dispossession of the Rarabe in 1835', *Kleio*, XXX, 1998, 38.

86 The 'Sixth Frontier War' is still referred to by Xhosa as 'Hintsa's War'.

87 PRO, CO, 48/185, Court of Inquiry into Hintsa's Death; Peires, *The House of Phalo*, 110–12; Pretorius, *British Humanitarians*, 178–258.

88 Quoted in Elbourne, *To Colonize the Mind*, 307.

89 CA, GH 1/22, Glenelg to D'Urban, 26 Dec. 1835.

90 *Ibid.*

91 T. W. Lacquer, 'Bodies, Details, and Humanitarian Narrative', in L. Hunt (ed.) *The New Cultural History*, University of California Press, Berkeley, Los Angeles and London, 176–204.

92 Pretorius, *British Humanitarians*, 198.

93 CA, GH 1/114, no. 1720, Glenelg to D'Urban, 1 May 1837; CA, GH 1/107, no. 1588, Glenelg to D'Urban, 26 Dec. 1835. See also Vigne, '"*Die Man Wat Die Groot Trek Veroorsaak het*"', 37–9.

94 Quoted in Pretorius, *British Humanitarians*, 197.

95 Quoted in *ibid.*, 194–5.

96 *John Bull*, 9 Aug. 1835, quoted in *ibid.*, 207. The references to 'Southey the younger' refer to official confusion as to which of the two Southey brothers accompanying Smith as scouts actually shot Hintsa.

97 *Missionary Chronicle*, June 1836, quoted in Elbourne, *'To Colonize the Mind'*, 311.

98 *Edinburgh Review*, Jan. 1836, quoted in Pretorius, *British Humanitarians*, 207.

99 It was the settlers' ally, King William IV, finding the humanitarian domination of the Select Committee in London unacceptable, who insisted that the proceedings be held at the Cape. This was in order that officials and soldiers on the spot would have a better chance of defending themselves.

100 *Report from the Select Committee: Minutes of Evidence*, evidence of Col. Wade, 394.

101 Pretorius, *British Humanitarians*, 210–11.

102 PRO, CO 48/185 (167), Court of Enquiry into Hintsa's Death.

103 Pretorius, *British Humanitarians*, 212.

104 PRO, CO 48/185 (167), Court of Enquiry into Hintsa's Death.

105 *Ibid.*, Opinion of Court of Enquiry.

106 *Report from the Select Committee*, 44.

107 CA, A 519, vol. 4, address given by Smith, 7 Jan. 1836.

108 Smith, *Autobiography*, 92, 94 and 89 respectively.

109 *Ibid.*, 72.

110 For examples of these depositions, all of which had a similar structure and a phraseology suspiciously characteristic of that of Smith himself, see CA, CO 4382, Chiefs of Kongo tribe to Smith, 27 July 1836 and the various testimonies contained in CA, GH 28/12/1. See also CA, A 519, vol. 4, Smith to D'Urban, 1 Aug. 1836. For Smith's descriptions of Xhosa lamentation at his and his 'popular' wife's departure, see *Autobiography*, 98 and 100.

111 For examples of these attempts see CA, A 519, vol. 5, minutes of conversation with Macomo's counsillor [sic]; CA, GH 28/12/1, Macomo to D'Urban, 27 July 1836. Mhala's message, supposedly written on 27 July 1836 particularly strains credibility. See also CA, LG 616, Stockenström to D'Urban, 3 Nov. 1836.

112 Smith, *Autobiography*, 106.

113 For D'Urban's wariness concerning Smith, see N. Mostert, *Frontiers: The Epic of South Africa's Creation and the Tragedy of the Xhosa People*, Jonathan Cape, London, 762–75. See also CA, LG 54, D'Urban to Stockenström, 1 Aug. 1836 and Pretorius, *The British Humanitarians*, 294.

114 He went a step further when, as we saw in chapter 3, he assigned Donald Moodie to reconstruct the colony's entire history so as to legitimate his attempt at direct British rule. CA, CO 4382, copies of correspondence with D. Moodie, 23 Oct. to 19 Dec. 1836.

115 Pretorius, *British Humanitarians* 133–4.

116 Quoted in Pretorius, *British Humanitarians*, 133.

117 *Ibid.*, 137.

118 *Ibid.*

119 *Report from the Select Committee: Minutes of Evidence*, evidence of Captain Beresford, 270. However, on the whole, Beresford did not fare particularly well when questioned by the Select Committee. When Sir George Grey pressed him as to what exactly constituted the 'scenes of devastation' that D'Urban reported encountering on his visit to Albany in the wake of the recent Xhosa attack, Beresford had to admit to seeing only one destroyed farmhouse and noticing an absence of sheep. He was unable to report seeing any settler corpses. This contrasted with Philip's report that 'during a ride of perhaps 20 miles, I did not find a single Caffre Kraal or hut which had not been burnt or otherwise destroyed by the [colonial] military': evidence of Rev. John Philip, 553. It was largely from Beresford's evidence that the Committee was able to establish that the British forces in the recent war had invaded Gcaleka territory without sufficient provocation, that they had inflicted disproportionate losses and an 'ungentlemanly' scorched earth policy on the resisting Xhosa, and that it was all too easy for colonists to claim captured Xhosa cattle as their own stolen beasts in the aftermath of the war: 252–8.

120 See *Report from the Select Committee: Minutes of Evidence*, evidence of W. G. Atherstone (1837), 24.

121 *Report from the Select Committee: Minutes of Evidence*, evidence of Col. T. F. Wade (1837), 27.

122 This refers to a Captain Blakeman, who had been posted at Fort Wilshire from 1819 to 1822. He testified before the Committee that in the early 1820s Xhosa men and women had been lured across the colonial border by soldiers to trade, only to be shot in accordance with instructions that those Xhosa found in the colony without passes were to be fired upon. Furthermore, a particular patrol in 1821 had attacked an unoffending Xhosa kraal, killing women and children as well as men, and throwing one woman alive into a burning hut. Having forwarded reports on these atrocities to the Colonial Office in London, via the military secretary at the Cape, Blakeman was removed from duty, his papers confiscated and, upon his return to England, confined as an inmate of Hanwell Lunatic Asylum: *Report from the Select Committee, Minutes of Evidence*, Captain R. Blakeman, 143–6.

123 *GTJ*, 11 Feb. 1836.

124 *GTJ*, 19 Jan. 1837, letter from 'A Farmer'.

125 *GTJ*, 12 Jan. 1837. As we saw, the dominant view of the Committee was that a further extension of British authority was needed to protect Aborigines from the devastating activities of degraded Britons in these territories. Not all of the humanitarians interviewed by the Committee, however, agreed. Coates of the Church Missionary Society felt that 'though I do not conceive colonisation to be necessarily productive of destructive consequences, yet it has so generally led to that result, that there is nothing that I should deprecate more than the colonisation of New Zealand by this country': *Report from the Select Committee: Minutes of Evidence*, evidence of D. Coates, Rev. John Beecham and Rev. William Ellis, 513.

126 *GTJ*, 22 Dec. 1836.

127 *GTJ*, 4 Aug; 8 Sept., address to Stockenström and 17 Nov. 1836, Retief's address to Stockenström. See also Le Cordeur, *Eastern Cape Separatism*, 79 and Pretorius, *British Humanitarians*, 296.

128 *GTJ*, 31 March, 28 Apr., 12 May and 8 Sept. 1836.

129 M. J. McGinn, *J. C. Chase – 1820 Settler and Servant of the Colony*, unpublished MA thesis, Rhodes University, 1975, 48–9. It was Wade who, in a rehearsal of subsequent anti-humanitarian arguments (such as those of Thomas Carlyle), suggested that 'leniency' only encouraged the 'natural vices' of men who were irremediably different from Europeans. He gave as his 'proof' the 'fact' that 3,500 head of cattle and 20 horses had been stolen by the Xhosa annually during the period from 1826 to 1829 in which Acting Governor Bourke had tried his more humane frontier policy. Given the Xhosa's inherent incapacity for restraint, their removal from Queen Adelaide Province 'was an act of mercy' since it would remove them 'from the temptations which must attach to their close proximity to the borders of the settlement'. Similarly, giving colonial troops the order to fire upon all Xhosa found within the colony was 'a humane regulation' because it saved them from succumbing to their predilection for depredation: *Report from the Select Committee: Minutes of Evidence*, evidence of Colonel Wade, 280, 293, 313. By the time he gave his testimony before a second session of the Committee in 1836, Wade had had a chance to write to colleagues in the Cape, including Henry Somerset and Duncan Campbell, informing them of the deliberations of the first session in 1835 and to receive written depositions from them which he could then present as part of his own evidence: 299–303.

130 *Report from the Select Committee: Minutes of Evidence*, evidence of T. Philipps, 179. Donkin was particularly condemnatory of missionary 'meddling' in political affairs. He had been personally embarrassed as Acting Governor when, having acceded to Philip's request to have farmers prosecuted for their abuse of Khoesan servants, insufficient evidence could be employed to secure their convictions: see *Report from the Select Committee: Minutes of Evidence*, evidence of Rev. John Philip, 648–9.

131 CA, GH 23/11, D'Urban to Glenelg, 9 June 1836.

132 *Ibid.* See also *Report from the Select Committee: Minutes of Evidence*, evidence of Major Dundas, 140–1. Most settlers remained convinced long afterwards that Philip had demonically prompted the Xhosa to attack in 1834. Indeed, it was partly in order to attack such enduring notions that Macmillan wrote *Bantu, Boer and Briton* (preface to the second edition).

133 See M. J. McGinn, *J. C. Chase*, 43–4.

134 *Report from the Select Committee: Minutes of Evidence*, evidence of Major Dundas, 141.

135 *GTJ*, 26 May 1836.

136 Quoted in McGinn, *J. C. Chase*, 173.

137 *Ibid.* D'Urban assisted Chase in his compilation of the Natal Papers, sending him private copies of various documents. As McGinn writes, the governor 'probably regarded Chase as a very convenient mouthpiece in his own campaign to vindicate his policy': 182. See also Galbraith, *Reluctant Empire*, 122.

138 *GTJ*, 25 Aug. 1836.

139 CA, GH 1/121, Southey to Napier, 10 Oct. 1837 and *GTJ*, 28 July and 4 Aug. 1836.

140 For *The Times'* political stance, see Briggs, *Age of Improvement*, 273.

141 *The Times*, 5 Jan. 1836, quoted in *GTJ*, 7 Apr. 1836.

142 See Pretorius, *British Humanitarians*, 175.

143 *GTJ*, 16 June 1836.

144 CL, MS 17043, vol. V, Cory transcript, Glenelg to D'Urban, 29 July 1837.

145 C. Hummel (ed.) *F.G. Kayser: Journal and Letters*, Maskew Miller Longman, Cape Town, 1990, 117.

146 CA, GH 23/11, D'Urban to Glenelg, 9 June 1836. See also CA, GH 28/12/1, D'Urban to Glenelg, 19 June 1835, enclosure no. 13.

147 *Ibid.*

148 See Boyce, *Notes on South African Affairs*, 56.

149 CA, GH 1/107, Glenelg to D'Urban, 26 Dec. 1835.

150 *Report from the Select Committee: Minutes of Evidence*, evidence of D. Coates, Rev. John Beecham and Rev. William Ellis, 495; *Watchman*, 21 Oct. 1835, quoted *GTJ*, 4 Feb. 1836 and CA, GH 1/114, Glenelg to D'Urban, 1 May 1837.

151 *GTJ*, 25 Feb. 1836.

152 H. Fast (ed.) *The Journal and Selected Letters of Rev. William Shrewsbury, 1826–1835, First Missionary to the Transkei*, Witwatersrand University Press, Johannesburg, 1994, 176–7 and CA, GH 28/12/1, D'Urban to Glenelg, 19 June 1835, enclosure no. 14, Shrewsbury's 'Thoughts on the Principles to be Adopted in Reference to the Kafir Tribes', 10 Jan. 1835; Boyce, *Notes on South African Affairs*, 48.

153 By contrast, Smith remained a firm advocate of settler representations: Smith *Autobiography*, 94–5.

154 D'Urban's personal hurt is evident in the annotations that he made to Glenelg's decisive despatch, sealing the fate of Queen Adelaide Province: CA, GH 1/107, Glenelg to D'Urban, 26 Dec. 1835. Du Toit and Giliomee note the same expedient response in Afrikaner representations of the period: *Afrikaner Political Thought*, vol. 1, 197. The *Graham's Town Journal*, as we have seen, did this at times too, but inconsistently.

155 CA, GH 23/11, D'Urban to Glenelg, 9 June 1836. Bowker used the Mfengu liberation to 'prove' the benevolence of the settlers: *Speeches, Letters and Selections from Important Papers*, 4. While Glenelg believed that the Mfengu were oppressed by the Xhosa and could not be abandoned to them, he refused to recognise D'Urban's grander parallel of slave emancipation: Pretorius, *British Humanitarians*, 170.

156 Quoted in Pretorius, *British Humanitarians*, 134, 136.

157 CA, GH 23/11, D'Urban to Glenelg, 9 June 1836; CA, GH 28/12/1, Shepstone to D'Urban, 28 July 1836.

158 *Report from the Select Committee*, 82.
159 CA, A 519, vol. 4, Stockenström to D'Urban, 17 Sept. 1836; Pretorius, *British Humanitarians*, 299. In a last gasp attempt to ward off the withdrawal, the *Graham's Town Journal* refused to believe that the official notice of the abandonment, dated 5 December, was genuine because it was merely posted on the church door in Graham's Town: *GTJ*, 2 Feb. 1837.
160 CA, LG 408, Rawstorne to Hudson, 17 Oct. 1836, appended note by Stockenström.
161 *GTJ*, 26 Jan. and 2 Feb. 1837.
162 Smith was fully aware of this, writing that their 'trade [which] I had again so brightly re-established' would be threatened by the withdrawal from the province: Smith, *Autobiography*, 103.

6 Imperial contests and the conquest of the frontier

1 Quoted in N. Mostert, *Frontiers: The Epic of South Africa's Creation and the Tragedy of the Xhosa People*, Jonathan Cape, London, 1992, 1105.
2 T. Holt, *The Problem of Freedom: Race, Labor, and Politics in Jamaica and Britain, 1832–1938*, Johns Hopkins University Press, Baltimore and London, 1992, 280.
3 C. Bolt, *Victorian Attitudes to Race*, Routledge & Kegan Paul, London, University of Toronto Press, Toronto, 1971, 78–9; Holt, *The Problem of Freedom*, 115–77.
4 Holt, *The Problem of Freedom*, 116–7, 146.
5 Quoted in M. Kale, '"When the Saints Came Marching In": The Anti-Slavery Society and Indian Indentured Migration to the British Caribbean', in M. Daunton and R. Halpern (eds) *Empire and Others: British Encounters with Indigenous Peoples, 1600–1850*, UCL Press, London, 1999, 331–2. For more on the 1840 convention, see D. A. Lorimer, *Colour, Class and the Victorians: English Attitudes to the Negro in the Mid-Nineteenth Century*, Leicester University Press, London, Holmes and Meier, New York, 1978, 35.
6 C. Hall, 'William Knibb and the Constitution of the New Black Subject', in M. Daunton and R. Halpern (eds) *Empire and Others: British Encounters with Indigenous Peoples, 1600–1850*, UCL Press, London, 1999, 320.
7 Holt, *The Problem of Freedom*, 285, 37, 116–17.
8 *Ibid.*, 280.
9 Quoted in D. Lambert, 'Little Englandist Discourse and Policy in Colonial Barbados', Paper presented at the Islands: Histories and Representations Conference, University of Kent, 21–3 April 1999, 10.
10 *John Bull*, 24 Dec. 1859, quoted in Lorimer, *Colour, Class and the Victorians*, 123.
11 Holt, *The Problem of Freedom*, 280.
12 For the relative success that former slave-owners had in maintaining productivity in the Cape, see R. Ross, 'Rather Mental Than Physical: Emancipation and the Cape Economy', in N. Worden and C. Crais (eds) *Breaking the Chains: Slavery and its Legacy in the Nineteenth-Century Cape Colony*, Witwatersrand University Press, Johannesburg, 1994.
13 A. Bank, 'Losing Faith in the Civilizing Mission: The Premature Decline of Humanitarian Liberalism at the Cape, 1840–60', in M. Daunton and R. Halpern (eds) *Empire and Others: British Encounters with Indigenous Peoples, 1600–1850*, UCL Press, London, 1999, 374.
14 Quoted in *ibid.*
15 Quoted in R. Ross, *Status and Respectability in the Cape Colony, 1750–1870: A Tragedy of Manners*, Cambridge University Press, Cambridge, 1999, 155.
16 C. Hummel (ed.) *F. G. Kayser: Journal and Letters*, Maskew Miller Longman, Cape Town, 1990, 173.
17 *Ibid.*, 172.

18 *Ibid.*, 165, 170. See also Bank, 'Losing Faith', 373.

19 Quoted in *ibid.*, 155.

20 Bank, 'Losing Faith', 373.

21 Aborigines Protection Society, 1842, quoted in R. Rainger, 'Philanthropy and Science in the 1830s: The British and Foreign Aborigines' Protection Society', *Man*, 15, 1980, 709; other quotes from P. Brantlinger, 'Victorians and Africans: The Genealogy of the Myth of the Dark Continent', in H. Louis Gates, Jnr (ed.) *Race, Writing and Difference*, University of Chicago Press, Chicago and London, 1986, 192–3.

22 Lorimer, *Colour, Class and the Victorians*, 116.

23 C. Dickens, The Niger Expedition', *Works*, 20 vols, New York, 1903, 18, 64, quoted in Brantlinger, 'Victorians and Africans', 193.

24 Bank, 'Losing Faith', 367.

25 I am using 'Albany' here as shorthand for those British colonists who subscribed to the settler identity that I described in chapter 3. Many of these individuals and their offspring no longer lived in Albany itself, having business interests and homes in places such as Cradock, Somerset, Colesberg, Caledon and George.

26 A number of these petitions can be found in C. H. Grisbrook, *Letter Pending on the Kafir Question*, 1846, CL 968/SOU, vol. 52.

27 M. Taussig, 'Culture of Terror – Space of Death: Roger Casement's Putumayo Report and the Explanation of Torture', in N. B. Dirks (ed.) *Colonialism and Culture*, University of Michigan Press, Ann Arbor, 1992.

28 Quoted in J. M. Bowker, *Speeches, Letters and Selection From Important Papers*, Godlonton and Richards, Grahamstown, 1864, 104. See also T. Kirk, *Self-government and Self-defence in South Africa: The Inter-relations Between British and Cape Politics, 1846–1854*, D.Phil. thesis, Oxford University, 1972, 61, 63–4.

29 Quoted in S. Dagut, 'The Migrant Voyage as Initiation School: Sailing From Britain to South Africa, 1850s-1890s', paper presented at the International Conference on New African Perspectives: Africa, Australasia and the Wider World at the End of the Twentieth Century', University of Western Australia, Perth, 26–9 November, 1999, 11.

30 Quoted in A. E. Du Toit, *The Cape Frontier: A Study of Native Policy with Special Reference to the Years 1847–1866*, Government printer, Pretoria, 1954, 52–3.

31 *South African Commercial Advertiser*, 3 July 1839, quoted in Bank, 'Losing Faith', 368.

32 Stretch quoted in J. B. Peires *The House of Phalo: A History of the Xhosa People in the Days of Their Independence*, University of California Press, Berkeley, 1982, 127.

33 *The Times*, 7 Feb. 1838.

34 Quoted in Kirk, *Self-government*, 128; Peires, *House of Phalo*, 125–6.

35 *GTJ*, 9 Jan 1847, reprinted in R. Godlonton, *Case of the Colonists*, Richards, Slater and Co., Grahamstown, 1879, 103.

36 Quoted in McGinn, *J. C. Chase*, 82.

37 After a series of Xhosa military successes at the beginning of the war, Stockenström was hauled out of retirement to lead the colonial commandos. His plan of merely restoring the former balance of power along the frontier, however, was over-ruled by the British military, who wanted the Xhosa to be completely crushed. Having defended the colony most effectively, Stockenström resigned from his military post in disgust at the colonial government's endeavours to recruit more volunteers by promising them that they could keep any 'booty' that they managed to capture from Xhosa kraals. During the fighting, a number of leading settler farmers and businessmen such as Thomas Holden Bowker, William Cock and L. H. Meurant drew vast sums of money from the colonial war chest to pay and equip volunteer 'levies' who, in fact, continued to work on their own farms for their customary wages. Not content with such profiteering, some of these same individuals tried

(unsuccessfully) to implicate Stretch and Stockenström for fraud. See B. A. Le Cordeur and C. Saunders, *The War of the Axe*, Raven Press, Johannesburg, 1981; Kirk, *Self-government*, 185–6. As it is in so many respects, Mostert's account of the war in *Frontiers*, 870–90, is the most detailed.

38 When colonial troops stormed Tshatshu's Great Place, they were disgusted to find in his hut a copy of Justus's *Wrongs of the Caffre Nation*. They blamed local and metro-politan humanitarians accordingly for inciting the Xhosa to war: Mostert, *Frontiers*, 873–4.

39 W. M. Macmillan, *Bantu, Boer and Briton: The Making of the South African Native Problem*, Clarendon Press, Oxford, 1963, 291.

40 Bank, 'Losing Faith', 369. See also his *Liberals and Their Enemies: Racial Ideology at the Cape of Good Hope, 1820–1850*, Unpublished Ph.D. thesis, University of Cambridge, 1995, 349–56.

41 Quoted in Kirk, *Self-government*, 138. It was Gladstone who, in 1846, allowed a Masters and Servants Ordinance drawn up in 1841 to be implemented in the Cape. Modelled on British precedents, it reimposed many of the controls that had been used to regulate the Khoesan labour force before Ordinance 50, only in a new, non-racial guise: *ibid.*, 150.

42 Kirk, *Self-government*, 76–7.

43 Quoted in Mostert, *Frontiers*, 872.

44 *South African Commercial Advertiser*, 14 Oct. 1846. See Bank, *Liberals and Their Enemies*, 228–36; H. Botha, *John Fairbairn in South Africa*, Historical Publication Society, Cape Town 1984, chs 6 and 7; T. Keegan, *Colonial South Africa and the Origins of the Racial Order*, Leicester University Press, London, 1996, 216–17.

45 Quoted in Kirk, *Self-government*, 151.

46 *Ibid.*, 57.

47 Grisbrook, *Letter Pending on the Kafir Question*, 3.

48 *Ibid.*, 5. Grisbrook argued that the Xhosa should be treated in the same way as the recently conquered Sikhs, who were 'a similar profligate and invading confederacy': 9.

49 Philip Quoted in Bank, 'Losing Faith', 375; Laing quoted in Mostert, *Frontiers*, 873.

50 Keegan, *Colonial South Africa*, 82, 127, 167–8 and 214–18.

51 Earl Grey, Memorandum, The Kafir War, 18 Feb. 1852, reprinted in D. Throup (ed.) *British Documents on Foreign Affairs, Part 1, series G, Africa, vol. 1: Cape Province and Eastern Frontier, 1848–1856*, University Publications of America, 1995, 230–1.

52 Quoted in Du Toit, *The Cape Frontier*, 21.

53 Pottinger claimed the honour of having forced open the Chinese ports to British opium traders in 1842. He went to the Cape on the condition that he would subsequently be granted an Indian appointment: Kirk, *Self-government*, 167.

54 Quotes from Mostert, *Frontiers*, 904, 915.

55 *Ibid.*, 926.

56 Quoted in Kirk, *Self-government*, 169. Grey's plans to arm 'friendly' Xhosa chiefdoms as allies, along the lines being adopted in India, was opposed by Russell on the grounds of the innate differences between Indians and Africans. 'A people civilized to effeminacy', he wrote, 'are easily conquered, and may again be raised into spirit and courage by discipline and example'. But 'wild and savage tribes . . . are not so easily subdued, and are not lightly to be trusted with arms': quoted in *ibid.*, 173–4.

57 Bank, 'Losing Faith', 378.

58 Quoted in Mostert, *Frontiers*, 930.

59 See *ibid.*, 932–6.

60 In reporting the speech, *The Graham's Town Journal*, 15 Jan. 1848, commented: 'There is perhaps no one living who has such peculiar talents as His Excellency

possesses for acquiring a hold on the native mind. Persons ignorant of the peculiar cast of the native's ideas are apt to think lightly and even to ridicule the style adopted by H.E. in addressing these people'. Smith was particularly concerned to effect the public, bodily humiliation of important Xhosa individuals. Upon his arrival in Algoa Bay, he unexpectedly caught sight of Maqoma in the crowd that had come to welcome him. When the chief approached Smith to greet him, he was made to lay on the ground while, to the delight of the settler audience, the governor placed his foot on his neck. Similarly, upon releasing Sandile from imprisonment, Smith told him 'You may approach my foot and kiss it, but not until you repent the past will I allow you to touch my hand.' Such rituals, of course, were intended to symbolise a kind of personal power which it was possible for such an individual to attain only in the colonial service. See Du Toit, *A Study of Native Policy*, 29; Mostert, *Frontiers*, 932.

61 Du Toit, *A Study of Native Policy*, 29.
62 Quoted in Kirk, *Self-government*, 205.
63 Du Toit, *A Study of Native Policy*, 36. In 1857, the Mfengu would be granted certificates of colonial citizenship. These exempted them from pass laws but did not extend to giving them the vote under the Cape's non-racial constitution, since they generally held land communally and therefore did not meet the personal property qualification. After 1864, Xhosa could also qualify for the certificates if they could prove that they had worked in the colony for 10 years without committing any misdemeanours: *ibid.*, 285–6.
64 Macmillan, *Bantu, Boer and Briton*, 300.
65 Du Toit, *A Study of Native Policy*, 43. Xhosa drinkers evaded the prohibition by buying their liquor from the free trade area around the port of East London, which was annexed as part of the Cape Colony proper and therefore subject to different laws.
66 Kirk, *Self-government*, 200–1.
67 Quoted in Mostert, *Frontiers*, 950.
68 *Ibid.*, 950.
69 Du Toit, *A Study of Native Policy*, 39–40.
70 *Ibid.*, 48–9.
71 *Ibid.*, 47.
72 Quoted in *ibid.*, 53.
73 Quoted in *ibid.*, 58. The metropolitan colonial reformer Sir William Molesworth blamed Smith directly for the Xhosa uprising. He wrote, 'Sir Harry . . . harangued the Kaffirs in speeches full of bombast and rodomontade . . . by playing up to all manner of fantastic and mountebank tricks, by aping the manners of the savage, Sir Harry thought to civilise the Kaffirs and to impose upon them; but the Kaffirs laughed at him, turned him into ridicule, and imposed upon him.' Quoted in *ibid.*, 63.
74 See C. Crais, *White Supremacy and Black Resistance in Pre-Industrial South Africa: The Making of the Colonial Order in the Eastern Cape, 1770–1865*, Cambridge University Press, Cambridge, 1992, 175–88; T. Keegan, *Colonial South Africa*, 233–40; M. Legassick, 'The State, Racism and the Rise of Capitalism in the Nineteenth Century Cape Colony', *South African Historical Journal*, 28, 1993, 348–54.
75 Quoted in Macmillan, *Bantu, Boer and Briton*, 305.
76 Quoted in Mostert, *Frontiers*, 988–9.
77 J. B. Peires, *The Dead Will Arise: Nongqawuse and the Great Xhosa Cattle-Killing Movement of 1856–7*, Ravan Press, Johannesburg, 1989, 8.
78 Against this figure, 818 men remained 'loyal': Mostert, *Frontiers*, 1082.
79 See sources cited in fn. 74.

80 Quoted in Crais, *White Supremacy*, 151. For Chase's efforts at local segregation in Albert to the north, see McGinn, *J. C. Chase*, 108–10.

81 See also H. M. Zituta, The Spatial Planning of Racial Residential Segregation in King William's Town, 1826–1991, unpublished MA, Rhodes University, 1997; and, for South African projects of urban spatial control more generally, J. Robinson, *The Power of Apartheid: State, Power and Space in South African Cities*, Butterworth-Heinemann, Oxford, 1996.

82 In Uitenhage and Beaufort, as well as Graham's Town, local officials evicted 'coloured squatters' from Crown Lands 'with a ruthless efficiency which the central government seemed incapable of matching': Kirk, *Self-government*, 141.

83 *British Parliamentary Papers: Report from the Select Committee on Aborigines (British Settlements)*, reprinted Irish University Press, Shannon, 1968, *Minutes of Evidence*, evidence of James Read, 600.

84 Quoted in Kirk, *Self-government*, 180.

85 *Ibid.*, 181.

86 Quoted in Mostert, *Frontiers*, 1102.

87 Du Toit, *A Study of Native Policy*, 36.

88 Quoted in Kirk, *Self-government*, 180.

89 For the various other pressures brought to bear on the Kat River settlement before the war, see Crais, *White Supremacy*, 168–9.

90 Quoted in Mostert, *Frontiers*, 987.

91 Matroos, the son of an escaped slave and a Xhosa, is a particularly intriguing character. His biography would be revealing of the fluidities as well as the rigidities of identities along the Cape frontier during the mid-nineteenth century. Before becoming a British army translator with landholdings in the Kat River as a reward for his services, he was a Ngqika councillor. My thanks to Robert Ross for correcting some of the misconceptions about Matroos contained in the first draft of this chapter. See R. Ross, 'The Kat River Settlement in the Frontier Wars, 1835–1853: Hintsa's War, the War of the Axe and Mlanjeni's War', unpublished paper presented to the conference on War and Violence in Africa: Historical and Anthropological Perspectives, Siegburg, Germany, 2000.

92 Ross, *Status and Respectability*, 156. Following Trapido, Ross interprets the Kat River rebellion as an expression of an incipient Khoikhoi nationalism, mobilised partly through the endeavours of their missionary defenders, although I am not sure of the extent to which such a national consciousness was enduringly inscribed in the subjectivities of the rebels and of those who remained passive in the war. See S. Trapido, 'The Emergence of Liberalism and the Making of "Hottentot Nationalism", 1815–1834', Collected Seminar Papers of the Institute of Commonwealth Studies, University of London: The Societies of Southern Africa in the Nineteenth and Twentieth Centuries, 17, 1992; R. Ross, 'The Kat River Rebellion and Khoikhoi Nationalism: The Fate of an Ethnic Identification', *Kronos: Journal of Cape History*, 24, 1997, 91–105, and 'Missions, Respectability and Civil Rights: The Cape Colony, 1828–1854, *Journal of Southern African Studies*, 25, 3, 1999, 333–46.

93 E. Elbourne, *'To Colonize the Mind': Evangelical Missionaries in Britain and the Eastern Cape, 1790–1837*, unpublished D.Phil. thesis, Oxford University, 1991, 315–16.

94 Of course, for the majority of Khoesan not fortunate enough to have gained access to land after 1828, servitude had been a continuing experience.

95 Bank, 'Losing Faith', 371–2.

96 Du Toit, *A Study of Native Policy*, 64.

97 Quoted in Elbourne, *'To Colonize the Mind'*, 320.

98 Quoted in *ibid.*, 319–20. Botha's sentence was later commuted and, after LMS missionaries campaigned on his behalf, he was eventually pardoned: Mostert, *Frontiers*, 1149.

99 Mostert, *Frontiers*, 1109.

100 C. A. Bayly, 'The British and Indigenous Peoples, 1760–1860: Power, Perception and Identity', in M. Daunton and R. Halpern (eds) *Empire and Others: British Encounters with Indigenous Peoples, 1600–1850*, UCL Press, London, 1999, 30–1.

101 See J. Osterhammel, 'Britain and China, 1842–1914', in A. Porter (ed.) *The Oxford History of the British Empire, Vol. III, The Nineteenth Century*, Oxford University Press, Oxford and New York, 1999.

102 M. Lynn, 'British Policy, Trade and Informal Empire in the Mid-Nineteenth Century' in A. Porter (ed.) *The Oxford History of the British Empire, Vol. III, The Nineteenth Century*, Oxford University Press, Oxford and New York, 1999, 107.

103 *Ibid.*

104 Palmerston quoted in L. James, *The Rise and Fall of the British Empire*, Abacus, London, 1994, 177.

105 As Robert Kubicek points out, the steamship (available from the 1840s), new weaponry and later, the land–sea telegraph 'fostered the creation and transmission of powerful images of peoples and places. In conjunction with techniques used to produce books and newspapers, they provided for the . . . provocative reports of "crises" on the periphery of empire': R. Kubicek, 'British Expansion, Empire and Technological Change', in A. Porter (ed.) *The Oxford History of the British Empire, Vol. III, The Nineteenth Century*, Oxford University Press, Oxford and New York, 1999, 256.

106 A. Porter, 'Introduction: Britain and the Empire in the Nineteenth Century', in A. Porter (ed.) *The Oxford History of the British Empire, Vol. III, The Nineteenth Century*, Oxford University Press, Oxford and New York, 1999, 6.

107 E. Stokes, *The English Utilitarians and India*, Oxford University Press, Delhi, 1959, xii. See also U. S. Mehta, 'Liberal Strategies of Exclusion' in F. Cooper and A. L. Stoler (eds) *Tensions of Empire: Colonial Cultures in a Bourgeois World*, University of California Press, Berkeley and London, 1997.

108 R. Hyam, *Britain's Imperial Century, 1815–1914: A Study of Empire and Expansion*, Macmillan, London, 1993, 140.

109 B. Porter, *The Lion's Share: A Short History of British Imperialism, 1850–1995*, Longman, Harlow, 1996, 37.

110 J. Walvin, 'Freedom, Slavery and the Shaping of Victorian Britain', *Slavery and Abolition*, 15, 1994, 250.

111 N. Stepan, *The Idea of Race in Science: Great Britain 1800–1960*, Macmillan, London 1982, 178–83.

112 C. Brownlee, *Reminiscences of Kaffir Life and History*, Lovedale Press, Lovedale, 1896, 202.

113 J. Belich, *The New Zealand Wars and the Victorian Interpretation of Racial Conflict*, McGill-Queen's University Press, Montreal and Kingston, 1989, 304.

114 *Ibid.*, 328.

115 *Southern Cross*, 1863, quoted in *ibid.*, 328.

116 Quoted in Du Toit, *A Study in Native Policy*, 291.

117 For the shaping of Eyre's personal constructions of racial difference through his experiences in Australia, New Zealand, Britain and Jamaica, see C. Hall, 'Histories, Empires and the Post-Colonial Moment', in I. Chambers and L. Curti (eds) *The Post-Colonial Question: Common Skies, Divided Horizons*, Routledge, London and New York, 1996.

118 C. Bolt, *Victorian Attitudes to Race*, Routledge & Kegan Paul, London, University of Toronto Press, Toronto, 1971, xi.

119 See B. Semmel, *The Governor Eyre Controversy*, MacGibbon and Kee, London, 1962. See also C. Hall, 'Imperial Man: Edward Eyre in Australasia and the West Indies, 1833–1866' in B. Schwarz (ed.), *The Expansion of England: Race, Ethnicity and*

Cultural History, Routledge, London, 1996 and '"From Greenland's Icy Mountains to Afric's Golden Sand": Ethnicity, Race and Nation in Mid-Nineteenth-Century England', *Gender and History*, 5, 2, 1993, 226.

120 Quoted in C. Hall, 'Rethinking Imperial Histories: The Reform Act of 1867', *New Left Review*, 208, 1994, 21.

121 Stokes, *The English Utilitarians*, 292.

122 Bolt, *Victorian Attitudes to Race*, 83.

123 Quoted in Lorimer, *Colour, Class and the Victorians*, 181.

124 *Ibid.*, 22. One of Eyre's critics, E. S. Beesly wrote: 'I protest I am no negro-worshipper . . . there can be no doubt that they belong to a lower type of the human race than we do.' But, he continued, 'there is no reason why the negro should work cheaper for us because he is ugly . . . when the upper classes see how . . . injustice to labour, even in a distant colony, is resented by the working men of England, they will be careful how they trifle with similar interests at home'. Quoted in Bolt, *Victorian Attitudes to Race*, 83. The metropolitan context in which the Eyre debate was conducted, and its important connections with colonial events will be examined below.

125 *The Times*, 18 and 13 Nov. 1865, quoted in Bolt, *Victorian Attitudes to Race*, 77, 76.

126 Holt, *The Problem of Freedom*, 305.

127 Bolt, *Victorian Attitudes to Race*, 90.

128 R. Young, *Colonial Desire: Hybridity in Theory, Culture and Race*, Routledge, London and New York, 1995, 124.

129 C. Hall, '"From Greenland's Icy Mountains"', 224; Lorimer, *Colour, Class and the Victorians*, 13.

130 Lorimer, *Colour, Class and the Victorians*, 149–50.

131 The reports of the London Anthropological Society, which included a Confederate Agent on its council, quoted American sources 'confirming' that the South's freedmen had been better off as slaves: Bolt, *Victorian Attitudes to Race*, 33.

132 *Ibid.*, 58.

133 *Belfast Northern Whig*, 23 Dec. 1864, quoted in *ibid.*, 48. For radical exceptions within the press coverage, see 100.

134 P. D. Curtin, *The Image of Africa: British Ideas and Action, 1780–1850*, University of Wisconsin Press, Madison Wis. and London, 1964, 372. For the broader impact of the US Civil War on metropolitan debates over race, see Lorimer, *Colour, Class and the Victorians*, 162–77.

135 Bayly, 'The British and Indigenous Peoples', 34.

136 *The Times*, 30 Jan. 1866, quoted in Bolt, *Victorian Attitudes to Race*, 94. See also Lorimer, *Colour, Class and the Victorians*, 13.

137 Belich, *The Victorian Interpretation*, 327.

138 Quoted in Lorimer, *Colour, Class and the Victorians*, 199.

139 Hall, '"From Greenland's Icy Mountains"', 216.

140 Quoted in Bolt, *Victorian Attitudes to Race*, 91. Although I have not examined the discursive effects of Fenianism in Ireland here, they will be touched upon below, where racialised representations of the white Irish are mentioned as being indicative of a new late nineteenth-century hegemonic discourse of race and class difference, founded upon colonial 'experience'.

141 Holt, *The Problem of Freedom*, 306–7.

142 Bayly, 'The British and Indigenous Peoples', 33. See also Brantlinger, 'Victorians and Africans', 201.

143 E. J. Evans, *The Forging of the Modern State: Early Industrial Britain, 1783–1870*, Longman, London and New York, 1996, 223.

144 Holt, *The Problem of Freedom*, 180.

145 L. Davidoff and C. Hall, *Family Fortunes: Men and Women of the English Middle Class, 1780–1850*, Routledge, London, 1987, 23.

146 Quoted in J. Saville, *The Consolidation of the Capitalist State, 1800–1850*, Pluto Press, London and Boulder, Colorado, 1994, 39, 37–8.

147 *Ibid.*, 70–75; F. M. L. Thompson, *The Rise of Respectable Society: A Social History of Victorian Britain, 1830–1900*, Fontana, London, 1988, 328–32.

148 Evans, *The Forging of the Modern State*, 293.

149 Lorimer, *Colour, Class and the Victorians*, 105.

150 Quoted in Hall, 'Rethinking Imperial Histories', 18.

151 See Hall, 'Rethinking Imperial Histories', '"From Greenland's Icy Mountains"' and 'Histories, Empires'. The debate over the Reform Act was also framed with the US Civil War in mind. As Bolt argues, 'From the moment Republicans took an interest in the Negro vote, British writers became aware of the impatience which might be generated among the disfranchised classes at home': Bolt, *Victorian Attitudes to Race*, 62. The metropolitan radical John Bright, certainly 'linked the liberation of the slaves [in America] with the proper recognition of the political rights of respectable working men' in Britain: Hall, 'Rethinking Imperial Histories', 15.

152 Holt, *The Problem of Freedom*, 306.

153 *Pall Mall Gazette* and *Saturday Review*, quoted in Bolt, *Victorian Attitudes to Race*, 87.

154 Quoted in Lorimer, *Colour, Class and the Victorians*, 199.

155 Hall, 'Rethinking Imperial Histories', 18.

156 See G. Stedman Jones, *Outcast London: A Study of the Relationship Between Classes in Victorian Society*, Penguin, London, 1984.

157 Women, of course, could be ambivalently positioned as respectable in ways that the poor and the Irish, for instance, were not, and yet were still disfranchised: Hall, 'Rethinking Imperial Histories', 5.

158 Quoted in Holt, *The Problem of Freedom*, 38.

159 *Wesleyan-Methodist Magazine*, quoted in Lorimer, *Colour, Class and the Victorians*, 80. For the discourses of social control developed in relation to the 'residuum', see F. Driver, 'Moral Geographies: Social Science and the Urban Environment in Mid-Nineteenth Century England', *Transactions of the Institute of British Geographers*, 13, 1988, 277, Lorimer, *Colour, Class and the Victorians*, 81 and Stedman Jones, *Outcast London*.

160 For specifically scientific constructions of class, gender and ethnic-based difference within mid-nineteenth-century Britain, and the ways in which these scientific constructions intersected with political discourses, see N. L. Stepan, *The Idea of Race in Science: Great Britain, 1800–1960*, Macmillan, London, 1982, 84, 101–3.

161 S. Dubow, *Scientific Racism in Modern South Africa*, Cambridge University Press, Cambridge, 1995, 15, 27–8. In 1866, Knox wrote: 'If we are to hold places within the tropics, it can only be as military masters lording it over a sort of serf population, and under the continual fear of whose terrible vengeance we must always live. If such be really the case, then all schemes of philanthropy and of brotherhood by Act of Parliament and stump oratory, which delude us and take us off our guard, should at once be deprecated'. Quoted in Bolt, *Victorian Attitudes to Race*, 22. For Knox's profound contribution to the development of scientific racism in Britain, see Stepan, *The Idea of Race in Science*, 41–3. For his contribution to metropolitan thinking on Africa, see P. Brantlinger, '"Dying Races": Rationalizing Genocide in the Nineteenth Century', in J. Nederveen Pieterse and B. Parekh (eds) *The Decolonization of Imagination: Culture, Knowledge and Power*, Zed Books, London and New Jersey, 1995, 43–56.

162 Quoted in Bolt, *Victorian Attitudes to Race*, 6.

163 *Ibid.*, 15. Herbert Spencer argued in the late 1860s that women's individual evolution was arrested earlier than that of men's to permit conservation of their energies

for reproduction. Accordingly, the Darwinist Karl Pearson asserted that 'If child-bearing women be intellectually handicapped, then the penalty to be paid for race predominance is the subjection of women.' Domestic male supremacy over females was thus constructed as being essential to Britons' superiority over colonised peoples: J. Lewis, *Women in England 1870–1950: Sexual Divisions and Social Change*, Wheatsheaf Books, Sussex, Indiana University Press, Bloomington, 1984, 82–3. Although they challenged specific constructions of gendered difference within Britain, even the terms of metropolitan women's struggle to be included within the body politic through the 1867 Act contributed to new discourses of irremediable racial difference. In the early nineteenth century, feminist writers had made connections between their own subjection and that of colonial slaves, empowering themselves by representing these racial others (See M. Ferguson, *Subject to Others: British Women Writers and Colonial Slavery 1670–1834*, Routledge, London and New York, 1992). By the mid-1860s, though, Millicent Fawcett among others was arguing that 'women in England could not be compared with women of "savage races" with "little better lives than beasts of burden"': Hall, 'Rethinking Imperial Histories', 26. Although most women reformers still held that blacks were potentially reclaimable, some early feminists thus staked their claim to citizenship within the metropole by emphasising their differentiation from 'races' who really were unfit for self-government in the colonies.

164 For other ways in which British nationhood became further embroiled in imperial ventures in the late nineteenth century, see F. Harcourt, 'Gladstone, Monarchism and the "new" Imperialism, 1868–74', *Journal of Imperial and Commonwealth History*, XIV, 1, 1985, 20–51.
165 Hall, 'Rethinking Imperial Histories', 12.
166 Holt, *The Problem of Freedom*, 280–2.
167 Quoted in *ibid.*, 281–2.
168 Hall, 'Rethinking Imperial Histories', 12.
169 *Ibid.*, 12.
170 Quoted in Holt, *The Problem of Freedom*, 281; Hall, 'Rethinking Imperial Histories', 12.
171 Lorimer, *Colour, Class and the Victorians*, 113. For Charles Dickens' and Charlotte Brontë's ridicule of missionary humanitarianism, see J. Comaroff and J. Comaroff, *Of Revelation and Revolution: Christianity, Colonialism and Consciousness in South Africa*, University of Chicago Press, Chicago, 1991, 50–1.
172 Hall, '"From Greenland's Icy Mountains"', 218.
173 Carlyle, quoted in Bowker, *Speeches, Letters*, 123. Carlyle's greater sympathy for the English weaver could, of course, be reconciled with his belief that the weaver was best led by other social classes more fitted for government.
174 Bowker, *Speeches, Letters*, 249.
175 *Ibid.*, 131.
176 See Hall, 'Rethinking Imperial Histories', 13.
177 The remainder of this section is heavily indebted to Jeff Guy's 'Class, Imperialism and Literary Criticism: William Ngidi, John Colenso and Matthew Arnold', *Journal of Southern African Studies*, 23, 2, 1997, 219–41.
178 J. W. Colenso, *The Pentateuch and the Book of Joshua Critically Examined*, Longman, Green, Longman, Roberts and Green, London, 1862, vol. 1, 150, quoted *ibid.*, 232.
179 *Ibid.*, 219, 221.
180 M. Arnold, 'The Bishop and the Philosopher', *Macmillan's Magazine*, VII, 1863, 43, quoted in *ibid.*, 234.
181 *Ibid.* Guy points out that Arnold subsequently toned down this line of attack.
182 *Ibid.*, 239.

183 A. L. Stoler, *Race and the Education of Desire: Foucault's History of Sexuality and the Colonial Order of Things*, Duke University Press, Durham, N.C., 127, 128.

7 Epilogue and conclusion

1 C. Brownlee, *Reminiscences of Kaffir Life and History*, Lovedale Press, Lovedale, 1896, 200.
2 Quoted in A. E. Du Toit, *The Cape Frontier: A Study of Native Policy With Special Reference to the Years 1847–1866*, Government printer, Pretoria, 1954, 63.
3 R. Ross, *Status and Respectability in the Cape Colony, 1750–1870: A Tragedy of Manners*, Cambridge University Press, Cambridge, 1999, 161.
4 S. Dubow, *Knowledge and the Politics of Colonial Identity*, unpublished MS, 2000, no pagination.
5 For these struggles, see S. Trapido, 'The Origins of the Cape Franchise Qualifications of 1853', *Journal of African History*, 5, 1964, 37–54. For the attempt by Albany settlers to secure a separate eastern Cape government, see B. A. Le Cordeur, *Eastern Cape Separatism, 1820–1854*, Oxford University Press, Oxford, 1981..
6 Cited in A. Bank, 'Losing Faith in the Civilizing Mission: The Premature Decline of Humanitarian Liberalism at the Cape, 1840–60', in M. Daunton and R. Halpern (eds) *Empire and Others: British Encounters with Indigenous Peoples, 1600–1850*, UCL Press, London, 1999, 377.
7 T. Kirk, *Self-government and Self-defence in South Africa: The Inter-relations Between British and Cape Politics, 1846–1854*, D.Phil. thesis, Oxford University, 1972, 506.
8 *Ibid.*, 58.
9 M. Winer and J. Deetz, 'The Transformation of British Culture in the Eastern Cape, 1820–1860', *Social Dynamics*, 16, 1, 1990, 55–75.
10 L. Davidoff and C. Hall, *Family Fortunes: Men and Women of the English Middle Class, 1780–1850*, Routledge, London, 1987, 403.
11 For more on communications improvements and their cultural effects in the Cape, see Dubow, *Knowledge and the Politics of Colonial Identity*, to which this section is indebted. See Dubow's work in particular for the enormous individual contributions made by Andrew Geddes Bain and W. G. Atherstone to the new intellectual, political and material connections between the eastern and western Cape.
12 Davidoff and Hall, *Family Fortunes*, 447. See Dubow, *Knowledge and the Politics of Colonial Identity*, and K. MacKenzie, *Gender and Honour in Middle-Class Cape Town: The Making of Colonial Identities, 1828–1852*, D.Phil., Oxford University, 1997.
13 Dubow, *Knowledge and the Politics of Colonial Identity*.
14 T. Keegan, *Colonial South Africa and the Origins of the Racial Order*, Leicester University Press, London, 1996, 288. As Governor of New Zealand, Grey had successfully persuaded the British government that defeat at the hands of the Maori in the Northern War of 1845–6 was actually a magnanimous British victory: J. Belich, *The New Zealand Wars and the Victorian Interpretation of Racial Conflict*, McGill-Queen's University Press, Montreal and Kingston, 1989, 30.
15 Grey's utilitarian philosophy of colonial government is scathingly investigated in J. B. Peires, *The Dead Will Arise: Nongqawuse and the Great Xhosa Cattle-Killing Movement of 1856–7*, Ravan Press, Johannesburg, 1989, and in Dubow, *Knowledge and the Politics of Colonial Identity*. Grey summarised it himself in 1861: 'to enable the European race in South Africa to occupy such territory as they really require on such terms as are mutually advantageous to both races, is to build up and consolidate great and prosperous communities, wealthy and strong enough to maintain themselves': quoted in Du Toit, *A Study of Native Policy*, 157–8. One of the best treatments of Grey's philosophical inspirations can be found in N. Mostert, *Frontiers: The Epic of South Africa's Creation and the Tragedy of the Xhosa People*, Jonathan Cape, London,

1992, 1165–7. See also L. D. Berg, 'Reading (Post)Colonial History: Masculinity, "Race", and Rebellious Natives in the Waikato, New Zealand – 1863', *Historical Geography*, 26, 1998, 101–27.

16 Quoted in du Toit, *A Study of Native Policy*, 79.

17 Mostert, *Frontiers*, 1178. With these strategically vital areas under colonial control, the confinement of the Xhosa to new locations, together with natural population increase, meant that their population density within British Kaffraria was now 33 persons per square mile, compared with the already relatively high 10 to 11 people per square mile within Queen Adelaide Province in 1836: *ibid.*, 1167–8.

18 Quoted in du Toit, *A Study of Native Policy*, 238.

19 E. Stokes, *The English Utilitarians and India*, Oxford University Press, Delhi, 1959, 55.

20 *Ibid.*, 58, 75, 242.

21 *Ibid.*, 249. See also C. A. Bayly, 'The British and Indigenous Peoples, 1760–1860: Power, Perception and Identity', in M. Daunton and R. Halpern (eds) *Empire and Others: British Encounters with Indigenous Peoples, 1600–1850*, UCL Press, London, 1999, 31, and Peires, *The Dead Will Arise*, 46, 48–9, where Grey's utilitarian beliefs are linked to those applied to the government of India.

22 Quoted in du Toit, *A Study of Native Policy*, 88.

23 When Grey first toured the frontier districts, he took with him an evangelical Maori who told the assembled Xhosa that the Maoris had been cannibals until they were saved through the kindness of Grey and the British missionaries: Peires, *The Dead Will Arise*, 59.

24 Quoted D. M. Schreuder, 'The Cultural Factor in Victorian Imperialism: A Case Study of the British "Civilising Mission"', *Journal of Imperial and Commonwealth History*, 4, 3, 1976, 290.

25 Quoted in Mostert, *Frontiers*, 1168.

26 du Toit, *A Study of Native Policy*, 88.

27 Mostert, *Frontiers*, 1172.

28 Arguments over the causes and classed and gendered characteristics of the Cattle Killing have been rehearsed in Peires, *The Dead Will Arise*; H. Bradford, 'Women, Gender and Colonialism: Rethinking the History of the British Cape Colony and its Frontier Zones, *c.* 1806–70', *Journal of African History*, 37, 1996, 351–70; J. Lewis, 'Materialism and Idealism in the Historiography of the Xhosa Cattle-Killing Movement, 1856–7', *South African Historical Journal*, 25, 1991, 266 and Mostert, *Frontiers*, 1222–3.

29 Quoted in Peires, *The Dead Will Arise*, 247.

30 J. B. Peires, 'Sir George Grey versus the Kaffir Relief Committee', *Journal of Southern African Studies*, 10, 2, 1984, 158.

31 Quoted in Du Toit, *A Study in Native Policy*, 254.

32 *Ibid.*, 256–7.

33 *Ibid.*, 253, 91.

34 C. Crais, *White Supremacy and Black Resistance in Pre-Industrial South Africa: The Making of the Colonial Order in the Eastern Cape, 1770–1865*, Cambridge University Press, Cambridge, 1992, 213.

35 Du Toit, *A Study of Native Policy*, 260.

36 *Ibid.*

37 *Ibid.*, 94–9, 104.

38 Quoted in Bank, 'Losing Faith', 380.

39 As Deleuze and Guattari have argued, 'all the fugitive forces that European states since the early modern period have sought to contain and destroy' are embodied in the figure of the mobile nomad. 'The nomad sums up everything that has remained counter to the state, including knowledges that resist bureaucratic codification . . .

peoples that defy national concentration . . . armies that evade defeat . . . entire societies that inhibit the formation of power centres': cited in T. Richards, *The Imperial
Archive: Knowledge and the Fantasy of Empire*, Verso, London and New York, 1993.

40 Quoted in Du Toit, *A Study in Native Policy*, 105. See also Crais, *White Supremacy*,
150–1.

41 Quoted in *ibid.*, 105.

42 *Ibid.*, 107.

43 For the intentions behind the school and the power relationship and resistances that
developed within it, see J. Hodgson, *Princess Emma*, A. D. Donker, Craighall, 1987.

44 Du Toit, *A Study in Native Policy*, 242–3.

45 Peires, *The Dead Will Arise*, 60; D. Gordon, 'Science, Superstition and Colonialism:
Disease and Therapy at Kingwilliamstown, Xhosaland, 1847–91', unpublished paper.

46 S. Dagut, 'The Migrant Voyage as Initiation School: Sailing From Britain to South
Africa, 1850s–1890s', paper presented at the International Conference on New
African Perspectives: Africa, Australasia and the Wider World at the End of the
Twentieth Century', University of Western Australia, Perth, 26–9 November,
1999, 16.

47 Quoted in Mostert, *Frontiers*, 1169.

48 Peires, *The Dead Will Arise*, 69.

49 Quoted in Du Toit, *A Study of Native Policy*, 174.

50 C. Brownlee, *Reminiscences of Kaffir Life and History*, Lovedale Press, Lovedale, 1896,
189.

51 *Ibid.*, 183.

52 Du Toit, *A Study in Native Policy*, 106–7.

53 *Ibid.*, 193.

54 *Ibid.*, 194.

55 *Ibid.*, 70.

56 See A. Stoler, *Race and the Education of Desire: Foucault's History of Sexuality and the
Colonial Order of Things*, Duke University Press, Durham, N.C., 1995.

57 C. Hall, '"From Greenland's Icy Mountains . . . to Afric's Golden Sand": Ethnicity,
Race and Nation in Mid-Nineteenth-Century England', *Gender and History*, 5, 2,
1993, 227.

58 A. McClintock, *Imperial Leather: Race, Gender and Sexuality in the Colonial Contest*,
Routledge, London and New York, 1995, 16. For an imperial historian's recent
analysis of these 'myriad encounters', which approaches, but does not quite approxi-
mate, the concept of an imperial network described here, see J. Darwin, 'Imperialism
and the Victorians: The Dynamics of Territorial Expansion', *English Historical Review*,
June 1997, 614–42.

59 Homi Bhabha seems to ascribe ambivalence within a singular, if fractured, colonial
discourse to the contradictions inherent in a rather universal colonising pysche:
H. Bhabha, *The Location of Culture*, Routledge, London and New York, 1994. But,
as Sara Mills has argued, 'in focusing attention on the colonial psyche, we risk ignoring the political and economic bases on which those psyches were constructed':
S. Mills, 'Gender and Colonial Space', *Gender, Place and Culture*, 3, 2, 1996, 126.

60 In clarifying my own use of the term discourse, I have found it useful to turn to
critiques of one of the founding texts of postcolonialism, Edward Said's *Orientalism:
Western Conceptions of the Orient*, Penguin, London, 1995 (originally 1978). Although
Said defined what he meant by 'Orientalism' in a number of ways, he actually seems to
use the term to describe 'an enormous system or inter-textual network of rules and
procedures which regulate anything that may be thought, written or imagined
about the Orient': L. Gandhi, *Postcolonial Theory: A Critical Introduction*, Edinburgh
University Press, Edinburgh, 1998, 76–7. It is this all encompassing use of the
concept of discourse which has attracted most criticism from historians (see

C. A. Breckenridge and P. van der Veer, 'Orientalism and the Postcolonial Predicament', in C. A. Breckenridge and P. van der Veer (eds) *Orientalism and the Postcolonial Predicament*, University of Pennsylvania Press, Philadelphia, 1993, 5–6, and J. MacKenzie, *Orientalism: History, Theory and the Arts*, Manchester University Press, Manchester and New York, 1995 especially xv). However, rather than rejecting Said's overall premise about the power of cultural representation, I would suggest that these critiques highlight the imperative for more complicated, spatially differentiated and precise uses of the term 'discourse', such as those deployed in F. Cooper and A. L. Stoler (eds) *Tensions of Empire: Colonial Cultures in a Bourgeois World*, University of California Press, Berkeley and London, 1997; J. Duncan, *The City as Text: The Politics of Landscape Interpretation in the Kandyan Kingdo*m, Cambridge University Press, Cambridge, 1990, and N. Thomas, *Colonialism's Culture: Anthropology, Travel and Government*, Polity, Cambridge, 1994.

61 See D. Kennedy, 'Imperial History and Post-Colonial Theory', *Journal of Imperial and Commonwealth History*, 24, 3, 1996, 345–63.

62 T. J. Barnes and J. S. Duncan, 'Introduction' in T. J. Barnes and J. S. Duncan (eds) *Writing Worlds: Discourse, Text and Metaphor in the Representation of Landscape*, Routledge, London, 1992, 9. Such a conception has the effect of recognising the power of individual agency by assuming that people are capable of appropriating elements of certain discourses and rejecting others.

63 See J. Jacobs, *Edge of Empire: Postcolonialism and the City*, Routledge, London and New York, 1996, 3–5.

64 See Bhabha, *The Location of Culture* among others.

65 G. Prakash, 'Introduction: After Colonialism', in G. Prakash, (ed.) *After Colonialism: Imperial Histories and Postcolonial Displacements*, Princeton University Press, Princeton, N.J., 1995, 9.

66 D. Ludden, 'India's Development Regime', in N. B. Dirks (ed.) *Colonialism and Culture*, University of Michigan Press, Ann Arbor, 1992, 265.

67 J. L. Comaroff, 'Reflections on the Colonial State, in South Africa and Elsewhere: Factions, Fragments, Facts and Fictions, *Social Identities*, 4, 3, 1998, 341.

Index

Significant information in notes is indexed as 123n4, i.e. note 4 on page 123